JACQUES MARITAIN and his wife Raïssa—who died in 1960—lived for many years in America where he taught first at Columbia University and then at Princeton. During this time he also traveled frequently to Toronto to lecture at the Pontifical Institute of Mediaeval Studies. In 1945, at the request of General de Gaulle, he accepted the post of French Ambassador to the Vatican and spent the next three years in Rome. M. Maritain returned to Princeton in 1948 where he remained until his retirement, as professor emeritus, in 1953. Born in Paris in 1882, he and his late wife—whom he married in 1904—converted to Catholicism after coming under the dynamic influences of Henri Bergson, Charles Péguy, and Léon Bloy. He has devoted his life to study, teaching, writing, and lecturing. At present, he is in retirement but still actively engaged in writing in Toulouse, France, where he is associated with the Little Brothers of Jesus. He was honored by Pope Paul VI at the closing session of the Second Vatican Council in December 1965.

Long accepted as the greatest Catholic philosopher of the twentieth century, and highly honored and respected throughout the world, M. Maritain has devoted his life to the evolving of a contemporary Christian philosophy which can reconcile the seeming differences between faith and reason, and between religion and science. It is largely through his efforts that there has been a rebirth of interest in the philosophy of St. Thomas Aquinas, in scholasticism, and in philosophical realism.

A stimulating teacher and gifted stylist, M. Maritain has today almost as many admirers outside the Catholic faith as within it. He is the Catholic philosopher par excellence for our times and unquestionably one of the greatest philosophers of the twentieth century.

A MARITAIN READER

SELECTED WRITINGS OF

JACQUES MARITAIN

EDITED WITH AN INTRODUCTION

BY DONALD AND IDELLA GALLAGHER

BOSTON COLLEGE

IMAGE BOOKS

A DIVISION OF DOUBLEDAY & COMPANY, INC.

GARDEN CITY, NEW YORK

Image Books edition: 1966
Image Books edition published September 1966

First Edition

Library of Congress Catalog Card Number 66–21024
Copyright © 1966 by Doubleday & Company, Inc.
All Rights Reserved
Printed in the United States of America

Grateful acknowledgment is made to the following for permission
to include the following copyrighted material in A *Maritain Reader*.

THE ARCHABBEY PRESS. From *Man's Approach to God* by Jacques
Maritain, Wimmer Lecture V, pp. 1–23. Published 1960 by Archabbey Press, Latrobe, Pennsylvania. Reprinted by permission of
the publisher.

BEACON PRESS. "The Immortality of Man" from *Man's Destiny in
Eternity* by Jacques Maritain. Copyright 1949 by F. Lyman
Windolph and Farmer's Bank and Trust Co. of Lancaster, trus-
tees under the will of M. T. Garvin, deceased. Reprinted by permission of the publisher.

GEOFFREY BLES, LTD. From *Scholasticism and Politics* by Jacques
Maritain. Reprinted by permission of Geoffrey Bles, Ltd., Publishers.

BOLLINGEN SERIES. From *Creative Intuition in Art and Poetry* by
Jacques Maritain, Bollingen Series XXV.1, Pantheon. Reprinted by
permission of Bollingen Series.

THE BRUCE PUBLISHING COMPANY. From *God and the Permission of
Evil* by Jacques Maritain. Reprinted by permission of the publisher.

THE COMMONWEAL. "That Suffer Persecution" by Jacques Maritain.
From The Commonweal for October 11, 1946, Volume 44,
No. 26. Reprinted by permission of the publisher.

CONFERENCE ON SCIENCE, PHILOSOPHY AND RELIGION. Originally
printed as "Science, Philosophy and Faith," Chapter X, pp. 162–
84, *Science, Philosophy and Religion: A Symposium*, Conference
on Science, Philosophy and Religion and Their Relation to the
Democratic Way of Life, Inc., New York, 1941, and reproduced
with the permission of the copyright holder.

HARPER & ROW, PUBLISHERS, INC. Pp. 72–82 from *Approaches to God* by Jacques Maritain, translated from the French by Peter O'Reilly. Copyright 1954 by Jacques Maritain. Reprinted with the permission of the publisher.

DAVID MCKAY, INC. "The Divine Significance of the Dispersion of Israel" from *A Christian Look at the Jewish Question* by Jacques Maritain. Reprinted by permission of the publisher.

THE NEWMAN PRESS. From *The Sin of the Angels* by Jacques Maritain, published 1959. Reprinted by permission of the publisher.

PHILOSOPHICAL LIBRARY. "The Freedom of Song" from *Art and Poetry* by Jacques Maritain. Reprinted by permission of the publisher.

PHILOSOPHY TODAY. "Love and Friendship" by Jacques Maritain, copyright © 1966 by The Messenger Press. To be published in *Philosophy Today*. Reprinted by permission of *Philosophy Today* and Jacques Maritain.

RANDOM HOUSE, INC. From *Existence and the Existent* by Jacques Maritain, copyright 1948 by Pantheon Books, Inc. Reprinted by permission of Random House, Inc.

CHARLES SCRIBNER'S SONS. From the following works by Jacques Maritain: "Art and Beauty" from *Art and Scholasticism and Frontiers of Poetry*, pp. 23–37, copyright © Jacques Maritain; "The Majesty and Poverty of Metaphysics" from *The Degrees of Knowledge*, pp. 1–18, copyright © 1959 Jacques Maritain; "Brief Remarks in Conclusion" from *Moral Philosophy*, pp. 449–62, copyright © 1964 Jacques Maritain; "On Contemporary Atheism" copyright 1952 Jacques Maritain, "The Ways of Faith" copyright 1949 Jacques Maritain, "Christian Humanism" copyright 1942 Jacques Maritain from *The Range of Reason*, pp. 103–20, 205–17, 185–99; "Human Equality" and "Who is My Neighbour" from *Ransoming the Time*, pp. 17–32, pp. 115–40, copyright 1941 Charles Scribner's Sons; "The Christian in the Modern World" from *True Humanism* pp. 105–20. Reprinted by permission of Jacques Maritain and the publisher.

SHEED & WARD, INC. From *A Preface to Metaphysics* by Jacques Maritain. Published by Sheed & Ward, Inc., New York. Reprinted by permission of the publisher.

UNIVERSITY OF CHICAGO PRESS. From *Man and The State* by Jacques Maritain. Reprinted by permission of the publisher.

CONTENTS

INTRODUCTION

THE CHRISTIAN PHILOSOPHY
OF JACQUES MARITAIN

Since his conversion to Catholicism half a century ago, Jacques Maritain has labored to make the wisdom of St. Thomas Aquinas a living ferment in contemporary culture. He looks upon his own philosophy as a Christian philosophy, neither separated from theology nor a disguised form of it, but an enterprise of reason situated in the climate of faith.

There are some Catholic thinkers who regard "Christian philosophy" as a mélange of faith and reason, an indefinable something neither fish nor fowl. And there are contemporary philosophers like Martin Heidegger who call it "a round square," asserting that a religious philosophy can never face up to the question: why are there *essents* rather than nothing? In response to such criticisms the Christian philosopher will point out that historically Christian philosophers, while following a properly philosophical method, have philosophized within the Faith, and that without the light afforded by Revelation on the problem of creation the question posed by Martin Heidegger might never have been raised by the philosophers of the Western world.[1]

That there is something paradoxical about the state in which Christian philosophy finds itself is recognized by Jacques Maritain. Yet the more he reflects upon the problem of Christian philosophy, he tells us in *True Humanism*, the more he is convinced that it occupies a central place in the history of modern times and will continue to do so in the age to come.

What manner of philosophy is this "Christian philosophy"? And what manner of philosopher is Jacques Maritain, who has been acclaimed by so many as an apostle of truth and condemned by others as a sign of contradiction? This Introduction is an attempt to answer these questions, and the selections in A *Maritain Reader* are intended to illustrate the major themes running through the more than threescore books and the hundreds of articles written by this Christian philosopher during his long career.[2]

II

The philosophical achievements of Jacques Maritain are the fruit of his passionate quest for the meaning of life, his tireless pursuit of wisdom in philosophy, theology, and spiritual experience, and his ever-deepening conviction that his intellectual calling is to work for a philosophy united with every source of light and experience in the human mind, a philosophy able "to ransom the time, and to redeem every human search after truth."[3] Like other philosophers of his generation—Heidegger, who looks upon modern man as one forgetful of being, astray in a world of unmeaning, or Gabriel Marcel, who revolts from abstract intellectualism in his search for concrete ways of approach to the mystery of being —Jacques Maritain sees in the modern world the progressive loss of the sense of love, of truth, and of being.

Since the publication of his earliest works, Maritain has been accused of excessive severity in his judgment of the modern world and of modern thought. In Bergsonian Philosophy and Thomism (1913; tr. 1955), Antimoderne (1922), and Three Reformers (1925), he condemned many modern trends. And in subsequent books he refers to the unhappy world passing to an end before our eyes, and calls for a new style of civilization as well as a new style of sanctity (see MR 14). Yet even in his early writings Maritain acknowledges the great accomplishments of the modern world and insists that he is not simply an "antimodern." He shows extraordinary insight into the problems and longings of modern man and an immense compassion over the "anguish of our time."

In one of his more recent books, Reflections on America (1958), Jacques Maritain displays a remarkable understanding of American life and culture. His views on America are decidedly optimistic. He does not hesitate to grant well-known faults, but he insists that the American people, far from being the most materialistic, are the most generous he has known. He discovers in this country a thirst for the contemplative life in the midst of practical concerns, and he discerns a new social and economic order in the making, stemming from a non-doctrinaire form of democracy with concrete humanist and personalist aspirations. His interpretation of American civilization undoubtedly reflects the broadened experience of democracy which his years of teaching and residence in the United States have afforded him. The new order "beyond capitalism and socialism," which he sees emerging, is a phenomenon in which he finds a confirmation of his argument that the so-called "modern" world is giving way to a new one.[4]

Of the many and varied historic gains that Jacques Maritain recognizes as having been won for culture and civilization by the modern world between 1500 and the early 1900s, there is one that encompasses them all. Since the Renaissance there has developed a growing awareness of human possibilities, a deepening self-consciousness on the part of man as poet, as scientist, and as worker. This aroused and heightened consciousness, this *prise de conscience*, is evident and stirring in every phase of man's activity and in every discipline he practices. Speaking of the growth of self-consciousness among the working class in modern times, both activated and distorted by Marxism, Maritain points out that this is but one manifestation of a widespread phenomenon of immense significance.

. . . all the great forms of progress of the modern age, be it a question of art, of science, of philosophy, of poetry, of the spiritual life itself, seem to exhibit this growth of self-consciousness, this awareness.[5]

The philosophies of this century, springing from the classic forms of modern philosophy, evince this sort of awareness in a highly reflective way. In this *prise de conscience*, in this awareness and the responsibilities it entails, Christian philosophy must share. Thanks to all the influences from which he has profited, thanks to his readiness to follow every lead given him and to seek the truth whatever the cost, Maritain has attained this awareness, and for this reason his is not only a genuinely contemporary philosophy but one looking to the future.

Jacques Maritain's critique of modern civilization does not emanate from one who has dwelt in some sort of medieval enclave. He has had experience at first hand of the social and cultural world he evaluates. Born in Paris in 1882, he was reared in the heart of French culture and educated in its schools. His father, Paul Maritain, was a lawyer from Burgundy; his mother, Geneviève Favre, was the daughter of Jules Favre, one of the founders of the Third Republic. At the Sorbonne Jacques studied under the most renowned scholars of the day, but their scientist and phenomenalist philosophy caused him to despair of reason. Recalling this period in his life, he tells us that he and Raïssa Oumansoff, whom he married in 1904, attended the lectures of Henri Bergson at the Collège de France and that it was Bergson who fulfilled "our deep desire for metaphysical truth by giving us back the sense of the absolute." The other great influences upon him and Raïssa at this time were Charles Péguy and Léon Bloy. A year after their first encounter with Bloy they were baptized in the Catholic Church choosing him as their godfather.[6]

It was not philosophy that brought Jacques and Raïssa Maritain to the truth for which they longed so ardently. It was grace and faith. Indeed, in his inexperience, the young Jacques feared that he might have to surrender his philosophy, for were not all things already settled in Catholicism? While he did not shrink from such a sacrifice for the priceless gift of faith, it was not long before he discovered the writings of St. Thomas Aquinas and experienced a kind of illumination of the intelligence. Ever since he has followed in this path,

> . . . with a feeling that I could understand more completely the gropings, the discoveries and the travail of modern thought, as I tried to throw upon them more of the light which comes to us from a wisdom which, resisting the fluctuations of time, has been worked out through the centuries.[7]

His vocation as a philosopher had become clear to Maritain, and all the things he had thought he might have to forego—his studies at the Sorbonne, his knowledge of Bergson, his passionate enthusiasm for art, literature, and music, his scientific research in Germany—became part of his philosophy and yielded up its treasure. There were losses, too, of friends, and of the close relationship he had enjoyed with his mother, who never became reconciled to his Catholicism, the antithesis of everything she valued. These wounds too entered his philosophy to make it more human, more aware of the sufferings of man.

Maritain's devotion to St. Thomas is evident throughout his works. In *St. Thomas Aquinas* (1930) he writes of the purity of the Saint's intelligence, dedicated to discovering and teaching truth in all its universality. In St. Thomas, perhaps never fully understood or appreciated until our day, Maritain beholds an apostle for modern times, a guide for the working out of a new Christian philosophy.[8]

III

The selections in Parts One and Two of *A Maritain Reader*, "The Pursuit of Wisdom" and "The Approach to God," are intended to illustrate the mind of Maritain where it is most at home, in metaphysics or the field of theoretical philosophy.

"A philosopher is not a philosopher if he is not a metaphysician," says Maritain, and it is in metaphysics that he has made some of his most significant contributions to philosophy. It is not an easy matter in a Reader of this type to choose selections that do justice to the metaphysics of Maritain. Among his writings deserving of careful study are those on what he calls "the difficult and controversial notion" of subsistence; on the three degrees or orders of abstraction; on perinoetic, dianoetic, and ananoetic intellection; on ontological and empiriological knowing. In "The Intuition of Being" (MR 3) he treats of a most fundamental subject, our knowledge of being, of which everyone has glimpses and which the metaphysician holds in a steady habitual grasp. To know all the riches implicit in the notion of being, he remarks, would require all the metaphysics ever elaborated or to be elaborated (MR 3). Yet even in this abstruse subject there are flashes of Maritain's poetic intelligence, as when he remarks that the intuition of being takes place only when we are sufficiently empty to *hear* what all things are whispering.

In his discussion of the existent and subjectivity ("Subjectivity and the Human Person," MR 10), Maritain addresses himself to a theme preoccupying contemporary philosophers. Indeed, from Kierkegaard and Nietzsche to Sartre and Buber the fundamental importance of the subjectivity of personal existence has been more and more recognized. The individual who is awake to the intuition of being, according to Maritain, is awake to the intuition of subjectivity, as when he grasps in a flash that he is a self. It is in the thinking self, which is a subject and not merely an object for itself that we are faced with subjectivity as subjectivity. Some of Maritain's most profound and original pages are devoted to this topic.

In *God and the Permission of Evil* ("The Innocence of God," MR 7) Maritain returns to the philosophical question, or rather metaphysical mystery, which had absorbed his mind for many years, to which he alludes in "The Freedom of Song" (MR 22) and which he took up formally in *Saint Thomas and the Problem of Evil* (1941).[9] The tragic import of the problem of evil, at the root of so many forms of contemporary atheism, must be fearlessly accepted but at the same time must be seen in the light of the absolute innocence of God. Jacques Maritain has expressed the hope that in his writings on this subject he may have made some contribution of lasting value to philosophy. His reflections on the divine innocence, brief but profound, suggest what that contribution is.

Unlike the great system-builders of classical modern philosophy, and in common with his contemporaries, Jacques Maritain has given us no monumental work elaborating a complete philosophical synthesis. His major work in speculative philosophy, *The Degrees of Knowledge* (1932), is a comprehensive work far-reaching in scope, but his aim here is only to clear the ground and push back the frontiers of Thomistic philosophy. It grew out of his conviction that a reflective and critical realism should discriminate and integrate the orders and degrees of the various kinds of knowing. In mapping out what he calls the metaphysical topology of the inner world of reflection, he touches upon philosophy and experimental science, critical realism and theory of knowledge, our knowledge of sensible nature, metaphysical knowledge, analogy and subsistence, mystical experience and philosophy, Augustinian wisdom and the doctrine of John of the Cross. *The Degrees of Knowledge* is not a systematic metaphysics but an epistemological study of the various levels of knowledge.

Like many other present-day philosophers, Jacques Maritain has devoted considerable attention to the relations between science and philosophy. He accords ample recognition to the intrinsic value and manifold benefits of the sciences but warns against the possible consequences of their hold on modern culture. Habits of thought prevalent in an industrial civilization, in which the manipulation of the world through science and technology plays a dominant role, result in a loss of the sense of being. This shrinkage of the intellect produces an inability to grasp any rational explanation of God's existence and weakens adherence to religious beliefs.[10] Maritain urges that philosophers and scientists learn to speak each other's language and to appreciate each other's insights.

The metaphysician's calling is an arduous one. He must be all things to all men of learning and at the same time intent on what matters most, namely, the contemplation of being itself. In this contemplation there is hidden an impulse toward something beyond metaphysics. Of this irrepressible and insatiable desire implanted in every man but aroused to poignant awareness in the metaphysician, Maritain writes in "The Grandeur and Poverty of Metaphysics" (1925), which constitutes the Introduction to *The Degrees of Knowledge* (MR 1), "It awakens a desire for supreme union, for spiritual possession completed in the order of reality itself and not only in the concept. It cannot satisfy that desire." One of man's glories is his capacity to attain some measure of human wisdom in metaphysics, but herein lies the poverty of that science.

By metaphysics, then, man can arrive at neither a knowledge of God as He is in Himself nor at living union with Him. Yet the metaphysician is properly concerned with the mystery of Subsisting Being and seeks to understand in the light of reason the causes of being. The thirst for being can never be quenched, as the history of metaphysics with its periods of renewal following those of stagnation amply proves. Nevertheless, Maritain calls attention to the fact that in the existential situation of our age there are many minds for whom philosophical explanations of God have little meaning and no attraction. God is not absent from the world, as Fr. Martin C. D'Arcy points out in *No Absent God,* but men have strayed far from Him. The Christian philosopher cannot rest satisfied with merely repeating or refining the five ways of St. Thomas. In *Approaches to God* (1954) Maritain considers the traditional arguments for the existence of God, taking into account advances in and difficulties arising from scientific knowledge, discusses new approaches drawn from connatural knowledge, e.g., poetic and moral experience, and proposes a "sixth way" (MR 5; also MR 4).

On a higher level, the problem we are considering is no longer simply philosophical but takes on theological dimensions. One is tempted to say that it is a matter not only of theology but of atheology. Can atheism really be lived? Jacques Maritain answers that if it could be lived down to its ultimate roots in the will it would disorganize and kill the will metaphysically.[11] In the penetrating study of contemporary atheism included in this Reader (MR 6), he probes this fateful problem and submits the atheistic mentality to a kind of phenomenological description. There was a time when Scholastic philosophers discussed in rather academic fashion whether atheism involved an inherent contradiction, but this approach fails to appreciate the full dimensions of the problem. The Christian philosopher has come to perceive that there is an atheistic attitude of mind bred by the very conditions of modern culture. Unconscious in people indifferent to religion, it may be latent even in lukewarm or routine believers. At length it issues into the open in the various species of atheist that Maritain examines. Alongside the lesser types, the Absolute Atheist as depicted by Maritain stands forth as an awesome figure, a sort of lost saint with demonic proportions. In him human liberty is pitted against divine, against a God vainly but passionately negated.

The philosophical knowledge the Christian philosopher possesses concerning God's existence and nature, and his capacity to discuss these questions with other philosophers are invaluable and indispensable. But in the altogether different dimension of the spirit we are considering here, the Christian philosopher knows that the absolute defiance of the atheist can be met only by the affirmation, equally absolute, of the saint. In writing of this dramatic and portentous confrontation Maritain reaches one of his philosophical and literary heights.

One of the most far-reaching themes in the philosophy of Jacques Maritain is that of liberty. The mystery of freedom and of the choices men face at crucial stages of their lives has never ceased to awe and evoke reflection in the philosopher's mind. An uncomplicated yet primordial and illuminating example is that of the child making his first genuine option for either good or evil.[12] Another example is afforded by the adolescent at the threshold of maturity deciding for one way of life over another, perhaps for or against the religion in which he was raised. The striking contrast between the saint and the atheist as Maritain portrays them brings into opposition two beings who in the secret recess of the soul have made their choice for or against God. These illustrations testify to what every one knows and has experienced in his personal life: the fact of free choice. The metaphysical roots of freedom exist in every human being but must be encouraged to grow in the psychological and moral order. "We are called upon to become in action," says Maritain in *Freedom in the Modern World*, "what we are already in the metaphysical order, persons. It is our duty to make ourselves persons by our own efforts, having dominion over our own acts and enjoying a wholeness of existence."

Maritain's treatment of the love of free option in *The Sin of the Angel* (1959) is exceptionally pertinent to an understanding of the mystery of free choice as exercised by the human will. In considering from the vantage point of the Christian philosopher the profound theological problem of the peccability of the angel—discussed in highly technical language as a controversial question by the theologians—he provides us with rewarding insights into the metaphysics of choice ("Freedom and the Love of God," MR 9). The study of the nature of the free act as possessed, as it were, in its purest form by an intelligent being that is "pure spirit," un-encumbered by bodily passions and weaknesses, yields a deeper understanding of the nature of choice in any created intellect whether embodied or disembodied.

The freedom of choice in which the destiny of the free creature is decided is ordered to a higher freedom, that of autonomy, fulfillment, or exultation.[13] This freedom of in-dependence, as Maritain also calls it, is dwelt upon in a number of studies (see "Human Freedom," MR 8). Each one of us knows it obscurely as something of supreme value, yet Maritain is one of the few philosophers who have ad-dressed themselves to its elucidation, and scarcely anyone else has written so illuminatingly on freedom. Like all great words, he says, freedom is laden with the riches, desires, dreams, and generosities of the human person.

IV

Societies, too, or we should rather say human persons dwelling in community and acting in concert, have their choices to make. In his works on social philosophy, Jacques Maritain stands out as the philosopher of freedom; he is concerned not only with the type of social and political order that contemporary man is called upon to build, but with the concrete attitude of the human being in the face of his des-tiny. Within the limits set down by the laws of nature, by heritage and tradition, and by the pressures of the material environment, there is ample room for man to choose the kind of society in which he desires to live. A truly human society promotes and fosters the conditions prerequisite to the flowering of the freedom of fulfillment or independence.

The selections contained in Parts Three, Four, and Five of A Maritain Reader, "The Image of Man," "Heroic Hu-manism and Democracy," and "Human Fellowship," illus-trate the principal themes of this practical philosophy, em-bracing moral, political, and social philosophy, and including also philosophy of history and philosophy of education. In these areas, as in those of theoretical philosophy, Jacques Maritain has blazed trails and pushed forward the boundaries of Christian philosophy. Among the many topics on which he has made lasting contributions and pointed the way for further research are the natural law and human rights, sovereignty and the nature of the state, authority and freedom, human equality (MR 16), the foundations of personalist democracy (MR 15), philosophy of education, and intellectual cooperation. (MR 16).

Of the numerous books and studies Maritain has devoted to these matters, the most important in the domain of social thought is undoubtedly *True Humanism* (1936, see MR 14), as *Man and the State* (1951, see MR 15) is in the domain of political theory and *Moral Philosophy* (1960, see MR 11) in that of ethics.[14] *True Humanism*, which Maritain regarded as a sketch of a more comprehensive work he hoped to write, contains his charter for a Christian social order, a New Christendom.[15] To the various forms of anthropocentric humanism rampant everywhere in the modern world, men of good will must oppose a theocentric humanism. A Christian social philosophy must be developed taking full cognizance of the economic and social questions of our time. Christians in particular are called upon to take positions of leadership in the field of action. Maritain expresses his amazement over the number of Christians who are content to sleep on unaware of the crisis threatening them. What is needed is a heroic humanism, but is this possible for man in the existential conditions of actual life? Maritain has compassion for the common man, he has confidence in the plain people, but he understands "the human condition" well, and knows that while man aspires to a heroic life, there is nothing less common than heroism.[16] Is a "humanism conscious of itself and free, capable of leading man to sacrifice and superhuman greatness" really possible? The Christian answer is in terms of a higher ideal, that of the Humanism of the Incarnation, which is directed toward the sociotemporal fulfillment of the message of the Gospels.

The pages in which Jacques Maritain treats the temporal mission of the Christian are drawn from *True Humanism*. A kind of document of and testament to the troubled times of the 1930s in which it was written, "The Christian in the Modern World" (MR 14), as this selection is herein entitled, rings with an urgent, prophetic, and compelling con-

temporary note. Maritain sheds light upon the secular failure
of a civilization once Christian but now only outwardly so,
and characterizes the temporal role of the Christian upon
whom is incumbent the inception of a new Christian order.
Without compromise he sets forth what must be discarded
of the old ways of acting and what virtues, heroic in scope,
must be fostered.

The personalism and "heroic humanism" of Maritain's social philosophy has had a strong attraction for people in the
developing countries of the world who clamor for greater
fraternal recognition and dialogue, and not simply for technical and material assistance. This is particularly true of
those lands with Christian traditions such as the republics
of Latin America. While the conservative elements have often
in the past repudiated his social thought as "revolutionary,"
it has been an inspiration to the Christian Democratic movement which is growing in many of these countries.[17]

For an understanding of the complex questions pertaining to the social, economic, political, and cultural orders,
there is need for a philosophy of history and of culture as
well as for a social and political philosophy. Herein lies one
of the greatest opportunities and challenges for the Christian
philosopher, for to his mind a pure philosophy of history can
scarcely be adequate. The proper climate for the growth and
development of a philosophy of history is that of Judeo-
Christian history. In the hands of a philosopher without faith,
says Maritain, the philosophy of history shrinks to an insignificant object and risks mystification, where would such a
man find the prophetic gifts required? An adequate philosophy of history is illuminated by the higher knowledge of
faith and theology; it is, in short, a Christian philosophy of
history. Evaluating Maritain's work in this field, Cardinal
Journet says that it constitutes for the first time a Christian
philosophy of history as distinguished from the theology of
history.[18]

A Christian philosophy of culture is confronted with similar tasks. It must pose the problems involved in culture and
civilization otherwise than do non-Christian philosophies. It
must recognize the importance of the economic factor in
history but seek to shed light upon deeper and more human

aspects of culture, especially as concerns the role played by spiritual forces.[19]

Maritain's social and political philosophy is impelled by its own principles of justice and friendship to call for cooperation with likeminded men. Long before it was fashionable to talk the language of dialogue and encounter, he was urging upon us the necessity of dialogue between believing and unbelieving philosophers. Such discussion is difficult because it involves different spiritual universes, yet it is not only possible and desirable but necessary if the unity of Western culture is to be preserved. Similar problems on a wider scale exist among peoples of different countries and civilizations, and Maritain treats of these in his studies on co-operation in a divided world.[20] His essay "Who is My Neighbour?" (MR 17) is one of his noblest statements on truth and human fellowship. In it he gives expression to his personal credo and manifests his ecumenical spirit. Maritain has personally sought to enter into fraternal dialogue with men of every creed and culture. His success is not to be judged by the number of converts he has made to the truth in which he believes but rather by the influence his zeal for truth and justice has had upon his contemporaries.

Of unique significance here is Maritain's concern with "The Jewish Question," which is, as he notes, not a mere *problem* composed of economic and political elements but a *mystery* related to that of the Cross (MR 18). His moving indictment of Anti-Semitism and his defense of all members of the human family as brothers under the Heavenly Father are among the pages for which history will do him most honor. He has condemned in season and out of season every form of racism and degradation of the human person. He has not merely preached these things, he has acted upon them repeatedly and at personal cost.

Throughout the selections on humanism, democracy, and fellowship in this Reader, the theme of a Christian philosophy in the making runs like a *leitmotif*. Maritain tells us that a realistic philosophy of human equality must draw upon the resources of the Judeo-Christian tradition to be sound and effective. He describes eloquently the lessons democracy has learned from the inspiration of the Gospels, and emphasizes

that the growing consciousness of the rights of the person
has at its origin the conception of man and of natural law
established by centuries of Christian philosophy.[21] Of all the
medieval philosophers, it was St. Thomas in particular who
clearly distinguished between theology and philosophy and
accorded autonomy to the philosophic disciplines.[22] But the
Christian philosophy thus established in principle was never
explicitly elaborated until our time, and is still only in the
process of development.[23] It is more a philosophy of the
future than of tradition.

v

Maritain's writings on the philosophy of art span a period
of more than forty years. Both in *Art and Scholasticism*
(1920; MR 21) and in *Creative Intuition in Art and Poetry*
(1955; MR 20) he seeks to effect a dialogue between peren-
nial philosophy and contemporary art.

Art and Scholasticism has become so much a part of our
Catholic culture that it is difficult for us to grasp how novel
it seemed at the moment of its appearance. The medieval
masters had touched upon the principles of art in their theology, but little or nothing had been written by recent Scholastics on modern aesthetics. Then came the work of Maritain, with its precise and lucid definitions, its concise and
luminous explanations. Beneath the austere simplicity and
artistic restraint of the book there throbs the ardor and enthusiasm of Maritain's first period as a champion of Thomistic philosophy. Who was this Scholastic who wrote on the
latest productions of the art world? Was he not, as he describes himself in his letter to Jean Cocteau (*Art and Faith*,
1926), the most unworthy and the latest of the disciples of
St. Thomas? Yet this man who speaks of himself with wry
humor writes about art and faith to Cocteau, and it was he
who wrote *Art and Scholasticism* with Rouault in mind![24]

In his first book on art, Jacques Maritain attempted to
clarify the nature of art as a virtue of the practical intellect;
in later years he became more and more intent upon scruti-
nizing the mysterious nature of poetic knowledge and ap-
propriating the precious substance it contains for philosophy.

This form of knowledge by connaturality he investigates in *Situation of Poetry* (1938, written in collaboration with Raïssa) and in *Creative Intuition in Art and Poetry*, his master work on the philosophy of art and beauty.

Every man enjoys or is capable of enjoying poetic experience whether or not he expresses it in a poem or work of art. A kind of poetic intuition comes into play, Maritain says, in science, philosophy, big business, religion, and revolution. There is a secret poetic intuition at work in the creative thinking of Plato, St. Thomas, and Hegel. The poetic intuitivity and imaginativeness of Maritain himself is evident in almost everything he writes, even in some of his most abstruse pieces. It is particularly evident in one of the most beautiful and profound essays he ever wrote, *La clef des chants*, ("The Freedom of Song" MR 22). Like a poet of the intelligence, he utters soaring words about poetry and music and their mysterious ontological correspondence with metaphysics and mysticism.

The selections on art and poetry, and on faith and contemplation included in Parts Six and Seven of *A Maritain Reader* are imbued with the authentic spirit of the creativity and the wisdom with which they are concerned because the author himself is a man of poetry and of faith. He has lived in close friendship with artists, enjoyed their company, and tried unceasingly to comprehend their work and give it a critical and philosophical interpretation. His life, though filled with practical concerns and charitable tasks, excursions into the world for the sake of men, has been profoundly inward, dedicated not only to habitual philosophic meditation but, above all else, to spiritual contemplation. One of the first books he wrote and one of his most recent, both in collaboration with his wife Raïssa, are devoted to prayer and contemplation.[25] When Maritain the Christian philosopher touches upon theological and spiritual questions in "Action and Contemplation" (MR 24) and "The Ways of Faith" (MR 23), he speaks as one who has knowledge firsthand. In his reflections on love and friendship (MR 25), written *en marge du Journal de Raïssa* (Paris 1963), and which he writes "not as a philosopher (which I am) nor as a theologian (which I am not)" but out of the experience of *un vieil homme*, there is both a fidelity to Catholic tradition and a glowing freshness of thought.

VI

In this Introduction we have briefly treated the work of Jacques Maritain in many areas of both practical and speculative philosophy and have pictured him at work, as it were, working out a Christian philosophy for the age to come. His calling, as Yves Simon saw it, has been that of a philosopher who considers philosophical issues in the particular *state* they assume by virtue of their relation to faith and theology.[26] This relation is so close and intimate that the full significance of Maritain's achievement in philosophy itself may be obscured. There should be no misunderstanding on this point. The greatness of Jacques Maritain as a *Christian* philosopher will be judged on philosophical grounds. And we believe that posterity will judge him to be a great philosopher. To clarify this matter, let us note the following points.

1. Maritain's philosophical writings, as the selections in this Reader should make clear, are fortified and steadied by theology and often soar to theological and even contemplative heights. Yet they possess a proper philosophical starting point, employ philosophical methodology, and arrive at specifically philosophical conclusions.

2. He has been called by a noted theologian who has known him for many years, *un théologien immense*. Here again the readings in this volume will show why such a judgment could be made. Yet even in those studies where he deals with theological as well as philosophical topics, he takes pains to point out that the study in question is in the philosophical order.[27]

3. In recent years, Jacques Maritain has become more and more emphatic about the philosophical objectives and character of his work, for example, in his *Moral Philosophy*.[28]

Many years ago, Maritain envisioned the Christian philosophy of the future and pointed out how essential an ingredient it would be in the constitution of a Christian social order.[29] Part of the task he foresaw then has been accomplished, but the future looms before us and much remains yet to be done.

Jacques Maritain has endeavored, as we have seen, to extend the frontiers of the Thomistic synthesis in theoretical philosophy. He has given us the grand outlines of such a philosophy suited to our age and, as far as we can foresee, to the age to come. There are various ways of assessing a philosopher's achievement and no one criterion suffices, but his own statement of what he aimed at accomplishing in *The Degrees of Knowledge* expresses an ideal and a goal shared by all those collaborating with him in the common task of furthering Christian philosophy, even by those, including some Thomists, who do not accept his conception of Christian philosophy. Maritain will be judged by his success in attaining that goal, and there is no doubt, in our view, that he has been successful.[30]

In the immense and variegated expanses of practical philosophy, Maritain has provided us with the grand outlines of a Christian social and political philosophy, for example in *Man and the State, True Humanism*, and a number of definitive studies of difficult and complex particular problems. The Christian philosophy of the future, as foreseen (as a concrete historical ideal to aim at) by Jacques Maritain, is one which will be an intellectual expression of, as well as a vehicle for, the ideas and ideals of the personalist, communitarian, and pluralist society he advocates in *Christianity and Democracy* and other works.

In this realm of practical philosophy, too, the thought of Jacques Maritain should be judged on its merits, for example, his doctrines on moral philosophy adequately considered, on the person and the common good, and on authority and sovereignty. His philosophy of freedom and equality is attainable in its completeness, as he has argued, only in terms of a Christian philosophy of man, but its worth as philosophy must be evaluated not in terms of any religious value it may have but in accordance with strict philosophical criteria.

It is not possible, nor would it be appropriate in this Introduction, to give an elaborate appraisal of Maritain's accomplishments. We may be permitted, however, to quote from a tribute paid him by Gerald B. Phelan, long associated with him in Toronto:

In the years that are not yet, Jacques Maritain will undoubtedly be known as one of the great philosophical figures of the twentieth century. He is actually so regarded
today, in his lifetime. I, personally, would speak in stronger
terms of his pre-eminence as a philosopher and I would
not restrict myself to the twentieth century.[31]

At the solemn closing ceremonies of the Second Ecumenical Vatican Council held in Rome on December 8, 1965, the
Holy Father's Messages to the World were read out by a
Cardinal and then presented by the Pope personally to the
representatives of the various groups addressed. To the men
of thought and science Pope Paul VI tendered a special sa-
lute, to those "seekers after truth," who were "pilgrims on the
way toward the light." Three noted scholars were present to
receive this message on behalf of the intellectuals of the
world. Foremost among them was a Christian philosopher
who had only recently attained the age of eighty-three,
Jacques Maritain.[32]

*   *   *

This Reader was originally conceived and in the making a
number of years before it took shape as A *Maritain Reader*.
To many friends and associates we owe thanks for their suggestions and assistance. For Professor Jacques Maritain are
reserved our warmest thanks for his personal interest in the
project and his many extremely helpful suggestions.

This Reader is not an anthology in the classical sense of a
nosegay of flowers culled from the garden of an author. It is
not a collection of beautiful passages or thought-provoking
excerpts. It does not pretend to give "all the best" in Jacques
Maritain's work. There is in a sense no "best," short of an
edition of his complete works. In A *Maritain Reader* we have
attempted merely to present a selection of the writings we
judged would best achieve the end we had in view, namely,
to make manifest at one and the same time the organic unity
and rich variety of his voluminous writings. We have not had
in mind specialists but rather educated readers, even scholars in other disciplines, who may be largely unfamiliar with
the philosopher's thought but desire to become acquainted

with it. It is our hope that such persons may find herein the inspiration to read further on their own and that this Reader may serve as a guide to facilitate their progress.

DONALD and IDELLA GALLAGHER
Boston College
Chestnut Hill, Massachusetts
June 1964

NOTES

1. See Heidegger's work, *An Introduction to Metaphysics* (New Haven: Yale University Press, 1959), Ch. I. *Being and Time* (London: SCM Press, 1962), pp. 41–48 on the task of destroying the history of ontology. On Christian philosophy from the historical point of view, see Etienne Gilson, *The Spirit of Mediaeval Philosophy* (New York: Charles Scribner's Sons, 1936) and *Christianity and Philosophy* (New York: Sheed & Ward, 1939). One of the best definitions of Christian philosophy to be found in the works of Jacques Maritain is in *The Degrees of Knowledge*, 308. See also his *An Essay on Christian Philosophy*. For the complete reference to the books by Maritain cited in these Notes, see the *Suggestions for Further Reading*. In the text of this Introduction the date of original publication is given after the title of a work. Note also that references to selections in this Reader are indicated by MR and the selection number.

2. In the Introduction to *The Achievement of Jacques and Raïssa Maritain, a Bibliography 1906–1961* (New York: Doubleday & Company, 1962), we attempted a kind of bio-bibliographical essay on the spirit and significance of their life-work which was a genuine collaboration, as Jacques Maritain has confirmed in the years following his wife's death in 1960. (See *Journal de Raïssa*, publié par Jacques Maritain, Paris: Desclée de Brouwer, 1963). The present Introduction is not an account of Maritain's spiritual and intellectual itinerary but of the dominant themes of his Christian philosophy.

3. *Ransoming the Time*, p. ix.

4. Maritain's personal acquaintance with this country goes back to the period of his first lectures here and in Canada in 1933; he resided in the United States during World War II from 1940 to 1945 and later from 1948 to 1961. For a chronology of the lives of Jacques and Raïssa Maritain, see *The Achievement of Jacques and Raïssa Maritain*, pp. 37–42.

5. *True Humanism*, p. 225. Compare *The Situation of Poetry*, pp. 37–38.

6. For this account, see the personal credo or "confession of faith" by Maritain himself in *I Believe*, ed. C. Fadiman (New York: Simon and Schuster, 1939). *Confession de foi* was published in 1941. See also *The Social and Political Philosophy of Jacques Maritain*, ed. J. W. Evans and L. R. Ward (New York: Charles Scribner's Sons, 1955; Image Books, 1965), Ch. 25.

7. *Ibid.*

8. In the Preface written in 1958 for the new English edition of *St. Thomas Aquinas*, Maritain describes the great effort undertaken by a group of philosophers and theologians to rediscover the doctrine of St. Thomas and make it "enter the general realm of culture."

9. *Dieu et la permission du mal* (Paris: Desclée de Brouwer, 1963) was translated into English by Joseph W. Evans and published by The Bruce Publishing Company, Milwaukee, in 1966. In *The Meaning of Evil* (New York: P. J. Kenedy & Sons, 1963; French edition, 1961), Cardinal Journet refers to fifteen other works in which Maritain considers the question of evil (pp. 295–96; see also pp. 242–46, 269–74). He states (p. 14) that the writings of Jacques Maritain on this subject are "rich and coherent, traditional yet full of innovation, and containing the most penetrating teaching on evil written in our own times from the Christian viewpoint."

10. See "God and Science" in *On the Use of Philosophy* (1961).

11. *True Humanism*, pp. 52–53.

12. See *The Range of Reason*, Ch. VI, "The Immanent Dialectic of the First Act of Freedom." This study is one of the most important which Maritain has devoted to the topic of freedom.

13. One of Maritain's finest studies on this subject is "The Conquest of Freedom," reprinted in *The Education of Man: the Educational Philosophy of Jacques Maritain*. See also *Freedom in the Modern World*, p. 30. Compare *The Degrees of Knowledge*, pp. 232–33.

14. Maritain describes *Moral Philosophy* as doctrinal not historical, yet it is devoted "to the historical and critical examination of a certain number of great systems which are, in my opinion, the most significant ones with respect to the development and the adventures of moral philosophy." He projected the systematic explanation of the basic problems of ethics for a second volume, of which "a central fragment in outline form" exists in *Neuf leçons sur les notions premières de la philosophie morale* (1950).

15. The original title of *True Humanism* conveys forcibly Maritain's notion that an authentic humanism must be integral, complete. In *Humanisme intégral* he endeavored to take into account all that man has received from God, not only human nature but also the gifts of Christ's grace.

16. Compare Maritain's penetrating reflections upon the human condition in MR 11.

17. The Christian Democratic Party of Chile, for example, is nonconfessional, but its leaders, notably President Eduardo Frei (in *Maritain entre nosotros*, 1964, co-authored with Ismael Bustos, and in a number of other works), have acknowledged the inspiration they have received from Maritain's Christian humanism. His conception of the temporal order is described by Frei and Bustos as *comunitario, personalista y peregrinatorio*. A distinguished Latin American prelate, Bishop Manuel Larrain of Chile, has also pointed out that the thought of Jacques Maritain was an important influence in the deliberations of the Second Vatican Council.

18. See his study in *Jacques Maritain, the Man and His Achievement*, ed. J. W. Evans (New York: Sheed & Ward, 1963). This book is hereafter referred to as *Jacques Maritain*. See also Cardinal Journet's article "D'une philosophie chrétienne de l'histoire et de la culture" in *Jacques Maritain: son oeuvre philosophique* (*Revue thomiste* XLVIII, 1948).

19. See *Religion and Culture* (1930) and also "The Philosopher in Society" in *On the Use of Philosophy*.

20. *The Range of Reason*, Chs. XIII and IV.

21. See *The Rights of Man and Natural Law*, p. 81.

22. See "The Philosophy of Faith," *Science and Wisdom*, pp. 70–133. This study is Maritain's charter for the Christian philosophy of the future.

23. *Ibid.* Compare Note 14 above on his book *Moral Philosophy*, in which he points out that moral philosophy conceived in the light of the principles of St. Thomas and capable of illuminating modern problems has yet to be developed.

24. See *We Have Been Friends Together and Adventures in Grace —The Memoirs of Raïssa Maritain* (Image Books Edition, 1961), p. 194.

25. *Prayer and Intelligence* (1922) and *Liturgy and Contemplation* (1959).

26. "Jacques Maritain: the Growth of a Christian Philosopher" in *Jacques Maritain*, ed. Evans.

27. He makes such an explicit statement in "Natural Mystical Experience and the Void," *Ransoming the Time*, Ch. X. See Alan Watts, *The Supreme Identity*, (New York: The Noonday Press, 1957), p. 190, for a criticism of Maritain's position, and also MR 11, pp. 188–90 below.

28. See Note 20.

29. In his social and political philosophy Maritain advocates pluralism as an essential element in democratic theory; it is also an es-

sential factor in the ideal of a vitally Christian order he portrays in *True Humanism*. On this question see J. W. Evans, "Jacques Maritain and the Problem of Pluralism in Political Life," *Jacques Maritain*.

30. See J. F. Anderson, "The Role of Analogy in Maritain's Thought," *Jacques Maritain*, for an excellent study of Maritain the metaphysician.

31. See Phelan's Medalist's Address in the *Proceedings of the American Catholic Philosophical Association*, Vol. XXXIII. Jacques Maritain was the first recipient of the Cardinal Spellman-Aquinas Medal in 1951. (See *Proceedings A.C.P.A.*, Vol. XXV).

32. For the text of the closing messages of the Council, see *The Documents of Vatican II*, ed. Walter M. Abbott, S.J., and Msgr. Joseph Gallagher (New York: Angelus Books, 1966), pp. 728–37, especially pp. 730–31.

A MARITAIN READER: SOURCES

PART ONE
THE PURSUIT OF WISDOM

"We preach a different wisdom—scandal for the Jews, madness for the Greeks. This wisdom, far surpassing all human effort, a gift of deifying grace and free endowments of Uncreated Wisdom, has as its beginning the *mad love* that Wisdom *Itself* has for each and all of us, and as its end, the union of spirit with it. Only Jesus crucified gives access to it—the Mediator raised up between heaven and earth."

The Grandeur and Poverty of Metaphysics

1. THE GRANDEUR AND POVERTY
OF METAPHYSICS

To Charles Du Bos

In periods when shallow speculation is rife, one might think that metaphysics would shine forth, at least, by the brilliance of its modest reserve. But the very age that is unaware of the grandeur of metaphysics, likewise overlooks its poverty. Its grandeur? It is wisdom. Its poverty? It is human science.

It names God, Yes! But not by His Own Name. For it is not possible to paint a picture of God as it is to draw a tree or a conic section. You, True God, the Saviour of Israel, are veritably a hidden God! When Jacob asked the angel early in the morning: "Tell me, what is your name?",[1] He replied: "Why do you ask My Name?" "It is impossible to utter this truly wondrous name, the name that is set above every name that is named either in the present world or in the world to come."[2]

A deep vice besets the philosophers of our day, whether they be neo-Kantians, neo-positivists, idealists, Bergsonians, logisticians, pragmatists, neo-Spinozists, or neo-mystics. It is the ancient error of the *nominalists*. In different forms, and with various degrees of awareness, they all blame knowledge-through-concepts for not being a supra-sensible intuition of the existing singular, as is Spinoza's *scientia intuitiva*, Boehme's theosophic vision, or that of Swedenborg, which Kant so regretfully denounced as illusory. They cannot forgive that knowledge for not opening directly upon existence as sensation does, but only onto essences, possibles. They cannot forgive it for its inability to reach actual existence except by turning back upon sense. They have a basic misunderstanding of the value of the abstract, that immateriality which is more enduring than things for all that it is untouchable and unimaginable, that immateriality which mind seeks out in the very heart of things. But why this incurable nominalism? The reason is that while having a taste for the real indeed, they nevertheless have no sense of being. Being as such, loosed from the matter in which it is incorporated, being, with its pure objective necessities and its laws that prove no burden, its restraints which do not bind, its invisible evidence, is for them only a word.

How is it possible to speculate about geometry in space if figures are not seen in space? How is it possible to discourse on metaphysics if quiddities are not *seen* in the intelligible? Difficult acrobatics are undoubtedly required of the poet; so, too, are they demanded of the metaphysician. In both cases, however, no venture is possible without a primary gift. A Jesuit friend of mine claims that since the fall of Adam, man has become so ill suited to understanding that the intellectual perception of being must be looked upon as a mystical gift, a supernatural gift granted only to a few privileged persons. That is obviously a pious exaggeration. Yet, it does remain true that this intuition is, as far as we are concerned, an awakening from our dreams, a step quickly taken out of slumber and its starried streams. For man has many sleeps. Every morning, he wakes from animal slumber. He emerges from his human slumber when intelligence is turned loose (and from a sleepy unconsciousness of God when touched by God). There is a sort of grace in the natural order presiding over the birth of a metaphysician just as there is over the birth of a poet. The latter thrusts his heart into things like a dart or rocket and, by divination, sees, within the very sensible itself and inseparable from it, the flash of a spiritual light in which a glimpse of God is revealed to him. The former turns away from the sensible, and through knowledge sees within the intelligible, detached from perishable things, this very spiritual light itself, captured in some conception. The metaphysician breathes an atmosphere of abstraction which is death for the artist. Imagination, the discontinuous, the unverifiable, in which the metaphysician perishes, is life itself to the artist. While both absorb rays that come down from creative Night, the artist finds nourishment in a bound intelligibility which is as multiform as God's reflections upon earth, the metaphysician finds it in a naked intelligibility that is as determined as the proper being of things. They are playing seesaw, each in turn rising up to the sky. Spectators make fun of their game; they sit upon solid ground.

"You are," I was once told, "a sort of dispenser of black magic, one who would bid us to fly with our arms." "No! I am asking you to fly with your wings." "But we have only arms." "Arms? No! They are really atrophied wings. And that is quite another matter. They would spring up again if you had but the courage, if you but understood that the Earth is not our sole support, and the air is not the void."

To raise a simple factual impossibility, a certain historical state of intelligence, as an objection against a philosopher's undertaking, and say to him: "Perhaps what you are offering on our market *is* the truth, but our mental structure has become such that we can no longer think in terms of that truth of yours because our mind 'has changed as well as our body,'"[3] that, as an argument, is strictly null and void. It is, however, the best objection that can be raised against the present revival of metaphysics. True, timeless metaphysics no longer suits the modern intellect. More exactly, the latter no longer squares with the former. Three centuries of empirio-mathematicism have so warped the intellect that it is no longer interested in anything but the invention of apparatus to capture phenomena—conceptual nets that give the mind a certain practical dominion over nature, coupled with a deceptive understanding of it; deceptive, indeed, because its thought is resolved, not in being, but in the sensible itself. By advancing in this fashion, not by linking new truths to already acquired truths, but by substituting new apparatus for outmoded apparatus; by handling things without understanding them; by gaining ground against the real bit by bit, patiently, through victories that are always piecemeal and provisory—by acquiring a secret taste for the matter with which it conspires—thus has the modern intellect developed within this lower order of scientific demiurgy a kind of manifold and marvellously specialized touch as well as wonderful instincts for the chase. But, at the same time, it has wretchedly weakened and disarmed itself in the face of the proper objects of the intellect, which it has abjectly surrendered. It has become quite incapable of appreciating the world of rational evidences except as a system of well-oiled gears. Henceforth, it has to take its stand either against all metaphysics (old-fashioned positivism) or in favour of a pseudo-metaphysics (new-styled positivism). Indeed, intellect must choose one of those counterfeits for metaphysics in which the experimental process stands revealed in its grossest form, among pragmatists and pluralists, in its subtlest guise, in Bergsonian intuition, in its religious habit, in the integral action of the Blondellians and their attempt to suffer all things in a mystical fashion and thereby invade the realms of pure understanding.

That is all very true. The slope of modern intelligence is slanted against us. Well, slopes are made to be climbed. The intellect has not changed its nature; it has acquired habits. Habits can be corrected. Second nature? But the first nature is always there; and the syllogism will last as long as man does.

It is less bothersome for the philosopher to be out of intellectual step with his time than it is for the artist. Besides, things happen quite differently in the one case than in the other. The artist pours out his creative spirit into a work; the philosopher measures his knowing-spirit by the real. It is by leaning for support, at first, on the intellect of his age, by concentrating all its languors and fires in a single focal point, and then driving it to the limit, that the artist has the opportunity to refashion the whole mass. But the concern of the philosopher is, above all, to seize upon the object, to cling to it desperately, with such tenacity that a breakthrough is finally effected in the mass which confronts him, achieving a regrouping of forces and a new course of action.

It is also very true that metaphysics is of no use in furthering the output of experimental science. Discoveries and inventions in the land of phenomena? It can boast of none; its heuristic value, as they say, is absolutely nil in that area. From this point of view, there is nothing to be expected of it. There is no tilling of the soil in heaven.

For several thousand years we have known that herein precisely lies the majesty of metaphysics. Old Aristotle said that metaphysics is useless; it is of no service because it is above and beyond all service; useless because *super-useful*, good in and for itself. Note, then, that if it were to serve the science of phenomena, to assist in its output, it would be vain by definition since it would aim to go beyond such science and yet would not be better than it. Every metaphysic that is not measured by the mystery of what is, but by the state of positive science at such and such an instant, is false from the beginning, whether it be the metaphysic of Descartes, Spinoza, or Kant. True metaphysics can, in its own way and in due proportion, also say: My kingdom is not of this world. As for its axioms, it seizes upon them in spite of this world, which strives to hide them from it. What does the world of phenomena say, that false flux of the raw empirical, if not that what is, is not, and that there is more in the effect than in the cause? As for its conclusions, metaphysics contemplates them by ascending from the visible to the invisible; it hangs them from a stable order of intelligible causations found enmeshed, indeed, in this world but none the less transcending it, an order which in no way runs counter to the system of sensible sequences studied by experimental science, yet which remains strictly alien to it. The movement of my pen on paper, hand, imagination and internal senses, will, intellect, the first Agent, without whose impulse no created thing would act—such a series of causes is in no way opposed to, but is, on the other hand, of no assistance in determining, the vasomotor changes or the associations of images at work while I am writing. Metaphysics demands a certain purification of the intellect; it also takes for granted a certain purification of the will and assumes that one has the courage to cling to things that have no use, to *useless* Truth.

However, nothing is more necessary to man than this uselessness. What we need is not truths that serve us but a truth we may serve. For that truth is the food of the spirit. And, by the better part of ourselves, we are spirit. Useless metaphysics puts order—not any sort of police order, but the order that has sprung from eternity—in the speculative and practical intellect. It gives back to man his balance and his motion, which, as is well known, means to gravitate, head first, to the midst of the stars, while he hangs from the earth by his two legs. Throughout the whole extent of being, metaphysics reveals to him authentic values and their hierarchy. It provides a center for his ethics. It binds together in justice the whole universe of his knowledge by guaranteeing the natural limits, harmony, and subordination of the different sciences. And that is more important to the human being than the most luxuriant proliferation of the mathematics of phenomena. Indeed, what does it profit to gain the whole world and lose the integrity of reason? Besides, we are so weak that the limpid peace dispensed by a healthy metaphysics may quite well be less favorable to experimental discovery than the musings or the eagerness of a mind buried deep in the sensible. The sciences of nature may very well enjoy fishing in troubled waters; but perhaps, too, we have a right to deem ourselves amply surfeited by the benefits of that dissipation.

Metaphysics sets us down in the midst of the eternal and the absolute; it causes us to pass from the show of things to the knowledge of reason (in itself stronger and more certain than mathematical certitudes, even though less adapted to our grasp), to the knowledge of the invisible world of divine perfections spelled out from their created reflections.

Metaphysics is not a means; it is an end, a fruit, a good at once self-justifying and delightful, a knowledge for the free man, the freest and naturally most regal knowledge, the door to the leisure of that great speculative activity in which intellect alone can breathe, set, as it is, on the very peak of causes.

And yet that is not even the most remote outline of the joys of the fatherland. This wisdom is acquired after the manner of science: and there is in it a great burden of toil and affliction of the spirit. For the old curse, *maledicta terra in opere tuo*, weighs more tragically upon our reason than upon our hands. Yes, apart from a privilege given by that good Fortune upon which the pagans did well to meditate, what the explorations of the highest intelligibles chiefly holds out to us is the useless toil and frightful sadness of messed-up truths.

The gods envy us metaphysical wisdom (the doctrinal inheritance which alone allows us to attain that wisdom without too grievously mingling error with it, is itself constantly misunderstood); man never holds it except on a precarious claim. And how could it be otherwise? What more beautiful

paradox than a science of things divine achieved by human
means, an enjoyment of liberty, proper to spirits, gained by
a nature which is "a slave in so many ways"? Metaphysical
wisdom is at the purest degree of abstraction because it is
farthest removed from the senses; it opens out onto the immaterial, onto a world of realities which exist or can exist
separately from matter. But our means of making the ascent
must also mark our limits. By a kind of natural necessity,
abstraction, the lot of all human science, brings with
it, along with a multiplicity of partial and complementary
insights, the rigid law of logical movement, the slow elaboration of concepts, the complexity and vast mechanism, weight-
ier than air, of the winged apparatus of discourse. Metaphysics would like to contemplate in the purest way, to reach
beyond reasoning and to enter the realm of pure intellection;
it aspires to the unity of simple vision. It comes close to it, as
to an asymptote. It does not reach it. What metaphysician,
not to mention the old Brahmins, has more keenly felt this
burning desire for sublime unity than Plotinus? But Plotinus'
ecstasy is not the highest exercise of metaphysics; it is rather
its vanishing-point. And metaphysics, left to itself alone, is
not able to achieve it. This happy event, which Plotinus knew
four times during the six years Porphyry lived with him,
seemed like a brief contact with an intellectual light naturally more powerful, the spasm of a human spirit brushed by
a pure spirit in its passage. If we believe Porphyry when he
tells us that his master was born in the thirteenth year of the
reign of Severus, that he listened to Ammonius at Alexandria,
that he came to Rome at the age of forty, that he died in the
Campagna; if we believe him when he tells us of his rules of
health and his way of living, his kindness toward orphans
entrusted to his care, his way of teaching, of composing
works, of pronouncing Greek, of arranging his spelling, and
the rest, why should we not believe him when he tells us that
the philosopher was inspired by a higher daemon who dwelt
within him and who showed himself upon his death in sensible guise? "At that moment, a serpent glided under the bed
upon which he was reclining and slid into a hole in the wall;
and Plotinus gave up his soul."[4] Indeed, it would be surprising if the metaphysical *eros*, wherever Christ does not dwell,

did not call for some kind of collusion with superhuman intellectual natures, the *rectores hujus mundi*.

But let us take up our task once more. I am saying that metaphysics suffers not only from the common necessity of abstraction and discourse; it also suffers a weakness proper to itself. It is a natural theology; its object is, above all, the Cause of causes. The Principle of all that is—that is what it would know. And since that alone is fully satisfying, how could it help wanting to know it in itself, in its essence, in that which properly constitutes it? If the desire of seeing the first Cause is natural to man (while remaining "conditional" and "ineffectual," precisely because it does not arise from a source within us naturally proportioned to its object), it is natural to the metaphysician for a special reason because he, if he is worthy of his name, cannot fail to feel its spur. Now metaphysics makes God known to us only by analogy, known, I say, not in those things which are His very own, but in the commonness of transcendental perfections which exist at once in Him and in things—though in infinitely different modes. It is true knowledge, certain and absolute, the highest pleasure of reason, and worth being a man for; but it still falls infinitely short of vision and makes mystery all the more crushingly felt. *Per speculum in aenigmate*. We can all too readily understand that the most perfect fruit of the intellectual life still leaves man unsatisfied.

It is true to say, then, as a general thesis, that intellectual life is not enough for us. It needs a complement. Knowledge draws all forms and all that is good into our soul. But there they are stripped of their proper existence and reduced to the condition of objects of thought. They are there as so many graftings upon us, but in a mode of being that is essentially incomplete. They demand completion. They arouse forces of gravity within us. We desire to rejoin them in their own real and proper existence, to possess them no longer in an idea but in reality. Love thus arising, impels the soul to a union in the real order, a union which intellect left all to itself, cannot achieve except in the extreme case of the vision of God.[5] It is inevitable then—unless some inhuman deviation intervene—that intellectual life, as it is in us, must finally admit its poverty and, one day, pour itself out in desire.

It is the problem of Faust. If human wisdom does not spill upwards into the love of God, it will fall downwards toward Marguerite. Mystical possession in Eternal love of the Most Holy God, or physical possession, in the fleetingness of time, of a poor fleshly creature (for, great wizard as one may be, that is where it all ends up)—there lies the choice that cannot be avoided.

That, then, is the poverty of metaphysics (and yet its majesty, too). It awakens a desire for supreme union, for spiritual possession completed in the order of reality itself and not only in the concept. It cannot satisfy that desire.

We preach a different wisdom—scandal for the Jews, madness for the Greeks. This wisdom, far surpassing all human effort, a gift of deifying grace and free endowments of Uncreated Wisdom, has as its beginning the *mad love* that Wisdom Itself has for each and all of us, and as its end, the union of spirit with it. Only Jesus crucified gives access to it— the Mediator raised up between heaven and earth. When al Hallâj, his hands and feet cut off, and crucified on the gibbet like Him, was asked: "What is mysticism?" he replied, "You see here its lowest stage." "And its highest level?" "You cannot gain entrance to it; and yet tomorrow, you will see what it will become. For it is in the Divine mystery, wherein it exists, that I bear witness to it and that it remains hidden to you."[6] Mystical wisdom is not beatitude, the perfect spiritual possession of Divine reality. But it is a beginning of it. It is an entering into incomprehensible life even here below, a taste, a touch, a sweetness of God that will not pass away, for the seven gifts will continue in vision what they here begin in faith.

We cannot pardon either those who deny it or those who corrupt it, led astray as they are by an inexcusable metaphysical presumption, for while recognizing the Divine transcendence, they will not adore it.

Those doctrines that certain Occidentals suggest to us in the name of the wisdom of the Orient (I am not speaking of Oriental thought itself, whose interpretation requires a whole host of distinctions and shades of meaning), arrogant and facile doctrines, are a radical negation of the wisdom of the saints. In claiming to attain supreme contemplation by metaphysics alone, in seeking the soul's perfection outside of charity (the mystery of which remains impenetrable to them), in substituting a so-called secret tradition inherited from unknown masters of Knowledge in the place of supernatural faith and the revelation of God by the Incarnate Word (*unigenitus Filius, qui est in sinu Patris, ipse ennaravit*)—in all this they are lying, for they are telling man that he can add to his own stature and gain entrance into the superhuman by himself. Their esoteric hyperintellectualism, apt in its very structure to put true metaphysics on the wrong scent, is but a specious and harmful mirage. It leads reason to absurdity, the soul to a second death.

Vain philosophy can also be an enemy of wisdom in still another way: not, indeed, by suppressing the wisdom of the saints by metaphysics, but by more-or-less mixing the two together and, in the most serious instances, by brashly confusing it with metaphysics—and that is to fundamentally corrupt its nature. It is thus that an attentive and penetrating mind, after fifteen years of zealous research and unstinted efforts devoted to the most careful and intense erudition, has been led to disfigure in a tragic way the mystical hero whose inner drama he had undertaken to retrace. Alas! How could a philosopher with the sole help of a fund of historical information, even supposing it were exhaustive, and aided by the most intuitive Bergsonian sympathy, penetrate the heart of a saint? How could he relive John of the Cross in himself? Every one of philosophy's false keys is shattered for the very good reason that there is no lock; entrance to it is gained only through a wall. Despite my friendship for you, my dear Baruzi, I must confess that in turning a Leibnizian light on John of the Cross, you have erred. In wrenching his contemplation from that which was the life of his life (infused grace and the working of God within him), in making of him some sort of ineffectual giant of the metaphysics to come, still held in "extrinsicist" superstitions, yet aiming above all to reach (through a process of self-spoliation, in which man's mind did the whole job) a less and less crude intellectual comprehension of God, and succeeding so well in that task that he has led us "to some extent beyond Christianity"[7]—in all this you have traced out a picture of the saint which the latter would have held in abomination and one whose glaring falsity, coupled with such great zeal, is a subject of astonishment and sadness[8] for us. Your just man *does not* live by faith. This *theopath* does not suffer things Divine, but a disease of the Sorbonne.

The contemplation of the saints is not the line of metaphysics; it is the line of religion. This supreme wisdom does not depend on the intellect's effort in search of the perfection of knowing but on man's gift of his entire self in search of a perfect rectitude in respect to his End. It has nothing to do with the "stultification" which Pascal advised the proud to cultivate (if it is there, it is because pride has already fallen). Rather, it knows so well that it no longer dreams of knowing. This highest kind of knowing supposes that knowing has been foregone.

The saints do not contemplate to know, but to love. They do not love for the sake of loving but for the love of Him Whom they love. It is for the love of their first beloved, God, that they aspire to that very union with God that love demands whilst they love themselves only for Him.[9] For them, the end of ends is not to bring exultation to their intellect and nature and thus stop at themselves. It is to do the will of Another, to contribute to the good of the Good.[10] They do not seek their own soul. They lose it; they no longer possess it. If in entering into the mystery of Divine filiation and becoming *something of God*, they gain a transcendent personality, an independence and a liberty which nothing in the world approaches, it is by forgetting all else so that they do not live, but the Beloved lives in them.

I would willingly agree that the antinomies the "new mystics"[11] discover in traditional mysticism (because they construct an artificial idea of it, an idea vitiated by solemn modern prejudices about the life of the spirit) actually do characterize many philosophical pseudomysticisms. (And the *new mysticism* itself will have difficulty avoiding them.) But when referred to an authentically mystical life, those antinomies lose all meaning. In genuine mystical life there is neither "creative will" seeking direct exaltation in pure adventure or endless surpassing, nor "magic will" seeking self-exaltation in mastery over the world and in complete possession. Here there is love (our philosophers forget it, yet it is the very thing that does accomplish everything); here there is charity, which uses knowledge—which love itself makes delectable and present through the action of God's spirit—to adhere more fully to the Beloved. Here the soul does not wish to exalt itself and it does not want to be destroyed: it wishes to be joined to Him who first loved it. For here there is a God who is not a name, but a reality; there is a Real, and indeed, a Super Real which first exists, before us and without us— one that is capable of being grasped neither humanly nor angelically, but divinely, and one who makes us divine for that very purpose—a Superspirit the attaining of Whom does not limit us but removes the limits from our finite spirit —You the living God, our Creator! Before discussing mysticism, there is a question, John Brown, that you must first answer: "Has your Mr. Peter Morhange been created?"

The contemplation of the saints does not issue from the spirit of man. It issues from infused grace. (Let us talk theology, since we cannot answer the questions troubling our day except through recourse to notions from sacred science.) I say that contemplation is indeed the perfect fruit of our own acts, but only according as we are born of Water and the Spirit. A supernatural work in its very essence, as indeed it is, it none the less truly emanates from the depths of our substance and from our natural powers of activity only, however, to the extent that our substance and our activity (which are passive before the omnipotent God) are, through Him and the gifts He engrafts upon them, raised up to face a divine object which in itself is absolutely inaccessible to the energies of nature if left to themselves.[12] It is a supremely personal work, a free and active work, a life which springs up to eternity. Yet it is a life that is more like an inactivity and a death because being supernatural, not only in its object but also in its very way of proceeding, it emanates from our spirit moved by God alone and depends upon *operative grace* in which the whole initiative belongs to God. And because faith is the root and foundation of all supernatural life, such a work is inconceivable without faith, "outside of which, there is no proximate and proportioned means" of contemplation.[13]

Finally, the contemplation of the saints is not only *for* divine love; it is also *through* it. It not only supposes the theological virtue of Faith, but the theological virtue of Charity and the infused gifts of Understanding and Wisdom as well; and these do not exist in the soul without charity. Love as such attains immediately and in Himself the very God attained in faith in an obscure manner and, as it were, at a distance. This is so because as far as understanding is concerned, there is distance when there is not vision, while love unites us in our heart to Him who is hidden in faith. Mystical wisdom, moved and actually regulated by the Holy Ghost, experiences the Divine things thus imbedded in us by charity, God becomes ours by charity. Through and in that Love which, so to speak, gives itself to us within our very selves, and, "in virtue of an incomprehensible union,"[14] it knows that Love affectively. It knows it in a night above all distinct knowledge, above every image and every idea, as though infinitely transcending all that any and every creature could ever think of Him. *Vere tu es Deus absconditus, Deus Israel Salvator.* This secret wisdom which secretly purifies the soul attains God as a hidden God, a saving God, one who is the more a saviour the more hidden He is. It remains, however, all the while under the supervision of theology.[15] It constantly depends in respect to its earthly human conditions and foundations on many notions and conceptual signs wherein Divine Truth is revealed to our understanding (without, of course, abandoning revealed dogma in the least! Quite the contrary!). It knows better than by concepts that very thing in which the conceptual formulae of dogma communicate to human understanding. How, then, could it help but surpass every distinct notion and expressible sign so as to cling, in the very experience of love, to that reality which is the first object of faith? In this, we are poles apart from Plotinus. Here it is not a question of mounting intellectually beyond the intelligible, of climbing by metaphysics and its cleverly regulated dialectical scale right up to the abolition —still natural—of natural understanding in a superintelligible, or to an angelic ecstasy. Rather, is it a question of rising lovingly beyond the created, of renouncing self and all else so as to be carried off by charity into the transluminous night of faith, transported by a Divine activity, and borne to a sovereign supernatural knowledge of the unlimited supernatural, or of being transformed into God by love. For "in the final analysis we have been created for this love alone."[16]

No, metaphysics is not the doorway to mystical contemplation. That door is Christ's humanity, for by Him we have been given grace and truth. *I am the way,* He has said of Himself, *if anyone enters by Me, he will be saved, and he will pass inside, and he will pass outside and he will find pasture.* Having gained entrance through Him, the soul climbs and penetrates the dark and bare contemplation of pure Divinity, and it descends once more and goes out to the contemplation of sacred humanity. And in both instances, it finds pasture and is nourished by its God.[17]

There are two things to consider in every sign, concept, or name: the object it makes known and the way in which it makes it known. In all the signs our intellect uses to know God, the *way* of signifying is defective and unworthy of God since it is not proportioned to God but to that which is not God, i.e., to the way in which perfections, which in their pure state pre-exist in God, exist in things. In the same imperfect way in which created things represent God from Whom they proceed, our concepts (which primarily and directly attain the created) make God known. The perfection they signify, the perfection which—if it belong to a transcendental order—can exist in an uncreated state as well as in a created state, must be signified essentially as it exists in a created, limited, and imperfect condition. So, too, all the names by which we speak of God, while signifying a single self-same reality which is inexpressibly one and simple, are still not synonyms because they signify according to the mode in which those perfections, pre-existing in God in a state of sovereign simplicity, are participated and divided in creatures. God is subsistent Goodness just as He is subsistent Truth and subsistent Being. Yet, if the Idea of Goodness, of Truth, and of Being subsisted in a pure state, it would not be God.

Whence it follows that names and concepts which properly belong to God, in being applied to Him, retain their whole intelligible value and all their meaning: the thing signified is *entirely* in God, and in Him it is present with all that constitutes it for the intellect ("formally" say the philosophers): in saying that God is good, we qualify the Divine Nature intrinsically and we know that everything that goodness necessarily implies is to be found there. But within this perfection as it is in pure act (which is God Himself), there is still infinitely *more* than is signified by its concept and name. It exists in God in a way which infinitely surpasses our way of conceiving ("eminently," say the philosophers). For in knowing that God is good, we still do not know what Divine Goodness is because He is good as nothing else is good, true as nothing else is true; He *is* as nothing else we know is. "Thus," says St. Thomas, "when the name wise is said of man, it in some way *describes* and envelops the thing signified: but not so when it is said of God; for then, it leaves the thing signified, as it were, uncontained and uncircumscribed, and exceeding the signification of the name."[18]

Thus, all knowledge of God by notions or concepts, whether acquired, as in metaphysics and speculative theology, or infused, as in prophecy, in short, all purely intellectual knowledge of God, short of the Beatific Vision, even though it be absolutely true, absolutely certain, and constitute an authentic wisdom, desirable above all things, is still irreparably defective, lacking due proportion to the object known and signified, in its very manner of grasping and signifying.

It is clear, then, that although we can be given a knowledge of God, not *sicuti est*, that is, by His essence and in vision, but at least in accordance with the very transcendence of his Deity, that is, by making use of a mode of knowing appropriate to the object known, such a knowledge cannot possibly be obtained in a purely intellectual way. To transcend every method of conceiving while still remaining in the line of human understanding, and, consequently, of the concept, is a contradiction in terms. We must pass through love. Love alone, and I am speaking of supernatural love, can effect this overreaching. Here below, intellect can enter the realm that lies beyond all method only by a renunciation-of-knowing in which God's Spirit, by making use of the connaturality of charity and the effects produced in affection by Divine Union, grants the soul a loving experience of that very being which no notion approximates or can approximate. "And then, released from the world of sense and intellect, the soul enters into the mysterious darkness of a holy ignorance, and, renouncing every scientific datum, it loses itself in Him who cannot be seen or grasped. It now belongs entirely to this sovereign object without belonging either to itself or to others. It is united to the unknown through its noblest part because it has renounced knowledge. Finally it draws from this absolute ignorance a knowledge that understanding could never win to."[19]

It seems that the trend of modern times is set under the sign of a disjunction between flesh and spirit, or a progressive dislocation of the shape of human things. It is only too clear that the march of humanity under the sway of money and mechanics[20] marks a progressive materializing of intellect and of the world. On the other hand, as though in compensation for this phenomenon, the spirit (with which our discursive and social activity has less and less to do and is thus freed from guaranteeing the organic functions of human life) undergoes a kind of deliverance—at least, a virtual one. "Photography has set the art of painting free." This expression of Jean Cocteau can be applied to every realm. Printing has freed the plastic arts from the pedagogical function that was incumbent upon them in the day of the cathedrals. Sciences of phenomena have freed metaphysics from the trouble of explaining things of sensible nature, and from so many illusions which had followed upon it for Greek optimism. We must congratulate ourselves on this purification of metaphysics. It is less pleasant to state, however, that in the practical order, the government of earthly things, to the extent that it demands a heavier material work of intellect, is more and more separated from the life it leads beyond time. The earth is no longer in need of a moving angel; man pushes it by the strength of his arm. Spirit ascends to heaven.

Yet, man is flesh and spirit, not held together by a thread, but substantially united. The fact that human affairs cease to be cut to the measure of man (since some of those affairs take their rhythm from the energies of matter, while others look for their standards to the exigencies of a disincarnate spirituality) constitutes for man a frightful metaphysical disjunction. It is quite believable that the shape of this world will pass away on the day that this tension becomes so great that our heart will break.

As for the things of the spirit themselves, "to liberate" them is to run the risk of perpetuating an illusion—even worse than slavery. The constraints imposed on spirit in its service of man were good for it; they hampered it but they gave to it its natural weight. But the "angelizing" of art and knowledge? Will all this purity, possible to the spirit, be lost in a brutal frenzy? No! But it will be found and truly exist only in the sheepfold of Spirit. There where the Body is, the eagles will gather. Although the Christendom of days gone by has been undone, yet Christ's Church has continued to rise. It, too, has been set free little by little and delivered from the care for civil communities that reject it, from the temporal providence it once exercised in accordance with its rights to heal our wounds. Despoiled, stripped of everything, when she flees into a solitude she will take with her all that remains in the world not only of faith and charity and true contemplation, but of philosophy, poetry, and virtue. And all these will be more beautiful than ever.

The pressing interest of the present crisis arises from the fact that, being more universal than any other, it forces us all to make decisive choices. Here we have come to the parting of the ways. In virtue of the West's failures (for it has abused Divine graces and allowed the gifts it had to render fruitful for God to be lost) it discovers that, being no longer supported by the order of charity, the order of reason is corrupted through and through and is no longer good for anything. The evil wrought by the rationalist has produced a tension between nature and the *form of reason*. Thenceforth, it has become very difficult to cling to what is human. Its stake must either be set above reason and still on its side, or below reason and against it. Now the theological virtues and the supernatural gifts are the only things that are above reason. On all sides—even in the ranks of the new humanists or the partisans of dialectical materialism (as in days gone by amongst the followers of Barrès)—the cry is heard: spirit, spirituality! But upon what spirit are you calling? If it is not the Holy Spirit, you might just as well call upon the spirit of wood alcohol or the spirit of wine. The whole so-called spiritual, all the self-styled suprarational which does not exist in charity only serves animality in the final reckoning. Hatred for reason will never be anything but a revolt of the genus against its specific difference. Dreaming is quite the contrary to contemplation. If purity consists in a perfect releasing of life in accordance with the trends of its own mechanisms, it exists more truly in the brute than in the saint.

The world—that world for whom Christ did not pray—has made its choice in advance. To be delivered from the *forma rationis*, to flee far from God in an impossible metaphysical suicide, far from the cruel and saving order set down by eternal Law—that is the desire with which the flesh of the old man tingles; it was the desire of the Devil of old when he fell from heaven like thunder. To express it in an absolute fashion and as fully as possible to a being who, most of the time, does not know what he is doing, a kind of heroism is required. (The Devil has his own martyrs.) A testimony without promise, a testimony given to what is worse than death! . . . As for the great mass of men, if we can judge it by the ordinary conditions of human nature, it would be easy to believe that they would follow the same downward course, but without will or courage, hypnotized by the ideal. This course is such an easy one!

It is a mistake, however, to judge according to nature alone. Grace is there and it always holds in reserve its own surprises. For even as this old world continues to slip, the true new world comes forth—the secret, invincible coursing of Divine sap in the Mystical Body which endures and does not grow old, the blessed awakening of souls under the sign of the Virgin and the Spirit. O Wisdom which reaches with strength from one end of the world to the other and makes extremes one! O promise which makes beauty of these times of misery, and renders us joyful! Though baptized nations, unfaithful to their calling, cut themselves off from the Church, blaspheme the name of Christ on all sides by presenting as a Christian civilization what is nothing but its corpse, the Church still loves those nations. She has no need of them. They are the ones that need the Church. It is for their welfare that the Church, by using the only culture in which human reason very nearly succeeded, has tried for so long to impress a Divine form on earthly matter, to raise man's life and reason and so to maintain them in their perfection, under the most gentle sway of grace. If European culture comes to the brink of danger, *She* will save its essentials and will know how to lift up to Christ everything that can be saved in other cultures. She hears, rumbling at the roots of history, an unforeseen world, a world that will undoubtedly persecute Her as much as the ancient world did. (Is not Her mission a mission of suffering?) But She will find in it new possibilities of action.

If Hilaire Belloc means that Europe would be nothing without the faith and that its very reason for being has been, and still is, to dispense faith to the world, he is right in saying that Europe is the faith. But absolutely speaking, No! Europe is not the faith and the faith is not Europe; Europe is not the Church, and the Church is not Europe. Rome is not the capital of the Latin world; Rome is the capital of the world. *Urbs caput orbis*. The Church is universal because it is born of God. All nations are at home in it. Their Master's arms on the cross are stretched out over all races and all civilizations. It does not bring *the benefits of civilization* to people, but rather, Christ's Blood and supernatural beatitude. It seems that a kind of wondrous epiphany of its catholicity is being readied in our times, and the steady growth in missionary countries of a native clergy and a native episcopacy can be considered a prophetic sign of it.

For a long time the East has remained asleep on the fringes of history, but now, touched by madness, it is today as sick as the West. But, East or West, wherever the living faith has taken root, we shall see that adherence to what is truly beyond reason, to uncreated Truth, to the wisdom of the saints, will bring in its train a restoration (not, it is true, without some effort) of the very order of reason itself, a restoration implied by supernatural life as a condition of its existence. Thus do the Gospel and philosophy, mysticism and metaphysics, the Divine and the human, go hand in hand. The great plan of Brahmanandav, taken up once more by his disciple, Animananda, is not the plan of a European, but of a Bengali. This plan was to establish in Bengal a contemplative congregation whose members, religious mendicants on the order of the Hindu *sannyasis*, would set, for the whole of India, an Indian example of Catholic holiness, and, without overlooking the Vedanta, would base its intellectual life on the doctrines of Thomas Aquinas.[21] I cherish this tribute to the strength of Thomism. Though a gift made to the whole world by mediaeval Christianity, it neither belongs to one continent nor to one century; it is universal as is the Church and truth.

I would never scorn the distress nor the waiting of those who feel that all is lost and await the unexpected. But what is it they really expect? That is the important thing. Is it anti-Christ or the Parousia? We look for the resurrection of the dead and the life of the world to come. We know what we are waiting for and that it surpasses all understanding. There is a difference between not knowing what one hopes for and knowing that the thing one hopes for cannot be conceived.

"Adrian, while still a pagan, asked the martyrs, 'For what reward do you hope?' They replied, 'Our mouth cannot speak it nor our ear hear it.' 'And so, you have learned nothing of it? Neither by the law nor the prophets? Nor any other writing?' 'The prophets themselves did not know it as it should be known, for they were only men who adored God, and they have told in words the things they received from the Holy Ghost. But concerning that glory, it is written: "Eye has not seen, nor ear heard, nor has it entered into the heart of man what the Lord has prepared for those who love him."'. . .

"On hearing that, Adrian immediately jumped down into their midst and said, 'Count me among those who confess the faith with these saints, for behold I, too, am a Christian.'"[22]

NOTES

1. *Genesis* 32:29.
2. Denys, *On the Divine Names* I, 6. St. Thomas' lect. 3. Cf. St. Paul, *Eph.* 1:21.

3. Ramon Fernandez, "L'intelligence et M. Maritain," *Nouv. Revue Française*, June 1, 1925.

4. Porphyry, *Life of Plotinus*, II, 25. A little further along (C.10) Porphyry tells us how an Egyptian priest, who had come to Rome, suggested to Plotinus that he would let him see the spirit that dwelled within him, and that he had called up this daemon, who turned out to be a god. "It was impossible," he adds, "to question the daemon or keep him present to sight for long because one of his friends, a spectator at the scene, and to whom the birds had been entrusted and who was holding them in his hand, suffocated them in jealousy, or, perhaps, in terror. Plotinus, then, was attended by one of the most divine daemons; he constantly directed his mind's divine eye towards him. It was for this motive that he wrote his treatise *On the daemon we have received as our portion*, wherein he was compelled to give reasons for the differences between the beings that attend man."

5. In that vision the soul becomes God "intentionally" (*secundum esse intelligibile*), not substantially. But it is joined to him in a real (*secundum rem*) union, inasmuch as *through the very infinite essence of God*, immediately actuating the intellect in the intelligible order, it grasps Him and sees Him. Once the intellect has been rendered supernatural by the light of glory it is as the hand by which the blessed grasp God.

6. Louis Massignon, *Al Hallâj martyr mystique de l'Islam, exécuté à Bagdad, le 26 mars 922* (Paris: Geuthner, 1922), t. I, pp. 9, 306. We are quoting al Hallâj at this point because, insofar as a conjecture may be ventured about the secrets of the heart, everything leads us to think that this great Moslem mystic, who was condemned because he taught the union of love with God and who gave testimony to the very end of his desire to follow Jesus, had grace and infused gifts (and belonged to the "soul" of the Church) and could, as a result, have been raised to authentic mystical contemplation. Fr. Maréchal rallies to this conclusion in his review of Mr. Louis Massignon's admirable work (J. Maréchal, *Recherches de Science Religieuse*, May–August 1923). Cf. below, Chap. VI, § 26, p. 272.

7. Jean Baruzi, *Saint Jean de la Croix et le problème de l'expérience mystique*, 2nd ed., p. 230.

8. Cf. Dom Phil. Chevallier, *Vie Spirituelle*, May 1925, and R. Garrigou-Lagrange, *ibid.*, July–August 1925; and Roland Dalbiez's little work, *Saint Jean de la Croix d' après M. Baruzi* (ed. of *Vie Spirituelle*).

9. But then the love of self *secundum rationem proprii boni* does not vanish, but its act gives place to the act of the love of charity wherein man loves himself *propter Deum et in Deo* (*Sum. Theol.*, II-II, 19, 6; 19, 8 and 2; 19, 10), an act which, by perfecting him and raising him up, contains in itself the natural

love that every man bears towards his own being and even more than his own being towards God (I, 60, 5; II-II, 25, 4).

10. Cf. St. Thomas Aquinas, *Sum. Theol.*, II-II, 26, 3 ad 3: "Hoc quod aliquis velit frui Deo, pertinet ad amorem, quo Deus amatur amore concupiscentiae; magis autem amamus Deum amore amicitiae, quam amore concupiscentiae, quia majus est in se bonum Dei, quam bonum, quod participare possumus fruendo ipso; et ideo simpliciter homo magis diligit Deum ex charitate, quam seipsum." Cf. also Cajetan, in II-II, 17, 5.

11. Cf. Henri Lefebvre, "Positions d'attaque et de défense du nouveau mysticisme," *Philosophies*, March 1925.

12. Philosophers who speak of the *supernatural being superimposed*, in connection with the doctrine of "obediential power," have never read the Thomist theologians—or, if they have read them, they have not understood them. Cf. John of St. Thomas, *Curs. Theol.*, I P., q.12, disp. 14, a. 2. (Vivès, t. II.)

13. Cf. St. John of the Cross, *Ascent of Carmel*, II, viii. See *The Degrees of Knowledge*, Chap. VIII, § 16, p. 329.

14. Denys, *On the Divine Names*, VII, 3.

15. At least in the communicable expressions in which human language translates mystical experience—i.e., as regards that which is no longer, properly speaking, mystical experience but, rather, the theology with which it is pregnant—it is a fact that mystical wisdom may be under the supervision of theology. Thus, the theologian does not judge the contemplative as contemplative, but only to the extent that the contemplative comes down to the level of conceptual expression and rational communication. An astronomer can, in the same way, judge a philosopher who is talking astronomy.

But mystical wisdom of itself is superior to theological wisdom, and the spiritual man is the one who judges the speculative theologian, not, to be sure, in the order of doctrine but in the realm of experience and life. *Spiritualis judicat omnia, et a nemine judicatur* (I Cor 2:15).

As far as really judging the secret and incommunicable substance of mystical experience itself is concerned, and discerning spirits, that is not in itself the speculative theologian's business. It is the concern of spiritual men themselves and of the theologian only insofar as he is himself a spiritual person and possessed of a practical knowledge (cf. Chap. VIII, §§ 7 and 8) of mystical ways: "This is really," wrote John of St. Thomas, "the apostolic rule: 'Believe not every spirit, but try the spirits if they be of God' (I John 4:1). And again: 'Despise not prophecies. But prove all things: hold fast that which is good' (I Thess. 5:20–21). . . . . This examination should usually be made in common . . . .

"This does not mean that therein the gift of the Holy Ghost is subject to the virtue of prudence or that it is inferior to it or receives its determination from it. For those who judge such revelations or virtues should not do so in accordance with the reasons of human prudence but, rather, according to the rules of faith to which the gifts of the Holy Ghost are subject, or according to the gifts themselves which can be more excellently present in some men than in others. But if human reasons or theological reasons are still used in examining things of this sort, they are taken into secondary consideration only, and then merely by acting as aides assisting in providing a better explanation of that which concerns faith or the instinct of the Holy Ghost.

"That is why, in examining things of the spirit, and matters mystical, recourse must not only be had to the scholastic theologians, but to spiritual men as well, to men who possess mystical prudence, who know spiritual paths and how to discern spirits" (John of St. Thomas, *Gifts of the Holy Ghost*, V, 22. French tr. by R. Maritain, pp. 201–2).

16. St. John of the Cross, *Spiritual Canticle*, 2nd ed. str. 28 (19), ed. by Allison Peers (London: Burns Oates, 1934), Vol. 2, pp. 341 ff.

17. Cf. St. Thomas Aquinas *Quodlib*. VIII a. 20; Joseph of the Holy Ghost, *Cursus theologiae mystico-scholasticae*, Disp. prima pro-oemialis, q. 2, §I (Bruges: Beyaert, 1924 ed.), t. I, p. 117.

18. St. Thomas Aquinas, *Sum Theol.*, I, 13.5.

19. Denys, *Mystical Theology*, Ch. I, 3.

20. Material techniques of themselves should have prepared the way for a life much more completely freed of matter, but in virtue of man's fault they actually tend to oppress spirituality. Does that mean that technique must be forsaken or that we must give ourselves up to vain regrets? That has never been our view. But in this case reason has to impose its human regulation. And if it succeeds in this without having to have recourse to purely despotic and, for quite other reasons, inhuman solutions, the materialization of which we have been speaking would have been overcome—at least for a time, anyway. We are not making any claim here to express the law of a necessary curve in events, we are merely trying to sift out, from the point of time in which we now exist, the significance of a tendency in the form of a curve which these have followed down to the present moment—and a tendency that human liberty *can* rectify.

21. Michel Ledrus, S.J., *L'Apostolat bengali* (Louvain, 1924). A completely Chinese Catholic congregation, the Little Brothers of St. John the Baptist, was founded in China in 1928 by Fr. Lebbe. In a general way, those who know China best think that in our day what is finest in its ancient spiritual tradition has, in

Catholicism, its only chance of escaping the basic materialism youth goes on seeking in the West.

22. Boninus Mombritius, *Sanctuarium seu vitae sanctorum*, new ed. by the monks of Solesmes (Paris: Fontemoing, 1910): *Passio sancti Adriani M. cum aliis 33 MM.*

2. SCIENCE, PHILOSOPHY AND FAITH

I shall use the two words *science* and *philosophy* in the sense which they have acquired in modern times, according to which science designates above all the mathematical, physico-mathematical and natural sciences, or, as one is also wont to say, the positive sciences, the sciences of phenomena; *philosophy* designating above all metaphysics and the philosophy of nature.

Truly speaking, the problems of science and philosophy have been renewed and become extraordinarily complicated in our time. First, the crisis in the growth of modern physics, while launching science itself on an entirely new path, has liberated it from many pseudo-dogmatisms and much pseudo-metaphysics, and especially from the materialism of the physicists "of the Victorian Age," as Eddington says, with their pretense to "explain," *some day*, the essence of bodies, according to mechanistic determinism, and even to account for the occurrence of every single event in the universe. This crisis has made physics more conscious of its own nature.

Secondly, and at the same time, a considerable work has also been accomplished by the theoreticians of science, by logicians and by logisticians. Finally, this crisis of growth has not only diminished the dogmatic pretensions of experimental science, it has also deeply transformed in this domain (and by contagion, in certain other spheres), the work and the methods of reason; it has taught reason a sort of exhilarating freedom, a *new and terrible freedom*, to repeat the words used by Dostoevski in quite a different manner. Yes, and as it were in compensation, a tendency toward systematic interpretation, imposing very rigorous rules and seeking a sort of logical purism, has been developed by certain theoreticians. I have in mind the logicians of the Viennese School. It is by referring to the theories of the Viennese School, which represent one of the most remarkable of contemporary trends in epistemology, that I should like to try to present the conceptions of science, philosophy and supra-rational knowledge which I believe to be true, and which are linked to the principles of what could be termed the critical realism of Aristotle and of Thomas Aquinas.

I shall divide this paper into four parts. In the first and longest part, I shall deal with the theory of the science of phenomena as it is offered to us by logical empiricism on the one hand, and by what I call critical realism on the other. Secondly, I shall try to characterize briefly supra-rational knowledge; thirdly, philosophical knowledge. Finally, in the fourth part, I should like to point out a few of the characteristic connections between the problems that concern degrees of knowledge, and the problems of civilization which occupy our thoughts at the present time.

I

Let us then begin with the theory of the science of phenomena, as it is presented on the one hand by the Viennese School, and on the other hand by the critical realism which takes its inspiration from Aristotle and Thomas Aquinas.

The name of "Viennese Circle" was first mentioned in 1929. At the outset it was meant to designate a philosophic association created in Vienna by Moritz Schlick, who has since met with a tragic death. It now designates a group of scientist-philosophers whose common orientation is a *logical empiricism* due to quite different historic influences, in particular to the influence of Mach and Avenarius, that of Poincaré and of Duhem, of Peano, of Russell and of James, and to that of Einstein. Besides Moritz Schlick, the chief representatives of this school are Rudolf Carnap, Philipp Frank, Otto Neurath, and Hans Reichenbach.

When, about twelve years ago, Einstein came to Paris for important scientific discussions at the *Collège de France*, I was very much interested in the manner in which, in answer to questions about time and simultaneity, he invariably replied: "What does this mean to me, a physicist? Show me a definite method by which measurements can be made physically certain, in terms of which this or that observed result will be given this or that name, and only then will I know what you are talking about." It seems to me that the same question underlies the researches of the Viennese School: *What does this mean to me as a scientist?* The main point for this school is to distinguish those assertions which *have a meaning* for the scientist from assertions which *have no meaning* for the scientist.

In pursuing this analysis, the Viennese logicians have thrown light upon the fact that assertions which *have a meaning* for science are not those which concern the nature or the essence of that which is, but rather regard the connections between the designations or symbols, which our senses, and especially our instruments of observation and measurement, enable us to elaborate concerning that which *appears to us* in our *Erlebnisse*, as the Germans say, that is, in our lived experiences. It is not with the being of things that science is occupied; it is with the mathematical links, which can be established between these designations taken from things, and which alone make possible—I say in the proper order and in the proper plane of science—a communication or a well-established language, an *intersubjectivation*, submitted to fixed rules of signification.

If I say *this table*, these words do not mean for the scientist a hidden substance, presenting itself to me under a certain image and with certain qualities, of which substance, moreover, he can know nothing as a physicist. They mean a certain set of perceptions, linked by expressible regularities—*the permanent possibility of sensation* of which John Stuart Mill spoke—linked to a certain number of mathematical and logistic designations, which render it *intersubjectivable*.

If I say *matter*, this word does not mean for the physicist a substance or a substantial principle, about the mysterious nature of which he might question himself and, if wise, answer with Du Bois-Reymond: *ignorabimus*. For the scientist, the word *matter* only means a certain set of mathematical symbols, established by microphysics and submitted, moreover, to continual revision, wherein certain highly designable observations and measurements are expressed according to the rules of differential calculus or of tensorial calculus and according to the syntax of certain general theoretical constructions, which are also of a provisional character, such as the quantum theory or the syntheses of wave-mechanics.

Generally speaking, all reference to *being*, or essence in itself, is eliminated as *lacking meaning for the scientist*; and naturally the rational necessities disappear at the same time. What philosophers call the first principles of reason express at best certain regularities likely to be verified in certain cases, and likely not to be verified in others, according to the logical treatment to which we submit our *Erlebnisse*. The discussions concerning scientific determinism and Heisenberg's principle of indetermination, have cast light on this point, in so far as the principle of causality is concerned, or more exactly speaking, so far as concerns the recasting of the idea of causality in the domain of experimental science.

All this means that the intellect is a sort of indispensable *witness* and regulator of the senses in scientific work, remaining all the while—if I may express myself thus—*external* to this work. The senses and the measuring instruments *alone see* in science, and the intellect is there only to transform, according to the rules of mathematical and logical syntax, the signs expressing what has thus been seen. The intellect is set up in the central office of the factory, where it checks, and submits to more and more extensive calculations, all the indications which are conveyed to it. It remains outside the quarters where the work is being directly accomplished, and is forbidden to enter.

The theory of experimental science offered by the Viennese School suffers, in my opinion, from certain peculiar errors which especially concern the notion of logical work and the notion of sign and above all, from that delusive purism to which every positivist conception of science is naturally exposed. The School of Vienna ignores what Meyerson has so acutely pointed out: the incurably realistic tendency of the science of phenomena. If it seems to give an account of the logical structure towards which science tends, as towards its ideal limit—science as already completed, and more and more perfectly rationalized—this school neglects certain profound characters of science *in the making*, that is, of the process of research and the work of scientific discovery. However scandalous for positivist orthodoxy, this work can be performed only with a feeling for the subjacent importance of the causes and essences of things, that is, in the climate, however obscure to the scientist himself, of the ontological mystery of the universe.

But, so far as a certain characteristic structure of science is concerned, above all of science completed and rationalized, this theory insists upon a fundamental truth which, in fact, the Viennese logicians have not discovered (rather they have received it from the scientists), and which is due to the self-awareness which modern science, and especially physics, has achieved. The truth is, that science—science in the modern sense of the word—is *not* a philosophy, and consequently claims, if I dare use this barbarism, to de-ontologize completely its notional lexicon. I should like to note, as regards this precise point, that the consideration of the sciences of phenomena, as they have developed in modern times—novel, indeed, by relation to the cultural state of antiquity and the medieval world—this consideration carried out in the light of the epistemological principles of the Aristotelian critical realism would lead us to general views strikingly similar to those of the School of Vienna.

Now, what is important, it seems to me, is to distinguish (and this the Viennese School has omitted to do) two ways of analyzing the world of sensible reality and of constructing the concepts relevant thereto. I have given these two kinds of analysis of sensible reality the following names: the one, *empiriological analysis*; the other, *ontological analysis*.

If we observe any kind of material object, this object is—while we observe it—the meeting point as it were, of two knowledges: sense knowledge and intellectual knowledge. We are in the presence of a kind of sensible flux, stabilized by an idea, by a concept. In other words, we are in the presence of an ontological or intelligible nucleus manifested by a set of qualities perceived *here* and *now*—I do not say *conceived*. I say *felt* qualities, objects of actual perception and observation.

As to the sensible reality, considered as such, there will thus be a *resolutio*, a resolution of concepts and definitions, which we may call *ascendant*, or ontological, towards intelligible being—a resolution in which the sensible matter always remains there and plays an indispensable role, but indirectly and at the service of intelligible being, as connoted by it; and there will be on the other hand a resolution *descending* towards the sensible matter, towards the observable as such, in so far as it is observable. Not that the mind ceases to refer to being, for that is impossible—being always remains there—but being passes into the service of what is sensible, of what is observable, and above all of what is measurable. It becomes an unknown factor assuring the constancy of certain sensible determinations and of certain measures. In fact, the new aspect which modern science presents is precisely this *descendant resolution*, a procedure which the ancients had not thought of making an instrument of science.

In this empiriological analysis, characteristic of science in the modern sense of the word, the permanent possibility of sensible verification and of measurement, plays the same part that essence does for the philosopher; the permanent possibility of observation and measurement is for the scientist equivalent to, and a substitute for, what essence is to the philosopher. One may here behold something like an effort against the natural slope of the intellect, because one must turn back, if one is to grasp what is essential and properly constitutive here, to the act of sense itself, to a physical operation to be performed, to an observation of a measurement. It is this observation to be made, this act of sense, which will serve to *define* the object.

If one understands this, one has understood the views of an Einstein, for instance, in physics, and the opposition more apparent than real between the philosopher and the scientist on such matters as time or simultaneity. This opposition is immediately solved, because the type of definition is essentially different in the two cases. For the physicist conscious of the epistemological exigencies of his discipline, science tends to construct definitions, not by essential ontological characters, but by a certain number of physical operations to be performed under fully determined conditions. On the other hand, all science tends in a certain way, and however imperfectly, to explanation and deduction, to a knowledge of the *why*. Therefore, empiriological science will necessarily be obliged to seek its explicative deductions in mere *ideal constructions*, though founded on the real, and which can be substituted, as well-founded explicative *myths* or *symbols*, for the *entia realia*, the real entities, those causes of ontological order which the intellect seeks when it follows its natural slope. Such an elaboration of ideal entities grounded in reality—the most significant examples of which are encountered in mathematical disciplines as experimental psychology, and through which real causes are reached in a blind fashion—such an elaboration is linked to the aspect of art or fabrication, whose importance in empiriological science has often been observed with reason. The *essence*, the *substance*, the *explicative reasons*, the real causes are thus reached in a certain fashion, in an oblique and blind manner, through substitutes which are well-grounded myths or symbols, ideal constructions, which the mind elaborates from the data of observation and measurement, and with which it goes out to meet things. Thus, these basic notions, primitively philosophical, are recast and phenomenalized.

It has been justly observed that in the image which the physicist makes of the world, "certain traits really express, not nature, but the structure of the real, and in this there is a certain adequation. For instance, the atom of Bohr signifies the table of Mendelieff; the undulatory theory signifies light's interference."[1] Thanks to ideal constructions, to *entia rationis*, the real is thus grasped.

I do not know how to translate this word, *ens rationis*; it designates certain objects of thought, as the universal, the predicate, the privation, the transfinite number, and so forth, which I conceive intelligibly, but which cannot exist outside my mind. Let us say, if you like, *ideal entity* or *logical entity* or *being of thought* or *being made in the mind, being not expressing a reality*, (though possibly grounded in reality).

Certain facile minds, which imagine themselves strong, have often scoffed at the *entia rationis* of the Schoolmen. Yet here we have seen that the theory of the *ideal entity grounded in reality* alone furnishes us with an accomplished and satisfactory interpretation of the paradoxical twofold character—at the same time *realist* and *symbolic*—of the sciences of phenomena, which makes them appear, at first glance, so disconcerting.

The misfortune of the Viennese is that they are philosophers. This can be immediately seen from the way they insist on the truths they have grasped, while they blunt their point, as Pascal says. By a positivist conceptualisation, by a bad conceptualisation, the School of Vienna impairs—a phenomenon often observed—a good intuition, the reflexive intuition by which modern science becomes more and more conscious of itself.

The essential error of this school is to confuse that which is true (with certain restrictions) of the *science of phenomena*, and that which is true of *all science* and of *all knowledge* in general, of all scientific knowing. It is to apply universally to all human knowledge that which is valid only in one of its particular spheres. This leads to an absolute negation of metaphysics, and the arrogant pretension to deny that metaphysical assertions have any meaning.

I have earlier referred to what has no meaning *for the physicist*. If one only simply suppresses these three little words,—"for the physicist"—one will declare: that which has no meaning *for the physicist* has no meaning *at all*. This is a uniformization, a brutal way of restricting human science, which is not preceded by a critical examination of the life of the mind, and which cannot be so (for one would then have to enter into metaphysics in order to deny its possibility); a uniformization which, finally, is based only on the positivist superstition concerning positive science. But metaphysics does not let itself be done away with so easily. Before deciding that the question, "Does a primary cause of being exist?" has no meaning, we should first ask ourselves whether the question, "Does the philosophy of the School of Vienna exist?" is not a question deprived of meaning.

The objection has been justly raised against the Viennese position that *if* the meaning of a judgment consists in its method of (experimental) verification—not only in the usage proper to experimental sciences, but in an absolute manner; *if* any judgment which cannot be thus verified is devoid of meaning—then this school's own theory has no meaning, because it is incapable of being verified in this manner. It is incapable, even in principle, of space-time verifications. The theory of the Viennese is in fact, a *philosophical* theory, a *philosophy of science*, and in my opinion, the principle which I have just mentioned, the principle of the necessity of logico-experimental verification, is true in regard to the function of judgment in the empiriological *sciences*; but it is true *only in this domain*. A philosophy which generalizes this principle and extends it to the entire field of knowledge, seeing in it an exigency of the nature of all judgments truly valuable for knowledge—such a philosophy thus destroys itself.

The Viennese entirely ignore the mode of resolving the concepts which we have described as *ontological*, and which occurs in the direction of intelligible being. They do not see that, if it is true that all knowledge properly speaking supposes an intersubjectivation submitted to fixed rules of significance, such an intersubjectivation is not met with only on the plane of scientific knowledge, but also on the philosophical plane, where it acts, however, in quite a different way, and refers above all, not to an operation of the external senses, but to an intelligible perception. The School of Vienna does not see that the meaning of a judgment is derived from the intelligible objects which it composes or divides in the act of being. If—in empiriological sciences—meaning implies a possibility of physical verification, it is because, in this particular case, the objects of such notions are themselves as I have said, conceived in relation to the operation of the senses. The chief point in criticizing neopositivism is a warning to us of the irremediable mistake caused by a *univocist* conception of knowledge, and as a reminder, by antithesis, of the great words by which St. Thomas condemned Descartes before his day: "It is a sin against intelligence to want to proceed in an identical manner in typically different domains—physical, mathematical, and metaphysical—of speculative knowledge."

II

It is remarkable, in fact, that logical neo-positivism looks at the degrees of knowledge of the supra-rational order with less disfavor than at the highest degrees of an order entirely rational, namely, metaphysics and philosophy. Generally speaking, the School of Vienna manifests no hostility towards religion, and certain representatives of this school, perhaps in memory of Bolzano and Brentano, show a certain sympathy for the work of the theologians, whom they prefer to university philosophers.

Led by this preference, I shall treat of the positions of critical realism with regard to knowledge taken in its fullest extent, by starting with the highest degrees of knowledge, those which deal with the supra-rational order. Thus I come to the second part of this paper, which will concern superrational knowledge.

According to the classical doctrine which corresponds to the common experience of the believer, faith is not a *science* or *perfect knowledge*, because its object is neither *seen* nor *proven* by the intelligence, but only *believed* from the testimony of the Primal Truth. Thus it still implies an inquiring movement of the intellect—a movement towards vision. But faith is a very real and *genuine knowledge*, and by means of revealed words it adheres virtually to the substance of things we hope for, to the actual *thing* which is its object, that is, the intimate and personal being of God. While concerning what infinitely overreaches our natural means of grasping and verifying, nevertheless these dogmatic formulae of divine origin, heard in our heart, have a meaning for us, a meaning at once dark and illuminating, thanks to what can be called the superanalogy of faith. For in the knowledge of faith, it is from the very core of the transintelligible mystery, from the very heart of the Deity, that knowledge descends in order to return thither—in other words, that the free generosity of God chooses, in the intelligible universe which affects our senses, objects and concepts which God reveals to us as analogical signs of what is hidden within Him, and which He uses to declare Himself to us in our language.

We are here facing a type of knowledge which absolutely transcends the empirical knowledge characteristic of the science of phenomena. It is of another order, a divine and supernatural order. The power of apprehension is not in this case the natural light of reason, but the light of a divine order received as a free gift. Within such a knowledge, the intelligence, under the action both of voluntary consent and of grace, knows, without seeing it, the Truth which will some day be its eternal joy.

Now, there are linked to divine faith two types of science

or of perfect knowledge, taking the word *science* not in its modern meaning, but in its classical and very ample meaning of: *knowledge through causes and necessary reasons*; two kinds of science which are at the same time wisdoms, that is to say where knowledge is brought about in the light of *primary* causes. They can be called the *wisdom of reasoning faith*, or discursive theology, and the *wisdom of loving faith*, or mystical theology.

Although discursive theology exists in us in an imperfect state, because it works on principles which it does not itself see, and which are seen only by the intelligence of the separated spirits who see God, it is nevertheless in its essence truly and actually *perfect knowledge*, a *science*, because it is capable to a certain extent of penetrating its object, which is God, with demonstrative certitude, and by means of causes and necessary reasons (that is to say, here, through God Himself). It is attached, through the intermediary of faith, to the knowledge which God has of Himself, and proceeds from the principles of faith by means of conceptual necessities. It is a communicable knowledge, a knowledge of the rational *mode*, but the *root* of which is supernatural, or supra-rational.

Above this knowledge, above discursive theology, is the wisdom of loving faith, or mystical theology. Let us note that the theologians of old insisted that it has the character of *perfect knowledge* or *science*. In point of fact, it also is able to penetrate its object, which is God, with proven certitude, and by means of causes and necessary reasons (that is to say, through God Himself). But here conceptual necessities are no longer the proper means of attaining knowledge. The means is rather the connaturality of love or the assimilation of love with God. And thus the very mode of knowing is here supernatural, or supra-rational. It is an incommunicable knowledge, a science which does not consist in learning, but in suffering the things divine, a supreme science, the darkest, the most humanly naked, and not for the wise but for the poor, because it is not founded on concepts but on the love of charity.

We were saying previously that in the science of phenomena the intelligence remained *outside* of the work of knowledge. Here, not only is man's intelligence *within* the knowledge, but so also are his love, his entire being, the whole human Ego, with the divine Persons abiding within it. I have wished also to dwell on the fact that although mystical contemplation is a nescience with respect to all our natural means of thought, and, as the pseudo-Dionysus and St. John of the Cross both said, a ray of darkness for the intelligence, it is nevertheless a knowledge and a science of a pre-eminent kind, a knowledge whose recognition as the highest in itself and as surer than the philosopher's knowledge, is the claim to greatness of such a mindful philosopher as Bergson; thus is made more obvious to us the analogical ampleness of the word *science* when it recovers its true meaning, and we see what a misery it is for the spirit to limit knowledge to the form which, although it is noble and worthy in itself, is still the lowest form of which this analogical ampleness is capable, the form of empiriological knowledge characteristic of physico-mathematical science, and generally of the sciences of phenomena.

III

Let us now consider the third point I mentioned at the beginning of this paper: what characterizes philosophical knowledge in the outlook of critical realism.

I have just noted that for Christian tradition there are in the supra-rational order, two kinds of wisdom—contemplation by union of love, and discursive theology—which are properly speaking, *scientiae*, knowledge of a perfected and completed type (not in the modern sense of the word *science*, but in the very ample sense of knowing well founded on causes or reasons of being).

Now, if contemplation and theology can be knowledges of a perfected and complete type, it is first of all because there can be in the rational order a knowledge which is a wisdom —a wisdom accessible to our natural powers of inquiry and demonstration. Is it possible that the intellect—which knows itself and judges itself, and which knows and judges reflexively the nature of science—should be unable to enter itself in the work of knowledge, that is to *see into* the nature of things? Can it be condemned to remain always on the outside of this work, in the role of a witness and a regulator of the senses, as happens in the science of phenomena? There must be such a science, a knowledge in which intellect is on the inside, and where it freely develops its deepest aspirations, the aspirations of intellect *as intellect*. That is metaphysics.

Metaphysical wisdom is in its essence a purely natural wisdom. It is in terms of natural and rational evidences that this wisdom is entirely developed. And though from the point of view of exercise, one should—as Plato said—philosophize with one's entire soul, from the point of view of specification it is the intellect alone of man which is here engaged. Metaphysical wisdom is illumined by the intelligibility of being disengaged and in a pure state (I mean without intrinsic reference to any construction of the imagination or to any experience of sense), at the highest degree of abstractive intuition. Its formal object is *being* according to its proper mystery—*being as being*, as Aristotle said.

If positivism old and new, and Kantism do not understand that metaphysics is authentically a science, a knowledge of a perfected and completed type, it means that they do not understand that the intellect *sees*. For them, sense alone is intuitive, the intellect having only a function of connection and of unification. Let them be silent! for we cannot say "I," we cannot utter a noun of the language, without testifying that there are objects in things, that is, centers of visibility, which our senses do not reach, but which our intellect does. Of course, there is no *angelistic*, intellectual intuition, in the sense of Plato and Descartes—I mean an intuition which does not need the mediation of the senses; of course, there is nothing in the intellect which does not originally derive from sensible experience. But it is precisely the activity of the intellect which disengages from this experience and brings to the fire of immaterial visibility in act, the objects which sense cannot decipher in things, and which the intellect sees. This is the mystery of abstractive intuition. And in these objects, which it sees, the intellect knows, without seeing them directly, the transcendent objects which do not exist in the world of sensible experience. This is the mystery of analogical intellection. The problem of metaphysics reduces itself finally to the problem of abstractive intuition and to the question whether, at the summit of abstraction, being itself, in so far as it is being—permeating the world of sensible experience, yet exceeding the world on all sides—is or is not the object of such an intuition. It is this intuition which makes the metaphysician. Everbody does not have it. And if we ask why positivism, old and new, and Kantism ignore this intuition, we shall be bound finally to admit that it is because there are philosophers who see, and philosophers who do not see.

I still have to indicate that in the perspectives of initial realism, metaphysics does not constitute the whole of speculative philosophy, but only its highest category.

Below metaphysics and above the sciences of the empiriological type, there exists another degree of knowledge, that of the *philosophy* of nature. The philosophy of nature knows the same world as the empiriological sciences, the world of change and movement, of sensible and material nature; but the resolution of concepts is made here in intelligible being, not in the observable and measurable as such. Here, again, the intellect perceives being abstractively, but not, this time, being according to its proper mystery; it perceives being in so far as the latter is invested with material motion and according to the proper mystery of the world of becoming; and it is clear, that, if human intelligence is capable of abstractive intuition, it must exercise this power first in that order which is most connatural to human intelligence, namely, the order of sensible nature. A philosophical knowledge of movement, of transitive action, of corporeal substance, of living organism, of sensitive life—helps thus to complete, by proceeding according to an entirely different noetic type and conceptual lexicon, the empiriological notions obtained about nature by the science of phenomena and of experimental detail—that is, by science in the modern sense of the word.

I will not dwell here further on the problems relative to the philosophy of nature. I shall end this discussion by repeating that if neopositivism is right, there is only one science, the science of phenomena. And there is no wisdom. Blinded by logical empiricism, the intellect is a slave in the service of sensitive apprehension.

If Thomist realism is right, all the truth that neopositivism has discerned concerning the sciences of phenomena is maintained and saved, just as is all the truth discerned by dialectical materialism concerning the movement of history and the evolution of the social concrete. But above the sciences of phenomena, there are other categories of science which are categories of wisdom, because they reach, in its very mystery, and yet in quite different ways, being itself, that being after which the intellect thirsts and hungers. And above the work of man in time, accomplished in order to subjugate material nature and eliminate from society the forms of servitude—above this work, there is the activity of man in the eternal, an activity of wisdom and of love, by which the intellect and the heart of man interiorize to themselves an infinite good—not dominated, not capable of domination, but which finally gives itself as the object of fruition.

IV

I have tried to outline what would be, according to the principles of Aristotle and Thomas Aquinas, the organization of the universe of knowledge. Whatever one's philosophical standpoint may be, if one does not admit of an internal differentiation and an internal hierarchy, arising from the distinction among determining intelligible objects in the world of knowledge, one would try in vain to recapture that unity to which the human spirit aspires.

Specialization and departmentalization in the realm of science as they approach infinity, make of the scientist competent in a fraction of a fraction of a part of knowledge an ignoramus before all other things, more of a stranger to the vast world than primitive man with his infantile mythology. Each one's conceptual equipment and vocabulary become incommunicable, and we thus become strangers to each other; human thought enters into the confusion of Babel. If it is to emerge from this confusion, and if conversation and collaboration are to be resumed among workers in the various scientific fields, it can be only on condition that the value of the higher disciplines and the internal hierarchies of knowledge be recognized anew; that a valid critique of knowledge and a valid philosophical training enable the theologian and the philosopher to listen to science, and the scientist to listen to philosophy and theology, and finally, that science and wisdom be reconciled.

But I have not forgotten that this conference of men of science stands for the defense of civilization and liberty. I shall conclude, therefore, by pointing out how the subject I have treated pertains to this cause.

There is no unity in the multiple without order in diversity, and therefore, without a hierarchy of degrees. In the world of politics, one of the ills of modern democracies was the false ideology which led many to believe that a democratic society must be a *non-hierarchical whole*. The most obvious practices of democratic societies belie this assertion, but it would be better for the inevitable differentiations and hierarchies to be accepted and understood by the mind than to be undergone in fact blindly and unwillingly.

In reality, the authentic democratic principle, for the very reason that it opens the political life to all men, and puts political justice and legal relations in first place, is a principle essentially organic. It tends towards an organization of liberties, which is in itself inconceivable without centers of organization that are relatively autonomous yet subordinated to each other. It tends towards hierarchies founded on liberty. A non-hierarchical social whole can never be anything but an anarchic land where each individual or each clan wants to be king, or a totalitarian conglomeration of slaves ruled by the demi-gods of the Party.

In the realm of social life, however, the principle of the organic hierarchy of liberties, necessary and right as it may be, puts our nature to the test. For all men are equal in their specific nature and in their essential dignity; there is no difference in essence between this one and that one. Thus, if the structure and the organic functions of the social body necessitate one man's being placed above another, man's reason must make an especially vigorous and realistic effort to recognize the justice of that superimposed functional inequality.

I say now: how will such discernment be possible in the human order, where we have to deal with individual subjects all of the same kind, if we are incapable of recognizing the differentiations and the organic hierarchies in the world of knowledge, where we deal with objects of the understanding, with intelligible natures which are different *in essence* from each other? There are certain minds which, because of a very curious prejudice, are shocked when it is asserted that in the degrees of knowledge theological knowledge occupies a higher place than philosophical knowledge, philosophical knowledge a higher place than mathematical knowledge, and mathematical knowledge a higher place than purely physical knowledge. Yet it is very clear that the architect's art, by virtue of the nature of its purpose, plays a regulating part towards the art of the painter, charged with decorating the walls of the house, notwithstanding the fact that the architect himself may be a non-entity and the painter a decorator of genius. An army in which anybody may be a general is not the army of democracy but of stupidity. A republic of knowledge in which each type of knowledge claimed for itself the architectonic rank, or where it was declared that no one body of knowledge had a higher rank than any other, or a superordinate regulative role, would be a republic of ignorance.

Let there be no misunderstanding here. Each scientific discipline is free in its domain and develops autonomously; that is clear, because, by definition, it alone is competent regarding its specifying object. Thus, when we say that philosophy is of a higher order than the sciences of phenomena, we do not mean, thereby, that philosophy can enter into the realm of these sciences and willfully decree what is true and what is false; it is not fitted for that. The confusion and tragedies caused during the Renaissance by a theology that wished to prevent the earth from turning and by a decadent Aristotelianism which decreed that it was wrong for the telescope to show spots on the sun, have put the scientific world on guard most rightly against dictatorship of this kind. What we do mean is that philosophy occupies a higher place in the edifice of knowledge because its object or purpose, which is concerned with primary causes, reveals to it realities that are more profound and more essential. This diversity of planes superordinate to each other is the basic condition for the autonomy of each order of knowledge. If all the disciplines, diverse in essence, hunted in the same fields, they would inevitably limit each other and collide, ending in a conflict which would soon be chaos. But because in reality, each one develops upon a distinct plane, each may progress to infinity upon this plane without ever meeting the others. The biologist may progress endlessly in the knowledge of the human being from the standpoint of its physiological and physico-chemical functions without ever coming into conflict with the philosopher who progresses, on his part, in the knowledge of the human being from the standpoint of the relation between soul and matter.

In what sense, however, do we say that the disciplines of higher rank have a regulating or architectonic role as regards the others? We mean by that three things: first, it is the metaphysician, for instance, who must know and justify the principles of the other sciences; not the mathematician but the metaphysician must examine the value of the principle of non-contradiction, or ask himself what constitutes the essence of quantity.

In the second place, it pertains to those disciplines whose object is more profound and more universal to prevent the mind when it works in disciplines of less elevated rank, from overstepping the objective limits of these disciplines and falling into errors foreign to them. Thus the paleontologist does not step out of his sphere when he establishes the hypothesis of evolution and applies it to the origin of a human being. But the philosopher must warn him that he is out of his field when he tries to deny for that reason that the human soul is a spiritual soul which cannot emanate from matter, so that if once upon a time the human organism was produced by a mutation of an animal organism, it was because of the infusion of a soul created by God.

Thirdly, the disciplines of wisdom protect the other disciplines against the hidden domination of unconscious metaphysics, and in that way safeguard their liberty and autonomy. For instance, it would not be difficult to show, along with M. Bergson, that the mechanistic bias and the doctrine of psycho-physical parallelism, which have so long fed parasitically upon modern physics and modern psychology, were, all unknown to themselves, in reality of metaphysical origin and arose from the unconscious domination of Spinoza's philosophy, which was automatically accepted without critical scrutiny. And it would be easy to multiply the number of such cases.

In truth, the need for order and for unity is inescapable. If one denies the conditions of a true and natural unity, in which the degrees of knowledge—each one autonomous at its level, each one having its own jurisdiction and its own specific truth to know—are distributed according to the nature of their objects, one would ultimately come to ask of the social or political obedience of the thinking subjects, or of their racial or national endowment, an absurd and despotic unity of spirit. One would dress physics, biology, mathematics, philosophy, and theology in the same brown or red shirt. One would proclaim, to the great shame of the human spirit—and we have heard of such things—the constitutional unity and the single dignity of sciences of pure Aryan or German blood, or of sciences of pure Marxist-Leninist persuasion. And they alone, once regimented, would have the right to exist.

If it is denied that there is a true and natural hierarchy of the degrees of knowledge, disposed according to their purpose, one will be led not to suppress all hierarchy, but to subordinate wisdom to science and to ascribe the regulative role to the sciences of a lower order, which actually amounts to refusing existence to the higher sciences and to wisdom, and to the truths which it is their mission to dispense among men. Let us not delude ourselves; an education in which the sciences of phenomena and the corresponding techniques take precedence over philosophical and theological knowledge is already, potentially, a Fascist education; an education in which biology, hygiene and eugenics provide the supreme criteria of morality is already, potentially, a Fascist education.[2]

In short, it is simply a question of knowing whether or not one believes in the truth. It is a question of knowing whether, in the different fields of knowledge, the dignity and entire value of our spirit consists in conforming itself to what is. To think that there is no such adequation to reality, that there is no truth, but only opinions all equally worthy of satisfying curiosity, is certainly economical and spares teachers headaches—until it causes the fall of those obstinate heads which would some day refuse adherence to the opinion that it would please a totalitarian Caesar to declare consistent with the conscience of the race or state.

That which constitutes the spiritual essence of totalitarianism is its absolute and active contempt for the truth. Nietzsche proclaimed the death of truth, but the totalitarian regimes understood better than poor Nietzsche what that meant. Truth is whatever is expedient to the interests, the hatreds and the lusts of the party, and it changes with them. A man who does not believe in the truth through sheer indolence of mind, skepticism or dilettantism, is what Lewis Mumford calls a passive barbarian. He who does not believe in the truth by virtue of an actual, absolute and working negation of it, and in order to achieve his will to power, has become an active barbarian, ready to sacrifice men's lives and freedom to his desires, just as he has sacrificed the truth.

If we who are gathered here, scientists, philosophers, and theologians, all believe in the truth, if it is truth which each one of us seeks in his own field of endeavor, then we know that there are many mansions, in the home of truth, and that the least of these mansions, humble as it may be, is naturally sacred. It is within truth that we wish to communicate with each other and co-operate. And in serving truth we know that we are serving liberty, human fellowship, and the cause of peoples who do not wish to be slaves.

NOTES

1. F. Renoirte, "Philosophie et Sciences," *Studies of the Thomist Society*, Vol. III, p. 35.
2. Editors' Note: At this time, "Fascism" referred not only to Mussolini's totalitarian regime but to the ruthless totalitarian mentality wherever it appeared.

3. THE INTUITION OF BEING

The being which is the subject matter of metaphysics, being as such, is neither the particularised being of the natural sciences, nor the being divested of reality of genuine logic, nor yet the pseudo-being of false logic. It is real being in all the purity and fullness of its distinctive intelligibility—or mystery. Objects, all objects, murmur this being; they utter it to the intellect, but not to all intellects, only to those capable of hearing. For here also it is true: He that hath ears to hear let him hear. *Qui habet aures audiendi audiat.* Being is then seen in its distinctive properties, as trans-objectively subsistent, autonomous and essentially diversified. For the intuition of being is also the intuition of its transcendental character and analogical value. It is not enough to employ the word being, to say "Being." We must have the intuition, the intellectual perception of the inexhaustible and incomprehensible reality thus manifested as the object of this perception. It is this intuition that makes the metaphysician.

As you know, to each science there belongs a distinctive intellectual virtue. There is, therefore, an intellectual virtue proper to the metaphysician. And this virtue, or habitus, corresponds to being as the object of the intuition just mentioned. We must therefore distinguish two "Lights" in scholastic parlance, one pertaining to the object, the other to the habitus, or intellectual virtue. The characteristic mode of intellectual apprehension or eidetic visualisation—the degree of immateriality, of spirituality in the manner in which the mind grasps the object and conforms to it, demanded by the very nature of trans-objective reality as it presents to the mind as its object a particular intelligible facet—constitutes what the ancients termed the *ratio formalis sub qua*, the objective light in which at a given degree of knowledge objects are knowable by the intellect. At the same time proportionate to this objective light there is a subjective light perfecting the subjective activity of the intellect, by which the intellect itself is proportioned to a given object, fitted to apprehend it. That is why Thomists say that the habitus is a *lumen*, a light, not in the objective but in the *effective* order. For it is concerned with the production or effectuation of the act of knowing.

Hence the metaphysical habitus is requisite, if we are to have the intuition of being as such, *ens in quantum ens*. Yet on the other hand it is this intuition that effects, causes, the metaphysical habitus. This reciprocal causation simply means that the metaphysical habitus, the intellectual virtue of the metaphysician, comes to birth at the same time as its proper and specific object is disclosed to it. Nevertheless the object is prior, not in time but in ontological rank. In the order of nature the intuition of being as such takes precedence over the inner habitus of the metaphysician. It is this perception of being that determines the first moment at which the habitus comes to birth, and it is by the operation of this same habit thus developed that the being which is the metaphysician's distinctive object is more and more clearly perceived.

Enough of this digression. We are confronted here with a genuine intuition, a perception direct and immediate, an intuition not in the technical sense which the ancients attached to the term, but in the sense we may accept from modern philosophy. It is a very simple sight, superior to any discursive reasoning or demonstration, because it is the source of demonstration. It is a sight whose content and implications no words of human speech can exhaust or adequately express and in which in a moment of decisive emotion, as it were, of spiritual conflagration, the soul is in contact, a living, penetrating and illuminating contact, with a reality which it touches and which takes hold of it. Now what I want to emphasize is that it is being more than anything else which produces such an intuition. The characteristics of intuition as I have just described them may seem at first sight those of M. Bergson's intuition. They seem so, in truth, but with the important difference that he denies that his intuition is intellectual. I, on the other hand, have just maintained that the object par excellence of intuition is being, but that that intuition is intellectual. This is remote indeed from the Bergsonian philosophy. Being does not produce the intuition such as I have described it, by means of that species of sympathy which demands a violent return of the will upon itself of which M. Bergson speaks, but evokes it from the intellect and by means of a concept, an idea. The concept, or notion, of being corresponds with this intuition. The term being is the correct term to express it, though obviously we cannot display by this poor word nor for that matter by the most skilful devices of language all the wealth contained in the intuition. It requires all the metaphysics hitherto elaborated or to be elaborated hereafter in its entire future development to know all the riches implicit in the concept of being. It is by producing in conjunction with reality a mental word within itself that the intellect immediately attains being as such, the subject-matter of metaphysics.

Thus we are confronted with objects and as we confront them, the diverse realities made known by our senses or by the several sciences, we receive at a given moment, as it were the revelation of an intelligible mystery concealed in them. Nor is this revelation, this species of intellectual shock, confined to metaphysicians. It is sometimes given to those who are not metaphysicians. There is a kind of sudden intuition which a soul may receive of her own existence, or of "being" embodied in all things whatsoever, however lowly. It may even happen that to a particular soul this intellectual perception presents the semblance of a mystical grace. I have quoted elsewhere (*Degrés du Savoir*, p. 552) a personal experience communicated to me.

"I have often experienced in a sudden intuition the reality of my being, the profound first principle which makes me exist outside nonentity. It is a powerful intuition whose violence has sometimes frightened me and which first revealed to me a metaphysical absolute."

A similar intuition is described in the autobiography of Jean-Paul Richter. "One morning when I was still a child, I was standing on the threshold of the house and looking to the left in the direction of the woodpile when suddenly there came to me from heaven like a lightning flash the thought: *I am a self*, a thought which has never since left me. I perceived my self for the first time and for good."

There are, therefore, metaphysical intuitions which are a natural revelation to the soul, invested with the decisive, imperious and dominant character, of a "Substantial word" uttered by reality. They reveal the intelligible treasure, the unforgettable trans-objective fact, which is either her own subsistence, the "Self" that she is, or being either her own or the being apprehended in objects. Evidently this intuition of which I am speaking does not necessarily present this appearance of a species of mystical grace. But it is always, so to speak, a gift bestowed upon the intellect, and beyond question it is in one form or another indispensable to every metaphysician. But we must also observe that although it is indispensable to the metaphysician, it is not given to everybody, nor to all those who engage in philosophy, nor even to all philosophers who desire to be or are believed to be metaphysicians. Kant never had it. What is the explanation of this? That it is difficult. It is not indeed difficult like an operation which it is hard to perform, whose successful performance demands expert skill. For there is nothing simpler. It was precisely because he sought it by a technique, an intellectual technique of extreme subtlety, that Kant failed to attain it.

Moreover, it is as true to say that this intuition produces itself through the medium of the vital action of our intellect, I mean as vitally receptive and contemplative, as to say that we produce it. It is difficult, inasmuch as it is difficult to arrive at the degree of intellectual purification at which this act is produced in us, at which we become sufficiently disengaged, sufficiently empty to *hear* what all things whisper and to *listen* instead of composing answers.

We must attain a certain level of intellectual spirituality, such that the impact of reality upon the intellect—or to use a less crude metaphor, the active attentive silence of the intellect, its meeting with the real—gives the objects received through our senses (whose *species impressa* is buried in the depths of the intellect) a new kind of presence in us: they are present in a mental word, another life, a living content which is a world of trans-objective presence and intelligibility. Then we are confronted within ourselves with the object of this intuition, as an object of knowledge, living with an immaterial life, with the burning translucence of intellectual nature in act.

Concrete approaches to this intuition

It is worth remarking at this point that there are concrete approaches which prepare for this intuition and lead up to it. They are different *paths* which, however, it is important to observe, are radically insufficient if we stop short at them, but which may prove useful to particular individuals if they will transcend them, if they will go further. Here I will mention three of these. One is the Bergsonian experience of duration. Within limits it is a genuine experience.

Duration is apprehended by an experience of motion in which, on a level deeper than that of consciousness, our psychic states fuse in a potential manifold which is, notwithstanding, a unity, and in which we are aware of advancing through time and enduring through change indivisibly, yet that we are growing richer in quality and triumphing over the inertia of matter. This is a psychological experience which is not yet the metaphysical intuition of being, but is capable of leading us up to it. For involved in this psychological duration and implicitly given by it there is indeed existence, the irreducible value of being, *esse*.

This intuition is therefore a path, an approach, to the perception of existence. The latter, however, is not yet nakedly displayed in its own intelligible form.

The German philosopher, Heidegger, assures us that no man can become a metaphysician who has not first experienced anguish, this anguish being understood not only psychologically but also as metaphysically as possible. It is the feeling at once keen and lacerating of all that is precarious and imperilled in our existence, in human existence. As the effect of this feeling, of this anguish, our existence loses its commonplaceness and acquires a unique value, its unique value. It confronts us as something saved from nothingness, snatched from nonentity.

Certainly such a dramatic experience of nothingness may serve as an introduction to the intuition of being provided it is taken as no more than an introduction.

My third example is not a thesis fully worked out, but suggestions put forward in preliminary sketches or in the course of conversation. Therefore I must speak of it with all due reserve and without committing its author to my interpretation. It would seem that M. Gabriel Marcel is seeking a method of approach to metaphysical being by deepening the sense of certain moral facts, such as fidelity.[1] As Heidegger attaches himself to a personal experience, a psychological experience such as anguish, while warning us that he is not concerned with psychology, so the notion of fidelity is here understood in a sense which does or should transcend ethics and conveys strictly metaphysical value and content. We may observe that the consistency, *steadfastness*, and victory over disintegration and oblivion contained in this virtue and suggested by the word fidelity are strictly dependent upon a certain *steadfastness* in reality itself in virtue of which I dominate the flux of my own life and possess my metaphysical consistence. Therefore, if I rightly understand M. Marcel's thought, if we follow its direction we shall conclude that a philosophy of life which confuses my *self* with the flux of my life is inconsistent with the experience of fidelity. The experience, the irreducible reality of what I experience and know as fidelity, is pregnant with an ontological realism.

These approaches are useful only if we take the decisive step

In these three instances we are, you see, confronted with so many concrete approaches to being. The first of these experiences, that of duration, belongs to the speculative order, and is at once psychological and biological. The two others belong to the practical and moral order, the psychological factor being invested with the ethical. If we stop here, we have not, I maintain, crossed the threshold of metaphysics. These philosophic explorations are certainly not to be despised or refused. They can perform most valuable service by directing towards being many minds hidebound by idealist prejudices or repelled by some textbook of so-called scholasticism. They can prepare them to recover the sense of being. But they can do this, only if we will travel further; cross the threshold, take the decisive step. Otherwise, whatever we do, we shall remain in psychology and ethics, which we shall then work up, swell out, enlarge or rarefy to make them mimic metaphysics. We shall then have, not genuine metaphysics, but a substitute which may certainly possess a very considerable philosophic interest, but is nothing but a substitute all the same. The utmost that can be achieved along these lines are solutions obtained by an indirect route which skirts the essential issue or by definitions based on external criteria, not the genuine solutions demanded by a science worthy of the name, by philosophic knowledge. Even if psychology and ethics enrich their own speech with metaphysical echoes or undertones, they will be but echoes.

But the most serious danger which all these methods of approaching being involve is the danger of remaining imprisoned in one or other of the concrete analogues of being, whichever one has chosen as a path to it. The experience in question gives information only of itself. This is indeed the drawback of pure experience in philosophy and the pitfall of every metaphysical system which attempts to be empirical. The experience, though valid for the domain covered by the particular intuition, cannot, save by an arbitrary procedure, be extended to a wider province of the intelligible world, and be employed to explain it. On the other hand, as I have just said, such experiences bring us to the threshold which it is then for us to cross by taking the decisive step. We do this by letting the veils—too heavy with matter and too opaque—of the concrete psychological or ethical fact fall away to discover in their purity the strictly metaphysical values which such experiences concealed. There is then but one word by which we can express our discovery, namely being. Let us have the courage to require our intellect, acting as such, to look the reality signified by the term in the face. It is something primordial, at once very simple and very rich and, if you will, inexpressible in the sense that it is that whose perception is the most difficult to describe, because it is the most immediate. Here we are at the root, at last laid bare, of our entire intellectual life. You may say, if you please, for I am here attempting to employ a purely descriptive terminology as a preliminary to the formation of a philosophic vocabulary, that what is now perceived is, as it were, a pure activity, a subsistence, but a subsistence which transcends the entire order of the imaginable, a living tenacity, at once precarious—it is nothing for me to crush a fly—and indomitable—within and around me there is growth without ceasing. By this subsistence, this tenacity, objects come up against me, overcome possible disaster, endure and possess in themselves whatever is requisite for this. These are metaphors, lamentably inadequate, which attempt to express not so much what my intellect sees, which is super-empirical, as my experience of the vision, and do not themselves enter the domain of metaphysics but which may make us aware that to the word "being," when it expresses a genuine metaphysical intuition, there must correspond a primary and original datum, of its essence above the scope of observation.

So true is it that the words "being," "existence," are pregnant with a metaphysical content which transcends observation, that, in order to free us from it, logical empiricists have proposed to abandon the term "existence." It is a bold though impossible solution, and moreover entirely consistent with the principles of empiricism, inasmuch as they demand the formation of a philosophic vocabulary completely divested of ontological reference. In the *Revue de Metaphysique et de Morale* (April–June, 1931) I read an article by Madame Christine Ladd-Franklin, entitled "La Non-Existence de l'Existence," in which she proposes, in order to satisfy the demands of a scientific method devoid of ontology, in fact, of a purely empirical metaphysic, to substitute for the word "existence" the phrase "*Event* in such and such a province of thought."

This metaphysical content, of which we are speaking, covers the entire domain of intelligibility and reality. It is a gift bestowed upon the intellect by an intuition which infinitely exceeds, I do not say in the intensity of its experience but in its intelligible value, the experience which may have led up to it.

Confirmatory rational analysis

I have spoken briefly of the intuition of being and of the paths which may lead to its threshold. I must add that it is both possible and necessary to show analytically that to arrive at this point is inevitable. We are now dealing with something totally different from those concrete approaches to being which I have just discussed. We are now concerned with a rational analysis establishing the necessity of being as such, *ens in quantum ens*, as the supreme object of our knowledge. Such an analytic proof presupposes, as taken for granted by common sense or as scientifically confirmed by the criticism of knowledge, what in general terms we may call the objective or rather trans-objective validity of understanding and knowledge, a non-idealist position. It is then easy to prove that it is only in appearance that we can dispense, as Madame Ladd-Franklin would have us do, with the notions of being and existence, even though we speak of "Event" and attempt to prove that we should substitute this choicer term for the word existence. The entire series of concepts employed to reach her conclusion witnesses at every turn to the primacy of the notion of being. It is argued, for example, that philosophers who employ the term existence *are mistaken* and that a sound scientific method *requires* the abandonment of ontological notions. But being is still there—not always the word but the object which it signifies. And at every turn the critic makes use, unawares, of this intelligible value of being, which it is claimed has been got rid of. Every attempt to eliminate the notion of being refutes itself.

In the second place it is easy to prove, as St. Thomas proves in the first article of his *De Veritate* that all our notions, all our concepts, are resolved in the concept of being. It is therefore the first of all our concepts, of which all the rest are determinations. Being is determined by the differences which arise within, not outside, itself. It is then to being that we inevitably reascend as to the fountain head. It is being which the intellect perceives first and before anything else. It is, therefore, being which the metaphysical intellect must disengage and know in its distinctive mystery.

It is, however, important to observe that the intuition of which I was speaking just now and the analysis with which I am at present concerned should accompany each other. Were we content with the intuition without the rational analysis we should risk being landed with an intuition unconfirmed by reason, whose rational necessity therefore would not be manifest. Were we content with the analysis—as we are liable to be when we teach philosophy—though the analysis would indeed prove that we must arrive at the intuition of being as the goal of a necessary regress, it would not of itself furnish the intuition. Thus the analysis is in the same case as the approaches of which I spoke earlier. The latter led up concretely, *in via inventionis*, to the metaphysical intuition of being. But it still remained to cross the threshold to which they had led us. It is the same with rational analysis. It leads us by logical necessity, and *in via judicii*, to the threshold which an intuitive perception alone enables us to cross, the perception of being as such. When the mind once has this intuition it has it for good.

Observe what an unforgettable event in the history of philosophy was Parmenides' discovery, imperfect though it still was, of being as such. It was on that account that Plato called him the father of philosophy, and when obliged to criticise him accused himself of parricide. Parmenides was, it would seem, the first western philosopher to have the perception, though still very imperfect as I have said, of being as such. It was imperfect, for he does not seem to have disengaged it in its naked metaphysical value. He appears, as his theory of the sphere indicates, to have amalgamated the metaphysical intuition of being with a physical perception of sensible reality and to have misunderstood or misinterpreted his intuition of being, when the inevitable moment arrived for him to explain it in terms of philosophic concepts, by understanding it univocally and thus falling into monism.

You will also see why the intuition of the principle of identity, every being is what it is, being is being, can possess such value for the metaphysician, can become the object of his enraptured contemplation. Common sense—and therefore the man in the street—makes use of the principle without scrutinising it. "A cat is a cat" says common sense—what more could it say?—so that, if the philosopher comes on the scene and enunciates the principle of identity in front of common sense, the latter will not *see* it, but will merely have the impression that an insignificant commonplace has been affirmed, in fact a tautology. The philosopher, on the other hand, when he enunciates the principle of identity enunciates it as an expression of the metaphysical intuition of being, and thus sees in it the first fundamental law of reality itself, a law which astounds him because it proclaims *ex abrupto*, the primal mystery of being, its combination of subsistence and abundance, a law which is exemplified by objects in an infinite number of different modes, and applied with an infinite variety. It is not as the result of a logistic process that the metaphysician perceives and employs the principle of identity, so that it compels him to reduce everything to a pure identity, that is to say, to obliterate all the diversities and varieties of being. For it is with its mode of analogical realisation that he apprehends the principle. When he apprehends being as such, being according to its pure intelligible nature, he apprehends the essentially analogous value of the concept of being which is implicitly manifold and is realised in diverse objects in such fashion as to admit differences of essence between them, complete and vast differences. The principle of identity secures the multiplicity and variety of objects. Far from reducing all things to identity, it is, as I have explained elsewhere, the guardian of universal multiplicity, the axiom of being's irreducible diversities. If each being is what it is, it is not what other beings are.

The intuition of being as such is an eidetic intuition.

It follows that the metaphysical intuition of being is an abstractive intuition. Abstraction, however, is an antique term rendered suspect to modern ears by the distortion of long use and by errors and misconceptions of every sort. Therefore instead of *abstraction*, I propose to speak of *eidetic or ideating visualisation*. I maintain then that the metaphysical intuition of being is an ideating intuition, that is an intuition producing an idea, and this in a pre-eminent degree. How could it be otherwise with the pure speculative operation of our human intellect? This intuition is at the summit of eidetic intellectuality. What do I mean by the phrase eidetic visualisation, *abstractio*? I mean that the intellect by the very fact that it is spiritual proportions its objects to itself, by elevating them within itself to diverse degrees, increasingly pure, of spirituality and immateriality. It is within itself that it attains reality, stripped of its real existence outside the mind and disclosing, uttering in the mind a content, an interior, an intelligible sound or voice, which can possess only in the mind the conditions of its existence one and universal, an existence of intelligibility in act. If being were the object of a concrete intuition like that of an external sense or of introspection, of an intuition centred upon a reality grasped concretely in its singular existence, philosophy would be compelled to choose, as it gave this intuition an idealist or a realist value, between a pure ontological monism and a pure phenomenalist pluralism. If, however, being is, as I have said analogous and if the principle of identity is the axiom of reality's irreducible diversities, it is because extramental being is perceived in the mind under the conditions of the eidetic existence which it receives there, and the imperfect and relative unity it possesses in the mind must be broken up, as also must be the pure and unqualified unity of the objects of univocal concepts, when we pass from its existence in the concept to its real existence. The higher degree in which the intuition of being as such "ideates" is precisely the condition and guarantee of its correct metaphysical employment.

At this point a gulf yawns between the scholastics and many modern philosophers of realist tendencies who attempt to construct an "Existential" philosophy and ontology. For many modern philosophers being is indeed the object of an intuition and a decisive encounter but of an empirical intuition and a concrete encounter, which however profound, mysterious and secret it may be supposed to be, always remains of the same nature as those procured by psychological or moral experience. It discovers a singular reality or presence actually existing and acting—in any case a reality which the intellect does not grasp by an eidetic visualisation in the transparence of an idea or concept. And it discovers it by a kind of affective and experienced connaturality.

It is therefore an idealist prejudice which prevents these philosophers from making a frank and deliberate use of the eidetic intuition. They fail to see that they do employ it all the same but on its lowest level and mingled with sensible and emotional factors, the level, namely, of psychological experience or experiences even more enveloped by the opacity of the senses.

Hence, although the various forms of experience of which I have been speaking, may serve as paths to the metaphysical perception of being, they cannot of themselves constitute it. This perception, this intuition is of a supremely eidetic order, is purely intelligible, not empirical. That is the reason why many who think themselves metaphysicians are in fact psychologists or moral philosophers and, though striving to reach metaphysics, mimic rather than attain the perception of which I am speaking.

Thomism, as I have already observed, merits the appellation of an existential philosophy, and this already in the speculative order, in what concerns the speculative portion of philosophy. But though Thomist metaphysics is an existential metaphysics, it is so by being and remaining metaphysics, a wisdom whose procedure is intellectual and in strict accordance with the demands of the intellect and its distinctive intuitiveness.

NOTE

1. *Editors' Note*: Jacques Maritain published A *Preface to Metaphysics* in French in 1934. Gabriel Marcel had already published his brief *Positions et Approches concrètes du Mystère Ontologique* (1933) (which appeared in English in his *Philosophy of Existence*, 1949). Since then he has written a number of major works in which his position is fully and richly elaborated, notably in the Gifford Lectures, *The Mystery of Being*, two volumes, London, 1950 and 1951. Martin Heidegger takes up "anguish" or "anxiety" (*Angst*) in *Being and Time* (London: SCM Press Ltd., 1962), pp. 225–73. See pp. 228–34 on "the basic state-of-mind of anxiety as a distinctive way in which Dasein is disclosed.

PART TWO

THE APPROACH TO GOD

"One day the hills will surrender themselves, everything will surrender itself to the intelligence of man on the day when the self-subsistent *Act of Existing* shall give Itself in vision."

Ecce in Pace

4. MAN'S APPROACH TO GOD

In order to get a sufficiently comprehensive notion of the problems which have to do with our knowledge of the existence of God, we must take into account both that approach to God which depends on the natural forces of the human mind and that approach to God which depends on the supernatural gift of faith. Only thus can we have a complete picture of the subject. Consequently, I shall have to complement my philosophical discussion with some considerations borrowed from theology.

Physics is today reigning unchallenged over our minds and culture. Its progress and achievements are actually wonderful and deserve deep admiration. What is badly needed is not to disparage physics and accuse it of atomizing us, but to be aware of its very nature, its true field of knowledge and its limitations. What is badly needed is to supplement physics with another type of knowledge, concerned with grasping being for its own sake. What is badly needed is a renewal of metaphysics.

No doubt there is no continuity between the world of physics and the world of metaphysics. The modern image of the atom—each day more complicated, more mysterious and more fecund in practical applications—is a mathematical image or ideal entity founded on reality, which gives us an invaluable symbolical or phenomenological knowledge of *how matter behaves*, but cannot instruct us philosophically or ontologically about *what matter is*. Yet the fact remains that the conceptions of modern science and the extraordinary progress of micro-physics provide the human intellect with a scientific imagery, an imaginable or supra-imaginable picture of nature which is incomparably more favorable to the edification of a philosophy of nature and more open to the deepening labor of metaphysical reason than the old Newtonian physics. The opportunity is now given for that reconciliation between science and wisdom for which the human mind thirsts.

The "existential" philosophies which are today in fashion

are but a sign of a certain deep want to find again the sense of Being. This want remains, however, unfulfilled, for these philosophies are still enslaved by irrationalism and seek for the revelation of existence, for ontological ecstasy, in the breaking of reason, in the experience of despair and nothingness, of anguish or absurdity. True existentialism is the work of reason.[1]

It is so because the primary reality grasped by the intellect is the act of existing as exercised by some visible or tangible thing; and because it is the intuition of being—disengaged for its own sake, and perceived at the summit of an abstractive intellection—it is the intuition of being—even when it is distorted by the error of a system, as in Plato or Spinoza—which causes a human intellect to enter the realm of metaphysics and be capable of metaphysical intelligence.

From Plato and Aristotle to St. Anselm and St. Thomas Aquinas, Descartes and Leibniz, philosophers offered proofs or demonstrations of God's existence, or, as Thomas Aquinas more modestly and accurately puts it, *ways* of making God's existence intellectually sure—all of them are highly conceptualized and rationalized, specifically *philosophical* ways of approach. Kant criticized the proof afforded by Descartes, the so-called ontological argument, and wrongly endeavored to reduce all other ways of demonstration to this particular one, so as to envelop them in the same condemnation.[2] This was a great mistake, for the five ways pointed out by Thomas Aquinas are totally independent of the ontological argument; they hold true before any criticism, and are unshakeably valid in themselves.

Yet I do not intend to consider now these highly conceptualized and rationalized, specifically *philosophical* ways of approach. When St. Paul asserted: "What is known about God is clear to them [namely, to the Gentiles], for God Himself has made it clear, for since the creation of the world His invisible attributes—His everlasting power and divinity—are to be discerned and contemplated through His works,"[3] he was not only concerned with the scientifically elaborated or specifically philosophical ways of establishing God's existence, but also, and first of all, with the natural knowledge of God's existence to which the vision of created things leads the reason of any man whatsoever, be he a philosopher or not. It is this natural knowledge of God's existence that I shall consider—a knowledge which is natural not only in the sense of rational or non-supernatural, but also in the sense of *naturally* or *pre*-philosophically acquired, or prior to any philosophical, scientifically rationalized elaboration.

In other words I submit that, before the human mind enters the sphere of perfectly formed and articulate knowledge, particularly the sphere of metaphysical knowledge, it is capable of a pre-philosophical knowledge which is *virtually metaphysical*. It is this pre-philosophical knowledge that I shall now try to outline, at least in a tentative way.[4]

What must be first of all stressed in this connection is, I think, the fact that, once a man is awakened to the reality of existence, once he has really perceived this tremendous fact, sometimes exhilarating, sometimes disgusting and maddening, namely: I *exist*, he is henceforth taken hold of by the intuition of Being and the implications it involves.

Precisely speaking, this prime intuition is both the intuition of *my* existence and of the existence of things. When it takes place, I suddenly realize that a given entity, man, mountain, or tree, exists and exercises that sovereign activity *to be* in its own way, totally self-assertive and totally implacable, completely independent from *me*. And at the same time I realize that I also exist but as thrown back into my loneliness and frailty by such affirmation of existence in which I have positively no part, to which I am exactly as naught. So the prime intuition of Being is the intuition of the solidity and inexorability of existence; and, secondly, of the death and nothingness to which *my* existence is liable. And thirdly, in the same flash of intuition, which is but my *becoming aware* of the intelligible value of Being, I realize that the solid and inexorable existence perceived in anything whatsoever implies—I don't know yet in what way, perhaps in things themselves, perhaps separately from them—some absolute, irrefragable existence, completely free from nothingness and death. These three intellective leaps—to actual existence as asserting itself independently from me; from this sheer objective existence to my own threatened existence; and from my existence spoiled with nothingness to absolute existence—are achieved within that same and unique intuition which philosophers would explain as the intuitive perception of the essentially analogical content of the first concept, the concept of Being.

Then—this is the second step—a quick, spontaneous reasoning, as natural as this intuition (and, as a matter of fact, more or less involved in it) immediately springs forth, as the necessary fruit of such primordial apperception and as enforced by and under its light. I see that my Being, *first*, is liable to death; and, second, that it depends on the totality of nature, on the universal whole whose part I am; and that Being-with-nothingness, as my own being is, implies, in order to be, Being-without-nothingness. It implies that absolute existence which I confusedly perceived as involved in my primordial intuition of existence. Now the universal whole, whose part I am, is Being-without-nothingness from the very fact that I am part of it; consequently it does not exist by itself. And thus, finally, since the universal whole does not exist by itself, there is another, separate whole, another Being, transcendent and self-sufficient and unknown in itself and activating all beings, which is Being-without-nothingness, that is, Being by itself.

Thus the inner dynamism of the intuition of existence, or of the intelligible value of Being, causes me to see that absolute existence or Being-without-nothingness transcends the totality of nature, and compels me to face the existence of God.

This is not a new approach to God. It is the eternal approach of man's reason to God. What is new is the manner in which the modern mind has become aware of the simplicity and liberating power, the natural and somehow intuitive characteristics of this eternal approach. The science of the ancients was steeped in philosophy. Their scientific imagery was a pseudo-ontological imagery. Consequently there was a kind of continuum between their knowledge of the physical world and their knowledge of God. The latter appeared as the summit of the former, a summit which was to be climbed through the manifold paths of the causal connections at play in the sublunar world and the celestial spheres. The sense of Being that ruled their universal thought was for them a too usual atmosphere to be felt as a surprising gift. At the same time the natural intuition of existence was so strong in them that their proofs of God could take the form of the most conceptualized and rationalized scientific demonstrations, and be offered as an unrolling of logical necessities, without losing the inner energy of that intuition. Such logical machinery was quickened instinctively by the basic intuition of Being.

We are in a quite different position now. In order to solve the enigma of physical reality and to conquer the world of phenomena, our science has become a kind of Maya—a Maya which succeeds and makes us masters of nature. But the sense of Being is absent from it. Thus when we happen to experience the impact of Being upon the mind it appears to us as a kind of intellectual revelation, and we realize clearly both its liberating and its awakening power and the fact that it involves a knowledge which is separated from that sphere of knowledge peculiar to our science. At the same time we realize that the knowledge of God, before being developed into logical and perfectly conceptualized demonstrations, is first and foremost a natural fruit of the intuition of existence, and forces itself upon our mind in the imperative virtue of this intuition.

In other words, we have become aware of the fact that human reason's approach to God, in its primordial vitality, is neither a mere intuition, which would be suprahuman, nor is it that artlike philosophical reasoning by which it is expressed in its achieved form, each step of which is pregnant with involved issues and problems. Human reason's approach to God in its primordial vitality is a *natural* reasoning, that is, intuitive-like or irresistibly vitalized by, and maintained within, the intellectual flash of the intuition of existence. Then the intuition of existence, grasping in some existing reality Being-with-nothingness, makes the mind grasp by the same stroke the necessity of Being-without-nothingness. And nowhere is there any problem involved, because the illumining power of this intuition takes hold of the mind and obliges it to see. Thus it naturally proceeds, in a primary intuitive flash, from imperative certainty to imperative certainty. I believe that from Descartes to Kierkegaard, the effort of modern thought—to the extent that it has not completely repudiated metaphysics, and if it is cleansed of the irrationalism which has gradually corrupted it—tends to such an awareness of the specific *naturality* of man's knowledge of God, definitely deeper than any logical process scientifically developed. It tends to the awareness of man's spontaneous knowledge of God, and of the primordial and simple intuitivity in which it originates.

I have just tried to describe the way in which this *natural* pre-philosophical knowledge spontaneously proceeds. It implies a reasoning, but an intuitive-like reasoning, steeped in the primordial intuition of existence. I would say that this natural knowledge is a kind of *innocent* knowledge—I mean pure of any dialectics. Such knowledge involves certitude, cogent certitude, but in an imperfect logical state; it has not crossed the threshold of *scientific* demonstration, the certitude of which is critical and implies the logical overcoming of the difficulties involved; and by the same token such natural knowledge is still blissfully ignorant of these difficulties, of all that burden of objections which St. Thomas puts at the beginning of his demonstrations. Because scientific certitude and objections to be met—and the answers to the objections —come into being together.

We see, then, that the philosophical proofs of the existence of God, say, the five ways of Thomas Aquinas, are a development and explication of this natural knowledge on the level of scientific discussion and scientific certitude. And they normally presuppose this natural knowledge, not as regards the logical structure of the demonstration, but as regards the existential condition of the thinking subject. Thus, if all the preceding observations are true, we should always— before offering the philosophical proofs, say, the classical five ways[5]—make sure that those we are addressing are awakened to the primordial intuition of existence and aware of the natural knowledge of God involved in it.

Let us mention now that there are two other pre-philosophical approaches to God—namely, through art and poetry, and through moral experience.

As concerns art and poetry, suffice it to quote the famous page where Baudelaire has translated into his own language a passage from a lecture by Edgar Allan Poe, on *The Poetic Principle*. It is the immortal instinct for beauty, he said, "which makes us consider the world and its pageants as a glimpse of, a correspondence with, Heaven. . . . It is at once by poetry and *through* poetry, by music and *through* music, that the soul divines what splendors shine behind the tomb, and when an exquisite poem brings tears to the eyes, such tears are not the sign of an excess of joy, they are rather a witness of an irritated melancholy, an exigency of nerves, a nature exiled in the imperfect which would possess immediately, on this very earth, a paradise revealed."[6] *Our art,* Dante said, *is the grandchild of God.* The poet completes the work of creation; he cooperates in divine balancings, he moves mysteries about; he is in natural sympathy with the secret powers that play about in the universe. A slide down the inclined plane of heaven, a push from grace: the sleeper will change sides, and will wake up with God.

In the last analysis all genuine poetry is religious. Even if a poet has no conceptual knowledge of God, even if he is or believes he is an atheist, it is toward the primary source of Beauty that in actual fact his spiritual effort is oriented. And thus, if no intellectual or moral hindrance thwarts this spiritual dynamism, he will naturally be led by poetry to some conscious notion and awareness of the existence of that God at Whom he is unconsciously looking, in and through his art and his work.

As concerns moral experience, we may observe that when a man experiences, in a primary act of freedom, the impact of the moral good, and is thus awakened to moral existence, and directs his life toward the good for the sake of the good, then he directs his life, without knowing it, toward the absolute Good, and in this way knows God vitally, by virtue of the inner dynamism of his choice of the good, even if he does not know God in any conscious fashion or by means of any conceptual knowledge.[7] Let us suppose that no intellectual prejudice, deformation, or illusion thwarts this spiritual dynamism, and that no erroneous representation causes what is implied in the dynamism in question to be seemingly denied by conceptual thought: then the man who has really chosen the good for the sake of the good will be led by moral experience to some conscious notion and awareness of that God at Whom he is unconsciously looking in and through his primary act of freedom.

Moral experience in which man deliberating about himself chooses the moral good, *bonum honestum*, the end of his life—artistic creation which engenders in beauty—intuitive grasping of the intelligible value of the act of existing—these three approaches are existential approaches; they plunge into real existence. But the privilege of the intuition of being is that it winds up directly in a conscious and conceptually expressed, irrefragable awareness of the existence of God.

It also carries along with itself another intuition, the intuition of the Self, of subjectivity as subjectivity, which is at the same time a discovery of the basic generosity of existence. For "it is better to give than to receive"; and that kind of spiritual existence which consists in love and the gift of oneself is the supreme revelation of existence for the Self.

But is it not impossible that the supreme cause of existence should not enjoy the supreme kind of existence? So man awakened to the sense of being does not only know that God exists and is self-subsisting Existence, he also knows that because of this very fact God is absolute ontological generosity and self-subsisting love; and that such transcendent love causes, permeates, and activates every creature.

Though human reason is helped in fact by revelation to know more perfectly these natural truths, reason is enough, the natural forces of the human mind are enough, for man to know that God is self-subsisting Love, as He is self-subsisting Intellection and self-subsisting Existence. And we also know, through the Gospel revelation, through faith, that, as far as the creature is concerned, God should not only be loved but that He loves, I mean with the distinctive *madness* of love, and that there can be relations of friendship, mutual self-giving, community of life, and the sharing of a common bliss between God and His intelligent creatures: a fact which implies the supernatural order of grace and charity.

5. A SIXTH WAY

The views which I propose here are based neither on a fact observed in the world of sense experience, nor on the principle "One cannot rise to the infinite in the series of causes," nor does the argument proceed with the royal simplicity of Thomas Aquinas. It may, indeed, appear too subtle, and for a long time I regarded it as belonging to the domain of research hypotheses. I have, however, come to think that it constitutes a genuine proof, a rationally valid way leading to a firmly established certitude.

Here again it is appropriate to distinguish two levels of approach—a *prephilosophic* level whereon certitude bathes in an intuitive experience, and a *scientific* or *philosophical* level whereon certitude emanates from a logically elaborated demonstration and from a rationally developed metaphysical justification.

We shall first take our stand on the prephilosophic level. Indeed it is the intuitive process that, in this case more than ever, matters first of all, although the intuition in question is of a much more peculiar sort than the primordial intuition of existing, and supposes experience of the proper life of the intellect. By feeling the impact of this intuitive experience, the mind discovers the approach to God which this experience brings along with it. Later it is led to formulate in logically conceptualized terms that which I call here a "sixth way."

The intuition of which I speak is related to the natural spirituality of intelligence. I shall try to describe it as it is in its primitive, and, so to speak, "wild" state, where it first begins to sprout. I am busy thinking. Everything in me is concentrated on a certain truth which has caught me up in its wake. This truth carries me off. All the rest is forgotten. Suddenly I come back to myself; a reflection is awakened in me which seems to me quite incongruous, altogether unreasonable, but whose evidence takes possession of me, in my very perception of my act of thought; *how is it possible that I was born?*

The activity of the mind develops in two quite different orders. It develops on the one hand in the order of the life which Aristotle called "life proportioned to man." Here the activity of the mind, as it happens in our train of ordinary social or occupational pursuits, is made up of a succession of operations immersed in time and which are for the most part operations of sense and imagination sustained and illuminated by the intellect.

On the other hand it develops in the order of the life which Aristotle called "life proportioned to the intellect." Here the activity of the mind, entirely withdrawn in thought, is centered above the sense and imagination, and is concerned with intelligible objects alone. It is when a man is thus engaged in an act of purely intellectual thought (to the extent that this is possible for a rational animal) that it happens that the intuition in question takes place: how is it possible that that which is thus in the process of thinking, in the act of intelligence, which is immersed in the fire of knowing and in the intellectual grasp of what is, should once have been a pure nothing, once did not exist? Where I am now in the act of intellection and of consciousness of my thought, was there once *nothing*? That is impossible; it is not possible that at a certain moment what is now thinking was not at all, was a pure nothing. How could this have been born to existence?

I am not here faced with a logical contradiction. I am facing a *lived* contradiction, an incompatibility of fact (known in *actu exercito*). It is as if I were in a room and, without my having left for an instant, someone were to say to me that I just came in—I know that what he says is impossible.

Thus, I who am now in the act of thinking have always existed. This view imposes itself on me and does not seem strange to me unless I draw myself back from it in order to consider it from without. And perhaps I express it in a deficient way; we shall see about that later. For the moment I speak as I can, and I cannot speak otherwise.

Yet I know quite well that I was born. True, I know it by hearsay, but I do know it with an absolute certainty, and besides, I remember my childhood. The certitude of having been born, common to all men, represses in us the blossoming forth—when the natural spirituality of intelligence is activated in us—of another certitude, that of the impossibility that our existence as thinking minds ever began or followed upon the nothingness of itself, and it prevents that other certitude from reaching our consciousness.

So here I am, in the grasp of two contrary certitudes. There is only one solution: I, who am thinking, have always existed, but not in myself or within the limits of my own personality —and not by an impersonal existence or life either (for without personality there is no thought, and there must have been thought there, since it is now in me); therefore I have always existed by a suprapersonal existence or life. Where then? It must have been in a Being of transcendent personality, in whom all that there is of perfection in my thought and in all thought existed in a supereminent manner, and who was, in His own infinite Self, before I was, and is, now while I am, more than I myself, who is eternal, and from whom I, the self which is thinking now, proceeded one day into temporal existence. I had (but without being able to say "I") an eternal existence in God before receiving a temporal existence in my own nature and my own personality.

What shall we say now if we transport ourselves onto the level of rational demonstration? Is it possible to justify philosophically the intuitive experience which we have just tried to describe?

What is important to consider first is that the intellect is above time, *intellectus supra tempus*: because the intellect is spiritual, and time, the perseverance of movement in being, or the continuity of perpetually vanishing existence proper to movement, is the proper duration of matter.

The operations of the human intellect are in time, and, indeed, subject to time, but in an extrinsic manner, and only by reason of the materiality of the senses and the imagination to whose exercise they are bound. In themselves they are not subject to the flux of impermanence. They emerge above time. They exist in a duration which is a deficient imitation of eternity, a succession of fragments of eternity, for it is the perseverance in being of spiritual acts of intellection or of contemplative gaze. Thus this duration is composed of instants superior to time, each of which may correspond to a lapse of time more or less long, but is in itself without flow

or movement or succession—a flash of permanent or nonsuc-
cessive existence. Such is the proper duration of thought.
Thought as such is not in time. The distinction between the
spiritual and the *temporal* appears here in its primary sense.
That which is spiritual is not subject to time. The proper place
of the spiritual is above temporal existence.

We find a noteworthy indication of this in the fact that
spiritual events are "metahistorical" events. Insofar as they
are occurrences, they take place in history, but their content
belongs in a region superior to history. This is why it is normal for history not to mention them. The word event itself
is therefore ambiguous. "What happens," in the case of
spiritual events, comes on the scene for an instant in temporal existence, but comes forever in the existence of souls and
of thought.

But actions or operations emanate from a subject or from
a person—*actiones sunt suppositorum*. And no operation is
more personal than thought. Thought is exercised by a certain
subject, a certain *self*, made of flesh and spirit.

This self exists in time and was born in time. But inasmuch
as it exercises the spiritual operation of thought, inasmuch as
it is the center of spiritual activity and capable of living or
existing by the immaterial superexistence of the act of intellection, it is also superior to time, as is thought itself. It
escapes the grasp of time.

This self began in time. But nothing begins absolutely.
Everything which begins existed before itself in a certain way,
to wit, in its causes. Insofar as it is material, the thinking self
existed before itself in time, namely, in the ancestral cells,
the physiochemical materials and energies utilized by life all
along the line from which the self has sprung. Whatever of
it existed before it pre-existed in time.

But as spiritual, as exercising the spiritual operations of
thought, as thinking, it could not have existed before itself
in time, because mind can come only from a mind, thought
can come only from a thought, and therefore from an existence superior to time.

Moreover, since thought is essentially personal, when it
arises in time as the operation of such and such a subject
born one day into temporal existence, it cannot come from

an existence superior to time unless the self which exercises it now pre-existed in a certain way beyond time.

The self is born in time. But insofar as it is thinking it is not born of time. Its birth is supratemporal. It existed before itself in a first existence distinct from every temporal existence. It did not exist there in its proper nature (since it began to exist in its proper nature by being born in time), but everything that there is in it of being and of thought and of personality existed there better than in itself.

This, however, would not be possible unless everything that exists in temporal existence were a participation of the first existence in question. The latter then must contain all things in itself in an eminent mode and be itself—in an absolutely transcendent way—being, thought and personality. This implies that that first existence is the infinite plenitude of being, separate by essence from all the diversity of existents. This means that it is not the act of existing of a thing which *has* existence, but the very act of existing itself, subsisting through itself. Thus we are necessarily led to the principle which no concept can circumscribe—Being in pure act, from which comes every being; Thought in pure act from which comes every thought; Self in pure act from which comes every self.

It is thus that the "sixth way" leads us to the existence of God. But it would remain incompletely elucidated if, after recognizing the existence of God, we should not ask ourselves how things exist in Him before being caused by Him in their own *esse*.[1]

Things pre-exist in God not in their proper natures but according as they are known to God, and, therefore, by that which renders them present to the divine intellect, that is to say by the divine essence itself, of which they are participations or likenesses, and which is itself the proper object of the divine intellect. In God they are the divine essence as revealing its participability. They live there, but without existing in themselves, by a life infinitely more perfect than the existence which they have in their proper natures. They live, in God who knows them, by the very life of God. They exist in the divine thought by the very existence of God which is in His act of intellection.

This is true of thinking subjects, of *selves*, endowed with intelligence, as it is of all other creatures. Before existing in themselves they exist eternally in God by the very existence of God, as participations or likenesses of the divine essence eternally known in that Essence. Therefore I can say that I, who am now in the act of thinking, always existed—I always existed in God. Care must be taken, however, to understand this proposition correctly. It does not mean that in God the human self has always exercised the act of thinking, or that in God it collaborates eternally in the act of divine thought. That makes no sense. In God the unique Self who thinks is the divine Self. The statement signifies rather that the creature which is now I, and which thinks, existed before itself eternally in God—not as exercising in Him the act of thinking, but as thought by Him. It bathed there in the light of God; it lived there by a suprapersonal (suprapersonal in relation to every created personality) and divinely personal life, by that life which is the eternal act of intellection of the divine Self itself, thinking itself.

Thinking subjects, *selves* capable of acting beyond time, which thus pre-exist in God, as do all those other participations of the Divine Essence which are created things— infinitely deficient in relation to their principle—are the most elevated of all things in the whole order of nature, because they are either purely spiritual creatures or creatures composed of matter and spirit, which, once they exist in their proper nature, resemble the divine Self in that they think and can be called, because of this, "images of God."

NOTE

1. Cf. *Summa Theologica*, I, 18, 4, corp. et ad 3.

6. THE MEANING OF CONTEMPORARY ATHEISM

The subject discussed in this chapter involves many deep and intricate problems. I do not pretend to dogmatize about them; the views that I shall put forward are no more than tentative views, which originate in a desire to look for the hidden spiritual significance which lies within the present agony of the world.

Various kinds of atheism

Let us try, first, to establish in a more systematic way the distinction between the diverse forms of atheism. This distinction can be made from either of two points of view: from the point of view of the attitude of the human being who professes himself to be an atheist; or from the point of view of the logical content of various atheistic philosophies.

From the first point of view, or with regard to the manner in which atheism is professed, there are, in the first place, *practical atheists*, who believe that they believe in God but who in actual fact deny His existence by their deeds and the testimony of their behavior. Then there are *pseudo-atheists*, who believe that they do not believe in God but who in actual fact unconsciously believe in Him, because the God whose existence they deny is not God but something else. Finally there are *absolute atheists*, who really do deny the existence of the very God in Whom the believers believe— God the Creator, Savior and Father, Whose name is infinitely over and above any name we can utter. Those absolute atheists stand committed to change their entire system of values and to destroy in themselves everything that could possibly suggest the name they have rejected; they have chosen to stake their all against divine Transcendence and any vestige of Transcendence whatsoever.

From the second point of view, that is, with regard to the logical content of various atheistic philosophies, I would divide atheism into negative and positive atheism.

By *negative atheism* I mean a merely negative or destructive process of casting aside the idea of God, which is replaced only by a void. Such a negative atheism can be shallow and empirical, like the atheism of the *libertins* in the XVIIth century—then it digs a hollow in the center of the universe of thought which has taken shape through the centuries around the idea of God, but it does not bother about changing that universe; it is merely concerned with making us live a comfortable life, enjoying the freedom of doing exactly as we please. On the other hand, negative atheism can be lived at a profound and metaphysical level: in which case the hollow it creates at the heart of things extends to and lays waste our whole universe of thought; the freedom it claims for the human Self is absolute independence, a kind of divine independence that this Self, like Dostoevski's Kirilov, has no better way of affirming than by suicide and voluntary annihilation.

By *positive atheism* I mean an active struggle against everything that reminds us of God—that is to say, anti-theism rather than atheism—and at the same time a desperate, I would say heroic, effort to recast and reconstruct the whole human universe of thought and the whole human scale of values in accordance with that state of war against God. Such positive atheism was the tragic, solitary atheism of a Nietzsche; such is today the literary, fashionable atheism of existentialism; such is the revolutionary atheism of dialectical materialism. The latter is of special interest to us, because it has succeeded in getting a considerable number of men to accept whole-heartedly this new kind of faith, and to give themselves to it with unquestionable sincerity.

Now when I speak of contemporary atheism, I have in mind atheism seen under the last aspect I have just mentioned; I consider it the most significant form of atheism, one which spells a new and unheard of historic event because it is an atheism at once *absolute and positive*. Human history has been confronted, for almost a century now, with the stormy bursting forth of an atheism which is both *absolute* (making man actually deny God Himself) and *positive* (anti-theism, demanding to be lived in full by man and to change the face of the earth).

The two-fold inconsistency of contemporary atheism

AN ACT OF FAITH IN REVERSE GEAR

After these preliminary signposts I should like to point out that today's absolute-positive atheism involves a dual inconsistency.

How does absolute-positive atheism come to birth in the mind of a man? At this point we are faced with a remarkable fact. A man does not become an absolute atheist as a result of some inquiry into the problem of God carried on by speculative reason. No doubt he takes into account the negative conclusions afforded in this connection by the most radical forms of rationalist or positivist philosophy; he does not neglect, either, the old platitude which will have it that the scientific explanation of the universe purely and simply got clear of the existence of God. But all that is for him a second-hand means of defense, not the prime propelling and determining incentive. Neither those philosophical conclusions nor that nonsensical commonplace does he submit to any critical examination. He takes them for granted. He believes in them. And Why? By virtue of an inner act of freedom, in the production of which he commits his whole personality. The starting point of absolute atheism is, in my opinion, a basic act of moral choice, a crucial free determination. If at the moment when he takes stock of himself and decides upon the whole direction of his life, a man confuses the transition from youth to manhood with the refusal not only of childhood's subordinations but of any subordination whatever; if he thus considers the rejection of any transcendent law as an act of moral maturity and emancipation; and if he decides to confront good and evil in a totally and absolutely free experience, in which any ultimate end and any rule coming from above are cast aside forever—such a free moral determination, dealing with the primary values of existence, will mean that this man has entirely excluded God from his own universe of life and thought. Here is, in my opinion the point at which absolute atheism begins in the depths of a man's spiritual activity.

But what is this I have just been describing if not a kind

of act of faith, an act of faith in reverse gear, whose content is not an adherence to the transcendent God but, on the contrary, a rejection of Him?

Thus it is that absolute atheism is positive atheism. As I stated elsewhere and this must be stressed once again: "It is in no way a mere absence of belief in God. It is rather a refusal of God, a fight against God, a challenge to God."[1] The absolute atheist is delivered over "to an inner dialectic which obliges him ceaselessly to destroy any resurgence in himself of what he has buried . . . In proportion as the dialectic of atheism develops in his mind—each time he is confronted with the natural notion of and tendency to an ultimate End, or with the natural notion of and natural interest in absolute values or unconditioned standards, or with some metaphysical anxiety—he will discover in himself vestiges of Transcendence which have not yet been abolished. He must get rid of them. God is a perpetual threat to him. His case is not a case of practical forgetting, but a case of deeper and deeper commitment to refusal and fight." He is bound to struggle against God without pause or respite, and to change, to recast everything in himself and in the world on the base of that anti-theism.

Now what does all this mean? Absolute atheism starts in an act of faith in reverse gear and is a full-blown religious commitment. Here we have the first internal inconsistency of contemporary atheism: it proclaims that all religion must necessarily vanish away, and it is itself a religious phenomenon.

AN ABORTIVE PROTEST AND RUPTURE

The second inconsistency is very like the first one. Absolute atheism starts as a claim of man to become the sole master of his own destiny, totally freed from any "alienation" and heteronomy, made totally and decisively independent of any ultimate end as well as of any eternal law imposed upon him by any transcendent God. According to atheistic theorists, does not the idea of God originate in an alienation of human nature separated from its true subject, and transmuted into an ideal and sublimated image whose very transcendence and sovereign attributes ensure man's submission to an en-

slaved state of existence? Is it not by getting rid of that
sublimated image and of any transcendence, that human nature will achieve the fullness of its own stature and freedom
and bring about the final "reconciliation between essence
and existence?"

But what is the actual end-all of the philosophy of absolute
Immanence which is all one with absolute atheism? Everything which was formerly considered superior to time and
participating in some transcendent quality—either ideal value
or spiritual reality—is now absorbed in the movement of temporal existence and the all-engulfing ocean of Becoming and
of History. Truth and justice, good and evil, faithfulness, all
the standards of conscience, henceforth perfectly relativized,
become radically contingent: they are but changing shapes of
the process of History, just as for Descartes they were but
contingent creations of divine Freedom. The truth, at any
given moment, is that which conforms with the requirements
of History's begettings. As a result truth changes as time
goes on. An act of mine which was meritorious today will be
criminal tomorrow. And that is the way my conscience must
pass judgment on it. The human intellect and moral conscience have to become heroically tractable.

And what of the Self, the person, the problem of human
destiny? A total rejection of Transcendence logically entails
a total adherence to Immanence. There is nothing eternal in
man; he will die in the totality of his being; there is nothing
to be saved in him. But he can give himself, and give himself
entirely, to the Whole of which he is a part, to the boundless
flux which alone is real and which bears the fate of mankind.
By virtue of his decisive moral experience itself, and of that
primary moral choice—against any ultimate End—which I
have tried to describe, and which commits the human personality far more profoundly than individualistic egoism or
epicureanism can do, the absolute or positive atheist hands
himself over, body and soul, to the ever-changing and all-
engulfing Whole—be it the social or the cosmic totality. It is
not only that he is satisfied to die in it, as a blade of grass in
the loam, and to make it more fertile by dissolving in it. He
is also willing to make of his own total being, with all its
values and standards and beliefs, an offering given, as I said

above, to that great Minotaur that is History. Duty and virtue mean nothing else to him than a total submission and im-molation of himself to the sacred voracity of Becoming.

Here we are confronted with a new variety of mystical "pure love"—giving up every hope for personal redemption—a real unselfishness, self-denial and self-sacrifice, a total and absolute disinterestedness—but a monstrous one, paid for at the price of the very Self, and the existence and dignity of the human Person: at the price of that which, in each one of us, is an end in itself and the image of God. Christ had said: "He who loses his own soul for Me, shall find it,"[2] be-cause losing one's own soul for God is delivering it over to absolute Truth and Goodness and Love, to the eternal Law itself which transcends all the contingency and mutability of Becoming. The positive atheist delivers over his own soul—and not in order to save it—to a worldly demiurge crazy for human minds to bend and bow and yield at the event's sweet will.

I am not belittling the spiritual significance of the moral attitude of the absolute atheist. On the contrary, I am em-phasizing the kind of mystical disinterestedness, and the ele-ments of greatness and generosity which are implied in it. But I say that this moral attitude also involves a basic incon-sistency, and that the whole process is in the end a failure. That rupture with God began as a claim to total independ-ence and emancipation, as a proud revolutionary break with everything that submits man to alienation and heteronomy. It ends up in obeisance and prostrate submission to the all-powerful movement of History, in a kind of sacred surrender of the human soul to the blind God of History.

The atheist and the saint

THE INITIAL ACT OF RUPTURE BROUGHT ABOUT BY THE SAINT

The failure I have just mentioned reveals to us a fact which has, to my mind, a deep significance: I mean the fact that absolute atheism has a revolutionary power which ma-terially speaking is exceedingly strong, but spiritually speak-ing is very weak indeed, minute, and deceptive; I mean the fact that its radicalism is an inevitably self-deluded radical-

ism, for a genuinely revolutionary spirit does not kneel before
History, it presumes to make history; I mean the fact that
absolute atheism falls short of that uncompromising protest,
of that absolute non-compliance the semblance—and the
expectation—of which make it seductive for many people.

Thus, we arrive at the point I should like especially to discuss. Which of these two, the Atheist or the Saint, is the
more uncompromising and thoroughgoing, the harder, the
more intractable; which has his axe more deeply embedded
in the root of the tree? Which brings about the more complete and far-reaching, the cleaner and more radical break?

Let us try to imagine what takes place in the soul of a saint
at the crucial moment when he makes his first irrevocable decision. Let us consider St. Francis of Assisi when he threw
away his raiment and appeared naked before his bishop, out
of love for poverty; or St. Benedict Labre when he decided
to become a verminous beggar wandering along the roads.
At the root of such an act there was something so deep in the
soul that it hardly can be expressed, I would say a simple
refusal—not a movement of revolt which is temporary, or of
despair, which is passive—rather a simple refusal, a total,
stable, supremely active refusal to accept things as they are:
here it is not a question of knowing whether things and nature and the face of this world are good in their essence—to
be sure they are good; being is good insofar as it is being;
grace perfects nature and does not destroy it—but these truths
have nothing to do with the inner act of rupture, of break,
that we are now contemplating. This act is concerned with a
fact, an existential fact: Things as they are are not tolerable,
positively, definitely not tolerable. In actual existence the
world is infected with lies and injustice and wickedness and
distress and misery; the creation has been so marred by sin
that in the nethermost depths of his soul the saint refuses to
accept it as it is. Evil—I mean the power of sin, and the
universal suffering it entails, the rot of nothingness that
gnaws everywhere—evil is such, that the only thing at hand
which can remedy it, and which inebriates the saint with
freedom and exultation and love, is to give up everything,
the sweetness of the world, and what is good, and what is
better, and what is pleasurable and permissible, in order to

be free to be with God; it is to be totally stripped and to give himself totally in order to lay hold of the power of the Cross; it is to die for those he loves. That is a flash of intuition and of will over and above the whole order of human morality. Once a human soul has been touched by such a burning wing, it becomes a stranger everywhere. It may fall in love with things, it will never rest in them. To redeem creation the saint wages war on the entire fabric of creation, with the bare weapons of truth and love. This war begins in the most hidden recesses of his own soul and the most secret stirrings of his desire: it will come to an end with the advent of a new earth and new heaven, when all that is powerful in this world will have been humiliated and all that is despised will have been exalted. The saint is alone in treading the winepress, and of the peoples there is no man with him.[3]

And I would say that in that war of which I have just spoken his God has given him the example. For, in calling the intellectual creatures to share in His own uncreated life, God uproots them from the very life of which they are possessed as rooted in nature. And Jews know that God is a hidden God, Who conceals His name and manifests Himself to mankind in prodigies and in the stormy visions of the prophets, in order to renew the face of the earth, and Who has separated for Himself His people from all the nations of the world. And Christians know that God is both so dissatisfied with that lost world which He had made good and which evil has ruined—and at the same time so carried away by love —that He has given His Son and delivered Him over to men, in order to suffer and to die, and in this way to redeem the world.

THE GREAT GOD OF IDOLATERS

To this true God the saint is entirely given. But there are false gods; even as I shall shortly say, there is a spurious and distorted image of God that can be called the King or Jove of all false gods, the great god of the idolaters. With regard to *this* god, the saint is a thorough atheist, the most atheistic of men—just because he adores *only* God.

Let us dwell a moment on this point. And let us consider the merely rational, merely philosophical concept of God.

This concept is twofold: there is the true God of the philosophers, and there is the false god of the philosophers. The true God of the philosophers is but the true God Himself, the God of the saints, the God of Abraham, Isaac and Jacob —imperfectly and inchoatively known, known in those attributes only which can be reached by our natural forces: Such a merely rational notion of God is in actual fact open to the supernatural.

But now suppose for yourselves a merely rational notion of God which would know the existence of the Supreme Being, but would disregard at the same time what St. Paul called His glory, deny the abyss of freedom which is meant by His transcendence, and chain Him to the very world He has made. Suppose for yourselves a merely rational—and warped—notion of God which is closed against the supernatural, and makes impossible the mysteries that are hidden in God's love and freedom and incommunicable life. Here we would have the false god of the philosophers, the Jove of all false gods. Imagine a god bound to the order of nature who is no more than a supreme warrant and justification of that order, a god who is responsible for this world without the power of redeeming it, a god whose inflexible will, that no prayer can reach, is pleased with and hallows all the evil as well as all the good of the universe, all the trickery, wickedness and cruelty together with all the generosity which are at play in nature, a god who blesses iniquity and slavery and misery, and who sacrifices man to the cosmos, and makes the tears of the children and the agony of the innocents a stark ingredient of, and a tribute offered without any compensation to the sacred necessities of eternal cycles or of evolution. Such a god would be the unique supreme Being but made into an idol, the *naturalistic* god of nature, the Jupiter of the world, the great god of the idolaters and of the powerful on their thrones and of the rich in their earthly glory, the god of success which knows no law, and of mere fact set up as law.

I am afraid that such was the God of our modern rationalistic philosophy, the God perhaps of Leibniz and Spinoza, surely the God of Hegel.

Such was also, in quite another mood, not rationalistic,

but magical, the God of Pagan antiquity, or rather one of the countenances of that double-faced God. For the pagan God was ambiguous; on the one hand he was the true God of nature and reason, the unknown God of Whom St. Paul spoke to the Athenians: and on the other hand he was the false god of naturalism, the self-contradictory god I have just described, and who does get on very well with the Prince of this world.

It could be added that among Christian sects, some wild Gnostics, especially the followers of Marcion, who regarded the God of the Old Covenant as an evil world-maker in conflict with the Redeemer, mistook for the Creator the same false god I have been discussing, the same absurd Emperor of the world.

And this brings me to the point I want to drive home. The saint, when he brings about the great act of rupture which I stressed earlier, rejects by the same stroke, breaks and annihilates, with an irresistible violence, this spurious Emperor of the world, this false god of naturalism, this great god of the idolaters, the powerful and the rich, who is an absurd counterfeit of God, but who is also the imaginary focus whence the adoration of the cosmos radiates, and to whom we pay tribute each time we bow down before the world. With regard to this god the saint is a perfect atheist. Well, were not the Jews and the first Christians often called atheists by the pagans at the time of the Roman Empire? There was a hidden meaning in this slander.[4]

THE CASE OF THE ABSOLUTE ATHEIST

But let us turn at present to our modern atheists, our true and actual atheists—what can we say about them? I would suggest that, in the sense I have just emphasized, the absolute atheist is *not atheist enough*. He, too, is indignant against the Jupiter of this world, against the god of the idolaters, the powerful and the rich; he too decides to get rid of him. But instead of hurling against that false god the strength of the true God, and of giving himself to the work of the true God, as the saint does, the atheist, because he rejects the true God, can only struggle against the Jupiter of this world by calling on the strength of the immanent god of History, and by dedicating himself to the work of that immanent god.

It is indeed because he believes in the revolutionary disruptive power of the impetus of History, and because he expects from it the final emancipation of man, that the atheist delivers over his own soul to the blind god of History. Yet he is caught in a trap. Wait a while, and the blind god of History will appear just as he is—yes, the very same Jupiter of this world, the great god of the idolaters and the powerful on their thrones and the rich in their earthly glory, and of success which knows no law, and of mere fact set up as law. He will reveal himself as this same false god in a new disguise and crowned by new idolaters, and meting out a new brand of power and success. And it is too late for the atheist. As we saw at the beginning, he is possessed by this god. He is on his knees before History. With respect to a god who is not God, he is the most tractable and obedient of the devotees.

And so his break with this world of injustice and oppression was but a shallow and temporary break. More than ever he is subservient to the world. In comparison with the saint, who consummates in his own flesh his initial rupture with the world, and every day dies unto himself, and is blessed with the beatitudes of the poor and the persecuted and all the other friends of God, and who enjoys the perfect freedom of those who are led by the Spirit, the atheist is, it seems to me, a very poor replica of the liberated mind and the heroic insurgent. Nevertheless, as I have tried to point out, it is by an ill-directed longing for inner freedom and for non-acceptance of things as they are that he has been led astray. A somewhat paradoxical, yet, in my opinion, true statement about absolute atheism would be to say that it deprives God and mankind of some potential saints, in bringing to bankruptcy their attempt at heroic freedom, and turning their effort to break with the world into a total and servile subservience to the world. With all his sincerity and devotion, the authentic, absolute atheist is after all only an abortive saint, and, at the same time, a mistaken revolutionist.

The saint and temporal history

A LOST OPPORTUNITY

There is now another paradox, this time in an opposite direction. If we look at the saint, it seems that the inner act through which he achieves his total break with the world and total liberation from the world, making him free from everything but God, will inevitably overflow from the realm of spiritual life onto the realm of temporal life. Thus, if he is not dedicated solely to a contemplative state of existence, he will be led to act as a ferment of renewal in the structures of the world, as a stimulating and transforming energy in social matters and in the field of the activities of civilization.

And this is true, of course. As a matter of fact, it is what has been taking place for centuries. The Fathers of the Church were great revolutionaries. Thomas Aquinas in the order of culture, St. Vincent de Paul in the social field, were eminent examples of genuine radicals, whose initiative brought about decisive changes in the history of civilization. For centuries temporal progress in the world has been furthered by the saints.

Yet, here is the paradox that I just mentioned—the day when, in the course of modern history, a particularly inhuman structure of society, caused by the Industrial Revolution, made the problem of social justice manifestly crucial; when, at the same time, the human mind became aware of the *social* as a specific object of knowledge and activity, and when the first attempts to create workers' organizations provided the beginnings of a historical force capable of acting upon social structures—then was it not the moment for the saints to take the lead in the protest of the poor and in the movement of labor toward its historical coming of age? In actual fact, except for a few men of faith, like Ozanam in France and Toniolo in Italy (they are not yet canonized, but some day they might be), the task, as we know, was not conducted by saints. It even happened that atheists, instead of saints, took the lead in social matters, much to the misfortune of all.

Why such a tragic vacancy? It seems difficult not to see in it a kind of punishment of the Christian world, which for a long period has more or less failed Christianity in its practical behavior, and despised the lessons of the saints, and abandoned to their fate, here below, that great flock which also belongs to Christ, that immense herd of men whom destitution and unlivable conditions of existence kept chained to hell on earth. Let us not be mistaken. During the time of which I am speaking, saints were not lacking on the earth; there was a considerable flowering of saints in the last century. But they did not pass beyond the field of spiritual, apostolic or charitable activities: they did not cross the threshold of temporal, social, secular activity. And thus the gap was not filled, because in the historical age which is ours, the indirect repercussion of the inner renewal of conscience upon the external structures of society is definitely not enough, although it answers a basic need and has made progressively more possible such social changes as the abolition of slavery. A specifically social activity, an activity which directly aims at improving and recasting the structures of temporal life, is also needed.

Why has this kind of activity been neglected by a great many Christians in the past? Is it on account of their supposed contempt for the world, as people say? Nonsense! The saints break with the world, but they have no contempt for creation; that they leave to apprentices. As for the general run of Christians, one need but look at them—at ourselves—(as François Mauriac reminded us rather bluntly in the second *Semaine des Intellectuels Catholiques*[5]) to be assured that we do not despise the world in the least and that we are "of the earth", as it is said in the new devotional jargon. No; the reason for which activities directly aiming at the structural changes required by social justice have been lacking for so many centuries, is quite simple: the means of exercising such activities were non-existent. In the seventeenth century Saint Vincent de Paul could found hospitals but he could not found trade unions. It was only after the Industrial Revolution and the way in which it developed that the possibility of directly social activity could enter people's imaginations, and that such a directly social, and not only spiritual or charitable, activity has become a crying need.

Perhaps a concrete example will help to make clear the difference between the two kinds of activity I have mentioned. A poor priest named Cottolengo, who was a saint (though his name is not to be found in the *Encyclopaedia Britannica*) founded in Turin, in the first half of the past century, a hospital that rapidly grew into a sort of huge city of all kinds of infirmity and human misery; hundreds of the poor were fed and cared for every day. But Cottolengo had established the rule that none of the money contributed for the support of his Institute should ever be saved and invested. Money each day received from the Providence of God should be spent each day, for "sufficient unto the day is the evil thereof."[6] There is even a story that one evening, as he saw that his assistants had set aside a certain amount of money for the morrow, Cottolengo threw that money out of the window—which in our modern world is the height of insanity, and perhaps of sacrilege. This course of action was in itself perfectly revolutionary, and all the more revolutionary in that it succeeded (Cottolengo's work has thrived in an astounding manner; it is now one of the most important institutions in Turin). Yet such a course of action, for all its spiritual significance, remained of no social consequence. It transcended the social problem. The social problem must be managed and solved in its own order. For half a century men of good will have realized better and better that the temporal mission of those who believe in God is to take over the job. Still, we must not forget that, even in the simple perspective of the temporal community, Christian social action is not enough; political action is even less so, however necessary both of them may be. What is required of those who believe in God is a witness of God; and what the world demands and expects of the Christian is first and foremost to see the love of truth and brotherly love made genuinely present in and through man's personal life—to see a gleam of the Gospel shining in the one place where the crucial test and crucial proof are to be found, namely the obscure context of relations from person to person.

THE CHRISTIAN WORLD IS NEITHER CHRISTIANITY
NOR THE CHURCH

I have just spoken of the historical deficiencies of the Christian world. Parenthetically, in order to avoid any misunderstanding, I should like to point out that by these words, "the Christian world," I am designating a sociological category, which is involved in the order and history of temporal civilizations, and is a thing of this world. The Christian world is neither Christianity nor the Church. The failures of the Christian world have no power to tarnish the Church or Christianity.

There has been, moreover, a good deal of confusion on this score. Neither Christianity nor the Church has a mission to make men happy, their business is to tell them the truth—not to bring about justice and freedom in the political society, but to give mankind salvation and eternal life. No doubt this lays upon them the additional task of quickening the energies of justice and love in the depths of temporal existence and thus making that existence more worthy of man. Yet the successful accomplishment of such a task depends on the way in which the divine message is received. It is at this point that we are confronted with the responsibilities of the Christian world, that is, of the social groups of Christian denomination at work in secular history.

It is nonsense to reproach the Christians, as we often see it done today, with not having baptized "the Revolution," and with not having devoted their whole energies to "the Revolution." The messianic myth of "the Revolution" is a secularized perversion of the idea of the advent of God's Kingdom; it is apt to warp the course of human history, and to turn into failures the particular, genuine and genuinely progressive revolutions—the revolutions without a capital R—that are bound to follow one another as long as human history endures. But it is not nonsense to reproach Christians in the world with having failed to bring about at certain given times such needed particular revolutions. It is not nonsense to reproach them, more generally, with being sinners—they know very well that they are—who more or less always betray Christianity. Most important of all, it is certainly not nonsense to

reproach the many people in modern times who are paying
lip-service to the God in Whom they think they believe,
with being in fact practical atheists.

MEN TODAY NEED SIGNS

If a new age of civilization is to come rather than a new
age of barbarism, the deepest requirement of such an age
will be the sanctification of secular life, a fecundation of
social, temporal existence by spiritual experience, contemplative energies and brotherly love.

I dare say that we have not yet reached that stage. For
the moment we are at the lowest point; human history today
is in love with fear and absurdity, human reason with despair.
The powers of illusion are spreading all over the world,
throwing all compasses off direction. The faculty of language
has been so dishonored, the meaning of words so thoroughly
falsified; so many truths, met with at every corner in press or
radio reports, are at each moment so perfectly mixed with so
many errors similarly advertised, and trumpeted to the skies,
that men are simply losing the sense of truth. They have been
lied to so often that they have become addicted, and need
their daily dose of lies as a daily tonic. They look as if they
believed in all this; but they are beginning to lead a kind of
clandestine mental life in which they will believe nothing
they are told, but will rely only upon savage experience and
elementary instincts. They are surrounded on all sides by
spurious marvels and false miracles, which dazzle and blind
their minds.

Things being as they are, it seems clear that the wisest
reasonings and the most eloquent demonstrations and the
best managed organizations are definitely not enough for the
men of this time. Men today need *signs*. They need deeds.
Above all they need tangible signs to reveal to them the
reality of things divine. Yet there is everywhere a considerable
shortage of thaumaturges, though they probably are the kind
of commodity we need the most.

At this point I should like to bring back to our minds a
saying of Pascal. "We always behave," Pascal has said, "as if
we were called upon to make the truth triumph, whereas we
are called upon only to struggle for it."

It does not rest with us to give men miracles. It is up to us to practice what we believe.

Here it seems well to stress one of the deepest meanings of absolute atheism. As I put it in another essay, absolute atheism is "a translation into crude and inescapable terms, a ruthless counterpart, an avenging mirror, of the practical atheism of too many believers who do not actually believe."[7] It is both the fruit and the condemnation of practical atheism, its image reflected in the mirror of divine wrath. If this diagnosis is true, then we must go on to say that it is impossible to get rid of absolute atheism without first getting rid of practical atheism. Furthermore this has become clear to everyone that from now onwards a decorative Christianity is not enough, even for our existence in this world. The faith must be an actual faith, practical and living. To believe in God must mean to live in such a manner that life could not possibly be lived if God did not exist. Then the earthly hope in the Gospel can become the quickening force of temporal history.

NOTES

1. See *The Range of Reason* (New York: Charles Scribner's Sons, 1952), p. 98.
2. *Matth.* 10:39.
3. *Isaiah*, 63:3.
4. St. Justin said: "We are called atheists. And, yes, we confess it, we are atheists of those so-called gods." 1st *Apology*, VI, n. 1.
5. See *Foi en Jésus-Christ et Monde d'aujourd'hui* (Paris: Editions de Flore, 1949).
6. *Matth.* 6:34.
7. See *The Range of Reason*, pp. 99–100.

7. THE INNOCENCE OF GOD

The fundamental certitude, the rock to which we must cling in the question of moral evil, is the *absolute innocence of God*.

In proportion as the conscience of men, under the very influence of Christianity, became more sensible of the dignity of the human person and of the outrages which are inflicted on him by evil, while on the other hand the dimensions of evil, of injustice, of cruelty, of all the kinds of crimes at work in history were more and more revealed to it in depth as well as in extension (today one has only to open the newspaper to see the iniquities which pride or stupidity linked to hardness of heart cause to be committed at the four corners of the earth)—in proportion, consequently, as such a process developed, the problem of evil has taken on a more tragic importance for the human conscience. It is this problem which is at the origin of many forms of atheism, at the origin also of what one could call in many the bewildered Christian conscience.

Some great writers and poets have been much more deeply affected by the tragic importance of which I speak than have philosophers and theologians; in this way they have been prophets of a sort. The greatest of these prophets, the greatest of these bewildered and tortured souls, has been, in my opinion, Dostoevski (I am thinking especially of *The Brothers Karamazov* and *The Possessed*). One could also name poets like Jean-Paul Richter, and above all the author of *Chants de Maldoror*, Lautréamont, of whom Léon Bloy has said that he brought "the good tidings of damnation." Lautréamont sought all the possible means of insulting God, because he was enraged against the abomination of the world. I quote a passage (which, by chance, is not blasphemous, but highly typical, and besides it is very beautiful): "I am," he said, "the son of man and of woman, according to what I am told. This astonishes me—I thought I was more! Besides, what does it matter to me where I come from: If it could have depended on my own will, I would rather have wished to be the son of the shark's wife, whose hunger is the friend of the tempests, and of the tiger, who is renowned for his cruelty; *I would not be so wicked*."

It is advisable to be attentive to the warnings of such prophets. An old jack-of-all-trades curious about everything like Georges Sorel knew this well. That is why, as I note in *De Bergson à Thomas d'Aquin*, he said that if philosophers lived up to their calling in the new age into which we have entered, the crucial work for them would be to renew the theory of evil, that is to say, by examining it more profoundly.

In other words, the day of the theodicies *à la* Leibniz or of the justifications of God which have the aid of pleading mitigating circumstances is decidedly past. Something else is needed in order to meet contemporary atheism, the militant atheism of the Marxists as well as the infantile and pretentious atheism which the existentialists advance in competing with it.

And now, by a very remarkable paradox, it happens that the pure and simple affirmation that one must oppose to all this, and which must at no price be permitted to become obscured however so little, has been enunciated by Lautréamont himself. Violently retracting his past, at the end of his short life, he wrote in his *Préface à des Poèmes Futurs*, in his poet's language: "If one recollects the truth from which all other truths flow, *the absolute goodness of God and His absolute ignorance of evil*, the sophisms collapse of themselves. We do not have the right to interrogate the Creator about anything whatsoever." (And he added—let us note this sentence in passing—"All the water of the sea would not suffice to wash away a single intellectual bloodstain.")

Lautréamont expressed himself poorly in saying that *God is absolutely ignorant of evil*; God knows evil, to be sure, and he knows it perfectly, *through the good* of which evil is the privation. But what Lautréamont meant is that God is *absolutely innocent of evil*, and also that God does not have the *idea* or the invention of evil. There is in God, as Saint Thomas Aquinas teaches, no *idea*, no intelligible matrix of evil. This is a point to which we shall return later on.

Well, Saint Thomas recognized this absolute innocence of God, and affirmed and taught it, much better indeed than did Lautréamont. I would like to quote to you two texts of his, which in their simplicity sovereignly command the whole question, and which we should inscribe on our walls; let us call them our two most sacred axioms:

First axiom: *Deus nullo modo est causa peccati, neque directe, neque indirecte* (God *is* absolutely not the cause of moral evil, neither directly nor indirectly).[1] You notice the import of these words "nullo modo," absolutely not, and *"neque directe, neque indirecte,"* neither directly nor indirectly. Every shadow of indirect causality must be excluded.

Second axiom: *Defectus gratiae prima causa est ex nobis* (the first cause—he says indeed, the *first* cause—of the absence of grace comes from us).[2] It is in us, it is in the creature that the first cause of moral evil (first cause in the order of non-being or of nothingness) is to be found. The creature has the first initiative of moral evil; it is in the creature that the *initiative* and the *invention* of sin have their origin.

Here we have the two texts which command everything. The second one (the first cause of the absence of grace comes from us) had been enunciated at greater length by Saint Thomas in his *Commentary on the Sentences*, I, dist. 40, q. 4, a. 2: "It is . . . evident that the first cause of the absence of grace is purely and simply on the side of the man to whom grace is lacking, (because he has not been willing to receive it); on the side of God, there is no cause of this absence of grace, except once admitted that which is the cause on the side of man."[3]

Naturally every Thomist theologian, indeed every Catholic, whether simple man of faith, philosopher, or theologian, is ready to die for the two axioms which I have just mentioned. The misfortune is that at the same time, especially if they are learned people acquainted with the difficulties of things, they can happen unwittingly to compromise these axioms more or less seriously and to tarnish their lustre in the conceptualization that is made of them.

I remember having spoken of this absolute innocence of God, which was blasphemed by Hegel, with one of my friends, a renowned professor and a man greatly versed in the Bible. "Yes, yes, of course, that's true," he replied to me, "but in the end it is not so clear; there still remain the expressions that Holy Scripture uses so often, when it says, for instance, that God blinded Pharaoh, that He sent to this or that man a spirit of darkness, a spirit of error, etc." This professor knew very well that it is a question here only of turns of speech peculiar to the Semitic languages, and which amounted to saying that God had permitted that Pharaoh become blind, etc. However he let a kind of doubt insinuate itself into his mind, by the help of these expressions, and while holding that God is not the cause of moral evil he went and lodged in the obscurity of the divine transcendence a vague doubt on this matter.

Or else again, it is of this that I am thinking especially, one will find philosophers and theologians who also affirm, and certainly without doubting them in the least, the two most sacred axioms recalled a moment ago, but who, at the same time, seeking to reconcile them with other equally sacred truths, *explain* them by means of notions and reasons which in reality sap them at their very base, without the effort of conciliation to which they are attached, permitting them to be aware of this; or else, if they suspect in the least some inconsistency, they proceed, like the friend of whom I have just spoken, to lodge it in the obscurity of the divine transcendence.

Attention here! It is important for us to understand that the incomprehensible mystery of the things of God is not, as Hegel said of Schelling's absolute, a night in which all the cows are black, and in which we could shelter, under the pretext of the divine transcendence, theories which do harm to the primary certitudes which we propose to defend and to explicate.

The divine transcendence is obscure for us, it is a night for our reason. And it embraces truths which at first seem irreconcilable. But what we must do is to push to the extreme, to their divine extreme, these at first glance contradictory truths of which we seek some understanding; it is never to sacrifice one of them while pretending to save it and while hiding our misfortune in the obscurity of the divine mystery.

However obscure this mystery may be, the aseity or *absolute independence* of God on the one hand, and the *divine absolute innocence* on the other, shine there with a sovereign brightness, and it is this radiance itself which our eye has difficulty in enduring. Rather than sacrifice or destroy, however so little, one of these truths at the expense of the other, it would after all be better to confess that our reason is too weak to reconcile them.

I do not think that we are reduced to this here. But if we do not wish to spoil everything in the question of God and the permission of evil, we must from the beginning set down a principle which is like a beacon illuminating the whole debate: this is the principle of the *dissymmetry, the fundamental, irreducible dissymmetry, between the line of good and the line of evil.*

Ens et bonum convertuntur. The good is being, and plenitude or completion of being. When we reason in the line of good, we reason in the line of being, of that which exercises being or bears being to its accomplishment.

Evil, on the contrary, of itself or insofar as evil, is absence of being, *privation* of being or of good. It is a nothingness which corrodes being. When we reason in the line of evil, we reason in the line of non-being, for evil is in nowise being; evil is only a vacuum or a lack of being, a nothingness and a privation.

It follows, then, with absolute necessity that there will be a dissymmetry between our manner of looking at and explaining things in the perspective of good and our manner of looking at and explaining things in the perspective of evil.

It is a radical mistake to make use, in order to explain things in the line of evil, of types of explanation by which we explain and must explain things in the line of good.

Let me give a first example: in the line of good, God is the first and transcendent cause of our liberty and of our free decisions, so that the free act is wholly from God as first cause and wholly from us as second cause; because there is not a fibril of being which escapes the causality of God. Our liberty has the initiative of our acts, but this is a second initiative; it is God who has the first initiative. Yes, this is true for good acts; but for evil acts, or more exactly for the evil itself which vitiates these acts, it is just the contrary: in the line of evil we have our two very sacred axioms which I unite in one same statement: God is absolutely not the cause of the evil of our free acts, it is man who is the *first cause* and who has the *first initiative* of moral evil.

Second example. In the line of good: all that which God knows in created existence, He knows because He causes it. His science of vision is the cause of things. Yes, this is perfectly true in the line of being, or of good; but, in the line of evil, well! the evil accomplished by creatures is known by God, and yet God is absolutely not the cause of the evil, *neither directly nor indirectly.* There is, then, something (which is not a thing, a being, but a non-being, a lack or privation of being), which is known by God in created existence without having been caused by Him. Evil is known by God without having been in any way caused by God.

To deny or shake the two truths concerning the line of good which I have just mentioned is very serious—it is to meddle with something sacred, the divine aseity.

To deny or shake the two truths concerning the line of evil which I have also mentioned is *likewise serious,* and it is likewise to meddle with something sacred: the absolute innocence of God.

I shall further add, speaking for once in the manner of Hegel: there is no sense in tackling the problem of evil, one will make no advance at all, if one does not have the courage to *sojourn close to non-being* and to look it in the face—and to employ the conceptual equipment that is needed in order to treat of it; that is to say, to *take seriously,* without regarding them as mere figures of speech, these things that I call *to nihilate, initiative of nothingness, nihilating* or *nihilation, fissure of being,* etc.

For the fact is that in order to express anything at all of that which is most real but which belongs to the realm of non-being, we must inevitably have recourse to paradoxical statements which envelop, in the measure to which they seem to substantify non-being, the formation in our mind of a certain *auxiliary entity of reason.* Is not this already the case each time that we say *evil* (as if *evil* were a being)? Because, given the nature of our human intellect, we can conceive evil, and non-being, only *ad instar entis*, after the fashion of being. God alone knows this privation which is evil without having to form the slightest being of reason, and it is God's privilege.

Without this auxiliary entity of reason, presented in an idea, there is no means for us to know the lack of being that is evil. And this lack of being, itself, is in nowise a being of reason; it is indeed very real in things. It is in order to signify this, that we do not hesitate to say "evil" (which is a non-being, a privation) just as we say "intelligence" or "beauty" (which are beings). Why, when it is a question of signifying that we evade a motion, an influx of being coming from the first Cause, should we hesitate to say that we *nihilate*, that we *cause nothingness*?

And all this is true of that non-being which is simple *negation* (absence of a good *which is not due*) as well as of that non-being which is *privation* (absence of a due good). If I wish to express that a negation comes to occur in existence like a vacuum or a cavity, in other words, that it has an existential or existentialising value and not simply a grammatical or logical value, I shall be able to do so only by saying, for example, that it is (as in the case of the voluntary non-consideration of the rule) a "fissure of being" or a nihilation.

NOTES

1. "Deus . . . non potest directe esse causa peccati. Similiter etiam neque indirecte . . . Et sic patet quod Deus nullo modo est causa peccati." *Sum. Theol.*, I-II, 79, 1.

2. *Ibid.*, 112, 3, ad 2.

3. ". . . Istum autem carere gratia, ex duobus contingit: tum *quia ipse non vult recipere*, tum quia Deus non sibi infundit, vel non vult sibi infundere. Horum autem duorum talis est ordo, ut secundum non sit nisi ex suppositione primi . . .

"Patet ergo quod *hujus defectus absolute prima causa est ex parte hominis* qui gratia caret; sed ex parte Dei non est causa hujus defectus nisi ex suppositione illius quod est causa ex parte hominis."

PART THREE
THE IMAGE OF MAN

"To say that a man is a person is to say that in the depth of his being he is more a whole than a part and more independent than servile. It is to say that he is a minute fragment of matter that is at the same time a universe, a beggar who participates in the absolute being, mortal flesh whose value is eternal, and a bit of straw into which heaven enters. It is this metaphysical mystery that religious thought designates when it says that the person is the image of God."

The Conquest of Freedom

8. HUMAN FREEDOM

The two kinds of freedom

I would like to note at the very beginning of this essay that the word *freedom*,—like all big words for which men are ready to die, and which are laden, not only with the riches of the object, but with the desires, the dreams and the supreme generosities of the subject,—the word freedom conveys a great number of meanings; and yet these meanings, though widely different, have something in common.

If we seek to limit ourselves to the essential, we shall behold, by attentively considering this variety of meanings, two directions, two principal lines of significance. One of them concerns freedom as an *absence of constraint*; as a bird is *free* when it is not in a cage, which does not mean that the bird possesses free will. The other concerns freedom as an absence of necessity or of necessitation, which is precisely the case of free will: when Samuel Adams decided to throw the tea of the East India Company into the waters of Boston Harbor, his decision was not only a spontaneous act, an act without constraint, but it was also an act which neither outer nor inner circumstances, motives, impulses, inclinations, etc., had necessarily determined; he could indeed have made a contrary decision. What he did was an act of free will; no outer or inner necessity determined it.

One of the causes of obscurity and confusion in the elaborate discussions of freedom and grace which occupied the seventeenth century was the fact that the two lines of significance which I have mentioned were not clearly distinguished. It is these two lines and these two primordial meanings of the word, and of the concept, of freedom,—freedom of choice (absence of necessitation) and freedom of spontaneity (absence of constraint),—which we must first of all distinguish.

It is perhaps suitable to observe, concerning these two kinds of freedom, that the specialists in knowledge,—I have in mind the philosopher and the theologian,—are mostly interested in the freedom of choice, in free will, no doubt because this subject gives rise to the most arduous problems. Whereas the average man is mostly interested, not in free will,—about which he troubles himself very little, knowing he possesses it,—but in the other kind of freedom, the freedom of spontaneity in its highest forms, where it means emancipation and personal independence (in this case we shall call it freedom of autonomy and freedom of exultation); and this interest arises from the fact that this kind of freedom must be dearly and strenuously bought, and because it is continuously threatened.

Freedom of choice

Let us now, by placing ourselves in the perspective of Thomist philosophy, consider the mysterious nature of the *first freedom*, or human free will, I shall not discuss here its existence, as each of us knows by experience the existence of his own freedom. Moreover, the way in which St. Thomas clarifies for us the nature of free will, is at the same time the proof that the latter necessarily exists in every intelligent nature. Let us try to scrutinize the nature of the freedom of choice.

The ancients took care to emphasize primarily the *transcendence of the intellective appetite*, or of *the will*, with regard to every sort of good except happiness.

For St. Thomas, the will is an appetite, a power of desire and of inclination, creating in the soul spiritual weights which attract the whole of it; its primordial act is to love.

Now, all appetite is rooted in knowing or awareness. What the scholastics call sensitive appetite, the power of desire and emotion which is common to men and animals, has its root in the knowledge of the senses.

The will, that is, the power of spiritual appetition, is, on the contrary, rooted in the intellect. And it is because the intellect possesses the notion of *what is good*, of the good in itself, abstracted in its proper objectivity and in its universality, and co-extensive with the notion of being,—it is for this reason that in every intelligent nature, there must exist a power of desire and of love essentially distinct from the sensitive appetite, and tending toward the good known as such, in so far as it transcendentally imbibes all good things, toward the good intelligibly grasped, and not toward this or that particular good thing known only through the senses. And this power of desire and love is the rational appetite or will which has its root in the intellect.

Thus the will is grounded in nature and is itself a kind of *nature*. Hence it must have, as all nature has, a necessary determination,—*natura determinatur ad unum*. It must have an operation which is produced in a natural way, and as such necessarily determined. There is something which it must desire by virtue of what it is, something which it desires necessarily. As God loves necessarily His being and His goodness, because to love the infinite goodness, which is Himself, is His very essence; so also the intelligent creature necessarily loves, not this or that good, but the Good (I do not say the moral good, which relates to whatever suits the intelligent creature in the line of *its own final end*; I say the metaphysical good, which relates to what is capable of satisfying desire and of bringing joy in every line, and which is as boundless as being itself). Thus, what the will necessarily desires by reason of what it is, is a good which satisfies every desire, a good which suits in every respect all human aspirations: in short, beatitude. The most unhappy creature necessarily desires happiness and, no doubt, that is why he is so unhappy; for his plight is such that, according to natural conditions, he is normally led to despair of ever reaching this happiness. If I properly understand the thought of St. Thomas, it is in his view only through a revelation of faith that we can tell ourselves that some day we shall really be able to become *perfectly, absolutely happy*. This is astonishing news: 'Thou wilt be with me in paradise.'

Strictly speaking, if St. Thomas insists much more than Aristotle upon the absolutely plenary character of the good to which we naturally aspire, it is because he knows through faith that we can really aspire to it,—by means of divine grace, because it is supernatural. Necessarily and naturally we desire a *happiness that is absolute*: *happiness* by virtue of a desire which is unconditional and connatural, or tending toward something required by the capacities of our being; absolute happiness, by virtue of a desire which is conditional and transnatural, tending toward something superior to our natural limitations and concerning the constitution of which consequently, nature cannot possess the idea.

It is with the help of these distinctions that we have to understand the assertions of the Thomists concerning the human will.

But let us return to the nature of human will. It necessarily desires,—it cannot, as soon as it exercises itself, help desiring,—beatitude. That which necessarily determines it (even before knowing where this good is to be found, or whether it is possible to achieve it) is the absolute and complete good, happiness saturating every desire.

And what follows? Simply this, that toward every good which is not this absolute good, the will of man is naturally undetermined, is without natural and necessary propensity. If that which necessarily determines my will is a limitless good, and absolute good which completely satiates all my capacities of desire, it is evident that whatever is not this limitless, absolute good, cannot determine my will necessarily.

This is a surprising consequence! St. Thomas deduces freedom (here) from necessity (there). Because the will is internally and naturally necessitated to absolutely satisfying happiness, it is free with respect to everything else; that is to say, with respect to everything it can desire here on earth, —for where on earth is this perfect happiness, this complete satiety of desire?

It must be made clear that not only particular and partial goods, offered us by the finite world, but all the concrete goods which we may love and desire in this life, are thus the object of the will's free choice. Even the noblest good, even the divine good, is thus, and for the same reason, the object of the will's free choice. According to the teaching of the theologians, when the human intelligence shall behold God, not only will it know that for us beatitude can consist only in seeing God (I know this already through reason and faith), but it will grasp God, it will see Him and possess Him as He is actually in Himself; it will behold Him as actually satisfying, up to repletion and super-repletion, all the possibilities of desire of the human person, leaving him nothing, not even the shadow of a shadow, to be desired apart from Him. Then the will shall love God in a necessary manner, as necessarily and even more necessarily than it loves happiness on earth. But as long as God is not beheld face to face in the Beatific Vision, we may know well enough, through reason and through faith, that He is the absolute Good and that He is our real last end, this beatitude is not yet in our possession; the intellect does not grasp God as the beatitude which actually beatifies us; it knows Him through abstract knowledge as a beatitude which will beatify us. And there are many kinds of good, real and apparent, which for the time being we will have to renounce in order to attain to God. Many good and desirable things will continue to attract us outside the narrow path of the goods which are better for us, and which are directed toward God as the apex of the moral order.

By an apparent paradox, which it was the object of my previous remarks to explain, we necessarily desire the absolute Good (beatitude in general); and yet God,—this hidden God, who is the absolute Good and the subsistent beatitude and who, existing as the (transcendent) Whole and common Good of the universe, is naturally loved by every creature more than itself, even in spite of itself,—this God is longed for by us, and loved efficaciously above all, as being in His very nature Sanctity itself and the end of our life, and the goal of the whole order of our acts, yet only by virtue of a free option, which remains in our power to decline.

Here occurs a point of doctrine which clearly shows, it seems to me, the truly human amplitude and the universal bearing of the thought of St. Thomas. He teaches[1] that we make our first decision concerning our last end at the time when the life of reason and of personality matures in the child. This act can be accomplished in utter silence in our very depths, but it is in itself an extremely great event. And each time that a man takes himself in hand in order to deliberate over his ultimate end and to choose his destiny, he recovers in this act something of the absolute beginnings of his childhood. Now, when a man deliberating about his life chooses to love that which is good in itself, the *bonum honestum,* in order to link his life to it, it is toward God, whether he knows it or not, that he turns himself. And then, St. Thomas says, this man, whether grown up in the Christian faith or among the idolatrous and nourished in wild forests, has the grace of God, without which our wounded will cannot turn itself efficaciously towards God as the supreme end of our life.

Let us add that if the ethics of St. Thomas is an ethics of beatitude, it is nevertheless something entirely different from an interested eudemonism, because it is also an ethics of love; and, when we act rightly, that in which our happiness consists (which is to say, God, the transcendent whole), is loved by us for Himself, not for ourselves, and He is loved above all else, loved more than ourselves; it is by virtue of our love for Him that we ourselves want to be happy.

I have insisted upon the universal capacity of the will, on its infinite capacity to love, which is a consequence of the universal capacity of the intellect; and I have also insisted upon the indetermination or absence of a necessary propensity, which inevitably belongs to the will in respect to all good things which are not Beatitude, grasped as actually beatifying and saturating every desire.

This 'indifference' or indetermination (it is highly important to understand this) does not coincide at all with the potential or passive indetermination of that which, being imperfect and as if expecting a determination, can become this or that, can receive this or that actuation. In so far as there is such passive indetermination in the human will it testifies to the imperfection of all that is created. It does not constitute the freedom of human will.

There is in the human will a certain passive indetermination, from which it emerges sometimes *without our wishing it* (by non-deliberate movements for which we are not responsible and which surge up, before we reflect at all, at the simple perception of some good); and sometimes *by our wishing it,* by an act of free will; such a potential and passive indetermination is a mark of the weakness of the created being. It does not constitute liberty; it does not exist in the divine will.

The indetermination which is identical with free will is

quite another kind of indetermination, an *active and domi-*
nating indetermination. It consists in *the mastering by the*
will of the practical judgment which determines it.

Though, in fact, the intellect may speculatively declare
that such or such an action must be accomplished by virtue
of a law or of a rule which applies to human action in general
(the scholastics called this a speculatively practical judgment), yet this does not suffice to make me take a decision
in favour of this action. I need a practical decision, a practical
judgment of the intelligence, bearing upon the action to be
accomplished in so far as it is *properly mine*, as a concrete
and singular action related to my end and to my personal
and singular desire of my end, in the singular circumstances
in which I find myself (the scholastics called this a practically-practical judgment).

Now, if the intellect were left to itself, this practically-
practical judgment which is the immediately determining
principle of my act of willing, would itself remain undetermined. Such a judgment bears on the relation between my
act considered *hic et nunc* and that which I, who produce
this act, necessarily desire. Now, what I desire necessarily is
Happiness. And the act concerning which the intellect delib-
erates is a particular good, which consequently lacks certain
aspects of good, and therefore takes on the significance of
non-good; it is a good under one aspect and a non-good under
another aspect. I may continue to desire (that is to say, continue to desire Happiness), without wishing for that particular good, and the entire set of goods to which it is related,
and which I can challenge, if I wish, without ceasing to desire
Happiness. In one way it suits me to accomplish this act,
in another it suits me not to accomplish it; that is all that
the intellect alone, as a pure faculty of knowledge, can say
to me. Using the intellect alone, it is impossible for me ever
to decide: 'I must absolutely, here and now, accomplish this
act,'—this is due to the *invincible indetermination* which
characterizes the relation between this particular good considered in itself and the only thing which I necessarily desire
—Happiness.

Now, the will triumphs over this indetermination of the
intellect. It determines *itself*; that is, the will brings the intel-

lect to pass from the speculatively-practical judgment, incapable of determining efficaciously the act of willing, to a practically-practical judgment, which alone is capable of determining the act efficaciously. It is the will which intervenes by an act which rises from the depths of personality, *by an act of the person in so far as it is person,* and in which the practical *fiat* bears, in the creature, the greatest possible resemblance to the creative *fiat.* It is the will which intervenes and which, by its own exercise, specifies the practical judgment, the very judgment which determines it.

Here, indeed, is the very kernel of the problem of free will.

The intellect can express a practically-practical unconditioned judgment only as a function of the actual exercise and the actual movement of the will; as a function of *what is* actually the desiring and willing subject (not only in its natural being, but in the ultimate actuality of its spiritual being, and of its will); as a function of the line of finality to which it adheres and of the decisive proprieties that it thereby establishes between itself and such a good, or such a line of goods. And the will can exercise this actual movement only by being formally determined by the judgment which the will itself makes efficacious in this way. *Causae ad invicem sunt causae.*

As Aristotle said, the diverse causes that co-operate in producing one and the same act cause one another from different points of view. The free act appears thus as the common offspring of the intellect and the will vitally enveloping each other in one and the same instantaneous co-determination. The intelligence determines the will in the order of objective or formal-extrinsic causality; the will determines the intelligence in the order of efficient causality; or, to put it another way, *specification* (of the will by the intelligence) itself depends on the *exercise* of the will. The judgment which, in so far as it is efficaciously expressed, specifies and determines the act of willing, derives its actual value of existential efficacy from the will itself, which transfers, so to speak, to the particular good in question the excess of motivation which fills it through its determination by the infinite good. To be free means to be master of one's judgment.

The will is master of the very judgment which determines it, and *thus* has full mastery of its own actions.

It is not easy to draw an image from the spectacle of sensible things which can illustrate this metaphysical process. Let us, nevertheless, try to find a metaphor, however inadequate.

Every river flows between two banks; and it is determined by them, that is, by the conformations of the earthly crust. Well, let us imagine a spiritual river, which as yet exists only in the thought, and which is ready to spring forth into existence. Let us imagine that everything which concerns realization in existence also depends on it. Let us imagine that before it springs forth, angels present to it various conformations of soil, diverse possible banks. It cannot spring forth without being contained or determined by one or another pair of banks. But at the precise moment when it springs forth, it is the river itself which brings into existence, amongst the various possible courses presented to it, this or that earthly course and the banks which encase the waters. This image represents the act of free will. The will is as a torrent, mastering the banks which contain it.

We perceive in what sense it is correct to say with M. Bergson (yet in quite a different metaphysical context than the one he uses), that 'our motives are what we make them'. And, also, that 'our reasons determine us only at the moment when they have become determining, that is, at the moment when the act has been virtually accomplished'. This is because, truly, in the act of freedom, the will goes out to meet half-way an attraction which is incapable of quite reaching it by itself; and this is because the free act is a gratuitous answer, which has sprung forth from the very depths of the will, toward a powerless solicitation of a finite good. In the act of free will, wrote Cajetan, the famous commentator on St. Thomas, the *will bends the judgment in the direction it desires*.

Such is the character of the active and dominating indetermination which is free will, due to the spiritual amplitude of that which, put into action and into appetite by an infinity of joy, has no necessary connection with every object which is not presently infinite joy. In so far as one comprehends this notion of an active and dominating indetermination, one understands free will, the freedom of choice.

One understands that the free act is *in itself and essentially* something impossible to *foresee*. Given all the inner and outer circumstances, all the instincts and inclinations of a human being, all his motives and impulsions; given the speeches he delivers to himself, and the exhortations which carry him hither or thither, and the graces of God which attract him, and the passions which solicitate him; you may foresee what he is going to do with more or less probability. Moreover, if you deal with averages and large numbers, you can predict with certitude that in a town where all the citizens are ill-tempered, there will surely be some quarrelling. In a country where everyone has an inferiority complex, and manifests fear and trembling in the presence of corporals and captains, there will some day be a dictator. But to foresee with *certitude* what this *particular man* will do after inner reflexion and deliberation, and by the exercise of his free will, —that is something which you cannot do. It is this man's *absolute secret*, and it is a secret even *for himself*, a secret which he will learn only at the very moment when he makes his decision. The free act is not only the act of the person as such, it is moreover,—and this is perhaps the same thing—the revelation of the person to itself. Even with a 'super-comprehension of the causes', however perfect it may be supposed, you cannot foresee this act. Even God cannot do so. To be precise, God does not *foresee* our free acts, He *sees* them, all the moments of time being present to His creative eternity. And in so far as our free acts are good, He works them with us and causes them, for He is the primary cause of being. We have the initiative and the free initiative of our good acts and of our good acts in their entirety, but this is a *secondary* initiative, and not the *primary* one; the latter belongs to God alone. Our good acts are thus wholly from God as primary cause, and wholly our own as due to a secondary free cause. And this is easy to comprehend, once we have understood that freedom consists in an active and dominating indetermination and the mastery of will over judgment. How could this mastery and this high activity exercise themselves in me without the activating influx of the first Cause within me? And how could this activating influx, descending from the Life in Pure Act, destroy or diminish in me this dominating activity, at the very instant when it activates and vivifies it? It is great folly to seek the freedom of our will,—which is a supreme degree of activity,—in I know not what *asides*, isolating us from Him, without whom we can do nothing but evil and nothingness.

Sine me, nihil potestis facere, without Me you can do nothing. This text can be read in two different senses, and so it illuminates the problem of created freedom in relation to the Divine liberty. Without Me, you can do nothing: without Me you cannot execute the slightest movement which conveys being and goodness. So much for the line of good. But for the line of evil, this text must be read differently. *Sine me potestis facere nihil*: without Me nothingness, or nothing itself can be done by you. Without Me you can introduce into act and into being this *nothingness*, which wounds them, and which constitutes evil.

Freedom of Spontaneity

To be free, generally speaking, is to suffer no hindrance, is to be not bound. But this general notion can be realized, as I observed at the beginning of this chapter, according to two specifically different types. There is a freedom which consists in the *absence of necessity*; it is the freedom which I have just described, the freedom of choice. It implies not only spontaneity, but it also implies the absence of all necessity, even internal, and of all determinism.

There is another freedom which, on the contrary, consists merely in the *absence of constraint*, a freedom which is not a freedom of choice, not a free will, but which, however, deserves, in quite a different sense, the name of freedom. It is the degrees of this second freedom, the freedom of spontaneity, which I shall now consider.

One will agree that a stone *falls freely* when nothing hinders it from obeying the law of gravitation, which is a law of its nature. We are here at the lowest degree of spontaneity.

A second degree of spontaneity is represented by organic bodies having vegetative life; a third, by organisms possessing sensitive life. The animal is free with respect to the *structural conditions*, or the constitutive structures, which it has received from nature, in the sense that its activity in space depends on forms or patterns of movement which are perceptions, that is, acts of sensitive knowledge. Thus, says St. Thomas, the animal puts itself into motion by means of a form, serving as the principle of its movement, which it bestows upon itself through the immanent activity of its senses.

But it does not give itself the *ends* of its own activity. They are pre-established by nature. So the bird's flight, which we call free and which depends on the bird's perceptions, is accomplished according to the psychic structures and the instincts, which form a part of the *structural conditions* with which nature endows the bird.

The fourth degree of freedom of spontaneity is that of intellective life. The human being not only acts according to forms and patterns of activity which are not pre-established by nature, but which result from his own cognitive activity; in addition, the *ends of his acts* are not imposed upon him by nature, as in the case of the animal instinct. Able to exceed the realm of the sense, able to know being and intelligible natures, he knows both what he does and the ends of his activity, as such. By means of his own intellectual operations, he is able to envisage the ends of his activity.

Starting with this fourth degree of spontaneity, we enter into the world of spiritual things, which forms the supreme level of creation.

At this point, freedom of spontaneity becomes freedom of independence, for at this point we are concerned with persons endowed with free will, and masters of their actions,—persons, each of whom is as a whole or as a universe.

Through the intellect and the will, the entire universe enters the soul, becoming there, while existing according to intentional being and in an immaterial mode, the form and interior principle of the actions which the soul will freely proceed to carry out. The supra-physical nature of that which is intelligent and loving as such, will flourish in such a creature in an activity of superabundance, free from all external constraint; it will even be free, if I can speak thus, from that interior constraint constituted in each created being by its nature, its constitutive structure. Every external reality interiorizes itself in such an activity. 'Let all my activity spring from myself as from its source, and be regulated by me; let me be sufficient unto myself in order to live',—this is what the person demands, according to an inefficacious metaphysical aspiration. 'Let the supreme condition of the operation of intelligence and of love in its living flame be the condition of my entire existence!'

Independent in its metaphysical root, because it appears in creation as an intelligent substance and is endowed with liberty of choice, the person,—in so far as it is concerned in the pure line of its aspirations as a person,—wishes thus to pass to an ever higher degree of freedom of spontaneity and independence.

It seems to me that sometimes not enough emphasis has been laid on the dynamic aspect of the thought of St. Thomas. St. Thomas says clearly that a donkey does not have a natural desire to become a lion, because this would involve a desire to destroy what it is, that is to say, a donkey. But intelligence, love, personality, are not destroyed in passing from an inferior to a superior degree of being. Far from being destroyed, these transcendental perfections are then more than ever themselves. That is why there exists in us, as reasonable animals, a natural desire, which is not exactly of ourselves but of a transcendental element within us, to pass beyond the human condition: which does not take place, of course, without some accidents, and which too often makes us want to be unreasonable animals. But precisely because these desires to pass beyond the human state are not desires of our own specific nature, but are only the product of a transcendental element in us, they remain inefficacious and conditional. We have no right to have them granted; if they are granted to some extent it is only through grace. These aspirations tend to the super-human; they torment us without satisfying us. We cannot rightfully claim their fulfilment, because they are not specific (connatural) aspirations of human nature, but only metaphysical (transnatural) aspirations of a transcendental element within us. Truly speaking, it is only in God himself, in the uncreated Being, that these aspirations find their fulfilment.

At the fifth degree alone,—which is the divine degree,—freedom of spontaneity and independence, as well as personality, is absolutely perfect. Freedom as well as personality are perfect only when they are in pure act. God exists by Himself, by His own essence. What the theologians call *aseitas* is His privilege. His very essence is His very act of intellection and of love. There is for Him no specifying object, nor rule other than Himself. And through faith we know that He is a Trinity of Persons, each of whom is so purely person, and so free of all shadow of dependence, that he does not participate his essence, but is this essence itself. He is Freedom of Autonomy in self-subsistence; He is Personality in an absolutely pure state.

As to the human person, he is but a person in embryo. He is, as with all created persons, not only subject to realities other than himself as to the specifying objects of his knowledge and of his will, but he is also subjected to laws he has not made, as measures regulating his actions. And this is the first defeat, inflicted upon the aspirations of the person as such, a defeat far deeper in men than in angels.

Moreover, the human person is involved in all the miseries and fatalities of material nature,—the servitudes and the needs of the body, heredity, ignorance, selfishness, and the savagery of instincts. This is the second defeat, inflicted upon the person as such, and this defeat originates not in the transcendence of God, but in the burden of nature. The human person! This unfortunate being, threatened by the entire universe, which seems ready to crush him, pretends to be a whole, to be a person! He is, indeed, a whole and a person! He is a person in the metaphysical root of personality. But for subjects both spiritual and bodily, which participate in the same specific nature, which are opaque to themselves, and whose normal state is movement, this metaphysical root, hidden in the depths of being, manifests itself only through a progressive conquest of itself, accomplished in time. Man must win his personality, as well as his freedom, and he pays dearly for it, and runs many risks. He is a person in the order of doing only if his rational energies, and virtues, and love, give such a face to the torrential multiplicity which inhabits him, and freely imprint on him the seal of his radical, ontological unity. In this sense, the one knows real personality and real liberty, while the other does not.

Personality, which it is metaphysically impossible to lose, suffers many a defeat in the psychological and moral spheres. It risks contamination from the miseries of material individuality, from its pettiness, its vanities, its bad habits, its narrowness, its hereditary predispositions, from its natural regime of rivalry and opposition. For the same being who is a person, and subsists through the subsistence of his soul, is also an individual in a species, and dust in the wind.

The dynamism of freedom

These things being understood, one immediately perceives the consequence they entail from the point of view of what one can call the *dynamism of freedom*. The first freedom (freedom of choice) exists for the sake of the second freedom (freedom of spontaneity or of independence) toward which the aspirations of personality themselves tend. I have called this second freedom, freedom of spontaneity or of independence. In order now to describe it more clearly in its relation to the aspirations of the person, we can also call it *freedom of exultation* and, in the Pauline, not the Kantian, sense, *freedom of autonomy*.

The freedom of choice, the *free will*, is not its own end. It is ordained to the conquest of freedom in the sense of freedom of exultation or autonomy. And it is in this conquest, demanded by the essential postulates of human personality, that the dynamism of freedom consists.

In this dynamism are involved two essentially distinct forms, which I can only briefly discuss; a *social* form and a *spiritual* one. If we remember what has just been said about the two defeats inflicted in us in respect to the claims of personality in its pure formal line,—one by divine transcendence, and the other by the burden of nature,—we can say that the object of the social form of the dynamism of freedom is to remedy the defeat inflicted by nature; while the object of the spiritual form of this dynamism is to remedy the defeat inflicted by the transcendence of God.

In the order of social life, it thus appears that the end of civil life is a common earthly good and a common earthly undertaking, whose *highest values* consist in aiding the human person so that it may free itself from the servitudes of nature and achieve its autonomy in regard to the latter.

Civilization has its origin at once in the exigencies of our rational nature and in freedom, in the sense of freedom of choice or free will, thanks to which the constitution of the political community,—commenced, prepared and dictated by nature,—is completed as a human achievement of reason and virtue. And, through the *dynamism of freedom*, civilization, taking thus its point of departure in nature and liberty, tends toward freedom in the sense of *freedom of autonomy*,—the expansion and growing realization of human nature. It tends towards a *terminal freedom*, which is terminal only from a certain point of view and in a certain order of things (since it concerns but an infra-valent or intermediary end), which can be described as follows. Civilized life tends to grant the human person,—that is, the concrete person of each member of the multitude,—an increasingly larger measure of independence from the external and internal constraints of Nature; an independence growing according to the very tendencies and the intimate law of human nature itself, as human and endowed with reason; and assured by the economic guarantees of labour and property, by political rights, by civil virtues, and the culture of the mind. In this way, certain conditions and certain means are prepared, and certain beginnings of spiritual freedom, of the freedom purely and simply terminal, whose conquest and achievement transcend the proper order of nature and the civil community.

Thus we return to those considerations of political philosophy which have been already expounded, and we see how they have their root in a general philosophy of man and life.

With reference to a strictly theological question, concerning the kind of life mankind would have led, had Adam not eaten of the forbidden fruit, St. Thomas enunciates principles which, in my opinion, most usefully enlighten social philosophy and the problems of liberty and authority.

He asks: In the state of innocence would man have had an authority over man, one commanding and the other obeying? And he replies that the rule or authority of man over man can be understood in two ways: either as it is exercised over free men, or as it is exercised over men in a state of servitude.

The free man (in the sense of liberty of spontaneity or of autonomy) is one who disposes of himself and has mastery over his own life; the slave, the man in the state of slavery, or more generally, the man in the state of servitude, is one who is referred to or ordered to another man and to the proper good of this other man.

And thus one man commands another as a free man, when he directs him, not toward the good peculiar to him who is directing, but toward the common good of the body politic. Such authority is required by the nature of society in so far as it is human and that is why, according to St. Thomas, it would have existed even in the state of innocence. The children of an innocent Adam would have been governed, governed as free men, and directed toward the common good of the city. Such authority would have existed among them. I suppose, for the sake of my philosophy, that they would have lived under the regime of personalist democracy: the privilege of the state of innocence (a privilege, I fear, we must regard as definitively lost) being manifested in the fact that the best and wisest would always have been chosen to govern the others.

But there is another sort of rule or authority of man over man: it is that which is exercised, not over free men, but over men in the state of servitude. This occurs when he who directs refers the one directed to his *own utility*, to the utility peculiar to *the director himself*. And that is a real affliction for the person directed, says St. Thomas,—to give over to the good of another the good which ought to be his own. That is why such a domination of man over man is a punishment following on sin; it would not have existed in the state of innocence.

It seems to me that these remarks go very far. They pose, in the most precise way, the problem of servitude which concerns authority considered in the economic order, in relation to the administration of things and the functions of work. In Thomistic perspectives, I believe it must be said that slavery, or more generally servitude, taken in the most philosophical sense of this word, is a state where one man serves the *private utility* of another man, and in this respect becomes, as it were, *a part* or an organ of this other man; and that, although human work has always been bound, in a more or less extended way and in different degrees, to some form or other of servitude,—slavery, strictly speaking, serfdom, domesticity, proletariat,—nevertheless, this condition of servitude is repugnant to human nature. It is an affliction for man, which runs contrary to the aspirations proper to the person. As much as Karl Marx, St. Thomas is cognizant of the humiliation inflicted on man by what Marx calls the alienation of work for the profit of another, and which St. Thomas called more simply servitude. As much as Marx, he renders intelligible this desire which possesses us, this nostalgia for a state where human work would be liberated and all servitude abolished.

But in contra-distinction to Marx, he makes us understand that if the progress of human societies is to proceed in the direction of this liberation, it would be fully attained,—that is, every form and modality of servitude, of service to another for the peculiar or private good of another, would be abolished for all men,—only at the termination of the movement of human history. This will not be accomplished by a quick change and a messianic revolution abolishing private property, but by better and more human arrangements of private property. This progressive escape from servitude among men depends, on the one hand, on technical progress, notably on the services rendered by the machine, and on certain transformations and transferences in the regime of property; but it necessarily demands also, on the other hand, a progressive spiritualization of humanity caused by the forces of the soul and of liberty, and the gospel leaven at work in human history.

Thus I have outlined what constitutes, in its most general features, the dynamism of freedom in the order of social-temporal life. In the order of spiritual life this dynamism tends—by virtue of grace—toward what I called a moment ago freedom purely and simply terminal. Such a freedom coincides with the plenitude and perfection of love. St. Paul and St. John of the Cross teach us what is the supreme freedom of exultation and of autonomy by saying that where the spirit

of God abides, there is also liberty (II Cor., 3, 17), and that
if you are led by the spirit, you are no longer under the law
(Gal., 5, 18); that those that are moved by the spirit of
God, being really sons of God, are really and perfectly free,
and that they enter into the very life of the Divine Persons.
Such then is here below the term of the progress of the soul,
the penultimate end, wherein even before having that vision,
which union of a corruptible body forbids, time joins eternity. It is the freedom of God Himself that the perfect spiritual man enjoys, being independent of all external constraint
in so far as he depends only on the divine causality, which
is extraneous to nothing. He is sufficient unto himself because he has lost himself, and his life is the life of the subsistent Love, living in Him. Far more than the pagan sage, he
is a whole unto himself, because he forms but a single spirit
and a single love with the Divine Whole. 'Two natures in
one single spirit, and love', as St. John of the Cross puts it.

Thus we understand that freedom of choice is not an end
in itself, but that one chooses in order, finally, not to have to
choose. Freedom of choice tends, as to its end, to the terminal
freedom (terminal from a certain point of view and in a certain order of things) which, in the order of social and political life, remedies the defeat inflicted on the connatural
aspirations of the person by the burden of Nature; and to the
freedom purely and simply terminal which, in the order of
spiritual life, remedies by sanctity the defeat inflicted on
the transnatural aspirations of the person by the transcendence of God. Freedom of choice is *freer* than the freedom of
exultation or of autonomy, since it is free not only from constraint, but also from all necessity. It is *less perfect*, however,
since it is itself ordained to this other freedom.

Truly and definitively speaking, being or actuality, according to all the analogical amplitude of the internal perfections which it bears, is best of all. It is better than freedom. One does not die in the name of free will; one dies in
the name of freedom of autonomy or exultation. And when
a man dies in the name of freedom, although he sacrifices his
existence to it, this sacrifice is made in the name of a better
existence for his fellow-men. For this freedom, the freedom
of exultation and of autonomy, is but another name for the

plenitude and superabundance of existence. God exists *necessarily*. He knows Himself and loves Himself *necessarily*. And this infinite necessity is an infinite *freedom* of independence, of exultation and of autonomy. It is *aseitas*, the freedom of independence subsistent by itself.

To return, in conclusion, to metaphysical considerations: the creature has necessarily two origins—God and nothingness; and St. Thomas reminds us that 'things which are made of *nothing*, tend by themselves toward nothing.'

From this point of view one can say that freedom of choice is linked to nothingness in quite a special way, since it cannot exist in a creature without peccability and without the possibility of making nothingness. Herein consists evil.

The creature can enter into the joy of God only if it can love God as a friend; and it can love God as a friend only if it is an image of God, endowed, as God is, with the freedom of choice. And it can be endowed with the freedom of choice only if it possesses a fallible freedom, that is, if it can converse with God, not only obeying the flux of divine actions and motions, but also by resisting them, by saying No, impeding in itself the action of God.

It is this very condition of created freedom that God wishes to turn to good account. When by the virtue of God's grace and by means of this fallible and peccable free will, a creature will attain the ultimate term and will gain a consummate freedom of exultation and autonomy, and a freedom of choice henceforth supernaturally impeccable, then nothingness itself will have been conquered in the very line of freedom of choice.

NOTE

1. *Sum. Theol.*, I-II, q. 89, a. 6.

9. FREEDOM AND THE LOVE OF GOD

There is an analogous relation between the way in which an intelligent creature would arrive at the enjoyment of his ultimate end in the natural order and the way in which he arrives at the enjoyment of his ultimate end in the supernatural order; *but the entrance into the possession of the last end takes place in the two cases in a structurally different manner.* It would be a serious mistake merely to copy our (philosophical) idea of the final natural happiness of the intelligent creature from the idea which theology offers us of supernatural beatitude. It would be to misunderstand the unique privileges of the beatific vision and at the same time to falsify the structures of the natural order, as if the natural contemplation of God would procure final natural happiness in the same way that vision procures supernatural beatitude.

I am not thinking here solely of the fact that the final happiness of a human being, if he had been created in the state of pure nature, would have been a sort of felicity in motion, and not a beatitude fixed from the first moment in an immutable plenitude like that given by the vision of God. What I have in mind has a universal and more profound import. It is the fact that every natural contemplation of God, angelic as well as human, remains at an infinite distance from the vision of the divine essence. No natural contemplation of God, angelic or human, can by itself alone introduce the intelligent creature into the enjoyment of his final happiness of the natural order. It is unique in the case of the vision —called because of that *beatific*—that knowledge suffices to procure beatitude, because there it is a question of supernatural knowledge and beatitude, and because the knowledge of vision deifies the creature by making him possess God, see God as He sees Himself. On the contrary, in the natural order, the most lofty contemplation of God, angelic or human, is never possession of God or deification; and on the supposition that the intellectual creature had been created in the state of pure nature, it is necessary that by *love joined to knowledge* he would have entered into the enjoyment of his final happiness, angelic or human.[1]

For as long as God is not intuitively seen, *melior est amor Dei quam cognitio*, it is better to love Him than to know Him.[2] The highest natural contemplation of God, angelic or human, cannot be made final happiness except by the love which makes the contemplated object the supreme joy and delight of the one contemplating, just because it is loved above all.

If furthermore (always in the hypothesis of pure nature), that final happiness is inamissible, it is because the intelligent creature is fixed forever in the act of love for God above all. His liberty would have produced that act either in the instant in which his soul was separated from the body or in that in which the pure spirit made his choice.

Four Necessary Loves

St. Thomas teaches, in connection with the Angels,[3] that every creature naturally loves God more than itself just as the part naturally loves the whole more than itself. A natural tendency is a tendency determined *ad unum* (to one); and in that respect is necessary.[4] However, this necessity of tendency is found in things according to the various degrees of being and in typically varying manners. The thesis, then, that every creature naturally loves God as his supreme Whole or as Common Good of all more than he loves himself, *thus covers four quite different sorts of love, to which it applies in an analogical manner*. This will be the case according as it applies to forms of love which are themselves necessary (which from now on we shall call *love of nature*, determined *ad unum* and necessary with regard to the mode of emanation); or merely to the inclination, necessary and determined by nature, but not determining, toward that which we shall call *love of free option*.

We ought to remark that in our modern languages it is necessary to force somewhat the common meaning of the word *to love* in order to give it the analogical extension (as wide as that of being) according to which St. Thomas uses that word, since for him every agent, even irrational, and even inanimate, "loves" (at least by inclination or by spontaneous élan) the end to which it tends.

Let us note first of all, as a truth basic to the discussion, that every creature naturally loves the supreme Whole more than itself with a radical élan consubstantial with its essence. This is an *ontological love-of-nature* which is in reality one and identical with the being and the radical inclinations of the being (in the Angel and in man, with the very essence of the will and its radical inclination toward the good).

This ontological love of God above all does not proceed from any knowledge other than that proper to the Author of being who orders all things to their ends. It necessarily exists in *every creature, with or without senses or reason,* and is not free. It is inamissible; a being cannot lose it except by losing its nature and ceasing to exist. It continues to exist in the sinner and in the demon.

To that ontological love of which we have just spoken pertains the love by which agents incapable of knowledge love the supreme Whole more than themselves with spontaneous élan, by the mere fact that they tend in act toward their proper end.

To this ontological love belongs also the love through which *every creature capable of knowledge* loves the supreme Whole more than itself, instinctively or by a spontaneous élan and not because it knows Him, due solely to the fact that it loves necessarily, and with an *elicited*[5] love, whatever is its *good of nature.* In this way, the hen loves God, without knowing Him, in loving her chicks which she does know, and loves Him more than her chicks; and man loves God above all, without knowing Him, merely because he necessarily loves happiness, of which he does have some idea.[6] Just as nature cannot tend toward any end whatsoever without tending still more toward the supreme Whole through each of its single particular ends, so the will cannot love any good whatsoever without loving still more the supreme Whole, through the good in general and happiness, of which our intellect has an idea, and which we will and love in all that we will.[7]

Can one say that man, therefore, naturally loves God with a necessary elicited love proceeding from a confused knowledge of God under the species of good in general or of happiness? But *hoc non est simpliciter cognoscere Deum esse; sicut cognoscere venientem, non est cognoscere Petrum, quamvis sit Petrus veniens* (This is not to know simply that God exists; as to know that someone is coming is not to know Peter, though it is Peter who is coming).[8] Here there is no knowledge of God properly speaking, no idea of God from which an elicited love for God might proceed. (As for the Angel, he knows quite well that God, or the supreme Whole, is the final term of the impulse that constitutes his desire for happiness; nevertheless, it remains true that this élan which extends up to God does not proceed from the knowledge of God.) Consequently, it is better to say that the love of God included in the elicited love of happiness is an ontological love which goes beyond the specification of the elicited love within which it is involved or implied. We shall name it the *ontological intra-elicited* love of God above all. It constitutes one and the same act, one sole and single inclination, with the elicited love of happiness; but it goes beyond the specifying object of that elicited love.[9] It also is a necessary and inamissible love, a love which endures even in hell.

St. Thomas is thinking especially of this love in the article upon which we are commenting.

Next comes the *elicited love-of-nature* which, before any option or election, arises at once in every intellectual creature as a spontaneous, immediate movement of the rational appetite at the instant and by the mere fact that the intellect knows the existence of the Principle of all good, the Self-subsisting Good which is the common good of all.

The will, as a matter of fact, is not simply the power to choose; it is also and primarily appetite. And what we call *indeliberate movement* in man is found not only in the sense appetite but also in the will. As for the pure spirit, he has no passions; but he does experience love, joy, fear, admiration, etc., *secundum quod nominant simplices actus voluntatis* (insofar as they are simple acts of the will).[10] What is more, as we shall see at greater length in the third part of this study, it is necessary to admit that there existed in the Angel, at the first instant of his creation, something which corresponds analogically to our indeliberate movements of will at the mere presentation of the beautiful and of the good. It was an impulse of nature toward the divine goodness, which preceded, not the actual presence, of course, but the positive exercise of the freedom of the will and the first act of option.

The drive (or *élan*) of nature of which we speak, the elicited love-of-nature for the Principle of all good, is a movement *necessary in itself* or in regard to its mode of emanation; but, unlike the ontological love pure and simple and the intra-elicited ontological love, it *depends indirectly and extrinsically* upon the free will, insofar as it can be prevented by free will, like any other indeliberate motion of the elicited appetite.

In man, the elicited love-of-nature for the supreme Whole can arise at any moment and can, moreover, be a simple velleity. It is not involved in the natural love of oneself. This is not the case for the pure spirit, who from the first instant of his creation knows God by the same token that he knows himself. In him, as a consequence, from the first instant of his creation, an elicited love for the Source of all good, proceeding from that knowledge of God implied in the knowledge of himself, arises as a primary dynamism or élan of nature.

In the Angel, then, there is not only an intra-elicited ontological love for God above all, a love which is but one with the necessary and inamissible love-of-nature by which the good in general and happiness are willed in all that he wills; there is also in him an elicited love-of-nature for God above all, which bursts forth from nature necessarily (as far as its mode of emanation is concerned), but which is in itself impedible by freedom (even though it be not in fact impeded). This elicited love-of-nature for the supreme Whole above all is involved in the love-of-nature by which the Angel loves himself. It depends on that natural love of self, which it prolongs, but does not constitute with it one and the same act, one sole and identical inclination. It is distinct from the natural love of self. It can, consequently, cease to exist (through the intervention of free will) while the natural love of self endures. It is a love-of-nature whose extrinsic and indirect dependence upon free will renders it contingent, an amissible love-of-nature. The fallen Angel lost it in the second instant.[11] Even though it arises from nature with the type of necessity of that which is determined *ad unum*, it can be freely rejected. It does not continue to exist in the damned.

In every intelligent creature there exists a natural inclination (emanating necessarily from nature, but not imposing any necessity upon the will) to love the supreme Whole more than himself with an elicited love of *free option*. The intelligent creature is inclined by his nature to this love which is essentially free in its very mode of emanation. He is inclined or disposed, but not determined, to it by his nature, because it is essential to such an act of love (which goes to God not only according as He is the supreme Whole and the common good of all, but also according as He is infinitely separated from all in the mystery of His proper essence) to proceed positively and directly from liberty. As a result, the intelligent creature can, if he so wills, refuse to perform that act which is, nevertheless, natural for him in the sense which we have just indicated.

That is undoubtedly why St. Thomas, when he affirms that the Angel and every creature naturally loves God more than himself, does not feel the need of adding "with the exception of man in the state of fallen nature." For this inclination, to love God above all, of which we speak (and which is strongest in the Angel, without, however, being invincible), exists even in man in the state of fallen nature as it does in every creature; but in man it is so enfeebled and obstructed that without grace he cannot *de facto* love God more than himself.

Love of free option

FIRST FORMULATION

The *right moral life* of every intelligent creature, insofar as he does not have beatitude, depends upon the *love of free option* for God above everything else, and *not* on any sort of *natural and necessary* love for God above everything else.

It is precisely as the supreme Whole, as the Universal Good or Common Good of all, the *bonum commune omnium*,[12] that God is loved by every creature more than itself in a necessary manner, with one or other of the *loves-of-nature* discussed above. Only in the beatific vision, however, or on the very level of the transcendence of God, is the intellectual creature, who sees this God elevated above all and as the common good of all, necessarily drawn to Him in His absolute singularity and in the transcendence of His essence.[13] In other words, he is drawn to God as infinitely superior to every other being, with the same motion of natural love (and with an even more fundamental necessity) as he is drawn toward God as common good of all.[14] He loves the transcendent God as the Good who actually fulfills and more than fulfills every possibility of desire. Here it is by an absolute necessity of nature that the creature loves above all things God as such, as infinitely distinct from all else which exists—God in His absolute singularity and in the transcendence of His essence. And it is in this absolutely necessary love for God above all that all his acts of desire and of will take form, so that the very possibility of any tension or conflict between the Uncreated and the created in the movements of his affection is absolutely abolished.

On the contrary, however, for those who do not see the essence of God and do not know Him except through the mirror of created things, where He appears as one good among other goods, to love God above all as the end and rule of their moral life means *to choose* between that good which is God and those other goods which are not He. The intelligent creature who does not enjoy the vision of God cannot anchor his moral life in God as such (as infinitely distinct from all that which is, in God with all His demands loved more than self and above all) except on condition of an option, a sort of sundering where God is vanquisher of creature—*Quis ut Deus?* (Who is like to God?)—and where, for the sake of the Sovereign Good,[15] he renounces certain other goods which he could pursue. That is an absolutely universal law, which holds for the Angel as well as for man.[16]

Those who do not see God (if we consider the Angels in the instant of their creation) can, indeed, love God above all as supreme Whole with an elicited love-of-nature before establishing their moral life; and this love, involved in their first impulse of love for themselves, is natural in itself, and necessary in itself, though impedible by free will. But they cannot love Him above all in the very singularity and transcendence of His essence, and in such a way as to establish their moral life in Him, except by virtue of an option. Nature undoubtedly inclines them to make this option for God, rather than against Him; but it depends upon their free will to make it in one direction or the other. It is by a love of free choice alone that they can make their moral life depend upon God.

We cannot admit the possibility of a single case where the moral life of an intelligent creature who did not see God would, because of the natural perfection of the creature, be based on a love of God above all which was natural and necessary in the way that our desire for happiness is natural and necessary. The creature in question would not be able *not* to love God above everything else from the first instant of volitional activity and choice, regardless of the object. Such a creature would not have to bear witness to God's victory over creation, nor would he have to sacrifice to the love of the transcendent Good other possible loves (particularly the possibility of loving and enjoying without limit some limited thing which is in itself good and lovable). To admit the possibility of a single case of such a creature would be to attribute to nature something which is peculiar to glory.

SECOND FORMULATION

An intellectual creature cannot attain that love of God upon which all right moral life depends *solely by virtue of his creation, or by the élan of his nature at its first instant.*

As a matter of fact, when the intelligent and free creature loves God solely in virtue of his creation, or of the drive of his nature at its first instant, his love proceeds from the motion determined *ad unum* (to one) by his nature. Now the transcendence of God is such that the love by which the intelligent creature anchors his moral life in Him cannot, even in the purely natural order, proceed from the motion determined *ad unum* by nature. It is by proceeding from the motion of freedom (and, in the supernatural order, of grace) that such love goes to God.

Why is this so? In the order of specification (of "what" is loved),[17] the love of God which proceeds from the motion naturally determined *ad unum* is first concentrated upon a creature[18] (through which God is known and loved); and then this love extends on to God as supreme Whole and Common Good of all (in Whom the creature is good and lovable). Here we are dealing with a *mediated* love of God, involved or implied in a love for a creature. It is through the mediation of an act which is focused on a necessarily loved object belonging to this world—to the world of creation, of what has been made—that the creature thus loves God above all as the Common Good of all. Because it is bound to something of this world, such a mediated act does not enable the person to pass beyond this world in order to adhere directly to the Uncreated and to give himself to Him.

It is only (at least as long as he does not see God) when the intelligent and free creature loves God *in virtue of his freedom or by a positive act of freedom, in other words, with a love of free option,* that he loves Him above all as the object of a love which rests in Him independently of any created object, or which goes uniquely to God, insofar as He is separated from all in His absolute singularity ("direct" love of God, as an act apart, and without intermediary, from person to person). The reason for this is that the act of free will as such is not *of this world*. Even in the natural order it does not belong to the world of creation, to the world of that which has been made. That is why the Angels, although the knowledge of all that belongs to the world of creation is due to them, do not know the secrets of hearts.[19] The free will transcends the world of creation. Hence it can produce an act of direct or non-mediated love for God above all, by which the person, passing beyond this world and without intermediary, crosses the abyss between the created and the Uncreated to give himself to the Uncreated.

When this act of love is irrevocable (whether it be in the Angel at his second instant, or in man at the instant of the separation of soul and body), it makes the creature enter into the enjoyment of his ultimate end. It is an act *of grace and of freedom* which merits the beatific vision in the case of the creature elevated to the supernatural order; or an act *of freedom alone*—which not only merits the felicity proper to the creature *in statu termini* (in state of term), but also enters into its formal constitution[20]—in the case of the creature supposed in the state of pure nature.

It is the very transcendence of God which makes it impossible that the love for God upon which all right moral life depends should emanate from the intellectual creature (even in the natural order) by virtue solely of his creation, or of the dynamism of his nature at its first instant.[21]

COROLLARY

It is impossible that an intellectual creature *solely by virtue of his creation or by the dynamism of his nature at its first instant should arrive at the love of God by which he enters into the enjoyment of his ultimate end.*

We might remark here that it is normal for the intelligent and free creature (for the person) to attain his end by virtue of his freedom itself, and by meriting it. Thus it is that, although God by His absolute power could have placed the intelligent creature in the beatific vision and in the state of supernatural beatitude at the first instant of his creation, nevertheless He has *de facto* willed that the creature should merit supernatural beatitude, which is in no way due to him, by virtue of grace and charity.

But the essential argument goes much further. As we have just seen, it is based upon the fact that only when he sees the divine essence does the intelligent creature necessarily love God above all, not simply as supreme Whole, but even as He is separated from all in His absolute singularity. It is also based upon the fact that the love by which the person passes beyond this world and without intermediary crosses the abyss between the created and the Uncreated in order to give himself to God (by a natural love or by a supernatural love) can only be the love of God above all which proceeds from freedom, the love of free option.

Consequently, *hoc est impossibile aliquam creaturam esse voluntate immutabili adhaerentem Deo per propriam naturam* (It is impossible that any creature should by his own nature adhere to God with immutable will).[22]

NOTES

1. *Summa Theologiae* I[a], q. 108, a. 4.

2. I[a], q. 82, a. 3.

3. I[a], q. 60, a. 5.

4. *De Malo*, q. 16, a. 4, ad 5[um].

5. That is to say, with a love which bears upon an object first *known*, because it emanates from an appetitive power (sense appetite or will) which is itself by nature rooted in a cognitive power (sense or intellect).

6. Without doubt the will is free not to exercise any act at all (and thereby not to will happiness). But as soon as it acts and as far as it acts, it cannot not will happiness. The elicited love of good in general and of happiness, of oneself and of one's own being, is in that sense a purely and simply necessary love (though less totally necessary than the love of God by the blessed, in whom the will is not free even not to act).

7. It is the same for the Angel with this difference, that the Angel has an idea of the good *in communi* and of happiness which is not abstract but infused. On the angelic universal, cf. John of St. Thomas, *Curs. theol.*, in I[am], qq. 54–55, disp. 41, a. 3 and a. 4, Solesmes ed., p. 596, n. 56; p. 602, n. 7.

   Moreover, the Angel loves the supreme Whole not only with this *intra-elicited ontological love*, by the fact that he loves any good whatsoever. He also loves Him with an *elicited love-of-nature* which arises at the same time as his natural love of self in the first instant of his creation. Cf. further on pp. 154–56.

8. I[a], q. 2, a. 1, ad 1[um].

9. This is a particular case of the law of "hyperfinality," according to which every creature tends to its proper end by virtue of its love for the supreme End: for the inclination of the created agent toward its proper end and its inclination toward God is one and the same inclination; and therefore it goes—under the aspect of the intensity of exercise—first to God (with a priority of nature) and afterwards to the end proper to the agent; however, under the aspect of specification by the object, it goes first to the end proper to the created agent, and then on beyond to God.

10. I[a], q. 64, a. 3.

11. When St. Thomas writes: "his appetite in its natural aspects is not turned away from God" in *de Malo*, q. 16, a. 6, ad 17[um], or when he says that a certain love of God, "insofar as He is the source of natural perfections, which is natural love", remains in the damned (*Compendium theol.*, I, c. 174), he has in view what we call intra-elicited ontological love. It is clear that in turn-

ing away from God, the Author of grace, the free will of the Angel by the same fact turned away from God, the Author of nature, and thereby impeded or put a stop to the elicited natural élan which carried him to God loved above all.

12. Cf. I^a, q. 60, a. 5, corp. and ad 5um.

13. *Ibid.*, ad 5um.

14. *Ibid.*

15. *Ibid.*

16. Obviously, it is not any natural propensity opposed to the love of God above all which the Angel *in statu viae* has to sacrifice to that love, but the possibility of a purely free and voluntary disorder in the love and enjoyment of a true good.

17. See above, p. 4, n. 9.

18. Whether it is a question of one and the same act going beyond its immediate specifying object (as in the intra-elicited ontological love of nature) or of an act which is distinct but involved in the natural love of self and a function of it (as in the elicited love-of-nature in the Angel at the first instant).

19. Cf. I^a, q. 57, a. 4; *de Veritate*, q. 8, a. 13; *de Malo*, q. 16, a. 8; John of St. Thomas, *Curs. theol.*, in I^{am}, qq. 56–58, disp. 22, a. 3, de. Vives, IV, p. 831.

20. Cf. above, p. 1 ff.

21. Cf. III^a, *Suppl.* q. 70, appendix I, a. 2.

22. *De Ver.*, q. 24, a. 1, ad 16um.

10. SUBJECTIVITY AND THE HUMAN PERSON

What we call *subject* St. Thomas called *suppositum*. Essence is *that which* a thing is; suppositum is *that which* has an essence, that which exercises existence and action—*actiones sunt suppositorum*—that which subsists. Here we meet the metaphysical notion which has given students so many headaches and baffles everyone who has not grasped the true—the existential—foundation of Thomist metaphysics, the notion of *subsistence*.

We are bound to speak of this notion of subsistence with great respect, not only because of the transcendent applications made of it in theology, but because, in the philosophical order itself, it bears witness to the supreme tension of an articulated thought bent on seizing intellectually something which seems to escape from the world of notions or ideas of the intellect, namely, the typical reality of the subject. The existential subject has this in common with the act of existing, that both transcend the concept or the idea considered as the terminus of the first operation of mind or simple apprehension. We have seen how the intellect (because it envelops itself) grasps in an idea which is the first of its ideas, that very thing, the act of existing, which is the intelligible (or rather the super-intelligible) proper to the judgement, and not to simple apprehension. Now we are no longer dealing with the act of existing but with that which exercises that act. Just as there is nothing more commonplace in language than the word being (and this is the greatest mystery of philosophy) so there is nothing more commonplace than the 'subject' to which in all our propositions we attribute a predicate. And when we undertake a metaphysical analysis of the reality of this subject, this individual thing which maintains itself in existence, this supremely concrete reality, and undertake to do justice to its irreducible originality, we are forced to appeal to that which is most abstract and most elaborate in our lexicon of notions. How can we be astonished that minds which are fond of facility should regard as so many vain scholastic refinements and Chinese puzzles the elucidations in which Cajetan and John of St. Thomas show us that subsistence is distinct from both essence and existence, and describe it as a substantial mode? I concede that the style of their dissertations seems to carry us very far from experience into the third heaven of abstraction. And yet, in reality their aim was to form an *objective notion* of the *subject* itself or the suppositum, to reach objectively, within the ontological analysis of the structure of reality, the property which makes the subject to be subject and not object, and to transcend, or rather exceed in depth, the whole universe of objects.

When they explain that an essence or a nature, considered strictly, cannot exist ouside the mind as an object of thought, and that nevertheless individual natures do exist, and that consequently, in order to exist, a given nature or essence must be other than it has to be in order to be an object of thought, that is to say, it must bear in itself a supreme achievement which adds nothing to it in the line of its essence (and consequently does not enrich our understanding by any new note which qualifies it), but which *terminates* it in that line of essence (closes or situates it, constitutes it as an *in-itself* or an inwardness face to face with existence) in order that it may take possession of this act of existing for which it is created and which transcends it;[1] when they explain in this fashion *that by which*, on the plane of reality, the *quod* which exists and acts is other than the *quid* which we conceive, they attest the existential character of metaphysics, they shatter the Platonic world of pure objects, they justify the passage into the world of subjects or supposita, they rescue for the metaphysical intellect the value and reality of subjects.

God does not create essences to which He can be imagined as giving a last rub of the sandpaper of subsistence before sending them forth into existence! God creates existent subjects or supposita which subsist in the individual nature that constitutes them and which receive from the creative influx their nature as well as their subsistence, their existence, and their activity. Each of them possesses an essence and pours itself out in action. Each is, for us, in its individual existing reality, an inexhaustible well of knowability. We shall never know everything there is to know about the tiniest blade of grass or the least ripple in a stream. In the world of existence there are only subjects or *supposita*, and that which emanates from them into being. This is why ours is a world of nature and adventure, filled with events, contingency, chance, and where the course of events is flexible and mutable whereas the laws of essence are necessary. We know these subjects, we shall never get through knowing them. We do not know them as subjects, we know them by objectising them, by achieving objective insights of them and making them our objects; for the object is nothing other than something of the subject transferred into the state of immaterial existence of intellection in act. We know subjects not as subjects, but as objects, and therefore only in such-and-such of the intelligible aspects, or rather *inspects*, and perspectives in which they are rendered present to the mind and which we shall never get through discovering in them.

As we pass progressively to higher degrees in the scale of beings we deal with subjects of existence or *supposita* more and more rich in inner complexity, whose individuality is more and more concentrated and integrated, whose action manifests a more and more perfect spontaneity, from the merely transitive activity of inanimate bodies to the occultly immanent activity of vegetable life, the definitely immanent activity of sentient life, and the perfectly immanent activity of the life of the intellect.[2] At this last degree the threshold of free choice is crossed, and therewith the threshold of independence properly so-called (however imperfect it be) and of personality. With man, liberty of spontaneity becomes liberty of autonomy, the *suppositum* becomes *persona*, that is, a whole which subsists and exists in virtue of the very subsistence and existence of its spiritual soul, and acts by setting itself its own ends; a universe in itself; a microcosm which, though its existence at the heart of the material universe is ceaselessly threatened, nevertheless possesses a higher ontological density than the whole universe. Only the person is free; only the person possesses, in the full sense of these words, inwardness and subjectivity—because it contains itself and moves about within itself. The person, St. Thomas says, is that which is noblest and highest in all nature.

Subjectivity as subjectivity

By sense or experience, science or philosophy, each of us, as I said a moment ago, knows the environing world of subjects, *supposita*, and persons in their role as objects. The paradox of consciousness and personality is that each of us is situated precisely *at the centre* of this world. Each is at the centre of infinity. And this privileged subject, the thinking self, is to itself not object but subject; in the midst of all the subjects which it knows only as objects, it alone is subject as subject. We are thus confronted by subjectivity as subjectivity.

I know myself as subject by consciousness and reflexivity, but my substance is obscure to me. St. Thomas explains that in spontaneous reflection, which is a prerogative of the life of the intellect, each of us knows (by a kind of knowledge that is not scientific but experimental and incommunicable) that his soul exists, knows the singular existence of this subjectivity that perceives, suffers, loves, thinks. When a man is awake to the intuition of being he is awake at the same time to the intuition of subjectivity; he grasps, in a flash that will never be dimmed, the fact that *he is a self*, as Jean-Paul said. The force of such a perception may be so great as to sweep him along to that heroic asceticism of the void and of annihilation in which he will achieve ecstasy in the substantial existence of the *self* and the 'presence of immensity' of the divine Self at one and the same time—which in my view characterises the natural mysticism of India.[8]

But the intuition of subjectivity is an existential intuition which surrenders no essence to us. We know *that which* we are by our phenomena, our operations, our flow of consciousness. The more we grow accustomed to the inner life, the better we decipher the astonishing and fluid multiplicity which is thus delivered to us; the more, also, we feel that it leaves us ignorant of the essence of our self. Subjectivity *as subjectivity* is inconceptualisable; is an unknowable abyss. It is unknowable by the mode of the notion, concept, or representation, or by any mode of any science whatsoever—introspection, psychology, or philosophy. How could it be otherwise, seeing that every reality known through a concept, a notion, or a representation, is known as object and not as subject? Subjectivity as such escapes by definition from that which we know about ourselves by means of notions.

Yet it is known in a way, or rather in certain ways, which I should like briefly to enumerate. At the very beginning and above all, subjectivity is known or rather felt in virtue of a formless and diffuse knowledge which, in relation to reflective consciousness, we may call unconscious or pre-conscious knowledge. This is knowledge of the 'concomitant' or spontaneous consciousness, which, without giving rise to a distinct act of thought, envelops in fact, *in actu exercito*, our inner world in so far as it is integrated into the vital activity of our spiritual faculties.[4] Even for the most superficial persons, it is true that from the moment when they say *I*, the whole unfolding of their states of consciousness and their operations, their musings, memories, and acts, is subsumed by a virtual and ineffable knowledge, a vital and existential knowledge of the totality immanent in each of its parts, and immersed, without their troubling to become aware of it, in the diffuse glow, the unique freshness, the maternal connivance as it were, which emanates from subjectivity. Subjectivity is not known, it is felt as a propitious and enveloping night.

There is, secondly, a knowledge of subjectivity as such, imperfect and fragmentary of course, but in this instance formed and actually given to the mind, and which is thrown into relief by what St. Thomas calls knowledge by mode of inclination, sympathy, or connaturality, not by mode of knowledge. It appears before us under three specifically distinct forms: (1) practical knowledge, which judges both moral matters and the subject itself, by the inner inclinations of the subject; (2) poetic knowledge, in which subjectivity and the things of this world are known together in creative intuition-emotion and are revealed and expressed together, not in a word or concept but in a created work;[5] (3) mystical knowledge, which is not directed toward the subject but toward things divine, and does not of itself issue in any expression, but in which God is known by union and by connaturality of love, and in which this very love that becomes the formal means of knowledge of the divine Self, simultaneously renders the human self transparent in its spiritual depths. Let the mystic reflect an instant upon himself, and a St. Theresa or a St. John of the Cross will show us to what extent the divine light gives him a lucid and inexhaustible knowledge of his own subjectivity.

But in none of these instances is the knowledge of subjectivity as subjectivity, however real it be, a knowledge by mode of knowledge, which is to say, by mode of conceptual objectivization.

In none of these instances is it philosophical knowledge. It would be a contradiction in terms to seek to make a philosophy of that sort of knowledge, since every philosophy— like it or not—proceeds by concepts. This is the first point to which the consideration of subjectivity as subjectivity draws our attention; and it is a point of capital importance. Subjectivity marks the frontier which separates the world of philosophy from the world of religion. This is what Kierkegaard felt so deeply in his polemic against Hegel. Philosophy runs against an insurmountable barrier in attempting to deal with subjectivity, because while philosophy of course knows subjects, it knows them only as objects. Philosophy is registered whole and entire in the relation of intelligence to object; whereas religion enters into the relation of subject to subject. For this reason, every philosophical religion, or every philosophy which, like Hegel's, claims to assume and integrate religion into itself, is in the last analysis a mystification.

When philosophy, taking its start in the being of things, attains to God as the cause of being, it has then, thanks to ana-noetic knowledge,[6] rendered the divine Self an object of philosophical knowledge expressed in concepts. These concepts do not circumscribe the supreme reality presented by them. On the contrary, that divine reality infinitely overflows the banks of conceptual knowledge. But philosophy knows thereby, or ought to know, that the reality thus objectised 'through a glass, darkly,' is the reality of a transcendent Self inscrutable in its being and its goodness, in its liberty and its glory. And all the other intelligent *selves* who know it, from the instant that they know it, owe to it, as their first duty, obedience and adoration. St. Paul blamed pagan wisdom for not recognising that glory of God of which it was in fact aware. But in fact, to recognise that glory is already to adore it. It is something to know that God is a transcendent and sovereign Self; but it is something else again to enter oneself and with all one's baggage—one's own existence and flesh and blood—into the vital relationship in which the created subjectivity is brought face to face with this transcendent subjectivity and, trembling and loving, looks to it for salvation. This is the business of religion.

Religion is essentially that which no philosophy can be: a relation of person to person with all the risk, the mystery, the dread, the confidence, the delight, and the torment that lie in such a relationship. And this very relationship of subject to subject[7] demands that into the knowledge of uncreated subjectivity which the created subjectivity possesses there shall be transferred something of that which the latter is as *subjectivity*, i.e., as that uncreated subjectivity is in the mystery of its personal life. Whence all religion comports an element of revelation. Therefore in the true faith it is the First Truth in Person which makes known to man the mystery of the divine subjectivity: *unigenitus filius, qui est in sinu patris, ipse enarravit*.[8] This knowledge is still 'through a glass, darkly', and therein the divine subjectivity is still objectised in order to be grasped by us. But this time it is in the glass of the super-analogy of faith,[9] in concepts which God Himself has chosen as His means of speaking to us about Himself—until at the last every glass falls away and then we know truly as we are known. Then shall we truly know the divine subjectivity as subjectivity in the vision in which the divine essence itself actuates our intellect and transports us in ecstasy within itself. While awaiting this state, the connaturality of love gives us, in apophatic contemplation, a dim sort of substitute and obscure foretaste of such a union.

Generally speaking, to *situate* the privileged subject which knows itself as subject in respect of all other subjects, which it knows as objects; to situate the self, that thinking reed in the crowd of thinking reeds, sets a singular problem. Each of us is able to say with Mr. Somerset Maugham: 'To myself I am the most important person in the world; though I do not forget that, not even taking into consideration so grand a conception as the Absolute, but from the standpoint of common sense, I am of no consequence whatever. It would have made small difference to the universe if I had never existed.'[10] This is a simple remark; but its implications are very wide.

Being the only subject which is a subject for me in the midst of a world of subjects which my senses and my intelligence can know only as objects, I am at the centre of the world, as we observed a moment ago. With regard to my subjectivity in act, I *am* the centre of the world ('the most important person in the world'). My destiny is the most important of all destinies. Worthless as I know myself to be, I am more interesting than all the saints. There is me, and there are all the others. Whatever happens to the others is a mere incident in the picture; but what happens to me, what I myself have to do, is of absolute importance.

And yet, as regards the world itself, from the most obvious 'standpoint of common sense', I know perfectly well that 'I am of no consequence whatever' and that 'it would have made small difference to the universe if I had never existed.' I know that I am one of the herd, not better than the rest, worth no more than the rest. I shall have been a tiny crest of foam, here one moment, gone in the twinkling of an eye, on the ocean of nature and humanity.

These two images—of myself and of my situation in respect to other subjects—can positively not be superposed. These two perspectives cannot be made to coincide. I oscillate rather miserably between them. If I abandon myself to the perspective of subjectivity, I absorb everything into myself, and, sacrificing everything to my uniqueness, I am riveted to the absolute of selfishness and pride. If I abandon myself to the perspective of objectivity, I am absorbed into everything, and, dissolving into the world, I am false to my uniqueness and resign my destiny. It is only from above that the antinomy can be resolved. If God exists, then not I, but He is the centre; and this time not in relation to a certain particular perspective, like that in which each created subjectivity is the centre of the universe it knows, but speaking absolutely, and as transcendent subjectivity to which all subjectivities are referred. At such time I can know both that I am without importance and that my destiny is of the highest importance. I can know this without falling into pride, know it without being false to my uniqueness. Because, loving the divine Subject more than myself, it is for Him that I love myself, it is to do as He wishes that I wish above all else to accomplish my destiny; and because, unimportant as I am in the world, I am important to Him; not only I, but all the other subjectivities whose lovableness is revealed in Him and for Him and which are henceforward, together with me, a *we*, called to rejoice in His life.

I am known to other men. They know me as object, not as subject. They are unaware of my subjectivity as such; unaware not merely of its inexhaustible depth, but also of that presence of the whole in each of its operations, that existential complexity of inner circumstances, data of nature, free choice, attractions, weaknesses, virtues perhaps, loves and pains; that atmosphere of immanent vitality which alone lends meaning to each of my acts. To be known as object, to be known to others, to see oneself in the eyes of one's neighbour (here M. Sartre is right) is to be severed from oneself and wounded in one's identity. It is to be always unjustly known—whether the *he* whom they see condemns the *I*, or whether, as occurs more rarely, the 'he' does honour to the 'I'. A tribunal is a masquerade where the accused stands accoutered in a travesty of himself, and *it* delivers his acts to be weighed in the balance. The more the judges stray from the crude outward criteria with which formerly they contented themselves, and strive to take account of degrees of inner responsibility, the more they reveal that the truth of him whom they judge remains unknowable to human justice. Interrogated by such a tribunal, Jesus owed it to Himself to remain silent.

I am known to God. He knows all of me, me as subject. I am present to Him in my subjectivity itself; He has no need to objectise me in order to know me. Then, and in this unique instance, man is known not as object but as subject in all the depth and all the recesses of subjectivity. Only God knows me in this wise; to Him alone am I uncovered. I am not uncovered to myself. The more I know of my subjectivity, the more it remains obscure to me. If I were not known to God, no one would know me. No one would know

me in my truth, in my existence. No one would know me
—*me*—as subject.

What this comes to is that no one would render justice to
my being.[11] There could be no justice for me anywhere. My
existence would be immersed in the injustice of the knowledge of me possessed by all the others and by the world itself; and in my own ignorance of myself. But if there is no
justice possible with regard to my being, then there is no
possible hope for me. If man is not known to God, and if he
has profound experience of his personal existence and his
subjectivity, then he has also the experience of his desperate
solitude; and the longing for death—more than this, the
aspiration to total annihilation, is the sole spring that can
gush forth within him.

Finally, to know that I am known as subject in all the
dimensions of my being is not only to know that my truth is
known, and that in this knowledge justice is done me; it is
also to know that I am *understood*. Even though God condemns me, I know that He understands me. The idea that
we are known to Him who scrutinises the loins and the heart
dissolves us at first in fear and trembling because of the evil
that is within us. But on deeper reflection, how can we keep
from thinking that God Who knows us and knows all those
poor beings who jostle us and whom we know as objects,
whose wretchedness we mostly perceive—how can we keep
from thinking that God Who knows all these in their subjectivity, in the nakedness of their wounds and their secret
evil, must know also the secret beauty of that nature which
He has bestowed upon them, the slightest sparks of good and
liberty they give forth, all the travail and the impulses of
good-will that they drag from the womb to the grave, the recesses of goodness of which they themselves have no notion?
The exhaustive knowledge possessed by God is a loving knowledge. To know that we are known to God is not merely to
experience justice, it is also to experience mercy.

In any case, what I should like to say is that our acts are
tolerable to ourselves only because our consciousness of them
is immersed in the obscure experience of subjectivity. Our
acts are hatched in it as in a nest where everything, even
the worst rendings and the worst shames, connives with us

to emanate from us in the unique freshness of the present instant that we are living. They bathe in that maternal atmosphere emanating from subjectivity, of which I spoke earlier. There is nothing which crushes us so much as our own acts when, forgotten and then one day evoked by some relic of past time, they pass to the state of objects, separated from the living waters of subjectivity. Even if they were not specifically evil, we are no longer sure that they were good and that some unknown illusion or hidden impurity has not tainted them—those strangers who fling themselves upon us like the dead come forth from within to bring doubt and death to us.

It must be one of the natural features of the state of damnation that the subject, not seeing himself in God, and therefore not seeing his whole life in the eternal instant to which everything is present, all his good and evil acts come back upon him in the sterile endlessly questioning light of the memory of the dead, like enemy objects wholly detached from the actual existence in which subjectivity is definitively set, in the solitude of its ill-will which renders its own past a separate thing for it.

But when the subject reaches his end and sees himself in God and in divine eternity, all the moments of his past life are known to him in the actuality and the presentness of the instant in which they were lived, and all his acts (even the evil, now not only forgiven but leaving no spot nor shadow) are known as emanating presently out of the freshness of subjectivity, now itself become trans-luminous. And in the virtue of the vision in which his intelligence possesses the *Ipsum esse subsistens* he knows not only himself and all his life in a sovereignly existential manner, but also the other creatures whom in God he knows at last as subjects in the unveiled depth of their being.

The structure of the subject

To objectivise is to universalise. The intelligibles in which a subject objectivises itself for our mind are universal natures. It is in relation to the individuality itself of the subject (which the intelligence is not capable of grasping directly);

in relation to its subjectivity as subjectivity, as something unique and singular, incommunicable and unconceptualisable, and in relation also to the subject's own experience of its own subjectivity, that objectisation is false to the subject and that, known as object, it is unjustly known, as we have already observed. On the other hand, in relation to its essential structures, the subject is in no wise betrayed when it is made object. The objectivisation which universalises it and discerns in it intelligible natures, makes it known by a knowledge destined doubtless to continue to deepen, but not one that is in any sense unjust. Such a knowledge does no violence to the truth of the subject, but renders that truth present to the mind.

The subject, or suppositum, or person has an essence, an essential structure. It is a substance equipped with properties and which is acted upon and acts by the instrumentality of its potencies. The person is a substance whose substantial form is a spiritual soul; a substance which lives a life that is not merely biological and instinctive, but is also a life of intellect and will. It is a very simple-minded error to believe that subjectivity possesses no intelligible structure, on the ground that it is an inexhaustible depth; and to conceive of it as without any nature whatsoever for the purpose of making of it an absurd abyss of pure and formless liberty.

These observations allow us to understand why many contemporary philosophers, while they talk of nothing but person and subjectivity, nevertheless radically misunderstand those words. They remain lightheartedly ignorant of the metaphysical problem of *subsistence*. They do not see that personality, metaphysically considered, being the subsistence of the spiritual soul communicated to the human composite, and enabling the latter to possess its existence, to perfect itself and to give itself freely, bears witness in us to the generosity or expansivity of being which, in an incarnate spirit, proceeds from the spirit and which constitutes, in the secret springs of our ontological structure, a source of dynamic unity and unification from within.[12]

Because analysis wearies them, they are ignorant of what the proper life of the intelligence consists in, and in what the proper life of the will consists. They do not see that, because his *spirit* makes man cross the threshold of independence properly so-called, and of self-inwardness, the subjectivity of the person demands as its most intimate privilege communications proper to love and intelligence. They do not see that, even before the exercise of free choice, and in order to make free choice possible, the most deeply rooted need of the person is to communicate with *the other* by the union of the intelligence, and with *others* by the affective union. Their subjectivity is not a *self*, because it is wholly phenomenal.

I have already cited St. Thomas's aphorism, that the whole root of liberty is established in the reason. What reveals subjectivity to itself is not an irrational break (however profound and gratuitous it may be) in an irrational flow of moral and psychological phenomena, of dreams, automatisms, urges, and images surging upwards from the unconscious. Neither is it the anguish of forced choice. It is self-mastery for the purpose of self-giving. When a man has the obscure intuition of subjectivity, the reality, whose sudden invasion of his consciousness he experiences, is that of a secret totality, which contains both itself and its upsurge, and which superabounds in knowledge and love. Only by love does it attain to its supreme level of existence—existence as self-giving.

'This is what I mean: Self-knowledge as a mere psychological analysis of phenomena more or less superficial, a wandering through images and memories, is but an egotistic awareness, however valuable it may be. But when it becomes ontological, then knowledge of the Self is transfigured, implying intuition of Being and the discovery of the actual abyss of subjectivity. At the same time, it is the discovery of the basic generosity of existence. Subjectivity, this essentially dynamic, living and open centre, both receives and gives. It receives through the intellect, by superexisting in knowledge. It gives through the will, by superexisting in love; that is, by having within itself other beings as inner attractions directed towards them and giving oneself to them, and by spiritually existing in the manner of a gift. And "it is better to give than to receive." The spiritual existence of love is the supreme revelation of existence for the Self. The Self, being not only a material individual but also a spiritual personality, possesses itself and holds itself in hand in so far as it is spiritual and in so far as it is free. And to what purpose does it possess itself and dispose of itself, if not for what *is better*, in actual existence and absolutely speaking, or to give of itself? Thus it is that when a man has been really awakened to the sense of being or existence, and grasps intuitively the obscure, living depth of the Self and subjectivity, he discovers by the same token the basic generosity of existence and realises, by virtue of the inner dynamism of this intuition, that love is not a passing pleasure or emotion, but the very meaning of his being alive.'[13]

By love, finally, is shattered the impossibility of knowing another except as object. I have emphasised this impossibility above at length and noted that it directly concerns the senses and the intellect. To say that union in love makes the being we love another *ourself* for us is to say that it makes that being another subjectivity for us, another subjectivity that is ours. To the degree that we truly love (which is to say, not for ourselves but for the beloved; and when—which is not always the case—the intellect within us becomes passive as regards love, and, allowing its concepts to slumber, thereby renders love a formal means of knowledge), to this degree we acquire an obscure knowledge of the being we love, similar to that which we possess of ourselves; we know that being in his very subjectivity (at least in a certain measure) by this experience of union. Then he himself is, in a certain degree, cured of his solitude; he can, though still disquieted, rest for a moment in the nest of knowledge that we possess of him as subject.

NOTES

1. Cf. the *Further Elucidations on the Notion of Subsistence* which I wrote for the new translation of *The Degrees of Knowledge* (New York: Scribner's, 1957). Here are some excerpts from this essay:

"The *esse*, is perceived quite precisely—even as in their own order intellection and volition—as an *exercised act*, exercised by the thing or the existent subject, or as an activity in which the existent itself is engaged, an energy that it exerts. Existence is therefore not only received, as if by *esse* essences were pinned outside nothingness like a picture hung on a wall. Existence is not only received, it is also *exercised*. . . . But to exercise existence something besides the bare essence is necessary, namely the suppost or person. *Actiones sunt suppositorum*, actions are proper to supposts, and especially and above all the act of exercising existence. In other words, to exercise existence the essence must be completed by subsistence and thus become a suppost. . . . Since existence by its very notion demands, as we have just seen, that it be not only received but exercised, and since this exigency, pertaining as it does to the existential order, places us outside and beyond the order of essence, it must be said that (substantial) essence or nature can *receive* existence only by *exercising* it, which it cannot do as long as it remains in its own essential order. In other words, it can receive existence only on condition of being drawn at the same time from the state of simple essence and placed in an *existential state* which makes of it a quod capable of exercising existence. This *state* which completes, or rather surcompletes the essence—not at all in the line of essence itself, but in relation to a completely other order, the existential order—and permits the essence (henceforth suppost) to *exercise* existence is precisely subsistence. . . .

So the proper effect of subsistence is to place the individual nature in a state of *exercising existence*, with the incommunicability proper to the individual nature. . . . This is the promotion on to a new plane of the incommunicability which defines singularity. Subsistence renders the essence (become suppost) capable of existing *per se separatim*, because it renders an individual nature (become suppost) capable of exercising existence." (Pp. 436–38).

2. Cf. J. Maritain, *De Bergson à Thomas d'Aquin*, Chap. VI ('Spontaneity and Independence').

3. Cf. J. Maritain, *Quatre essais sur l'Esprit dans sa condition charnelle*, Chap. III. See "Natural Mystical Experience and the Void" in *Ransoming the Time* (1941).

4. Cf. J. Maritain, *De Bergson à Thomas d'Aquin*, pp. 160–61.

5. Cf. Jacques and Raïssa Maritain, *Situation de la poésie*, Paris, 1947; English tr. *The Situation of Poetry*, 1955.

6. Cf. *Les Degrés du savoir*, pp. 432–47, Eng. trans., pp. 218–26.

7. Is it necessary to explain that when we employ the word *subject* in speaking of God, we do not do so in the sense in which the word signifies receptivity as regards forms or accidents (for in this sense God is obviously not a 'subject': cf. *Sum. Theol.*, I, q. 3, a. 6 and 7), but in the sense in which, as the moderns employ it, the word signifies subsistence and Self? In this circumstance the word *subject* is like the word *hypostasis* which

has a similar etymology and which is predicated formally-eminently of God (cf. *Sum. Theol.*, I, q. 29, a. 3).

8. *John* I, 18.

9. Cf. *Les Degrés du savoir*, pp. 478–84, Eng. trans., pp. 241–44.

10. W. Somerset Maugham, *The Summing Up*, 1938, § 5.

11. See Franz Kafka, *Amerika*, New York, 1946, p. 174 (English translation by Edwin Muir).

12. Cf. J. Maritain, *La Personne et le Bien commun*, Paris, 1947, p. 34 (Eng. trans., N.Y., 1947, p. 31.).

13. Cf. J. Maritain, 'A New Approach to God,' in *Our Emergent Civilization*, ed. by Ruth Nanda Anshen, Harper and Brothers, N.Y., 1947, pp. 285–86. By permission of the publishers.

11. THE HUMAN CONDITION

Great challenges to accepted ideas took place in the course of the nineteenth century, from which the coarsest materialist metaphysics or anti-metaphysics at first tried to claim the profit. I am thinking of the three great intellectual shocks that shook the confidence of man in himself, and which in reality could be salutary and powerfully assist moral philosophy, if we knew how to understand things as they should be understood, and if modern man, instead of abdicating under humiliation, stood erect again in the two conjoined virtues of humility and magnanimity.

The first great disturbance was produced by Darwinism, with the theory of the animal origin of man. Such a shock can have a double result: a result ruinous for moral life, and which dehumanizes man, if one believes that man is only an evolved monkey; one has then the materialistic ethic of the struggle for life.

But the same shock can have a salutary result if one understands things in another way, if one understands that the matter out of which man is made is an animal matter, but an animal matter informed by a spiritual soul, so that there is biological continuity in the sense of the natural sciences between the universe of the animal and the universe of man, but irreducible metaphysical discontinuity. The scientific concept of evolution is then likely to lead us to a better appreciation of the vicissitudes and the progress of human history, and to an ethic more conscious of the material roots of the rational animal, of the depths of the dynamism of the irrational element in him, but also of the deeper depths of the dynamism of the spirit in him that makes his grandeur.

A second shock was that of Marxism, with its insistence on the economic substructure of our moral ideas and of our rules of moral behavior. Here again a double result is possible. The result is ruinous for human life if one fancies that all that is not the economic factor is only an epiphenomenal superstructure; one moves then towards a materialist ethic—

either towards a materialist ethic suspended from the myth of technocracy organizing human life on the basis of pure productivity; or towards a materialist ethic such as the Marxist ethic, suspended from the myth of revolution and from that of the self-creation of man manifested by the titanic struggle of the working class freeing itself through violence from a condition presumed to be irremediably servile, and by the final coming of a universal communist society.

The result can be salutary if the shock in question forces us to be aware of the interdependence and interaction, interpreted in an Aristotelian sense, of economic factors and moral or spiritual factors. Ethics becomes then more conscious of the concrete situation of man, and of the meeting of structures and conditionings dependent upon material causality with what, in the order of formal causality, constitutes morality. A new field of exploration is opened up for ethics, a field independent in itself of Marxist theory, which however supplied the impulse for this new problematic.

The third shock finally was that of the discoveries of Freud, bringing to light the autonomous life and the swarming activity of the unconscious, and the ruses by which it seeks to take control of human conduct.

The result is ruinous for human life if man is looked upon as a creation of mere infra-rational tendencies, of libido and of the unconscious of instinct, without reason being thought to possess any vitality and energy of its own or to exercise any control other than a purely extrinsic one over the forces in conflict in the determinism of nature, and without one's according any reality to the universe of liberty which is the very universe of morality.

The result is salutary if the shock in question tends to lead us to recognize the immense universe of instincts and tendencies at the point of which reason and liberty work. Then ethics becomes more conscious of the concrete situation (no longer social, but psychological) of man, and of the meeting of the precombined structures and disguises of the unconscious with moral conscience. Thence an ethic more truly human, in this sense that it will know better what is human, and in this sense that it will care with more pity for man and his wounds.

The great problem of the relations between the conscious and the unconscious will be one of its principal concerns. It will be a question of establishing a normal relation between the dreaming and sleeping part of man and the waking part. It can happen that the waking part may exercise no rule, no control, or a pseudo-control only, over the dreaming part. Man is then the plaything of unconscious tendencies, which a banal process of lying rationalization will endeavor only to justify.

It can also happen, on the contrary, that the waking part may mistrust the dreaming part, hold it in contempt, and fear it, to such a degree that it may wish at any price to become conscious of all that takes place in us, to light up forcibly all the innermost recesses and to put conscious reason and deliberate will at the origin of all the movements of the soul. It is to be feared that this second method succeeds mainly in developing neuroses and in bringing about the victory of the disguises and ruses of the unconscious.

In other words, a despotic regime with regard to the unconscious is no better than an anarchic regime. What should be sought is—to use one of Aristotle's words—a *politic* control, that is, a control exercising an authority that would be without violence and based on friendship, taming to the spirit the vital spontaneities, in short, supposing a certain confidence in the sleeping part of man and a progressive purification of it. Such a purification is not brought about by trying to make this unconscious emerge from sleep, but by being at once attentive to this sleep and respectful of it, and by recognizing with an entirely frank and pure glance, without fright and without connivance, all that emerges from this sleeping part.[1]

What would also be required, and first of all, is to recognize the existence in man of another unconscious[2] than the animal unconscious of instinct, desires and images, repressed tendencies and traumatic memories, which asks only to be closed up in itself as an inferno of the soul. This other unconscious is the unconscious or pre-conscious of the spirit, which is not separated from the world of conscious activity and the works of reason, but on the contrary is their living source. It is on the activating motions—when man does not betray them—and the radiance of this spiritual unconscious on the whole soul, that depends above all the long work through which the instinctive spontaneities can be, as I said above, *tamed* to the spirit.

The considerations that follow do not have to do with doctrines and systems, they bear on human conduct itself and on the most general options with which our attitude in life is linked. Every great moral system, indeed, is in reality an effort to ask man, in one manner or another and to one degree or another, to go beyond his natural condition in some way. But either these same great philosophical doctrines refuse to acknowledge the effort in question, or else they leave in a wholly implicit state the problem it envelops. To my mind, on the contrary, it is important to disengage the problem explicitly. One sees then that it concerns the moral life of each one of us in such a fundamental way, and involves so profoundly the individual subjectivity, that it depends, to tell the truth, on a sort of metaphysics of conduct which precedes moral theories and systematizations. If one tries to examine it in itself, reducing things to the essential, one is led, it seems to me, to distinguish the four different attitudes I am about to discuss, of which the first two, more or less outlined, in fact, in the lives of certain among us, but impossible to carry through, are too irrational to correspond to any definite doctrine; and of which the last two correspond, one to the thought of India, the other, inchoatively, to the Western philosophical tradition, and, under its perfected and really effective form, to Christian thought.

The fact is, I believe, that in the background of all our moral difficulties there is a fundamental problem which is ineluctably posed for each of us, and which in practice is never fully resolved, except in those who have entered into the ways of perfection: the problem of the relation of man to the human condition, or of his attitude in the face of the human condition.

This condition is that of a spirit united in substance with flesh and engaged in the universe of matter. It is an unhappy condition. In itself it is such a miserable condition that man has always dreamed of a golden age when he was more or less freed of it, and so miserable that on the plane of revelation, the Christian religion teaches that mankind was created, with the grace of Adam, in a superior condition in which it was free of sin, of pain, of servitude and of death, and from which it fell through its own fault. The Judeo-Christian tradition also teaches that after the end of history and in a new world the human condition will be supernaturally transfigured. Those who believe neither in the state of innocence nor in original sin put the golden age at the end of history, not at the beginning, and fancy that man will attain it in the last stage of his terrestrial adventure, through his own liberating effort, thanks to science and to radical social transformations; others, who want no part of consoling illusions, try to escape the spectacle of this planet by surrendering to some powerful passion which distracts them day after day from themselves and from the world, or by the ardor of a despairing pity which in a way appeases their hearts while it corrodes them little by little.

Indeed, the tragic perplexity in which we are placed consists in the fact that we can neither refuse the human condition nor accept it purely and simply. I will explain later on in what sense I understand the expression "to accept *purely and simply* the human condition". As to refusing the human condition, it is clear that it is a question there only of a moral disposition. Such a refusal belongs to the world of a dream; but man nourishes himself on dreams, and a dream which has its roots in the depths of the individual psychology of the subject can determine his fundamental attitude in life.

The temptation to refuse the Human Condition

It is solely in the perspective of nature that we shall consider things in this and the three following sections. We have just noted that the human condition is an unhappy condition. The state of intermediary species is in general a state little to be envied; and it is in a paradoxically eminent manner that the human species, at once flesh and spirit, is an intermediary species. The heavens tell of the glory of God, but the earth that He has made is dreadful to man. A "vale of tears", yes, and this is not a mere poetic image.

It is not a question here of any sort of Manichaeism. It is quite true that the material universe abounds in wonders and is resplendent with an inexhaustible beauty that makes apparent the mark of the Spirit Who created it; it is quite true that despite the cruelty and voracity which inhabit it the world of nature is penetrated with the goodness and the generosity of being, and embraces finally all things in the imperturbable peace of its great laws, and of its great rational necessities which superbly ignore us; it is quite true that in man himself the world of the senses, whatever bitterness it may harbor, is made first and above all to enchant us with its sweetnesses and its joys; it is quite true that human nature is good in its essence, and that for every living being, but eminently for man, to live is a marvellous gift. And yet, for all that, a spirit whose operations have need of matter surmounts matter only at a formidable price and by running immense risks, and is most often scoffed at by it. The spirit is immortal, and matter imposes the law of death on the body animated by it. Man has more grandeur than the Milky Way; but how easy evil is for him, how inevitable (if one considers the species collectively) it is, in a being in which sense and instinct, and the animal unconscious, ask only to elude or to twist the judgment of the mind. As for suffering, it is already a frightful thing to see an animal suffer, but the suffering of beasts is of small account in comparison with the suffering that pierces a flesh united to spirit, or spirit itself.

Thus we can understand that the temptation to refuse the human condition has a greater chance of worming its way into us when man has in one manner or another become better aware of the natural exigencies of the spirit in him—of that spirit which is his soul, and which reveals itself to him in the highest powers of the soul. Such a temptation does not exist in the primitives. We may believe that in the collective history of mankind it is largely this temptation which, at work in us without our being aware of it, makes the very progress through which civilization advances go side by side with delusions which impair it or degradations which corrupt it.

To refuse—in one's innermost heart—the human condition, is either to dream of leaving our limits and to wish to enjoy a total liberty in which our nature would expand through its own powers; or else to play the pure spirit (what I once called the sin of angelism); or else to curse and try to disown all that presents an obstacle to the life of the intellect, and to live in a state of interior revolt against the fact that one is a man; or else to flee by no matter what frenzy, even if it be in the folly of the flesh, this situation of a reason everywhere at loggerheads with matter which is a permanent challenge to the demands of the spirit in us. It is hardly surprising that those who devote themselves to the life of the intelligence, the poet in particular, and the philosopher, are more or less exposed to this temptation. The ancient sages of Greece succumbed to it when they said that the best thing for man is not to have been born.

In the life of an individual the most frequent occasion for this temptation—which does not justify it for all that—is that the man who endeavors, as Aristotle said, "to live according to the intellect", is more conscious than those who live "according to the human" of everything we said above concerning the misery of the human condition. Often even the man dedicated to meditation forgets that the spirit finds, through the senses, the source of its life in the very matter that torments it; he forgets too that the evils that matter causes are made transitory to a certain extent by matter itself, since it is a root principle of change.

But above all, if he pays attention to the lessons of history and to the long cry of the poor and the abandoned, he understands that naked suffering, horror, anguish without consolation—all this is the true background of the world for us, however generous nature may be, and however admirable the victories won by human generations to make things less hostile to man and the structures of his own life more worthy of him, through the progress of civilization, of art and of knowledge. It may be that for a long while we almost lose sight of this background of the world. But every now and then it reappears to us.

The man who has passed the threshold of the life according to the intellect understands all that is offensive and humiliating—for that spirit in which his specific difference itself and his dignity consist—in the radical contingency linked with matter and the dependence with regard to matter which constitute the metaphysical infirmity of our existence. In the eyes of material nature is a man worth any more than the sound of the brook? To pursue its work there the spirit struggles ceaselessly against the fortuitous and the useless; its very movement depends not only on the absolute values in which it has its proper object, it depends also on chance, on good and bad encounters; it advances from generation to generation enduring a perpetual agony, only to have in the end what it has produced here on earth fall—I mean with regard to men, and unless it is divinely protected—under the law of decay and futility which is the law of matter, and only to have what is immortal in itself be received by our species only at the cost of equivocations and misunderstandings that are perpetuated throughout time.

The fact remains that all that must be accepted. Even when they do not repeat in their own way, and however pitifully, the story of Faust, there is no sadder and more fruitless distress than the distress of men who under the pretext of wanting to live according to the intellect allow themselves to be carried away by the temptation to refuse the human condition. They are vanquished beforehand, and their defeat aggravates their subjection.

The temptation to accept purely and simply the Human Condition

Would the solution therefore be to accept *purely and simply* the human condition?—This pure and simple acceptance would be just as costly, and is no less impossible. It would be a betrayal of human nature not to recognize the demands, which are consubstantial to it, of the superhuman in man, and this nature's need of the progressive movement of the spirit, with its torments and its dangers, in other words, its need of perpetually going beyond the presently given moment of our condition on earth. And if we want to go beyond it, it is because to that extent we do not accept it without reserve.

It is fitting moreover to see the whole import of the expressions one uses. To accept the human condition is to accept—with all that life offers of the good and the beautiful and the pure, and with all the grandeurs of the spirit, and with "the call of the hero"—the radical contingency, the failures, the servitudes, the immense part of sorrow and (as regards nature) of inevitable uselessness of our existence, sickness, death, the different kinds of tyranny and hypocrisy which prey on social life, the stench of gangrene and the stench of money, the power of stupidity and of the lie. But if it is a question for a man of accepting *purely and simply* the human condition, why then, after all, in accepting all the evil of suffering that our nature entails, should he not accept at the same stroke all the evil of sin to which it is inclined? He has been made as he is, with the weaknesses of his flesh and the covetousness that is in him, with the longing for pleasure and power and the rage of desires, of that obsessing desire especially which does not come from him but from his species, to which his individual person matters little but which has need of his chromosomes in order to perpetuate itself. All that also is part of the human condition. To accept *purely and simply* (if that were possible) the human condition, means to accept it in its entirety, with the misery of sin as well as with the misery of suffering.

This cannot be, moreover, without a fundamental contradiction and without additional torments. For the social groups—horde or society—and the state of culture without which the human species cannot endure on earth require rules and taboos guaranteed by terrifying sanctions; and it is essential to the human condition that the sense of moral obligation, and of the distinction between good and evil, which exists naturally in the soul of each one of us (and which is in itself contradictory to the acceptance of moral evil as supposedly required by our nature), exert itself at least under the wholly exteriorized form of obedience to tribal prohibitions, and according as good and evil appear only as what is permitted or forbidden by the social group. To accept *purely and simply* the human condition is therefore an intrinsically contradictory moral disposition (although more or less outlined in fact in a great number of human beings)—a disposition to accept not only subjection to Sin as well as subjection to Suffering, but also subjection to the law of Fear, which forbids certain definite faults as infractions of the general conduct and the rules of the closed society.

Supposing that it could be fully carried out, such an acceptance of the human condition would make man live on the edge of animality; it is, as we have noted, as impossible in reality as the refusal of the human condition, because to accept fully subjection to moral evil, in whatever manner one conceives it, is not possible for the human being. What we are calling *pure and simple* acceptance of the human condition is only a limit to which, even in its most primitive representatives, our species has never attained. Indeed, it is in more or less approaching this limit that many among us seem to accept purely and simply the human condition. They accept it *almost* purely and simply. They not only have the code of their gang, their class or their accustomed social group (which implies already, though under a very inferior form, the prohibition of wrongdoing), they have also an outline at least, and often a great deal more than an outline, of authentic moral life, by reason of which they do not love the evil that they do. But even if their conscience has in other respects firm convictions, there are a certain number of domains—notably the domain of sex, and, in certain periods, that of "honor" (duel), and that of war—in which to act without taking account of the moral law seems normal in their eyes; it's the human condition that requires it, they believe that at this point it imposes another code on them. Perhaps however they will repent one day of the actions thus committed in contempt of the moral law (not to speak of many others among us who violate the law only in the pangs of remorse). To do evil and to repent of the evil that one does is the minimum of what the human being is capable of to testify that it is impossible to give in completely to the temptation to accept *purely and simply* the human condition.

The answer to Indian spirituality

What is asked of man is neither to accept purely and simply nor to refuse the human condition—it is to transcend it.[3] Here too however two very different ways can be envisaged. It can be a question of transcending the human condition in a manner which implies a certain refusal of it (because in this case it is through his own forces that man has to transcend his condition, he must then engage himself in an effort against the grain of nature); or it can be a question of transcending the human condition while consenting to it (because in this case a "new nature" has been grafted on human nature, and permits man to transcend his condition by going, not against the grain of nature, but higher than nature). The first way corresponds to what we shall call, to be brief, the Hindu-Buddhist solution; the second, to what we shall call the Gospel solution.

By abolishing, by means of a sovereign concentration of the intellect and the will, every particular form and representation, the wisdom of India adheres, through the void, to an absolute which is the Self in its pure metaphysical act of existing—experience conceived as leading at the same stroke either to the Transcendence of Being (Atman) or to total indetermination (nirvâna). All the forms of illusion in the midst of which our life is spent have disappeared, everything is denied and annihilated, there remains only the Self in contact with itself.

It is clear that to attain such an end (not to speak of the "powers" for which one is supposed to search without pause), is to transcend the human condition by dint of spiritual energy. But it is also clear that it is to transcend it by the means of refusal. The living delivered one gains a sort of interior omnipotence by falling back upon himself and separating himself from everything human; he enters into a solitariness incomparably more profound than the solitude of the hermit, for it is his soul itself which has broken with men and all the miseries of their terrestrial existence. To pass beyond illusion, and to deliver oneself from transmigration, or at least from all the sorrow that it carries with it and perpetuates, is at the same stroke to deliver oneself from the human condition. The refusal of this condition is there but a means of transcending it, it is not an act of revolt against it, a pure and simple refusal. It remains however essential to the spirituality of India. That is why, even when the sage, as in the Buddhism of the Great Vehicle (Mahayana), spreads his pity over men, it is as it were through the condescension of a being who no longer belongs to their species, and whose heart—by the very exigency of solitariness in nirvâna—is not wounded by their troubles and does not enter into participation with them.

How can we not see in the implicit refusal of the human

condition of which I have just spoken one of the weak points of the spirituality of India? If one considers in itself (independently of the graces which in fact can supervene in a soul of good will) this effort to escape the state in which we are naturally placed by our coming into the world, it manifests, along with an exceptional courage, an exceptional pride of spirit. Moreover such a refusal is in reality doomed, whatever victories it may bring, to a final defeat. Courage and pride are precisely two of the most profound features of the human condition. The Hindu or Buddhist sage quits the human condition only by showing in spite of himself his belonging to it—I mean, by the very negations to which he is led and all the apparatus of exercises and techniques he needs, and by the kind of never-ending *tour de force* by means of which he comes to transcend this condition. And the living delivered one still has to die like the others; he is not delivered from that which is the most tragically human in the human condition.

The Gospel answer

What of the Christian or Gospel solution? It takes us beyond pure philosophy and pure reason, and yet, by a strange paradox, it is in it and in the mystery that it proposes to us that an authentically rational attitude toward the human condition becomes possible for man.

I said above that every great moral system is in reality an effort to ask man, in one manner or another and to one degree or another, to go beyond his natural condition in some way. These systems in fact (let us mention here only those which have been examined in the present work) ask man—while he rejects moral evil but accepts the suffering to which the human condition is exposed—to go beyond the human condition: either, as with Plato, Aristotle, the Stoics, Epicurus, Kant, Sartre or Bergson, by attaching himself to a good superior to human life, or to a happiness in which human life is achieved rationally, or to virtue, or to pleasure decanted to the point of indifference, or to duty, or to liberty, or to the sovereign love to which the great mystics call us; or, as with Hegel, Marx, Comte or Dewey, by deifying nature. But even in those cases where the effort to go beyond the human condition is the most authentic, there is the question, except in Bergson (and, in the name of faith, in Kierkegaard) of truly transcending it. And the attempt to go beyond the human condition by the sole means of man remains in the last analysis doomed either to futility or to illusion. It is only with Christianity that the effort to go beyond the human condition comes to real fruition.

It is superfluous to remark that I am not speaking here of the average behavior of the mass of people of Christian denomination. I am speaking of the exigencies of Christianity such as they are proposed to every one—and almost completely realized only in saints.

The question for the Christian is to transcend the human condition but by the grace of God—not, as for the Indian sage, by a supreme concentration on oneself—and in consenting at the same time to this condition, in accepting it, although not purely and simply, without balking; for the Christian accepts it as to all that pertains to the evil of suffering proper to the human condition, not as to what pertains to moral evil and sin. Rupture with the human condition as to sin, acceptance of the human condition as to the radical contingency and as to the suffering as well as to the joys that it entails: that is demanded by reason, but is decidedly possible only by the configuration of grace to Him Who is sanctity itself because He is the Word incarnate. At the same stroke, the acceptance of the human condition ceases to be simple submission to necessity; it becomes active consent, and consent through love.

That in a certain measure every soul inhabited by the gifts of grace, and in a full measure the saint, the one who has entered into what we have called the regime of supra-ethics,* transcends the human condition—this is obvious to anyone who holds that grace is a participation in the divine life itself. It is the other aspect of the Gospel solution, the simultaneous acceptance (except as to sin) of the human condition that it is important for us to insist on here.

In the human condition thus transcended and accepted at

* See *Moral Philosophy*, pp. 364–70.

the same time, everything, to tell the truth, remains the same and everything is transfigured. If grace makes man participate in the divine life and if it superelevates his nature in its own order, nevertheless it is a nature still wounded which is thus superelevated, it is a man still devoured by weakness who shares in eternal life and in God's friendship. The human condition has not changed. It has not changed because the Word of God assumed it such as it was and such as it will remain as long as history endures. In taking upon Himself all the sins of the world, He who was without sin also took upon Himself all the languors of the world, and all the suffering that afflicts the human race, and all the humiliation of its dependence with regard to the contingent and the fortuitous. What matter henceforth the contingency and the metaphysical futility to which our existence is subjected, since the most insignificant of our acts, if it is vivified by charity, has an eternal value, and since the Son of God has accepted to undergo Himself the servitudes of our condition?

During His hidden life He was a poor village workman, and His activity as preacher and miracle-worker took place in an historical milieu which made weigh on Him all its circumstances of time and place and all its hazards. He willed to die as the most unfortunate of men died in His time. His passion was an atrocious condescension of all the agony and abjection attached to the human condition since the Fall.

Consequently, when what I called just now the true background of the world—the world of naked suffering, of horror, of anguish without consolation—reveals itself to the Christian and takes possession of him, this matter of accepting (as to the evil of suffering) the human condition takes on an entirely new sense for him, comes to enter into the redemptive work of the Cross, and to participate in the annihilations of Him Whom he loves.[4] No wonder the saints are desirous of suffering. Suffering, because it is for them a signature of their love, and co-operation in the work of their Beloved, has become for them the most precious of goods here on earth.

There they are, then, the saints, who by an apparent contradiction give thanks to God for all the goods He heaps upon them and for all the protections, consolations and joys He dispenses to them, and give thanks to Him at the same time for all the evils and afflictions He sends them. We who are wicked, do we give a stone to our children when they ask us for bread? And yet thanks be to God when He gives us bread, and thanks be to Him when He gives us a stone and worse than a stone. The evil of suffering, while remaining what it is, and while being fully experienced as such, is transvalued now in a superior good, one perfectly invisible besides, unless there appear for an instant some sign of the more than human peace that inhabits the tortured soul.

The unbeliever sees here only a ghastly facility that religion allows itself, playing on two boards at the same time. The believer sees here the supreme grandeur of a mystery accessible to faith alone, and which can—in faith—be attained in some fashion and stammered by the intelligence, but which remains in itself as incomprehensible as God Himself.

It is doubtless for the philosopher that this mystery is the most incomprehensible, because the philosopher knows too well that essences do not change, and that in the ordinary course of things, suffering, unless the one that it visits undertakes bravely to surmount it, degrades and humiliates the human being. He would be a fool however if he did not bow before the testimony of the saints. But in his perspective as a philosopher the best he can say is that God's love is as transcendent as His being, which is as no thing is; and that it is more difficult still for the heart of man to apprehend the transcendence of Love subsisting by itself than it is for the human intelligence to apprehend the transcendence of Love subsisting by itself than it is for the human intelligence to apprehend the transcendence of Being subsisting by Itself. "Believe that God loves you *in a way that you cannot imagine*," said Dostoevski.[5]

And here again can the philosopher refrain from asking some questions?

He is astonished by another apparent contradiction in the behavior of the saints. They desire suffering as the most precious of goods here below. After all, that's their affair, or rather an affair between God and them. But what about the others, those whom they love, and who comprise all men? Do they not desire for them also this most precious of goods here on earth? Yet this is not what they do, they spend their time trying to lessen the suffering of men and to cure them of their wounds. The answer, to the extent that one can catch a glimpse of it, concerns the very structure of the spirit.

In itself suffering is an evil, and will always remain an evil. How then could one wish it for those one loves? The simple knowledge possessed by the Christian (and so frequently re-called to his attention by the commonplaces of pious litera-ture) that suffering unites the soul inhabited by charity to the sacrifice of the Cross, superimposes on suffering, ideally and theoretically, a quality thanks to which this knowledge helps one to accept suffering; it cannot make it be loved or de-sired, it does not transvalue it. If there is real and practical transvaluation, it can only be in the fire of the actual and ab-solutely incommunicable love between the self of a man and the divine Self; and that remains a closed secret, valid only for the individual subjectivity. Thus the saints would keep for themselves alone what they consider to be the most precious of goods here on earth. Singular egoists! They want suffering for themselves, they do not want it for others. Jesus wept over the dead Lazarus, and over the sorrow of Martha and Mary.

But the philosopher has still other questions. What strikes him above all in the human condition is not the suffering of the saints, it is the suffering of the mass of men, the suffering they have not willed, the suffering that falls on them like a beast. How could he resign himself to the suffering of men?

He knows that the struggle against suffering is one of the aspects of the effort through which humanity goes forward, and that in this struggle the work of reason and the ferment of the Gospel, the progress of science and the progress of social justice, and the progress of the still so rudimentary knowledge that man has of himself, enable us constantly to gain ground. He is not tempted to adore the Great Being, but he renders thanks to the men—to the innumerable work-ers known and unknown who throughout the course of an im-mense history, by dint of inventive genius and sacrifice of self, have applied themselves and will always apply them-selves to making the earth more habitable. But the philoso-pher also knows that as one gains ground in the struggle against suffering, new causes of suffering begin to abound, so that man, despite all his progress, will never have done with suffering just as he will never have done with sickness.[6] Modern man suffers in other ways than the cave man. On the whole, one can wonder whether he suffers less; one can wonder whether all the victories gained in the struggle against suffering do not result in maintaining, by compensating the progress in suffering, a kind of middle level at which life as a whole is almost tolerable. However this may be, there will always remain enough suffering to put the heart and the intelligence in anguish.

Thus the answers that the philosopher gives himself in thinking about the suffering of men are valid but insufficient. There is another answer still, one that not only concerns terrestrial history but also and above all eternal life. It was given in the Sermon on the Mount.

If there is in humanity an immense mass of suffering which is not redemptive like that of Christ and His saints, it is in order that it may be redeemed, and that everywhere at least where human liberty does not intrude its refusal, those who have wept in our valleys may be consoled forever.

NOTES

1. See the remarks made on the *know thyself* (apropos Kierkegaard), *Moral Philosophy* (New York: Charles Scribner's Sons, 1964), Ch. XIII, pp. 355–56.
2. See my book *Creative Intuition in Art and Poetry* (New York: Pantheon, 1953), pp. 91–92; pocketbook edition (New York: Meridian Books, 1955), p. 67; (London: Harvill, 1954).
3. I am not speaking of the Hegelian-Marxist answer to the problem of the human condition. In this perspective it is not a question of transcending the human condition, but of transforming it and finally of deifying it, through the work of history and of man himself. Such a solution rests on a manifestly erroneously philosophical postulate, in which the notion of human nature gives way to that of process of self-creation of man by man.
4. "Our annihilation is the most powerful means we have of uniting ourselves to Jesus and of doing good to souls," wrote Father de Foucauld. Cf. Jean-François Six, *Itinéraire spirituel de Charles de Foucauld* (Paris: Seuil, 1958), p. 364.
5. Cf. Henri Troyat, *Sainte Russie* (Paris: Grasset, 1956), p. 149.
6. Cf. René Dubos, *Mirage of Health* (New York: Harper, 1959).

12. THE IMMORTALITY OF MAN

I

Let us think of the human being, not in an abstract and general way, but in the most concrete possible, the most *personal* fashion. Let us think of this certain old man we have known for years in the country,—this old farmer with his wrinkled face, his keen eyes which have beheld so many harvests and so many earthly horizons, his long habits of patience and suffering, courage, poverty and noble labor, a man perhaps like those parents of a great living American statesman whose photographs appeared some months ago in a particularly moving copy of a weekly magazine. Or let us think of this certain boy or this girl who are our relatives or our friends, whose everyday life we well know, and whose loved appearance, whose soft or husky voice is enough to rejoice our hearts. Let us remember—remember in our heart—a single gesture of the hand, or the smile in the eyes of one we love. What treasures on earth, what masterpieces of art or of science, could pay for the treasures of life, feeling, freedom and memory, of which this gesture, this smile is the fugitive expression? We perceive intuitively that nothing in the world is more precious than one single human being. I am well aware how many difficult questions come to mind at the same time and I shall come back to these difficulties, but for the present I wish only to keep in mind this simple and decisive intuition, by means of which the incomparable value of the human person is revealed to us. Moreover, St. Thomas Aquinas warns us that the Person is what is noblest and most perfect in the whole of nature.

Nothing, however, nothing in the world is more squandered, more wasted than a human being. Nothing is spent so prodigally, so heedlessly, as though a man were a bit of small change in the hand of careless Nature. Surely it is a crime to throw away human lives more cruelly and contemptuously than the lives of cattle, to submit them to the merciless will-to-power of totalitarian states or of insatiate conquerors. The present-day transportations of populations, concentration camps, wars of enslavement, are signs of a criminal contempt for mankind unheard of until now. Surely it is shameful as well to contemplate throughout the world the debasing standards of life imposed on so many human beings in their slums of distress and starvation. As Burke wrote a century and a half ago, "the blood of man should never be shed but to redeem the blood of man. It is well shed for our family, for our friends, for our God, for our country, for our kind. The rest is vanity; the rest is crime." Yet since the blood of man is well shed for our family, for our friends, for our country, for our kind, for our God, this very fact shows that many things are indeed worth a man's sacrifice of his earthly life. What things? Things of a truly human and divine value, things that involve and preserve that justice, that freedom, that sacred respect for truth and for the dignity of the spirit without which human existence becomes unlivable; things that a man may and should love more than his own flesh and blood, just because they pertain to the great task of redeeming the blood of man.

But what I should like to emphasize is the fact that in the obscure workings of the human species, in that immense network of solidarity each mesh of which is made of human effort and human risk, and advances in its small way the progression of the whole, there is an infinity of things, often of little things, for which men expose themselves to danger and self-sacrifice. Often the reasons for such lavish courage are not love or pure generosity, but only natural energy, or temerity, or longing for glory, or pleasure in confronting new difficulties, or desire for risk and adventure. All these, however, are carried away in that flood of superabundance and self-giving which springs from the sources of being, and which brings mankind towards its fulfillment. A scientist risks his life for a new discovery in the realm of matter, a pioneer to establish a new settlement, an aviator to improve our means of communication, a miner to extract coal from the earth, a pearl-fisher to filch from the ocean an ornament for the beauty of some unknown woman, a traveler to contemplate new landscapes, a mountain climber to conquer a bit of earth. What comparison is there between the result to be obtained, be it momentous or slight, and the price of human life which is thus wagered, the value of that being, full of promise, endowed with so many gifts and whom many hearts may love? Well, at each corner of human activity death lies in ambush. Every day we trust our life and the lives of our beloved to the unknown driver of a subway-train, of a plane, of a bus, or a taxi. Where there is no risk, there is no life. A wisdom or a civilization based on the avoidance of risk, by virtue of a misinterpretation of the value of the human being, would run the greatest of all risks, that of cowardice and of deadly stupidity. That perpetual risk which man takes is the very condition of his life. That squandering of the human being is a law of nature; it is also the proof of the confidence, the trust, and the elementary love we every day give to the divine principle from which we proceed, and the very law of which is superabundance and generosity.

Now we face a paradox: on the one hand nothing in the world is more precious than one single human person; on the other hand nothing in the world is more squandered, more exposed to all kinds of dangers than the human being—and this condition must be. What is the meaning of this paradox? It is perfectly clear. We have here a sign that man knows very well that death is not an end, but a beginning. He knows very well, in the secret depths of his own being, that he can run all risks, spend his life, and scatter his possessions here below, because he is immortal. The chant of the Christian liturgy before the body of the deceased is significant: Life is changed, life is not taken away.

II

As I have just noted, there is in men a natural, an instinctive knowledge of his immortality. This knowledge is not inscribed in man's intelligence, rather it is inscribed in his ontological structure; it is not rooted in the principles of reasoning, but in our very substance. The intelligence may become aware of this knowledge in an indirect way, and through some reflection, some turning back of thought upon the recesses of human subjectivity. The intelligence may also ignore this instinctive knowledge, and remain unaware of it, for our intelligence is naturally turned or diverted towards the being of external things. It may even deny the soul and immortality, by virtue of any set whatsoever of ideas and reasonings; yet, when the intellect of a man denies immortality, this man continues living, despite his rational convictions, on the basis of an unconscious and, so to speak, biological assumption of this very immortality—though it is rationally denied. Although such discrepancies are not infrequent among us, introducing many troubles, deviations or weaknesses into our behavior, they cannot disturb or annihilate the basic prerequisites of that behavior.

The instinctive knowledge of which I speak is a common and obscure knowledge. When a man is not an "intellectual" man—that is to say, when his intelligence, rarely busy with ideas, science and philosophy, follows for guidance only the natural tendencies of our species—this instinctive knowledge naturally reverberates in his mind. He does not doubt that another life will come after the present one. The possibility of doubt and error about what is most natural in the basic strata of human existence is the price paid for the progress of our species toward its rational fulfillment. Sometimes it is a very high price! The only solution, however, is not to try some sort of return to purely instinctive life, as D. H. Lawrence and many others have dreamed it. This regression, moreover, is quite impossible, and could only lead, not to nature, but to a perversion of civilized life. The only solution worthy of man is not a backward flight towards instinct, but a flight ahead towards reason, towards a reason which at last is well-equipped and knows the truth.

Of man's instinctive belief in his immortality, which is not a conceptual or philosophical knowledge, but a lived and practiced one, we have a striking sign in the behavior of primitive men. No matter how far back we look into the past, we always find the trace of funeral rites, of an extraordinary care about the dead and their life beyond the grave. What we know concerning the beliefs of primitive men shows us that their belief in immortality may assume the strangest and most aberrant forms. Sometimes, as in the old Chinese superstitions, the dead were terribly feared, and the living man was to take every precaution against their mischievousness. In any case, the ideas, the reasons and explanations by means of which primitive men sought to justify their belief and to imagine the survival of the dead seem to us very queer, often absurd. This oddness and absurdity of primitive mythologies, which Frazer emphasized with the naïveté of the civilized man, are easily explainable. On the one hand the mental climate of the primitive man is not the climate of reason, but that of imagination; the intelligence of primitive men—a very acute and awakened one, vitally immersed in nature—functions in a kind of dusk where the imagination rules. Their conceptions are regulated by the law of images. When this point is well understood, the myths of primitive men appear less absurd, much wiser even than some anthropologists believe. On the other hand, as regards belief in immortality, the conceptions of primitive man are not the result of any rational inquiry. On the contrary they only translate, according to the ebb and flow of the imaginative thought, a substantial—not intellectual—persuasion given him by nature. The more irrational and queer his myths of the soul and its survival appear, the more strikingly they give testimony to the fact that his certitude of survival is rooted in underground strata more profound and immovable, though less perfect and fertile, than the arable soil of reason.

How then can we explain the origin of the natural and instinctive knowledge of immortality? Here we must consider that the highest functions of the human mind, particularly the functions of judgment, are performed in the midst of a kind of consciousness which is vital and spontaneous and accompanies every achieved or perfected act of thought. This spontaneous or *concomitant* consciousness is to be carefully distinguished from the consecutive or *explicit* consciousness. The second one presupposes a special reflexive act, by means of which the mind comes back upon itself and produces special reflexive concepts, special reflexive judgments concerning what lies within itself. The concomitant consciousness does not do so. It only expresses the self-interiority, the self-involvement proper to the human mind; it is only the diffuse light of reflexivity—lived and practised, not conceptualized—within which every spiritual achievement is accomplished in the human soul. But such a spontaneous consciousness slips back to the very root and principle of our mental operations, attains this root as something unknown in itself, known only —and that is enough, moreover—as transcending all operations and psychic phenomena which proceed from it. The Self, the supraphenomenal Self, is thus obscurely but certainly attained by the spontaneous consciousness—in the night as regards every notion and conceptualization, with certainty as regards vital experience. This experience—not conceptually formulated, but practically lived by the intellect—of a supraphenomenal Self is the basic datum, the rock of spontaneous consciousness. Our intelligence knows that before thinking of that, this obscure knowledge is involved in every achieved act of thought, dealing with any matter whatsoever. When philosophical reflection forms and elaborates the idea of the Self, it attains thereby an object which human intelligence already knew—in a merely lived and unexpressed fashion— and now recognizes.

Human intelligence also knows—in the same obscure fashion—that this supraphenomenal Self, vitally grasped by spontaneous consciousness cannot disappear—precisely because it is grasped as a center which dominates all passing phenomena, the whole succession of temporal images. That is to say, the Self, the knower able to know its own existence, is superior to time. All perceptions and images which succeed one another, composing the fluent show of this world, may vanish, as happens when a man sleeps without dreaming. The Self cannot vanish, because death, as well as sleep, is an event in time, and the Self is above time. This vivid perception—even if it remains unformulated, in the state of some intellectual feeling rather than of any conceptualized statement—is, I believe, the very origin of that instinctive knowledge of man's immortality which we are now considering.

Another point must be added, concerning the aspirations proper to the Self rather than the spontaneous consciousness of it. When philosophers look upon this metaphysical reality which is called Personality, they establish that a Person is essentially a spiritual totality, characterized by independence. A Person is a universe to itself, a universe of knowledge, love and freedom, a whole which cannot be subordinated as a part, except with regard to such wholes to which it can be related through the instrumentality of knowledge and of love. Personality is an analogical and transcendental perfection, which is fully realized only in God, the Pure Act. Then philosophers are led to distinguish in the human Person two different types of aspirations. Certain aspirations of the Person are *connatural* to man. These concern the human Person insofar as it possesses a determinate specific nature. Other aspirations may be called *transnatural.* And these concern the human Person precisely insofar as it is a person and participates in the transcendental perfection of personality. Now, among the aspirations of the Person, the most obvious one is the aspiration toward not-dying. Death, the destruction of Self, is for the human Self not so much a thing to be feared as it is first of all a thing incomprehensible, impossible, an offence, a scandal. Not to be is nonsense for the person. This is so true that although we meet death at every step, although we see our relatives, our friends die, although we attend their burial, still the most difficult thing for us, is to believe in the reality of death. Man sees death; he does not believe in it. Yet the human Person does not escape dying, so it may seem that his aspiration toward immortality is thus deceived. How is this possible? We know very well that an aspiration which expresses only the very structure of a being cannot be deceived. The only way is to distinguish, according to the distinction I indicated a moment ago, what is connatural and what is transnatural in the aspiration with which we are dealing.

To the extent that it relates to the spiritual part of the human whole, to the soul, the aspiration toward not-dying is connatural to man, and cannot be deceived. To the extent that it relates to the whole itself, to the human Person made up of soul and body, this aspiration is a transnatural aspiration. It can be deceived. Yet, even when deceived, it remains within us, appealing to we know not what power, appealing to the very principle of being for we know not what kind of realization beyond death—beyond the corruption of that body which is an essential part of the human whole and without which the individual soul is not, truly speaking, a Person— beyond every evidence of the disappearance of the Person scattered amidst the glamourous appearances of Nature and the seasons—beyond this very world the existence and duration of which is linked with the generation and corruption of material substances and is therefore a denial of the human Person's very claim to immortality.

III

I have spoken of the instinctive and natural, lived and practiced belief in man's immortality. Now I should like to pass to philosophical knowledge, to that kind of knowledge, no longer instinctive and natural, but rational and elaborated, by means of which the human mind can achieve perfectly tested or demonstrated certitudes.

The philosophical knowledge of which I speak is not positivism, because positivism seems to be a despair of philosophy rather than a philosophy; however, the father of all modern positivists, Auguste Comte, felt so strongly the inescapability of the problem of immortality that he tried to answer it according to his possibilities, and granted a major part, in his positivist religion of Humanity, to what he called the *subjective* immortality, the immortality of everyone, in the memory, thought and love of those who knew him and appreciated him. Naturally, as regards Auguste Comte himself, the immortality he would thus enjoy was to be the eternal gratitude of all mankind. I am very far from despising this subjective immortality. To be preserved within a mind, to endure in minds as something known and told in song and story, is an enviable condition for material things, and precisely the kind of immortality they will enjoy. Events in human history groan after their epic and wait for their poet; this world will be immortal in the memories of immortal spirits, and in the stories they will tell one another about it. But if subjective immortality is something, it is precisely because there are immaterial minds which may receive in themselves the images of what is perishable. Subjective immortality would be nothing—or a derision—if objective immortality, genuine immortality, did not exist.

The philosophical reasons that testify to immortality may be expounded in the following way. First, human intelligence is able to know whatever participates in being and truth; the whole universe can be inscribed in it; that is to say, the object it knows has been previously deprived, in order to be known, of any conditions of materiality: What is the weight and volume of my idea of man? Does man possess any dimension or perform any transmutation of energy within my mind? Does the sun exert any heating action within my intellect? Nay more, intellectual knowledge is abstract and universal knowledge. This rose (which I am seeing) has contours; but being (which I am thinking of) is vaster than space. The object of intelligence is something universal, which remains what it is while being identified to an infinity of individuals. And that is possible only because things, in order to become objects of intellect, have been entirely separated from their material existence by the intellect itself. The objects known by human intelligence, taken not as things existing in themselves, but precisely as objects determining intelligence and united with it, are immaterial.

The second point: Just as is the condition of the object, so is the condition of the act that bears on it and is determined or specified by it. The object of human intelligence is as such immaterial; the act of the human intelligence is also immaterial.

The third point: Since the act of the intellectual power is immaterial, this power itself is also immaterial. Intelligence is in man an immaterial power. Doubtless it depends on the body, on the conditions of the brain. Its activity can be disturbed or hindered by physical trouble, by an outburst of anger, by a drink, a narcotic. But this dependence is an *extrinsic* one. It exists because our intelligence cannot act without the joint activity of memory and imagination, of internal senses and external senses, all of which are organic powers, residing in some material organ, in some special part of the body. As to intelligence itself, it is not *intrinsically* dependent on the body, since its activity is immaterial; human intelligence does not reside in any special part of the body. It uses the brain, since the organs of the internal senses are in the brain; yet the brain is not the organ of the intelligence, there is no part of the organism whose act is intellectual operation. The intellect has no organ.

And the final point: Since intellectual power is immaterial, its first substantial root, the very substance from which it emanates and which acts through its instrumentality is also immaterial. An immaterial soul must be the first substantial root of an immaterial psychic soul-power. It is conceivable that such an immaterial soul have, besides immaterial faculties, other powers and activities which are organic and material. For this immaterial soul is not only a spirit, but also a spirit made for animating a body, in Aristotelian terms a "substantial form," an *entelechy* which by its union with matter constitutes a particular corporeal substance, the human being. But it would be perfectly inconceivable that a material soul, a soul which informs a body—as the souls of animals and plants do, according to the biological philosophy of Aristotle—but which is not a spirit and cannot exist without informing matter, should possess a power or faculty (that is, should act through an instrumentality) which is immaterial, intrinsically independent of any corporeal organ and physical structure.

Thus the human soul is both a soul—that is the first principle of life in a living body—and a spirit, able to exist and to live apart from matter. The human soul has its own immaterial existence and its own immaterial subsistence: and it is by virtue of this immaterial existence and subsistence of the human soul that each element of the human body is human and exists as such. The radical immateriality of the highest operations of the human soul, of intellectual knowledge, of contemplation, of supra-sensuous love and desire and joy, of free will, is an evidence that this soul is spiritual in itself, and cannot cease existing and living. It cannot be corrupted, since it has no matter, it cannot be disintegrated, since it has no substantial parts, it cannot lose its individual unity, since it is self-subsisting, nor its internal energy, since it contains within itself all the sources of its energies. The human soul cannot die. Once existing, it cannot disappear, it will necessarily exist always, endure without end.

Each one of us is inhabited. With what wonderful respect we would look upon every human being, if we thought of that invisible Psyche who dwells within him and who causes him to be what he is, and who will endure longer than the world, endure always, after these poor bones are reduced to dust! How can our eyes contemplate any human person without seeking anxiously after the eternal mystery which is living in him? The first Christians kissed the breasts of their children with awe and veneration, thinking of that eternal presence within them. They had some idea, some awareness, less fickle than ours, of the immortality of the human soul.

I have just considered the immortality of the human soul. All the certitudes which the wisdom of philosophers brings forth concerning immortality deal with the immortality of the human *soul*, because non-cessation of being is the natural property of what is spiritual in us. But what of those aspirations of the human Person toward immortality that I emphasized a moment ago? These aspirations concern the very Person, Man himself, the natural whole made of flesh and spirit —not the human soul alone. About the aspiration of man to the immortality of *man*, not merely of the *human soul*, the philosophical reason has very little to say.

On the one hand, philosophical reason perceives that a separate soul is not a person, although it subsists in itself. It is not a person, because the notion of Person is essentially the notion of a complete and perfect whole. The body integrates the natural human totality, and the soul is only a part. What would be the life of separated souls, if they had to lead a merely natural life? They would live a truly pale life in a pallid paradise, like the Elysian Fields of the Ancients, with their pallid asphodels. Separated souls in a merely natural condition would not see God face to face—which is a supernatural privilege; they would know God through the image of God which is themselves, and they would know themselves in an intuitive manner. They would be dazzled by their own beauty, the beauty of a spiritual substance, and they would know other things in a confused and imperfect way, through the instrumentality of their substance, in the measure in which the other things resemble them. But all this knowledge would remain in a kind of dusk, because of the natural weakness of human intellect. Moreover all the sensible powers of the human soul, sensible memory, imagination, instinct and passion, as well as the external senses, remain asleep in a separated soul—in such a way that if there were not a supernatural compensation and supercompensation for such a soul, the happy life it would live, according to its natural condition, would be a half life in happiness.

On the other hand, philosophical reason understands that since the human soul is naturally made to animate a body, a kind of unfulfillment, incompleteness and substantial dissatisfaction must remain in the separated soul, as regards that other half of the human being which the soul, by virtue of its very being, tends to use for its own purposes and operations, while giving it ontological consistence and activity. And in this way philosophical reason wonders whether such a desire for reunion with the body could not some day be fulfilled in the immortal soul. Yes, as regards God's omnipotence, there is no impossibility of some reembodiment of the soul into its flesh and bones, and some restoration of the human integrity. But human reason can only conceive this possibility; it cannot go farther, and therefore, as concerns the supreme aspiration of the human Person toward immortality, toward the immortality of Man, human reason stops, remains silent and dreams.

IV

This question, however, must be asked: In point of fact, will this aspiration toward the immortality of the human Person remain forever unsatisfied? Such a question transcends the philosophical domain, the domain of human reason. The problem is a religious one, it engages and puts into play the deepest, the most crucial religious conceptions of mankind.

Two great conceptions here confront one another. They represent the two types of religious interpretation of human life which are alone possible. One conception is the Indian conception, the other is the Judeo-Christian one.

The Indian conception surrenders the immortality of the person, and teaches metempsychosis or transmigration. The soul is immortal, but the soul transmigrates. At the death of the body, the soul passes to another body, like a bird to a new cage, a more or less noble, more or less painful new cage, according to the merits or demerits gathered by the soul during its previous life. Thus there is for the same soul a succession of personalities as well as a succession of lives; each of these personalities slips away forever, will never appear again, like outworn coats that a man throws away from season to season. The unlimited flux, the irremediable disappearance of the successive personalities, is the ransom for the immortality of the soul.

There are very impressive and definite philosophical arguments against the idea of transmigration. The essential argument is the following: transmigration implies that each soul preserves its own individuality and yet passes from one body to another. But that is possible only if the soul is not substantially one with the body. The negation of the substantial unity of man, and the negation of the fact that soul and personality are inseparably joined—such a soul, such a personality; such a personality, such a soul—these two negations are inevitably involved in the doctrine of transmigration. That is to say, there is transmigration if man is not man; or, as Aristotle said, if the art of the flute-player can descend into the harp and cause the harp to produce the sound of the flute. The basic truth concerning the human being, the substantial unity of man, is incompatible with the idea of transmigration.

But despite the strength of this philosophical evidence, the idea of transmigration remains a temptation for the religious consciousness of mankind. Why this temptation toward metempsychosis? In my opinion this temptation results from the conflict between the idea of the retribution for human acts and the idea of the brevity, distress and foolishness of human life. How is it possible that a man's unhappy life, with all its insignificance, its blundering, and its wretchedness should suddenly open out upon Eternity? How is it possible that an eternal retribution, an eternal and immutable end, may be fixed for us in virtue of some good or bad movements of so weak and queer, so dormant a free will as ours? The disproportion is too great between the End and the Means. I imagine that the mind of India was discouraged and frightened by such an idea, and therefore fell back, so to speak, into the infinity of time, as if a series of new lives offered to the same soul would somehow avail to attenuate the disproportion I just emphasized between the precariousness of the journey and the importance of its end.

Yes, but then there is no longer an end. Time continues always to be Time. The mind finds itself confronted with the horror of an endless series of reincarnations. The very law of transmigration becomes a terrible and intolerable law, of new suffering ceaselessly assumed, new trials, new pain amidst new vanishing and torturing appearances. The idea of Nirvâna will then occur as a way of escape. But Nirvâna is only a deliverance from Time. As it is conceived by Indian metaphysics (I do not say as it is lived in fact by such or such a contemplative soul) Nirvâna is only an escape, the self-annihilation of that very transmigration which was to bring about the immortality of the soul, and which now abolishes itself, and along with itself immortality. Transmigration was not a solution—it was an escape, a flight, and from which in turn escape must be sought.

The Judeo-Christian conception is a philosophy of the final end, and the philosophy of the final end is the exact contrary of the philosophy of transmigration. The pursuit of immortality through a horizontal movement all along a time without end, is quite different from, it is the exact opposite of, the vertical fulfillment of immortality by the attainment of an End which is eternal and infinite—just as Nirvâna is quite different from, and in a sense is the exact opposite of, the passage to eternity and the possession of everlasting life. And what makes the Judeo-Christian solution possible is in part a true appreciation of the relationship between time and eternity: lengthen time as much as you will, add years to years, hoard up lives upon lives, time will ever remain having no common measure with eternity; a thousand transmigrations are as little before eternity as is the short life of this particular poor little child; this short human life is as much before eternity as a thousand transmigrations. But what makes the Judeo-Christian solution possible is also and above all the fact that in it the philosophy of the last End is involved in the whole of the truths and mysteries of divine revelation. Let us understand that God is personal, Life and Truth and Love in Person; let us understand that there is a supernatural order, and that the least degree of grace—that is of participation in the inner life of God himself—is more valuable than all the splendor of this star-strewn universe; let us understand that God has taken flesh in the womb of a virgin of Israel in order to die for mankind and to infuse in us the life of His own blood; let us understand that the free initiatives and resources, the patience and the ingenuity of the mercy of God are exceedingly greater than the weakness or the wickedness of our human free will. Then we understand that that disproportion between the precariousness of the journey and the importance of the end, which I emphasized a moment ago, is in reality counter-balanced, and even exceedingly compensated for, by the generosity and the *humanity*, as St. Paul put it, of our Savior God. Man does not save himself through his own power. It is God and Christ who save man through the power of the Cross and of divine grace, by the instrumentality of Faith and Charity fructifying in good works.

The Judeo-Christian conception is not only a philosophy of the last End; but also, and by the same stroke, a philosophy of the immortality of Man. It asserts not only the immortality of the Soul, but also the immortality of the human Person, of the whole human subject—because grace perfects Nature and fulfills supereminently the aspirations of Nature, those aspirations of the human person which I have already called *transnatural*. What the sacred writings of the Jews constantly emphasized, what mattered most to them, was not so much the immortality of the soul as the resurrection of the body. It is the resurrection of the body that St. Paul preached in Athens, to the astonishment of the philosophers. It is the resurrection of the body that we Christians hope for: a resurrection which transcends all the powers of nature, and which is to be accomplished for the elect by virtue of the blood and resurrection of Christ, and by a miracle of justice for those who will have refused up to the end grace and redeeming life.

Such is the answer given not by philosophy alone, but by Faith and Revelation, to the question which we were led to ask a moment ago: In point of fact, will the aspiration of the human Person, of the entire man toward immortality remain forever unsatisfied? No, this aspiration will not remain unsatisfied, the soul and body will be reunited, this same Person, this identical human Person whom we knew and loved during our evanescent days is actually immortal; this undivided human totality that we designate by a man's name will perish for a while, yes, and will know putrefaction; yet in reality and when all is said and done he will triumph over death and endure without end. And this immortality of Man is inextricably engaged and involved in the drama of the Salvation and Redemption.

v

I have a few words to add in conclusion. I should like to come back to some considerations which I touched on at the beginning of this essay, concerning the value of human life, that value which is greater than anything in the world, except things which are divine or concern what is divine in man, and serve, as Burke said, to redeem the blood of man—and such things, in truth, are not of the world, although they may be in the world.

Here we face a strange paradox, and that kind of assertion which may be—with the same words but according to diverse meanings—at the same time perfectly true and absolutely false. *Nothing in the world is more precious than human life*: if I think of the perishable life of man, this assertion is absolutely false. A single word is more precious than human life if in uttering this word a man braves a tyrant for the sake of truth or liberty. *Nothing in the world is more precious than human life*: if I think of the imperishable life of man, of that life which will consist in seeing God face to face, this same assertion is perfectly true.

Human society can ask human persons to give and sacrifice their lives for it, as in the case of a just war. How is this possible? This is possible because the earthly common good of the earthly community is not a merely earthly good. Even this earthly common good involves supra-human values, for it relates indirectly to the last end of men, to the eternal destiny of the persons who compose society. Human society must tend toward its earthly common good, toward a good and happy common life, in such a way that the pursuit of eternal happiness—which is more than happiness, for it is beatitude, and God himself—may be opened and made feasible for each human person in the community. If the common good of human society were only and exclusively a set of temporal advantages or achievements, as the common good of a bee-hive or an ant-hill, surely it would be nonsense for the life of a human person to be sacrificed to it.

As regards human civilizations, or pseudo-civilizations, two mortal errors are to be pointed out in this connection.

A civilization which despises death because it despises the human person and ignores the value of human life, a civilization which squanders the courage of men and wastes their lives for business profits or for satiating covetousness or hate or for the frenzy of domination or for the pagan pride of the state, is not a civilization, but barbarism. Its heroism is heartless bestiality.

But on the other hand a civilization which knows the price of human life but which sets up as its main value the perishable life of man, pleasure, money, selfishness, the possession of acquired commodities, and which therefore fears death as the supreme evil and avoids any risk of self-sacrifice and trembles thinking of death, under the pretext of respecting human life—such a civilization is not a civilization, but degeneration. Its humanism is cowardly delicacy.

True civilization knows the price of human life but makes the imperishable life of man its transcendent supreme value. It does not fear death, it confronts death, it accepts risk, it requires self-sacrifice—but for aims which are worthy of human life, for justice, for truth, for brotherly love. It does not despise human life and it does not brutally despise death; it welcomes death when death, as pioneers and free men see it, is the accomplishment of the dignity of the human person and a beginning of eternity. Let me recall in this connection the words of the late Greek statesman, Mr. Metaxas, spoken to an American war correspondent. "We Greeks," he said, "being Christians, know that after all death is only an episode." An episode on the road of the immortal life of man. Such is Christian civilization, true civilization. Its heroism is genuine heroism, a heroism integrally human, because divinely grounded in the immortality of man.

13. CHRISTIAN HUMANISM

Every great period of civilization is dominated by a certain peculiar idea that man fashions of man. Our behavior depends on this image as much as on our very nature—an image which appears with striking brilliance in the minds of some particularly representative thinkers, and which, more or less unconscious in the human mass, is none the less strong enough to mold after its own pattern the social and political formations that are characteristic of a given cultural epoch.

In broad outline, the image of man which reigned over medieval Christendom depended upon St. Paul and St. Augustine. This image was to disintegrate from the time of the Renaissance and the Reformation—torn between an utter Christian pessimism which despaired of human nature and an utter Christian optimism which counted on human endeavor more than on divine grace. The image of man which reigned over modern times depended upon Descartes, John Locke, the Enlightenment, and Jean-Jacques Rousseau.

The secularization of the Christian man

Here we are confronted with the process of secularization of the Christian man which took place from the sixteenth century on. Let's not be deceived by the merely philosophical appearance of such a process! In reality the man of Cartesian Rationalism was a pure mind conceived after an angelistic pattern. The man of Natural Religion was a Christian gentleman who did not need grace, miracle or revelation, and was made virtuous and just by his own good nature. The man of Jean-Jacques Rousseau was, in a much more profound and significant manner, the very man of St. Paul transferred to the plane of pure nature—innocent as Adam before the fall, longing for a state of divine freedom and bliss, corrupted by social life and civilization as the sons of Adam by the original sin. He was to be redeemed and set free, not by Christ, but by the essential goodness of human nature, which must be restored by means of an education without constraint and reveal itself in the City of Man of coming centuries, in that form of state in which "everyone obeying all, will nevertheless continue to obey only himself."

This process was not at all a merely rational process. It was a process of secularization of something consecrated, elevated above nature by God, called to divine perfection, and living a divine life in a fragile and wounded body—the man of Christianity, the man of the Incarnation. All that boiled down to bringing back this man into the realm of man himself ("anthropocentric humanism"), to keeping a Christian make-up, while replacing the Gospel by human Reason or human Goodness, and expecting from Human Nature what had been expected from the virtue of God giving himself to his creature. Enormous promises, divine promises were made to man at the dawn of modern times. Science will liberate man and make him master and possessor of all nature. An automatic and necessary progress will lead him to the earthly realm of peace, to that blessed Jerusalem which our hands will build up by transforming social and political life, and which will be the Kingdom of Man, and in which we will become the supreme rulers of our own history, and whose radiance has awakened the hope and energy of the great modern revolutionaries.

The loss of religious and metaphysical bearings

If I were to try now to disentangle the ultimate results of this vast process of secularization, I should describe the progressive loss, in modern ideology, of all the certitudes, coming either from metaphysical insight or from religious faith, which had given foundation and granted reality to the image of Man in the Christian system. The historical misfortune has been the failure of philosophic Reason which, while taking charge of the old theological heritage in order to appropriate it, found itself unable even to maintain its own metaphysical pretense, its own justification of its secularized Christian man, and was obliged to decline toward a positivist denial of this very justification. Human Reason lost its grasp on Being, and became available only for the mathematical reading of sensory phenomena, and for the building up of corresponding material techniques—a field in which any absolute reality, any absolute truth, and any absolute value is of course forbidden.

As regards man himself, modern man knew truths—without *the Truth*; he was capable of the relative and changing truths of science, incapable and afraid of any supratemporal truth reached by Reason's metaphysical effort or of the divine Truth given by the Word of God. Modern man claimed human rights and dignity—without God, for his ideology grounded human rights and human dignity in a godlike, infinite autonomy of human will, which any rule or measurement received from another would offend and destroy. Modern man trusted in peace and fraternity—without Christ, for he did not need a Redeemer, he was to save himself by himself alone, and his love for mankind did not need to be founded in divine charity. Modern man constantly progressed toward good and toward the possession of the earth —without evil on earth, for he did not believe in the existence of evil; evil was only an imperfect stage in evolution, which a further stage was naturally to transcend. Modern man enjoyed human life and worshipped human life as having an infinite value—without a soul or the gift of oneself, for the soul was an unscientific concept, inherited from the dreams of primitive men. And if a man does not give his soul to the one he loves, what can he give? He can give money, not himself.

As concerns civilization, modern man had in the bourgeois state a social and political life, a common life without common good or common work, for the aim of common life consisted only of preserving everyone's freedom to enjoy private ownership, acquire wealth, and seek his own pleasure. Modern man believed in liberty—without the mastery of self or moral responsibility, for free will was incompatible with scientific determinism; and he believed in equality—without justice, for justice too was a metaphysical idea that lost any rational foundation and lacked any criterion in our modern biological and sociological outlook. Modern man placed his hope in machinism, in technique, and in mechanical or industrial civilization—without wisdom to dominate them and put them at the service of human good and freedom; for he expected freedom from the development of external techniques themselves, not from any ascetic effort toward the internal possession of self. And how can one who does not possess the standards of human life, which are metaphysical, apply them to our use of the machine? The law of the machine, which is the law of matter, will apply itself to him.

As regards, lastly, the internal dynamism of human life, modern man looked for happiness—without any final end to be aimed at, or any rational pattern to which to adhere; the most natural concept and motive power, that of happiness, was thus warped by the loss of the concept and the sense of finality (for finality is but one with desirability, and desirability but one with happiness). Happiness became the movement itself toward happiness, a movement at once limitless and increasingly lower, more and more stagnant. And modern man looked for democracy—without any heroic task of justice to be performed and without brotherly love from which to get inspiration. The most significant political improvement of modern times, the concept of, and the devotion to, the rights of the human person and the rights of the people, was thus warped by the same loss of the concept and the sense of finality, and by the repudiation of the evangelical ferment acting in human history; democracy tended to become an embodiment of the sovereign will of the people in the machinery of a bureaucratic state more and more irresponsible and more and more asleep.

But the world went on from force of habit

The process of secularization of the Christian man concerns above all the idea of man and the philosophy of life which developed in the modern age. In the concrete reality of human history, a process of growth occurred at the same time, great human conquests were achieved, owing to the natural movement of civilization and to the primitive impulse, the evangelical one, toward the democratic ideal. At least the civilization of the nineteenth century remained Christian in its real though forgotten or disregarded principles, in the secularized remnants involved in its very idea of man and civilization; in the religious freedom—as thwarted as this may have been at certain moments and in certain countries—that it willingly or unwillingly preserved; even in the very emphasis on reason and human grandeur which its freethinkers used as a weapon against Christianity; and finally in the secularized feeling which inspired, despite a wrong ideology, its great social and political improvements.

But the split had progressively increased between the real behavior of this secularized Christian world and the moral and spiritual principles which had given it its meaning and its internal consistency, and which it came to ignore. Thus this world seemed emptied of its own principles; it tended to become a universe of words, a nominalistic universe, a dough without leaven. It lived and endured by habit and by force acquired from the past, not by its own power; it was pushed forward by a *vis a tergo*, not by an internal dynamism. It was utilitarian, its supreme rule was utility. Yet utility which is not a means toward a goal is of no use at all. It was capitalistic, and capitalist civilization enabled the initiatives of the individual to achieve tremendous conquests over material nature. Yet, as Werner Sombart observed, the man of capitalism was neither "ontologic" nor "erotic"; that is to say, he had lost the sense of Being because he lived in signs and by signs, and he had lost the sense of Love because he did not enjoy the life of a person dealing with other persons, but he underwent the hard labor of enrichment for the sake of enrichment.

Despite the wrong ideology I have just described, and the disfigured image of man which is linked to it, our civilization bears in its very substance the sacred heritage of human and divine values which depends on the struggle of our forefathers for freedom, on Judeo-Christian tradition, and on classical antiquity, and which has been sadly weakened in its efficiency but not at all destroyed in its potential reserves.

The Marxist revolt against despair

The great revolutionary movements which reacted against our secularized Christian world were to aggravate the evil and to bring it to a peak. For they developed toward a definite break with Christian values. Here it is less a question of doctrinal opposition to Christianity than of an existential opposition to the presence and action of Christ at the core of human history.

A first development continued and climaxed the trend of secularized reason, the "anthropocentric humanism," in the direction which it followed from its origin, in the direction of rationalistic hopes, now no longer constituted solely as philosophical ideology but as a lived religion. This development arises from the unfolding of all the consequences of the principle that man alone, and through himself alone, works out his salvation.

The purest case of this tendency is that of Marxism. No matter how strong some of the pessimistic aspects of Marxism may be, it remains attached to this postulate. Marxist materialism remained rationalistic, so much so that for it the movement proper to matter is a *dialectical* movement.

If man alone and through himself alone works out his salvation, then this salvation is purely and exclusively temporal, and must be accomplished without God, and even against God—I mean against whatever in man and the human world bears the likeness of God, that is to say, from the Marxist point of view, the likeness of enslavement; salvation demands the giving up of personality, and the organization of collective man into one single body whose destiny is to gain supreme dominion over matter and human history. What becomes then of the image of man? Man is no longer the creature and image of God, a personality which implies free will and is responsible for an eternal destiny, a being which possesses rights and is called to the conquest of freedom and to a self-achievement consisting of love and charity. He is a particle of the social whole and lives by the collective conscience of the whole, and his happiness and liberty lie in serving the work of the whole. This whole itself is an economic and industrial whole, its essential and primordial work consists of the industrial domination of nature. There is here a thirst for communion, but communion is sought in economic activity, in pure productivity, which is engulfed in a demiurgic task of fabrication and domination over things. The human person is sacrificed to industry's titanism, which is the god of the merely industrial community.

The Nazi repudiation of reason and humanism

Another development, depending upon a quite opposite trend of mind, may be ascribed as an utter reaction against any kind of rationalism and humanism. Its roots are pessimistic, it corresponds to a process of animalization of the image of man, in which a larvated metaphysics avails itself of every misconception of scientific or sociological data to satisfy a hidden resentment against Reason and human dignity. Following this trend of mind the human species is only a branch which sprouted by chance on the genealogical tree of the monkeys; all our systems of ideas and values are only an epiphenomenon of the social evolution of the primitive clan; or an ideological superstructure determined by, and masking the struggle for life of class interests and imperialistic ambitions; all our seemingly rational and free behavior is only an illusory appearance, emerging from the inferno of our unconsciousness and of instinct, all our seemingly spiritual feelings and activities, poetic creation, human pity and devotion, religious creed, contemplative love, are only the sublimation of sensuality or sexual libido. Man is unmasked, the countenance of the beast appears. The human specificity, which rationalism had caused to vanish into pure spirit, now vanishes in animality.

Yet the development of which I am speaking has its real sources in something much more profound, which began to reveal itself from the second half of the last century on; anguish and despair, as exemplified in Dostoevski's *Possessed*. A deeper abyss than animality appears in the unmasking of man. Having given up God so as to be self-sufficient, man has lost track of his soul. He looks in vain for himself; he turns the universe upside down trying to find himself; he finds masks and, behind the masks, death.

Then was to be witnessed the spectacle of a tidal wave of irrationality, of hatred of intelligence, the awakening of a tragic opposition between life and spirit. To overcome despair, Nietzsche proclaimed the advent of the superman of the will to power, the death of truth, the death of God. More terrific voices, the voices of a base multitude whose baseness itself appears as an apocalyptic sign, cry out: we have had enough of lying optimism and illusory morality, enough of freedom and personal dignity and justice and peace and faithfulness and goodness which made us mad with unhappiness. Let us give ground to the infinite promises of evil, and of swarming death, and of blessed enslavement, and of triumphant despair!

The purest case of this tendency was Nazi racism. It was grounded not in a fanaticism of reason hating every transcendent value, but in a mysticism of instinct and life hating reason. Intelligence for it was of use only to develop techniques of destruction and to pervert the function of language. Its demonic religiosity was more irremediable than atheism itself, for it tried to pervert the very nature of God, to make of God himself an idol. It invoked God, but as a spirit protector attached to the glory of a people or a state, or as a demon of the race. A god who will end by being identified with an invincible force at work in the blood was set up against the God of Sinai and against the God of Calvary, against the one whose law rules nature and human conscience, against the Word who was at the beginning, against the God of whom it is said that he is Love.

Here, too, man is no longer the creature and image of God, a person animated by a spiritual soul and endowed with free will, and responsible for an eternal destiny, who possesses rights and is called to the conquest of freedom and to a self-achievement consisting of love and charity. And now this disfigured image of man is rooted in a warring pessimism. Man is a particle of the political whole, and lives by the *Volksgeist*, yet even for this collective whole there is no longer any decoy of happiness and liberty and of universal emancipation, but only power and self-realization through violence. Communion is sought in the glorification of the race and in a common hate of some enemy, in animal blood, which, separated from the spirit, is no more than a biological inferno. The human person is sacrificed to the demon of the blood, which is the god of the community of blood.

If it is true that in the dialectic of culture, communism is the final state of anthropocentric rationalism, we understand that by virtue of the universality inherent in reason—even in reason gone mad—communism dreams of an all-embracing emancipation and pretends to substitute for the universalism of Christianity its own earthly universalism. But racism, on its irrational and biological basis, rejects all universalism and breaks even the natural unity of the human family, so as to impose the hegemony of a so-called higher racial essence. There is no human regeneration to be expected either from communism or from racism, yet racism is more irremediably destructive. A Nazi people were led away from Nazi paganism only by a crushing defeat of Nazism in its undertakings of world conquest; it is not inconceivable that a communist people may be led away from communist atheism by internal changes, however hard this evolution may be. If we have any hope of a spiritual transformation in the Russian people, this is due not to communism but to their deep inherent religious and human resources. . . .

The need for a new Christian civilization

If the description which I outlined above is accurate, it appears that the only way of regeneration for the human community is a rediscovery of the true image of man and a definite attempt toward a new Christian civilization, a new Christendom. Modern times sought many good things along wrong tracks. The question now is to seek these good things along right tracks, and to save the human values and achievements aimed at by our forefathers and endangered by the false philosophy of life of the last century, and to have for that purpose the courage and audacity of proposing to ourselves the biggest task of renewal, of internal and external transformation. A coward flees backward, away from new things. The man of courage flees forward, in the midst of new things.

Christians find themselves today, in the order of temporal civilization, facing problems similar to those which their fathers met in the sixteenth and seventeenth centuries. At that time modern physics and astronomy in the making were at one with the philosophical systems set up against Christian tradition. The defenders of the latter did not know how to make the necessary distinctions; they took a stand both against that which was to become modern science and against the philosophical errors which at the outset preyed upon this science as parasites. Three centuries were needed to get away from this misunderstanding, if it be true that a better philosophical outlook has actually caused us to get away from it. It would be disastrous to fall once again into similar errors today in the field of the philosophy of civilization. The true substance of the nineteenth century's aspirations, as well as the human gains it achieved, must be saved, from its own errors and from the aggression of totalitarian barbarism. A world of genuine humanism and Christian inspiration must be built.

In the eyes of the observer of historical evolution, a new Christian civilization is going to be quite different from medieval civilization, though in both cases Christianity is at the root. For the historical climate of the Middle Ages and that of modern times are utterly diverse. Briefly, medieval civilization, whose historical ideal was the Holy Empire, constituted a *"sacral"* Christian civilization, in which temporal things, philosophical and scientific reason, and the state, were subservient organs or instruments of spiritual things, of religious faith, and of the Church. In the course of the following centuries temporal things gained a position of autonomy, all of which was in itself a normal process. The misfortune has been that this process became warped and instead of being a process of distinction for a better form of union, progressively severed earthly civilization from evangelical inspiration.

A new age of Christendom, if it is to come, will be an age of reconciliation of that which was disjoined, the age of a *"profane"* Christian civilization, in which temporal things, philosophical and scientific reason, and the state, will enjoy their autonomy and at the same time recognize the quickening and inspiring role that spiritual things, religious faith, and the Church play from their higher plane. Then a Christian philosophy of life would guide a vitally, not decoratively, Christian community, a community of human rights and of the dignity of the human person, in which men belonging to diverse racial stocks and to diverse religious creeds would commune in a temporal common work truly human and progressive.

In the last analysis, I would say that from the end of the Middle Ages—a moment at which the human creature, while awakening to itself, felt itself oppressed and crushed in its loneliness—modern times have longed for a rehabilitation of the human creature. They sought this rehabilitation in a separation from God. It was to be sought in God. The human creature claims the right to be loved; it can be really and efficaciously loved only in God. It must be respected in its very connection with God and because it receives everything —and its very dignity—from him. After the great disillusionment of "anthropocentric humanism" and the atrocious experience of the antihumanism of our day, what the world needs is a new humanism, a "theocentric" or integral humanism, which would consider man in all his natural grandeur and weakness, in the entirety of his wounded being inhabited by God, in the full reality of nature, sin, and sanctity. Such a humanism would recognize all that is irrational in man, in order to tame it to reason, and all that is suprarational, in order to have reason vivified by it and to open man to the descent of the divine into him. Its main work would be to cause the Gospel leaven and inspiration to penetrate the secular structures of life—a work of sanctification of the profane and temporal.

Personalistic democracy

This "humanism of the Incarnation" would care for the masses, for their right to a temporal condition worthy of man and to a spiritual life, and for the movement which carries labor toward the social responsibility of its coming of age. It would tend to substitute for bourgeois civilization, and for an economic system based on the fecundity of money, not a collectivistic economy but a "personalistic" democracy. This task is joined to today's tremendous effort for victory over the armies of the Pagan Empire, and to a future work of reconstruction which will require no less vigor. It is also joined to a thorough awakening of the religious conscience. One of the worst diseases of the modern world, as I pointed out in an earlier essay,* is its dualism, the dissociation between the things of God and the things of the world. The latter, the things of the social, economic, and political life, have been abandoned to their own carnal law, removed from the exigencies of the Gospel. The result is that they have become more and more unlivable. At the same time, Christian ethics, not really permeating the social life of people, became in this connection—I do not mean in itself or in the Church, I mean in the world, in the general cultural behavior—a universe of formulas and words; and this universe of formulas and words was in effect vassalized in practical cultural behavior by the real energies of this same temporal world existentially detached from Christ.

In addition, modern civilization, which pays dearly today for the past, seems as if it were pushed, by the self-contradictions and fatalities suffered by it, toward contrasting forms of misery and intensified materialism. To rise above these fatalities we need an awakening of liberty and of its creative forces, of which man does not become capable by the grace of the state or any party pedagogy, but by the love which fixes the center of his life infinitely above the world and temporal history. In particular, the general paganization of our civilization has resulted in man's placing his hope in force alone and in the efficacy of hate, whereas in the eyes of an integral humanism a political ideal of justice and civic friendship, requiring political strength and technical equipment, but inspired by love, is alone able to direct the work of social regeneration.

By the gift of himself man attains his life's peak

The image of man involved in integral humanism is that of a being made of matter and spirit, whose body may have emerged from the historical evolution of animal forms, but whose immortal soul directly proceeds from divine creation. He is made of truth, capable of knowing God as the Cause of Being, by his reason, and of knowing him in his intimate

* *Scholasticism and Politics* (New York: Macmillan, 1940), Chapter I, page 22.

life, by the gift of faith. Man's dignity is that of an image of
God, his rights derive as well as his duties from natural law,
whose requirements express in the creature the eternal plan
of creative Wisdom. Wounded by sin and death from the
first sin of his race, whose burden weighs upon all of us, he is
caused by Christ to become of the race and lineage of God,
living by divine life, and called upon to enter by suffering
and love into Christ's very work of redemption. Called upon
by his nature, on the other hand, to unfold historically his
internal potentialities by achieving little by little reason's
domination over his own animality and the material universe,
his progress on earth is not automatic nor merely natural, but
accomplished in step with freedom and together with the
inner help of God, and constantly thwarted by the power of
evil, which is the power of created spirits to inject nothingness
into being, and which unceasingly tends to degrade human
history, while unceasingly and with greater force the creative
energies of reason and love revitalize and raise up this same
history.

Our natural love for God and for the human being is fragile; charity alone, received from God as a participation in his
own life, makes man efficaciously love God above everything,
and each human person in God. Thus brotherly love brings
to earth, through the heart of man, the fire of eternal life,
which is the true peacemaker, and it must vitalize from
within that natural virtue of friendship, disregarded by so
many fools, which is the very soul of social communities.
Man's blood is at once of infinite value and must be shed all
along mankind's roads "to redeem the blood of man." On the
one hand, nothing in the world is more precious than one
single human person. On the other hand, man exposes nothing more willingly than his own being to all kinds of danger
and waste—and this condition is normal. The meaning of that
paradox is that man knows very well that death is not an
end, but a beginning. If I think of the perishable life of man,
it is something naturally sacred. Yet man can be required to
sacrifice it by devotion to his neighbor or by his duty to his
country. Moreover a single word is more precious than human
life if in uttering this word a man braves a tyrant for the sake
of truth or liberty. If I think of the imperishable life of man,

of that life which makes him "a god by participation" and, beginning here below, will consist in seeing God face to face, nothing in the world is more precious than human life. And the more a man gives himself, the more he makes this life intense within him. Every self-sacrifice, every gift of oneself involves, be it in the smallest way, a dying for the one we love. The man who knows that "after all, death is only an episode," is ready to give himself with humility, and nothing is more human and more divine than the gift of oneself, for "it is more blessed to give than to receive."

The community of freedom and fraternity

As concerns civilization, the man of Christian humanism knows that political life aims at a common good which is superior to a mere collection of the individual goods and yet must flow back upon human persons. He knows that the common work must tend above all toward the improvement of human life itself, enabling everyone to exist on earth as a free man and to enjoy the fruits of culture and spirit. He knows that the authority of those who are in charge of the common good, and who are, in a community of free men, designated by the people, originates in the Author of Nature and is therefore binding in conscience, and is binding in conscience on condition that it be just. The man of Christian humanism cherishes freedom as something he must be worthy of; he realizes his essential equality with other men in terms of respect and fellowship, and sees in justice the force of preservation of the political community and the prerequisite which, "bringing unequals to equality," enables civic friendship to spring forth. He is aware both of the tremendous ordeal which the advent of machinism imposes on human history and of the marvelous power of liberation it offers to man, if the brute instinct of domination does not avail itself of the techniques of machinism, and of science itself, in order to enslave mankind; and if reason and wisdom are strong enough to turn them to the service of truly human aims and apply to them the standards of human life. The man of Christian humanism does not look for an industrial civilization, but for a civilization integrally human and of evangelical inspiration.

As regards, finally, the internal dynamism of human life, the man of Christian humanism has an ultimate end, God to be seen and possessed—and he tends toward self-protection, which is the chief element of that imperfect happiness which is accessible to him in earthly existence. Thus life has meaning and a direction for him, and he is able to grow up on the way, without turning and wavering and without remaining spiritually a child. This perfection toward which he tends is not the perfection of some stoic athleticism wherein a man would make himself impeccable, but rather the perfection of love, of love toward Another whom he loves more than himself, and whom he craves above all to join and love even more, even though in the process he carries with him imperfections and weaknesses. In such an evangelical perfection lies perfect freedom, which is to be conquered by ascetic effort but which is finally given by the very One Who is loved, and Who was the first to love us.

But this vertical movement toward divine union and self-perfection is not the only movement involved in human life's internal dynamism. The second one, the horizontal movement, concerns the evolution of mankind and progressively reveals the substance and creative forces of man in history. The horizontal movement of civilization, when directed toward its authentic temporal aims, helps the vertical movement of souls. And without the movement of souls toward their eternal aim, the movement of civilization would lose the charge of spiritual energy, human pressure, and creative radiance which animates it toward its temporal accomplishment. For the man of Christian humanism history has a meaning and a direction. The progressive integration of humanity is also a progressive emancipation from human servitude and misery as well as from the constraints of material nature. The supreme ideal which the political and social work in mankind has to aim at is thus the inauguration of a brotherly city, which does not imply the hope that all men will someday be perfect on earth and love each other fraternally, but the hope that the existential *state* of human life and the structures of civilization will draw nearer to their perfection, the standard of which is justice and friendship—and what aim, if not perfection, is to be aimed at? This supreme ideal is the very one of a genuine democracy, of the new democracy we are expecting. It requires not only the development of powerful technical equipment and of a firm and rational politico-social organization in human communities, but also a heroic philosophy of life, and the quickening inner ferment of evangelical inspiration. It is in order to advance toward such an ideal that the community must be strong. The inauguration of a common life which responds to the truth of our nature, freedom to be achieved, and friendship to be set up at the core of a civilization vitalized by virtues higher than civic virtues, all these define the historical ideal for which men can be asked to work, fight, and die. Against the deceptive myths raised by the powers of illusion a vaster and greater hope must rise up, a bolder promise must be made to the human race. The truth of God's image, as it is naturally impressed upon us, freedom, and fraternity are not dead. If our civilization struggles with death, the reason is not that it dares too much, and that it proposes too much to men. It is that it does not dare enough or propose enough to them. It shall revive, a new civilization will come to life, on condition that it hope, and will, and love truly and heroically truth, freedom, and fraternity.

14. THE CHRISTIAN IN THE MODERN WORLD

The secular failure of a once Christian world

We have thus come to a mighty question, one that is no longer theoretical but practical, that of the temporal mission of the Christian. I shall divide the study of this question into three sections, endeavouring first of all to characterise what can be called the secular failure of a Christian world which, in the course of the modern age and more particularly of the nineteenth century, has more and more become so only in appearance. I shall then try to indicate briefly (referring the reader to what I have already written on the theme[1]) the causes of this phenomenon, and shall next go on to a consideration of the temporal role of the Christian, treating this particularly in relation to the inauguration of a new Christian life in this world.

It is the office of spiritual things to vivify the things of time. Christianity should inform, or better, interpenetrate the world, not that this is its primary end (it is a secondary and indispensable one), and not that this world should become the Kingdom of God, but in order that the refraction of the world of grace should be more and more effective in it, and that man should live better his life in the things of time.

In large measure this was the case for mediaeval Christendom. Everyone knows the capital role played by the Church in the building up of the Christian world of the Middle Ages: a world full of defects but livable.

With the decadence of the mediaeval Christian order and the coming of modern times, we see, on the one hand, a progressive detachment of the world from Christ; and, on the other, the Church still plays a very great part, endeavouring to maintain what has already been won with regard to the realisation of the principles of the natural law in the secular order and with regard to the subordination of this order to spiritual ends. It was a defensive position which though necessary was thankless, since it ran the risk in some degree of creating an apparent solidarity between Christianity and the forms of a world which meanwhile was becoming more and more inhuman.

Nevertheless, the play of historic forces yet remained for long at a sufficiently normal level; and if the world of the *ancien régime* ended by becoming unlivable, its politico-social structure, with its three qualitative orders (the nobility, the clergy, the third estate) for long continued to be an organic structure adapted to the needs of life.

This situation only became tragic after the fall of the *ancien régime* had become inevitable, after the French Revolution and Napoleon, with the coming of the industrial and mercantile world, when society found itself cut in two, into two classes: the one living exclusively by its labour, the other which lives (or more truly lived) on the revenues of its capital, classes which have no other economic relation than the wage system, whereby work itself has become a mere commodity. While all the time preserving an element of Christianity in its ethical and cultural foundations, and while making great use, among the conservative elements and for interested political ends, of the name of Christianity and its moral vocabulary, a civilisation which in the mass has turned away from Christianity under the pressure of adverse forces, where the Christian sap has itself grown weak, came, even in its Christian elements, to accept the inhuman position created for the proletariat by an uncontrolled capitalism, and so became totally absorbed in the blind movement of a social materialism which practically and in action proclaims by what it is the ruin of the Christian spirit.[2]

There is no need here to bring capitalism to book; its condemnation has become a commonplace that minds with an objection to platitude fear to reiterate. I shall content myself with the brief comment that if, taken in itself, the ideal mechanism of the capitalist system is not essentially evil and unjust as Marx held it to be,[3] yet, when we consider the *spirit* which makes concrete use of that mechanism, and which determines its concrete forms and particular realisations, it must be said that it hides a radical disorder. The energy which stimulates and drives this economy has been progressively soiled by a 'capital' sin: not certainly a sin which does to

death the souls of the individuals compelled to live in such a
world and utilise its machinery, but a sin which little by little
brings about the temporal death of the social body: the cult
of earthly riches which has become the form of civilisation.
The objective spirit of capitalism is a spirit of the exaltation
of men's active and inventive powers, of human dynamism
and individual initiative; but it is a spirit of hatred of poverty and of contempt for the poor: the poor man only exists
as an instrument of production, a 'hand', not as a person. The
rich man, on the other hand, does not exist as a person, but as
a consumer (for the benefit of the capital involved in this
same production): and the tragedy of such a world is that
the working and development of this frankenstein of a usuri-
ous economy should necessarily tend to make all men consumers or rich, while at the same time, if there are no poor,
no instruments or 'hands', the whole economy stops and dies:
and it equally dies, as we see to-day, if there are not enough
consumers (in act)[4] to bring the 'hands' into work.

But is not the fact that such a system has been able to
develop freely its most inhuman potentialities a singularly
grave sign of decadence in the world that issued from the
dissolution of Christendom, a world which long since has repudiated its own principles and denied its own God? And in
this decadence of a world which sociologically and culturally,
despite the power and variety of the forces of unbelief which
it deploys, can still be called Christian by reason of its historical foundations, is not there also a responsibility which
falls on the Christians themselves? Does this not imply a
bankruptcy of the 'Christian world' in the strictest sense of
that term, i.e. the social elements and formations gathered
together under the names of religious and christian? I am
well aware that it would be unjust to reproach Christians
with not having prevented the development of the new forms
of life and new economic structures which the errors and the
evils proper to the capitalist age have deflected and deformed,
but which in essence and abstractly considered are not evil
and correspond to a normal progress. But in the purely ethical
order of the personal use which they have made of these new
economic structures (in other words, in the social order as
envisaged from the standpoint of the private virtues) there is

ample space for deploring the indifference shown by so many Christians, since the barbarous and victorious days of early capitalism, to the laws of Christian conduct in their social bearing. A social system which, concretely taken, is in itself not good, has thus progressively worsened to the point of becoming intolerable. And we have equal need to deplore the fact that, in the social order as envisaged from the point of view of social life itself and the activities of earthly civilisation, the place which socialism found vacant, and took and planted with mighty errors, had not been taken and used by forces of Christian inspiration, calling into play a social philosophy based on truth; and giving the signal for the movement of emancipation among the workers. We are faced by the question of explaining this double failure.

Some reasons for this failure

Many reasons could be suggested: first of all, the *dualism* of the modern age, whose extreme results are here seen in the form of that division of labour between God and Mammon, of which I have already spoken.

In the second place it may be pointed out that, generally speaking, it is natural that there should be more 'bad Christians' than 'good Christians' in a Christian civilisation: and hence by a gradual decline a sociological *naturalization* of religion is too often achieved and a utilisation of Christianity for wholly secular ends.

There is yet a third cause, which belongs rather to the intellectual order, and which makes apparent to what an extent modern civilisation, even where it still calls itself Christian, has suffered from the lack of a Christian *philosophy*. In the Christian world of the Middle Ages, despite enormous obstacles, civilisation was orientated, as though unconsciously and by the spontaneous instinct of faith, towards a realisation of Christianity not only in the life of souls but in the socio-temporal order as well.

'When with the "reflective age" the inner differentiation of culture became a leading feature of life, when art, science, the State began each to be conscious (with what an awful consciousness) of itself, it is perhaps not inaccurate to say that there was no similar awakening of consciousness with respect to the social order as such or of the reality which properly constitutes it. How indeed could there be in a world which was to grow up under the ascendancy of Descartes? . . . It was not that the spirit of the Gospels was wanting in living and saintly members of the christian world, but an explicit and proper awareness was lacking of one of the areas of reality to which that spirit should be applied. And though the claim of Auguste Comte to be the inventor of social science is largely inadmissible, it may fairly be argued that the "scientific" illusions of sociology—and likewise of socialism—have assisted the children of light by obliging them to explore by the aid of philosophic reflection these areas of human life and activity.'[5]

These considerations may contribute to an explanation of why the transformation which little by little substituted the system of lending at interest and of capitalism for the economic system of the Middle Ages, although it has, from the beginning and at various subsequent stages, as M. Groethuysen has reminded us,[6] roused the hostility of the Church and set many questions to the Christian intellect concerned with the individual conscience and the confessional, has yet, for so long a time, not been thought out or measured by that intellect in terms of its veritable social significance and value: so that the capitalist system was able to establish itself in the world and encountered a passive resistance and dumb hostility in Catholic social formations, but without provoking any efficacious efforts to redress the balance or an active and deliberate opposition in the heart of the Christian world or of the 'Christian temporal order', even in Catholic circles.

'One ought, however, to observe that the Catholic conscience did not fail to make its protest heard. In the nineteenth century in particular, at the very time when capitalism was reaching maturity and taking possession of the world, men like Ozanam and Vogelsang and La Tour du Pin raised up their voices. And above all the Church itself made good the shortcomings of Christian society by formulating the principles and essential truths that govern the whole field of economic affairs and that the established order of modern societies largely fails to recognise.'[7]

The Christian's temporal part in the transformation of the social system

I wish here to bring forward certain considerations concerned with the temporal role to be played by the individual Christian in the work of transforming the social system. First of all let it be said that the *dualism* of the previous age is at least for Christian thought now at an end. For a Christian, separatism and dualism, whether of the school of Machiavelli or of Descartes, have had their day. An important process of integration is taking place, a return to a wisdom which is at once theological and philosophic, a return to a vital synthesis. There is much need for a similar integration to ethics of the things in the domain of politics and economics, due regard being had for their respective natures.

Again, that *social consciousness* which was more or less lacking in the Christian world at the beginnings of the modern period is at long last coming into existence. This is a phenomenon of considerable importance, all the more so as this consciousness is informed and will be more and more informed by a just understanding of modern history and its normal processes which were vitiated yesterday by capitalist materialism and are vitiated to-day by the communist materialism which has succeeded it.

At the same time light has been thrown on the proper part to be played by Christian activities in the things of time, with regard to the world and its culture. From this angle one may say that, while the Church itself, above all anxious not to become the adjunct of any one particular system, has been more and more freed, not from the necessity of judging things from above, but of administering and directing the temporal things of this world, the individual Christian finds himself more and more engaged in exactly these things, not so much as a member of the Church, but as a citizen of the earthly city, i.e. as a *Christian citizen*, conscious of the task incumbent on him of working for the inauguration of a new secular order.

But as soon as things are looked on in this light at once a new series of problems arise.

It will be necessary to elaborate a social, political and economic philosophy, which will not rest content with universal principles, but which must be capable of coming down to the details of concrete realisation; a task which presupposes an immense amount of work, both vast and delicate. A beginning has already been made in the encyclicals of Leo XIII and Pius XI, which lay down the general principles. I may point out that this is a question of a work of reason, of reason indeed illuminated by faith, but a work of reason, in which, as soon as we quit the principles to come down to their particular application, it will be vain to look for a unanimous agreement. If there are diverse schools of dogmatic theology there will inevitably be a like diversity among the schools of Christian sociology and of Christian politics, divisions which will only increase the more with each approach to the concrete. Nevertheless a common doctrine can doubtless be formulated, at least in what is concerned with more general truths: and for the rest, what is important is that a general plan which is truly precise and practical should be elucidated for a sufficient number of minds.

But the Christian conscious of these things must also approach the point of political and social action, not only, as has always been the case, in devoting his professional gifts to the service of his country according to his capacities, but also and more particularly in order to work, as I have said, towards a transformation of the temporal order.

But, since it is clear that social Christianity is inseparable from spiritual Christianity, it is impossible that a vitally Christian transformation of the temporal order can take place in the same way or by the same means as other temporal transformations and revolutions. If this is to be, it will be a fruit of christian heroism.

'The social revolution will be moral or it will be nothing.' This famous saying of Charles Péguy can be entirely misunderstood. 'It does not mean that before a reform of the social order can be made effective all men must first be converted to virtuous living. Interpreted in that way, the saying would be merely a pharisaical pretext for avoiding any effort at social reform. Revolutions are the work of comparatively small groups of men who devote all their energies to the task:

it is to these men that the words of Péguy are addressed. His meaning is: you can only transform the social order of the modern world by effecting at the same time and first of all within your own soul a renewal of moral and spiritual life: by digging down to the moral and spiritual foundations of human existence, and reviving the moral ideas that govern the life of the social body as such; and by awakening a new impulse in the secret sources of its being. . . .

'But has the true and perfect heroism, the heroism of love, no lesson to offer? Once the Christian conscience comes to realise the essential character of social life, with its distinctive being and reality and technique, will not Christian sanctity have to enter and labour in the same field in which the Hammer and the Sickle and the Fasces and the Swastika have severally pursued their heroic task? Is it not high time that sanctity should descend from the heaven of cloistered life that four centuries of the baroque spirit had reserved for it, descend to the world of secular culture and labour in social and political affairs with a view to the reform of the temporal order of mankind? Yes indeed; on condition that it retains its sanctity and does not lose its character on the way. There is the rub.

'The Christian body has at such a time as ours two opposite dangers that it needs to avoid: the danger of seeking sanctity only in the desert, and the danger of forgetting the need of the desert for sanctity; the danger of enclosing in the cloister of the interior life and of private virtue the heroism it ought to share among mankind, and the danger of conceiving this heroism, when it overflows into social life and endeavours to transform it, in the same manner as its materialist opponents: according to a purely external standard; which is to pervert and dissipate it. Christian heroism has not the same sources as heroism of other kinds. It has its source in the heart of a God scourged and turned to scorn and crucified outside the city gate.

'It is time for Christian sanctity again as in the centuries of the Middle Ages to put its hand to the things of earth but with the consciousness that its strength and majesty are from elsewhere and of another order.'[8]

A vitally Christian social renewal will thus be a work of

sanctity or it will be nothing: a sanctity, that is, which has turned its energies on the things of time, of this world, of secular culture. Has the world not known heretofore leaders of the people who were saints? If a new Christendom is to arise in history it will be the work of such leaders and such sanctity.

A *new style of sanctity*

We have thus come to a new and final problem: if these observations are exact, we have the right to look forward to an impulse of a new-style sanctity.

Do not let us talk about a 'new type of sanctity'; the phrase is more than ambiguous: there is only one type of sanctity recognized by Christians, once and forever manifested in Christ. But the changing conditions of history allow of new ways, new styles of sanctity. The sanctity of St. Francis has a different physiognomy from that of St. Simeon Stylites. Jesuit spirituality, Dominican spirituality, Benedictine spirituality have each their different modes. We are thus justified in thinking that the Christian's awareness of his social and temporal office calls for a new way of sanctity, one which may be primarily characterised as a sanctity and sanctification of *secular* life.

But, indeed, this new way is new primarily in regard to certain erroneous and materialised preconceptions. This is so since—as often happened in the age of classical humanism —the well-known distinction between the two states of life (the religious and the secular), when subject to a form of sociological depression, is understood in a materialistic and inexact sense; the religious life, i.e. the life of those vowed to the search for perfection, is then regarded as the state of the perfect and the secular state as that of the imperfect, so that in a way it becomes the duty and metaphysical function of the imperfect to be imperfect and to stay so: to lead a good, not too pious, worldly life, solidly grounded on a social naturalism (above all in family ambition). On these terms it would be scandalous for lay folk to seek to live otherwise; their business is from their material resources to make prosperous, by means of pious foundations, the religious who in exchange will win them a way into heaven, whereby all the claims of order will be satisfied.

This way of conceiving of lay humility seems to have been widely enough extended in the sixteenth and seventeenth centuries. It was for this reason that the explanatory catechism of the dominican Carranza, who was, moreover, Archbishop of Toledo, was condemned by the Spanish Inquisition at the direction of the celebrated theologian, Melchior Cano. This latter declared that 'it is entirely wrong to claim to give the faithful a form of religious instruction which is only suitable to priests. . . . He was equally in arms against the reading of the Gospel in the common tongue, against those who made it a duty all the day long to confess their faith. The zeal of spiritual directors for frequent confession and communion among the faithful was to him highly suspect, and the saying is attributed to him in a sermon that in his eyes one of the signs of the approach of Anti-christ was this general frequentation of the sacraments'.[9]

Going deeper into the matter, and thereby coming to a very important question for cultural philosophy, it can be said that there is a way of seeing this distinction between the sacred and the profane which is not Christian, but pagan.

For pagan antiquity what was *holy* was synonymous with the *sacred*, i.e. with what physically, visibly, socially belonged to God. And it was only in the degree to which these sacred functions entered into human life that the latter had any value before God. The Gospel changed all this profoundly, by setting in the heart of man, in the secret and invisible relations between the Divine personality and the human, the core of the moral life and life of sanctity. Henceforth the secular is no longer opposed to the sacred as the impure to the pure, but as a certain order of human activities with a temporal specific end is in opposition to another order of human activities socially built up for a specific end which is spiritual. And the man who is engaged in this profane and temporal order can and should, like the man engaged in the sacred order, tend towards sanctity,—so as to himself attain to union with the divine, and also to bring about the fulfilment of the divine Will in the entire order to which he belongs. In fact this secular order, as a collective form, will

always be deficient,[10] but we ought thereby to wish and to
strive all the more that it be the best that may be. For the
justice of the Gospels claims to penetrate all things, to be
concerned with all things, to affect the lowest things as the
highest. More, it can be pointed out that this evangelical
principle is only progressively manifested and translated in
concrete terms, and that the process of this realisation is by
no means complete.

The foregoing remarks should have made clear the significance of this new style of sanctity, that new stage in the
sanctification of what is profane, of which I have been speaking. Let it be added that this new mode, which touches pure
spirituality, will probably have the stamp of certain particular specifically spiritual characteristics—for example, an insistence on simplicity, on the value of ordinary means, on that
specifically Christian trait of perfection being the perfection,
not of a stoic athleticism of virtue, but of the *love* between
two persons, created personality and the Person of God;
finally, an insistence on that law of the uncreated love into
the depths of the human, to transfigure without annihilating it, characteristics of which certain contemporary saints
seemed charged to show us the importance. It is, moreover,
in the order of things that it is not in the secular life, but in
certain souls hidden from the world, some living in the world,
some on the crest of the highest towers of Christendom, in
other words in the supremely contemplative orders, that the
first light of the dawn of this way of sanctity, of this new
impulse of spirituality, is breaking; to spread from thence into
all our temporal and secular ways of life.

The mystery of this world

I shall reserve for later that question of the world and its
significance which is a capital one for Christian philosophy,
and of which the multiple problems call for deeper study.
In this chapter I have only been able to touch on it from the
outside, and to indicate certain general positions which strike
me as of primary importance. To make a brief résumé of
these: while yet in anticipation of that hour beyond history
when the Kingdom of God will be fully manifest in glory,

the Church is already the Kingdom of God in what we call the *spiritual* order and in a state of pilgrimage and crucifixion; and the world, the so-called *temporal* order, the world enclosed in history, is a divided and ambiguous domain, —belonging at one and the same time to God, to mankind and to 'the Prince of this world'.

The Church is holy, the world is not holy; but the world is saved in hope, and the blood of Christ, the vivifying principle of the Redemption, acts already within it. A divine and hidden travail works in history, and in each age of civilisation, beneath each 'historic heaven', the Christian must strive for some proportionate realisation (in expectation of that final realisation which is beyond time), for some realisation of the claims of the Gospel and of practical Christian wisdom in the socio-temporal order,—a realisation which is thwarted in fact and more or less masked and deformed by sin: but that is another matter.

Since men taken collectively live more often according to the senses than by reason, this work of which I speak (when the Christians to undertake it are not lacking, otherwise it is the opposing forces which take charge under the banner of destruction) meets, in the ordinary course of things, stronger resistance and more frequent betrayal the more it succeeds in establishing itself in existence. Hence the necessity of beginning again, of starting once more at the lowest rung, obliges history perpetually to surpass itself "from fall to fall" until the hour strikes that brings it to an end.

NOTES

1. Cf. *Freedom in the Modern World*.
2. See R. H. Tawney, *Religion and the Rise of Capitalism*, 1926, pp. 286–7.
3. See *Religion and Culture*, note 2, on the fecundity of money. *Editors' Note:* In a later work, *Reflections on America* (1958) Prof. Maritain reiterates his view that the inner logic of the industrial regime of capitalism is grounded on the fecundity of money and the primacy of profit but expresses his conviction that the American people are transforming this regime, going

beyond capitalism and inaugurating a new phase in modern civilization (pp. 21–23). See Introduction, pp. 9–10.

4. The unemployed are potential consumers. In the face of this mass of humanity in a state of privation, the existence of a mass of products in *apparent* over-production, because no connection can be established between the two, stands as the condemnation of an economy based on the capitalist theory of profit. At the time of writing, the world was still in the grip of a severe economic depression.

5. *Freedom in the Modern World*, pp. 123–24.

6. Bernard Groethuysen, *Origines de l'esprit bourgeois en France, I: l'Église et la Bourgeoisie*, Paris, N.F.R., 1927.

7. *Freedom in the Modern World*, p. 125.

8. *Ibid.*, pp. 142, 144–45.

9. Saudreau, 'Le mouvement antimystique en Espagne au XVIme siècle' *Revue du Clergé Français*, 1st August, 1917.

10. The order of sacred activities will also, in the degree to which it is a collective human form, be deficient here on earth. It is in so far as it is specially assisted by the spirit of God, and in the degree to which it is governed by its invisible Head (and by its visible head when he acts by right of his universal authority) that the Church is indefectible.

15. THE DEMOCRATIC CHARTER

The Democratic Secular Faith

In the "sacral" era of the Middle Ages a great attempt was made to build the life of the earthly community and civilization on the foundation of the unity of theological faith and religious creed. This attempt succeeded for a certain number of centuries but failed in the course of time, after the Reformation and the Renaissance; and a return to the mediaeval sacral pattern is in no way conceivable. In proportion as the civil society, or body politic, has become more perfectly distinguished from the spiritual realm of the Church—a process which was in itself but a development of the Gospel distinction between the things that are Caesar's and the things that are God's—the civil society has become grounded on a common good and a common task which are of an earthly, "temporal," or "secular" order, and in which citizens belonging to diverse spiritual groups or lineages share equally. Religious division among men is in itself a misfortune. But it is a fact that we must willy-nilly recognize.

In modern times an attempt was made to base the life of civilization and the earthly community on the foundation of mere reason—reason separated from religion and from the Gospel. This attempt fostered immense hopes in the last two centuries,—and rapidly failed. Pure reason showed itself more incapable than faith of ensuring the spiritual unity of mankind, and the dream of a "scientific" creed, uniting men in peace and in common convictions about the aims and basic principles of human life and society, vanished in our contemporary catastrophes. In proportion as the tragic events of the last decades have given the lie to the bourgeois rationalism of the XVIIIth and XIXth Centuries, we have been confronted with the fact that religion and metaphysics are an essential part of human culture, primary and indispensable incentives in the very life of society.

As a result, it seems likely that, if democracy enters its

next historical stage with sufficient intelligence and vitality, a renewed democracy will not ignore religion, as the bourgeois XIXth Century society, both individualist and "neutral," did; and that this renewed, "personalist" democracy will be of a *pluralistic* type.

Thus we would have—supposing that the people have regained their Christian faith, or at least recognized the value and sensibleness of the Christian conception of freedom, social progress, and the political establishment—we would have, on the one hand, a body politic Christianly inspired in its own political life. On the other hand, this personalist body politic would recognize that men belonging to most different philosophical or religious creeds and lineages could and should cooperate in the common task and for the common welfare, provided they similarly assent to the basic tenets of a society of free men. These common tenets, that is the subject matter which requests our attention and which I should like to discuss.

For a society of free men implies basic tenets which are at the core of its very existence. A genuine democracy implies a fundamental agreement between minds and wills on the bases of life in common; it is aware of itself and of its principles, and it must be capable of defending and promoting its own conception of social and political life; *it must bear within itself a common human creed, the creed of freedom.* The mistake of bourgeois liberalism has been to conceive democratic society to be a kind of list or arena in which all the conceptions of the bases of common life, even those most destructive to freedom and law, meet with no more than the pure and simple indifference of the body politic, while they compete before public opinion in a kind of free market of the mother-ideas, healthy or poisoned, of political life. Nineteenth Century bourgeois democracy was *neutral* even with regard to freedom. Just as it had no real *common good,* it had no real *common thought*—no brains of its own, but a neutral, empty skull clad with mirrors: no wonder that before the Second World War, in countries that fascist, racist, or communist propaganda was to disturb or to corrupt, it had become a society without any idea of itself and without faith in itself, without any *common faith* which could enable it to resist disintegration.

But the all-important point to be noted here is that this faith and inspiration, and the concept of itself which democracy needs—all these do not belong to the order of religious creed and eternal life, but to the temporal or secular order of earthly life, of culture or civilization. The *faith* in question is a *civic or secular faith*, not a religious one. Nor is it that philosophic substitute for religious faith, that adherence forced upon all by reason's demonstration, which the XVIIIth and XIXth Century philosophers sought in vain. A genuine democracy cannot impose on its citizens or demand from them as a condition for their belonging to the city, any philosophic or any religious creed. This conception of the city was possible during the "sacral" period of our civilization, when communion in the Christian faith was a prerequisite for the constitution of the body politic. In our own day it has been able to produce only the inhuman counterfeit, whether hypocritical or violent, offered by the totalitarian States which lay claim to the faith, the obedience, and the love of the religious man for his God; it has produced only their effort to impose their creed on the mind of the masses by the power of propaganda, lies, and the police.

What is, then, the object of the *secular faith* that we are discussing? This object is a merely practical one, not a theoretical or dogmatic one. The secular faith in question deals with *practical* tenets which the human mind can try to justify —more or less successfully, that's another affair—from quite different philosophical outlooks, probably because they depend basically on simple, "natural" apperceptions, of which the human heart becomes capable with the progress of moral conscience, and which, as a matter of fact, have been awakened by the Gospel leaven fermenting in the obscure depths of human history. Thus it is that men possessing quite different, even opposite metaphysical or religious outlooks, can converge, not by virtue of any identity of doctrine, but by virtue of an analogical similitude in practical principles, toward the same practical conclusions, and can share in the same practical secular faith, provided that they similarly revere, perhaps for quite diverse reasons, truth and intelligence, human dignity, freedom, brotherly love, and the absolute value of moral good.

We must therefore maintain a sharp and clear distinction between the human and temporal creed which lies at the root of common life and which is but a set of *practical conclusions* or of *practical points of convergence*—on the one hand; and on the other, the *theoretical justifications*, the conceptions of the world and of life, the philosophical or religious creeds which found, or claim to found, these practical conclusions in reason.

The body politic has the right and the duty to promote among its citizens, mainly through education, the human and temporal—and essentially practical—creed on which depend national communion and civil peace. It has no right, as a merely temporal or secular body, enclosed in the sphere where the modern State enjoys its autonomous authority, to impose on the citizens or to demand from them a rule of faith or a conformism of reason, a philosophical or religious creed which would present itself as the only possible justification of the practical charter through which the people's common secular faith expresses itself. The important thing for the body politic is that the democratic sense be in fact kept alive by the adherence of minds, however diverse, to this moral charter. The ways and the justifications by means of which this common adherence is brought about pertain to the freedom of minds and consciences.

Certainly, it is supremely important to the common good that the practical assertions which make up the charter in question be true in themselves. But the democratic State does not judge of that truth; it is born out of that truth, as recognized and asserted by the people—by each one of us, to the extent of his abilities.

What would be the content of the moral charter, the code of social and political morality which I am speaking about and the validity of which is implied by the fundamental compact of a society of free men? Such a charter would deal, for instance, with the following points: rights and liberties of the human person, political rights and liberties, social rights and social liberties, corresponding responsibilities; rights and duties of persons who are part of a family society, and liberties and obligations of the latter toward the body politic; mutual rights and duties of groups and the State; government of the people, by the people, and for the people; functions of authority in a political and social democracy, moral obligation, binding in conscience, regarding just laws as well as the Constitution which guarantees the people's liberties; exclusion of the resort to political coups (*coups d'état*) in a society that is truly free and ruled by laws whose change and evolution depend on the popular majority; human equality, justice between persons and the body politic, justice between the body politic and persons, civil friendship and an ideal of fraternity, religious freedom, mutual tolerance and mutual respect between various spiritual communities and schools of thought, civic history and heritage, and understanding of the various traditions that combine to create its unity; obligations of each person toward the common good of the body politic and obligations of each nation toward the common good of civilized society, and the necessity of becoming aware of the unity of the world and of the existence of a community of peoples.

It is a fact that in democratic nations, which, like the United States and France, have a hard historic experience of the struggles for freedom, practically everybody would be ready to endorse all the tenets of such a charter. Given that virtue of universality with which the civilization inherited from Christianity is endowed, as Toynbee has shown in a persuasive manner, we have good reason to hope that in all nations of the world the people—I say the people, whatever their governments may be—would be able to put forward the same endorsement.

I should like to add two remarks which do not deal directly with the issue that I just discussed, but rather with the problems that we shall consider in the next chapter.

First: as a matter of fact, the more the body politic—that is, the people—were imbued with Christian convictions and aware of the *religious* faith which inspires it, the more deeply it would adhere to the *secular* faith in the democratic charter; for, as a matter of fact, the latter has taken shape in human history as a result of the Gospel inspiration awakening the "naturally Christian" potentialities of common secular consciousness, even among the diversity of spiritual lineages and schools of thought opposed to each other, and sometimes warped by a vitiated ideology.

Second: to the extent that the body politic—that is, the people—were imbued with Christian convictions, to the same extent, as a matter of fact, the justification of the democratic charter offered by Christian philosophy would be recognized as the truest one—not at all as a result of any interference of the State, but only as a result of the free adherence which larger parts of the people would have given to Christian faith and Christian philosophy in actual fact.

And of course no religious pressure would be exercised by the majority. Non-Christian citizens' freedom to found their democratic beliefs on grounds different from those more generally accepted would by no means be jeopardized. What the civil authority and the State would be concerned with is only the common secular faith in the common secular charter.

Problems concerning authority

I have treated of authority in democracy in another book.[1] Yet it is necessary to sum up a few considerations of the subject in order to have our concept of the democratic charter sufficiently complete. I am not dissatisfied, moreover, to have an opportunity to make certain positions clearer and more definite—and truer, I hope—than in my previous essays.

Authority and Power are two different things: *Power* is the force by means of which you can oblige others to obey you. *Authority* is the *right* to direct and command, to be listened to or obeyed by others. Authority requests Power. Power without authority is tyranny.

Thus authority means right. If, in the cosmos, a nature, such as human nature, can be preserved and developed only in a state of culture, and if the state of culture necessarily entails the existence in the social group of a function of commandment and government directed to the common good, then this function is demanded by Natural Law, and implies a *right* to command and govern.

Furthermore, if the said function, which in direct democracy is exercized by the "multitude" or the people themselves, can be properly exercized, in larger and more differentiated societies, only on the condition that the people entrust it to certain men who will be henceforth especially concerned with the affairs of the whole, then those men, once put in charge of the direction of the community, have a *right* (received from and through the people) to be obeyed for the sake of the common good: in other words, the relation of authority among men proceeds from Natural Law. I mean here the relation of authority taken as yet indeterminately, and not in the sense that *some* in particular must command and *some* in particular must obey; but rather in the general sense that there must be people who command and people who obey, the mode of designation of those who shall command being a different matter to be determined later and according to reason.[2]

Finally, since authority means *right*, it has to be obeyed by reason of conscience, that is, in the manner in which free men obey, and for the sake of the common good.[3]

But by the same token there is no authority where there is no justice. Unjust authority is not authority, as an unjust law is not law. At the origin of the democratic sense, there is not the desire to "obey only oneself," as Rousseau put it, but rather the desire to obey only *because it is just*.

* * *

Whatever the regime of political life may be, authority, that is, the right to direct and to command, derives from the people, but has its primary source in the Author of nature. Authority derives from the will or *consensus* of the people, and from their basic right to govern themselves, as from a channel through which nature causes a body politic to be and to act.

These two statements, expressed as they are in the most general and still undetermined way, have been a matter of common agreement for a century-old tradition in political philosophy. But they have been understood in quite different and sharply opposed manners.

A first issue, dealing with the relationship between the people and God, has been: do the people receive from God the right to self-government and authority to rule themselves in a merely *transient and transitory* way? So that when they designate their rulers they act only as an *instrumental cause*[4] through which God alone (as principal agent) invests with authority the one or ones designated?

Or do the people receive from God the right to self-government and authority to rule themselves in an *inherent* manner? So that they are possessed of this right and this authority as a "principal agent" (though "secondary" or subordinate with respect to the Primary Cause) which through its own causal power—acting, as everything acts, in the virtue of God's universal activation—invests with authority the one or ones designated?[5] It is this second part of the alternative which has proved to be the true one.

And a second issue, dealing with the relationship between the people and their rulers, has been: do the people, when they invest certain men with authority, *divest themselves* of their right to self-government and their authority to rule themselves (whatever the way may be—transient or inherent —in which they have received these rights from God)? So that once the ruler or rulers have been put in charge, the people *lose* their right to self-government and their authority to rule themselves, which have been transferred to the ruler or rulers and are henceforth possessed by them alone?

Or do the people, when they invest certain men with authority, *keep* their right to self-government and their authority to rule themselves? So that they possess these rights, not only *inherently* with respect to the manner in which they receive them from God, but also *permanently* with respect to the manner in which they convey them to their rulers?

In modern history the age of the absolute kings, as we have seen in discussing Sovereignty,[6] has answered affirmatively the first part of this alternative, negatively the second. Yet the right answer is *no* to the first part of the alternative, and *yes* to the second. The realization of this basic verity (long ago pointed out by some great Schoolmen) has been a conquest of democratic philosophy. In this connection, whatever the political *régime* may be, monarchical, aristocratic, or democratic, democratic *philosophy* appears as the only true political philosophy.

The trouble has been that from the very moment when it took the upper hand, this philosophy was imperiled by a counterfeit ideology, the ideology of Sovereignty. Instead of getting clear of the concept of Sovereignty (which implies *transcendent* or *separate* supreme power, supreme power *from above*), Rousseau transferred to the people the Sovereignty of the absolute monarch conceived in the most absolute manner; in other terms he made a mythical people—the people as the monadic subject of the indivisible General Will —into a sovereign Person separated from the real people (the multitude) and ruling them from above. As a result, since a figment of the imagination cannot really rule, it is to the State—to the State which, in genuine democratic philosophy, should be supervised and controlled by the people,—that, as a matter of fact, Sovereignty, indivisible and not-accountable Sovereignty, was to be transferred. On the other hand, Sovereignty cannot be shared in; consequently, the people, or the Sovereign Person, could not invest any official with authority over them; only the people as a whole could make laws, and the men elected by them did not hold any real authority, or right to command. The elected of the people were only passive instruments, not representatives. As a matter of principle, the very concept of representative of the people was to be wiped away.

This concept, however, is absolutely essential to genuine democratic philosophy. It is on the notion of representation or vicariousness, by virtue of which the very right of the people to rule themselves is exercised by the officials whom the people have chosen, that all the theory of power in democratic society rests. As I shall emphasize further, the representatives of the people are "sent," missioned or commissioned, by the people to exercise authority because they are made by the people participants, to some given extent, in the very authority of the people, in other words because they are made by the people *images* of and *deputies* for the people.

Those who represent the people are not the image of God. The Pope in the Church, being the vicar of Christ, is the image of Christ. The Prince in political society, being the vicar of the people, is the image of the people. A great deal of confusion occurred in this regard in the age of absolutism, because the authority of the king was often conceived of on the pattern of the authority of the Pope, that is to say, as coming down from above, whereas in reality it came up from below. For another reason a great deal of confusion had previously occurred in the Middle Ages: because the solemn anointing or coronation of the king, by sanctioning from the sacred heights of the supernatural order his right to command in the natural order, conveyed to him, as servant or secular arm of the Church, a reflection of the supernatural royal virtues, bounty, justice, and the paternal love of Christ, Head of the Church. From this point of view the Middle Ages might regard the king as the image of Christ.[7] But in the natural order, which is the order of political life, he was not the image of Christ, he was the image of the people. Theologians, especially in the Thomist lineage, were able clearly to make that distinction. But mediaeval common consciousness remained enmeshed in an ambivalent idea of the Prince.

The civil power bears the impress of majesty: this is not because it represents God. It is because it represents the people, the whole multitude and its common will to live together. And by the same token since it represents the people, the civil power holds its authority, through the people, from the Primary Cause of Nature and of human society.[8] St. Paul teaches that "there is no authority that is not from God" and that those who bear the sword are "God's ministers" or "functionaries of God," "appointed by God" (let us understand, through the people) "to inflict his wrathful vengeance upon him that doth wrong."[9] Never did he teach that they were the image of God. What essentially constituted, in its own temporal or political order, the majesty of the king is the same as what the majesty of the President of a democratic nation consists of, especially when he is invested with such constitutional powers as those in this country. For the President, just as the king, can be a quite ordinary man deprived of any personal prestige; yet look at him when he acts in his capacity of supreme chief of the body politic: millions of citizens, with their collective power, their hopes, their trust, their century-old heritage of suffering and glory, their

prospective collective destiny, their collective calling in mankind's history, are there, in his person, as in a sign which
makes them present to our eyes. Here is majesty, here is the
essence of his political majesty. Not because he is a Sovereign! since in the political domain there is no such thing as
sovereignty. But because he is the image of the people, and
the topmost deputy of the people. And behind this majesty,
as its supreme foundation, there is the eternal Law of the
primary cause of being, source of the authority which is in
the people and in which the vicar of the people participates.
And if the man is righteous and faithful to his mission there
is reason to believe that, when the common good of the people is at stake, and when he acts in communion with the
people, he may somehow receive, in whatever obscure or even
tortuous way, some particular inspiration ("*grâce d'état*," aid
called for by one's vocational duty) from the One who is the
supreme governor of human history.

The majesty of which I am speaking exists also (in the
European parliamentary régimes it exists mainly) in the as-
semblies composed of the representatives of the people, insofar as they are a collective image of the people and a
collective deputy for the people. (They should be conscious
of that; when they themselves lose the sense of their inherent
majesty, and behave like a throng of irresponsible school-
boys or clan fighters at feud, this is a bad sign for democracy.)
And in each one of these representatives separately taken, as
deputy for a fragment of the people, part of that very
majesty, broken so to speak into pieces, still really exists.

*   *   *

Thus, in a democratic regime, the fundamental truth, recognized by democratic philosophy, that authority in the rulers
derives from the right to rule themselves inherent in the
people and permanent in them, is given a particular and
particularly appropriate expression in the typical structural
law of the body politic. Then authority deriving from the
people rises from the base to the summit of the structure of
the body politic. Power is exercised by men in whom authority, within certain fixed limits, is brought periodically to
reside through the designation of the people, and whose

management is controlled by the people: and this very fact is a sign of the continued possession, by the people, of that right to govern themselves, the exercise of which has entitled the men in question to be in command—in political command —of other men, in the virtue of the primary Source of all authority. I mean that the supremely just establishment of Uncreated Reason, which gives force of law, or of a just ordinance, to what is necessary for the very existence and common good of nature and society, causes the governing function of those men chosen by the people to be held *by right*, and, by the same token, obedience to them within the limits of their powers to be *required in justice*.

To understand these things correctly, we need, it seems to me, to sharpen the philosophical concepts traditionally used in this matter. In other words, I think that in order to bring to its full significance the political theory of Thomas Aquinas, which has been developed in so valuable a manner by Cajetan,[10] Bellarmine[11] and Suarez[12] in the XVIth and XVIIth centuries, we have still to add certain further clarifications, the principle of which is to be found in the very notion of *vicariousness*, as used by St. Thomas himself with respect to the Prince "vicar of the multitude,"[13] and elaborated by him in quite another field, namely the theory of the sign as "vicar" of the thing signified.[14]

Then two main points of doctrine, to which our preceding remarks have already alluded, would be clearly brought out. The first relates to the fact that in investing rulers with authority the people lose in no way possession of their basic right to self-government. The second relates to the fact that the representatives of the people are not mere instruments, but rulers invested with real authority, or right to command.

When I possess a material good, I cannot give it to another without losing by the very fact my possession of it. Conceiving things in that way has been the trouble with the classical theories of political power, especially, as we have seen, with the misleading theory of Sovereignty.[15] But when it is a question of a moral or spiritual quality, such as a right is, I can invest another man with a right of mine without myself losing possession of it, if this man receives this right in a vicarious manner—as a vicar of myself. Then he is made into an image of myself, and it is in this capacity that he participates in the very same right which is mine by essence. (Similarly, the disciple *as such* participates in the very same science which is in his teacher, and if he teaches in his turn—I mean in his mere capacity as a disciple, conveying the science of another —he will teach as a vicar, or an image of his teacher, and as a deputy for him;—and for all that, his teacher will not have divested himself of any bit of his own science.) The people are possessed of their right to govern themselves in an inherent and permanent manner. And the rulers, because they have been made into the vicars of the people, or into an image of them, are invested *per participationem*—to the extent of their powers—with the *very same* right and authority to govern which exists in the people *per essentiam*, as given them by the Author of nature and grounded upon His transcendent, uncreated authority. The people, by designating their representatives, do not lose or give up possession of their own authority to govern themselves and of their right to supreme autonomy.

Now there is a distinction between the *possession* of a right and the *exercise* of it.[16] It is the very exercise of the people's right to self-government which causes the rulers chosen by the people to be invested with authority, according to the duration of the office, and to the measure and the degree of their attributions: the very exercise of the right of the people to self-government restricts therefore to that extent, not this right itself, but the further *exercise* of it (in other words, the "power" of the people)—since the right of the people to self-government cannot be exercised in actual fact (except in the smallest groups or in the particular case of popular *referendum*) without placing certain men in public service, and, by the same token, having them invested with genuine authority. There is no lack of similar examples, where the very exercise of a right (for instance the right to choose one's vocation or state of life) restricts further exercise without causing to end, or lessening in any way, the possession of that right itself.

Thus we come to the second point. The representatives of the people are possessed of authority in a vicarious manner, in their capacity as vicars or image of the people, and deputies for them. But they are a living and active, not a dead image of the people, an image which is a human person, endowed with reason, free will, and responsibility. And they cannot *exercise* the vicarious authority of which they are possessed if not as human persons and free agents, whose personal conscience is committed in the performance of their mission. So the authority they exercise, which is the very same authority of the people participated in to some given extent and within certain given limits, is a vicarious but a genuine authority, held, like the people's authority, in the virtue of the primary Source of all authority; they really hold a right to command and to be obeyed. They are not mere instruments of a mythical general will; they are actual rulers of the people; they have to make their decisions conformably to the dictates of their conscience, to the laws of that specific branch of Ethics which is political Ethics, to the judgment of their virtue (if they have any) of political prudence, and to what they see required by the common good—even if by so doing they incur the displeasure of the people.

The fact remains that they are accountable to the people, and that their management has to be supervised and controlled by the people. The fact also remains that, since their authority is but the authority of the people vicariously participated in, they have to rule, not as *separated* from the people (except as regards the existential conditions for exercising authority),[17] but as *united* with the people in their very essence of deputies for them. Here is a difficult question, which I should like to try to make clear. I just said that the representatives of the people must be ready to incur the displeasure of the people, if their conscience demands it. Now I am saying that they must carry out their obligations in communion with the people. Are these two statements contradictory? They are not, on the condition that this expression "in communion with the people" be correctly understood.

In what can be called the common psyche of the people there is a huge variety of levels and degrees. At the most superficial level there are the momentary trends of opinion, as transient as the waves on the sea, and subjected to all winds of anxiety, fear, particular passions, or particular interests. At deeper levels, there are the real needs of the multitude. At the deepest level, there is the will to live together, and the obscure consciousness of a common destiny and vocation, and finally the natural trend of the human will, considered in its essence, toward the good. Furthermore—this is a point we shall meet in the next section—people are ordinarily distracted from their most capital aspirations and interests, as a people, by each one's everyday business and suffering. Under such circumstances, to rule in communion with the people means on the one hand educating and awakening the people in the very process of governing them, so as to demand of them, at each progressive step, what they themselves have been made aware of and eager for (I am thinking of a real work of education, grounded on respect for them and trust in them, and in which they are the "principal agent"[18]—just the contrary to selling them ideas through sheer propaganda and advertising techniques). It means on the other hand, being intent on what is deep and lasting, and most really worthy of man, in the aspirations and psyche of the people. Thus it is that in incurring the disfavor of the people a ruler can still act in communion with the people, in the truest sense of this expression. And if he is a great ruler, he will perhaps make that disfavor into a renewed and more profound trust. In any case there is nothing in common between despotically imposing one's own will on the people—as a ruler from above separated from them—and resisting the people, or becoming hated and rejected by them, while being united with them in one's inmost intentions, and heedful of keeping communion with their deepest human will, that they ignore.

If this question is intricate, it is because no relation is more complex and mysterious than the relation between a man and the multitude for whose common good he is responsible, precisely because the authority he possesses is a vicarious authority, ultimately grounded in God, which he exercises as a free and responsible agent, image of the multitude and deputy for it. If we are looking for the most significant—though too transcendent for our purpose—type of a Legislator, let us think of Moses and his relation with the Jewish people. But the rulers of our political societies are not prophets directly commissioned by God, and this makes their case a little more simple.

At this point it would perhaps be appropriate to use the distinction, which I have emphasized in another essay, between a *law* and a *decree*. "Law and decree belong to two specifically distinct spheres: law, to the sphere of the *structural forms* of authority; decree, to the sphere of the *existential exercise* of authority. . . . A *law* is a general and lasting rule (general, that is to say, which determines in the social body a certain *functional relation*; lasting, that is to say, which is directed to something beyond the present moment or circumstance, and *calculated not to change*). A decree is a particular ordinance, determining a *point of fact* in the framework of the law, and confronted with a given circumstance for a given time."[19] Then I would say that a decree can without too much drawback be promulgated contrary to the trends prevalent at the moment in the people, and forced upon a reluctant public opinion. But a law should normally be laid down (always supposing that it be just) in accordance with the common consciousness of the people as expressed in the mores or in collective needs and requests of organic groups of the population, or in spontaneous social and public service regulations in the making. Here could be saved the element of truth in Duguit's theory, unacceptable in itself, of "objective law." Contrary to this theory, the law is and will always remain a work of the reason of those who are in charge of the common good: but this same reason of the Legislator has to give shape to, or to express in a formed "word," an achieved *verbum*, what exists in the common mind in an inchoate, unformulated manner.

The prophetic shock-minorities

The last issue to be discussed no longer deals with the *people*, but with—how shall I designate them?—well, with the *inspired servants* or *prophets of the people*.

What I mean is that it is not enough to define a democratic society by its legal structure. Another element plays also a basic part, namely the dynamic leaven or energy which fosters political *movement*, and which cannot be inscribed in any constitution or embodied in any institution, since it is both personal and contingent in nature, and rooted in free initiative. I should like to call that existential factor a prophetic factor. Democracy cannot do without it. The people need prophets.

And those servants or prophets of the people are not—not necessarily—elected representatives of the people. Their mission starts in their own hearts and consciousness. In this sense they are self-appointed prophets. They are needed in the normal functioning of a democratic society. They are needed especially in the periods of crisis, birth, or basic renewal of a democratic society.

Truly speaking, something similar is to be found in every political regime. The kings of past ages were surrounded with *grands commis*, great stewards, favorite counsellors or ministers, in ruthless competition with one another; each one of them believed or alleged that his own views and endeavors expressed the hidden *real* will of the king. They took a risk. When they were mistaken, they were broken by the king, sometimes they were sent into exile or were hanged. The same story takes place in totalitarian States with rival high officials and political cliques in the bosom of the party.

In democratic societies the people play the part of the king, and the inspired servants of the people that of the great counsellors. As a rule they are prophets of emancipation—national, political, or social emancipation.

In the normal functioning of a democratic society the political animation thus proceeds from men who, feeling themselves designated for a vocation of leadership, follow the usual channels of political activity—they will become chiefs of political parties, they will come to power through the legal machinery of elections. The happiest circumstance for the body politic obtains when the top men in the state are at the same time genuine prophets of the people. I think that in a renewed democracy the vocation of leadership which I just mentioned,—a sinister image of which is offered us by the *unique Party* of the totalitarian States,—should normally be exercised by small dynamic groups freely organized and multiple in nature, which would not be concerned with electoral success but with devoting themselves entirely to a great social and political idea, and which would act as a ferment either inside or outside the political parties.[20]

But it is in periods of crisis, birth, or basic transformation that the role of the inspired servants, the prophets of the people, takes on full importance. Let us think, for example, of the fathers of the French Revolution or of the American Constitution, of men like Tom Paine or Thomas Jefferson; or of that John Brown—still a criminal for Southerners, a hero for Northerners—who was convinced he had a divine commission to destroy slavery by the force of arms, and who captured the arsenal at Harper's Ferry, to be hanged some months later, in December 1859:

> John Brown's body lies a-mouldering in the grave,
> But his soul goes marching on.

Or of the originators of the Italian Risorgimento,[21] or of the liberation of Ireland; let us think of Gandhi once again, or of the pioneers of unionism and the labor movement. The primary work of the inspired servant of the people is to awaken the people, to awaken them to something better than everyone's daily business, to the sense of a supra-individual task to be performed.

That is a quite vital and necessary social phenomenon. And it is a quite dangerous phenomenon. For where there is inspiration and prophecy, there are false prophets and true prophets; thieves aiming to dominate men and servants aiming to set them free; inspiration from dark instincts and inspiration from genuine love. And nothing is more difficult than what is called "discrimination between spirits." It is easy to mistake impure inspiration for unsullied inspiration; nay more, it is easy to slip from genuine inspiration to a corrupt one. And we know that *optimi corruptio pessima*, corruption of what is best is what is worst.

The political problem we are confronted with at this point is the problem of the prophetic pioneering minorities or shock-minorities,—I say shock-minorities as one says shock-troops—a problem which any theory of democracy should frankly face.

The people are to be awakened—that means that the people are asleep. People as a rule prefer to sleep. Awakenings are always bitter. Insofar as their daily interests are involved, what people would like is business as usual: everyday misery and humiliation as usual. People would like to ignore that they are *the* people. It is a fact that, for good or evil, the great historical changes in political societies have been brought about by a few, who were convinced that they embodied the real will—to be awakened—of the people, as contrasting with the people's wish to sleep. At the time of the Risorgimento, the great majority of Italians surely preferred not to be set free from the Austrian yoke. If a popular poll had been taken at the time of Samuel Adams, we may wonder whether the majority would have voted for the War of Independence. If a popular poll had been taken in France in 1940, it is highly probable that the majority would have voted for Marshal Pétain,—they believed he hated collaboration with the Germans as they did. In all these cases, the majority went wrong, and the shock-minorities were right.—Well, but we have also been able to contemplate how the makers of totalitarian States have used the power of vanguard insurgent minorities.

The question is: are the people to be *awakened* or to be *used?* to be awakened like men or to be whipped and driven like cattle? The prophetic minorities say *we the people* when in actual fact they alone, not the people, are speaking. Only the final decision of the people can prove whether that figure of speech was right or wrong. But each time a part speaks in the name of the whole, that part is tempted to believe that *it is* the whole. As a result the part will endeavor to substitute itself for the whole, or rather to oblige the whole to be "really" the whole, that is, what the part wills the whole to be. Thus the entire process will become rotten, and instead of awakening the people to freedom, as they believed or pretended they were doing, that prophetic shock-minority will dominate the people and make them more enslaved than they had been.

During the course of the XIXth Century a dreadful ambiguity existed in this regard in democratic ideology; concepts and trends inspired from genuine devotion to the people and genuine democratic philosophy were mixed up with concepts and trends inspired from spurious democratic philosophy and would-be dictatorial, mistaken devotion to the people. There were men who believed that, as Jean-Jacques Rousseau put it, they should *force* the people *to be free*.[22] I say they were betrayers of the people. For they treated the people like sick children while they were clamoring for the rights and freedom of the people. Those who distrust the people while appealing to the highest feelings and to the blood of the people cheat and betray the people. The first axiom and precept in democracy is to trust the people. Trust the people, respect the people, trust them even and first of all while awakening them, that is while putting yourself at the service of their human dignity.

The actual contempt for and distrust of the people involved in the principle "to force the people to be free" was to impair in some places the democratic mind and to develop a spurious philosophy of the mission of the self-styled enlightened minorities.

Let us summarize that spurious philosophy in the three following points. First, since the action of what I just called a prophetic shock-minority results in a showdown, and since only the fact, the event, can decide whether they were right or wrong in offering themselves as the personification of the people, then there is only one way to make good the risk that such a minority is taking, namely, *the out and out use of violence*, in order to succeed at any cost and by any means.

Second, once they have succeeded, they have to use *terror* to wipe out any possible opponent.

Third, given on the one hand the congenital dullness and infirmity of the people, on the other hand the indispensable role of prophetic shock-minorities in human history, the deep trend toward emancipation which is at work in that history requires *breaking of the law* as a perpetual and necessary condition of progress, and blossoms forth into the messianic myth of *the Revolution*. Thus the basic tenets of democratic faith were denied in the very name of democracy; and the myth of the Revolution, with a capital R, was to bring to naught the real changes of structure, let us say the particular revolutions (without a capital R) which could be possibly needed at certain given moments in human history, and which will be needed in actual fact as long as human history lasts.

How could we be surprised at seeing such spurious philosophy end up in totalitarianism, and the principle: *to force the people to be free*, reach its logical conclusion in the totalitarian dream: to force the people to be obedient in order that the State be free and all-powerful, or in order to make the people happy despite themselves, as Dostoevski expressed it in his Legend of the Grand Inquisitor?

The above-mentioned remarks, as well as the consideration of the present plight of the world, oblige us to take a serious view of the issue involved, and to ask from democratic philosophy a clear restatement of the theory of the role of prophetic shock-minorities. Such a restatement, as I see it, would emphasize the three following points, in accordance with the democratic charter.

First, the recourse to illegal activity is in itself *an exception*, not a rule, and should always remain exceptional; and it is only justified—as a lesser evil—when a prophetic shock-minority is confronted with a situation in which law has been already broken or suspended, that is, when it is confronted with some form of *tyrannical power*.

Second, just as exceptional as illegal activity, the use of force, or of hard measures of coercion, may be needed in such circumstances; but *justice* must always hold sway. The use of terror striking the innocent and the guilty indiscriminately is always a crime. Innocent persons can indirectly suffer from just public measures directed to the social group in which they belong; but no innocent person should ever be punished, put into captivity, put to death.

Third, it is true that only the fact, the event, can decide whether a prophetic shock-minority was right or wrong in offering itself as the personification of the people, but the only success which is to provide that test is the *free approval by the people*, as soon as the people can express their will. This means on the one hand that the use of force should always be provisional as well as exceptional, and the free consultation of the people always intended as an urgent, unpostponable aim; on the other hand, that the risk that a prophetic shock-minority is taking must be fairly taken, that this minority would betray itself as well as the people if it clung to power by any means whatever, and that it must be ready to lose the game if the people say so.

Finally what can be the weapons of the people to protect themselves and the body politic either against false servants of the people and genuine prophetic shock-minorities shifting from the struggle for freedom to the struggle for domination? Nothing can replace in this connection the strength of the common ethos, the inner energy of democratic faith and civil morality in the people themselves, the enjoyment by them of real freedom in their everyday life and of a truly human standard of living, and the active participation of them in political life from the bottom up. If these conditions are lacking, the door is open to deception.

Yet there is in any case a weapon which they should particularly treasure as a bulwark of their political liberties. Namely the freedom of expression and criticism. That's a new reason to confirm what has been said here about the vital necessity in democracy for the freedom of the press and of the means of expression of thought, even at the price of great risks,—still less great than the loss of liberty. A free people needs a free press, I mean free from the State, and free also from economic bondage and the power of money.

*   *   *

I have said that democracy cannot do without the prophetic factor, and that the people need prophets. I should like to conclude that this is a sad necessity; or, rather, that in a democracy which has come of age, in a society of free men, expert in the virtues of freedom and just in its fundamental structures, the prophetic function would be integrated in the normal and regular life of the body politic, and issue from the people themselves. In such a society inspiration would rise in the body politic from the starting point of their free common activity in their most elementary, most humble local communities. By choosing their leaders, at this most elementary level, through a natural and experiential process, as fellow-men personally known to them and deserving their trust in the minor affairs of the community, the people would grow more and more conscious of political realities and more ready to choose their leaders, at the level of the common good of the body politic, with true political awareness, as genuine deputies for them.

NOTES

1. *Scholasticism and Politics* (New York: Macmillan Co., 1940), chap. iv. (French corresponding text in *Principes d'une politique humaniste*, New York: Maison Française, 1944, Chap. ii).

2. Cf. Suarez, *De legibus*, Lib. III, c. 4, n. 5: "Unde potestas regia formaliter ut talis est de jure humano."

3. For a thorough discussion of the matter see Yves Simon, *Nature and Functions of Authority* (Milwaukee: Marquette University Press, 1940); and *Philosophy of Democratic Government* (Chicago: The University of Chicago Press, 1951). Professor Simon has rightly stressed the fact that the basic problem of authority (as a right of the people as a whole) comes prior to the problem of the necessity of having authority entrusted to a distinct governing personnel.

4. Instrumental, not with respect to the choice or designation made, but with respect to the transmission of authority.

5. Thus this authority comes from God as Primary Source and Primary Cause, even comes from Him "immediately," in the sense that human nature, naturally demanding what is necessarily implied in social life, immediately proceeds from God. Cf. Josephus Gredt, O.S.B., *Elementa philosophiae Aristotelico-Thomisticae* (St. Louis: Herder, 1946), t. II, n. 1029, 4: "Auctoritas politica immediate est a Deo seu a lege aeterna, quatenus immediate a Deo est humana natura naturaliter ad societatem ordinata."

6. See *Man and the State*, Chap. ii.

7. Cf. this passage from Bracton's *De rerum divisione*, quoted by Richard O'Sullivan in his Introduction to *Under God and the Law: Papers Read to the Thomas More Society of London, Second Series* (Oxford: Blackwell, 1949): The king "ought to be under the law since he is God's vicar, as evidently appears after the likeness of Jesus Christ whose representative he is on earth" (*cujus vices gerit in terris*).

8. And in a sense—a theologian would add—from Christ's universal kingship. But this no more makes him a representative of Christ than an image of God.

9. Rom. 13:1–7.

10. Cf. Cajetan, *Com. on Sum. Theol.*, I-II. 90. 3; *De comparatione auctoritatis papae et concilii* (Romae: Apud Institutum Angeli-

cum, 1936), c. 1, 12; c. 11, 190; c. 24, 359; c. 27, 415; *Apologia ejusdem tractatus* (in the same volume), c. 1, 449–50; c. 8, 533; c. 9, 550, 557–64, 572, 590; c. 16, 801.

11. Cf. Bellarmine, *Controversiarum de membris Ecclesiae liber tertius, De laicis sive secularibus,* c. 6; *Opera omnia* (Paris: Vives, 1870), III, 10–12. English translation by Kathleen E. Murphy, *De Laicis or the Treatise on Civil Government* (New York: Fordham University Press, 1928).

12. Cf. Suarez, *Defensio fidei catholicae et apostolicae adversus anglicanae sectae errores,* Lib. III: *De summi pontificis supra temporales reges excellentia, et potestate,* c. 2; *Opera* (Venetiis, 1749), fols. 114 ff.; *De legibus,* Lib. III, c. 4.

13. "*Vicem gerens multitudinis*" (*Sum. Theol.,* I-II. 90. 3.).

14. Cf. our chapter "Sign and Symbol," in *Ransoming the Time* (New York: Charles Scribner's Sons, 1941).

15. See *Man and the State,* Chap. ii. I am afraid such a concept remains in the background of some current Scholasticist views, which would finally reduce the democratic process to a moment of free choice, by the people, of their masters (just as Rousseau fancied that the representative system acted, when he condemned it). Cf. Gredt, *op. cit.,* t. II, nn. 1032, 1033.

16. See *Man and the State,* Chap. iv, pp. 101–3.

17. *Ibid.,* Chap. ii, pp. 34–35.

18. Cf. our book, *Education at the Crossroads* (New Haven: Yale University Press, 1943), pp. 29–31.

19. *Principes d'une politique humaniste,* Annexe to Chap. ii, "Pouvoir législatif et pouvoir exécutif."

20. Cf. *True Humanism* (New York: Charles Scribner's Sons, 1938), pp. 162 ff.

21. Cf. Carlo Rosselli, *Socialisme libéral* (Paris, 1930), pp. 47 ff.

22. Cf. *Contrat social,* Book I, Chap. vii: "*Quiconque refusera d'obéir à la volonté générale y sera contraint par tout le corps: ce qui ne signifie autre chose sinon qu'on le forcera d'être libre.*"

16. HUMAN EQUALITY

From a point of view that is neither nominalist nor idealist but realist, the unity or equality in nature among men is not a mere word nor a logical exigency of an abstract species fictitiously realized. It is ontological and concrete, just as much as the likenesses and affinities which in the external world serve as bases for that positive unity which the species has within our mind. For the universality of our ideas is grounded *in re*, in things, and it would be necessary to have angelic vision to measure the depth of the real relations and the real solidarity connoted by that maxim of the schools.

The equality in nature among men consists of their concrete communion in the mystery of the human species; it does not lie in an idea, it is hidden in the heart of the individual and of the concrete, in the roots of the substance of each man. Obscure because residing on the level of substance and its root energies, primordial because it is bound up with the very sources of being, human equality reveals itself, like the nearness of our neighbour, to every one who practices it; indeed it is identical with that proximity of all to each, and of each to all. If you treat a man as a man, that is to say, if you respect and love the secret he carries within him and the good of which he is capable, to that extent do you make effective in yourself his closeness in nature to and his equality or unity in nature with yourself. It is the natural love of the human being for his own kind which reveals and makes real the unity of species among men. As long as love does not call it forth, that unity slumbers in a metaphysical retreat where we can perceive it only as an abstraction.

In the common experience of misery, in the common sorrow of great catastrophes, in humiliation and distress, under the blows of the executioner or the bombs of total war, in concentration camps, in the hovels of starving people in great cities, in any common *necessity*, the doors of solitude open and man recognizes man. Man also recognizes man when the sweetness of a great joy or of a great love for an instant

clears his eyes. Whenever he does a service to his fellow men
or is helped by them, whenever he shares the same elementary actions and the same elementary emotions, whenever he
truly considers his neighbour, the simplest action discovers
for him, both in others and in himself, the common resources
and the common goodness—primitive, rudimentary, wounded,
unconscious and repressed—of human nature. At once the
realness of equality and community in nature is revealed to
him as a very precious thing, an unknown marvel, a fundamental basis of existence, more important than all the differences and inequalities superimposed upon it. When he
will have returned to his routine pleasures, he will have forgotten this discovery.

The authentic instinct of equality in nature, which naturally underlies and strengthens the fragile conception that our
heedless intelligence can gain of this same equality when we
retain that realist perspective which I have endeavoured to
describe, is no secondary tendency like pride or envy, no matter how deep-seated it is within us; it is a primary instinct,
the instinct of communication founded on a common membership in the same specific whole. The realist conception of
equality in nature is an inheritance of the Judeo-Christian
tradition; it is a natural prerequisite for Christian thought
and life. Just as there is in every being a natural love for God
above all else, without which charity would not serve to perfect nature but to destroy it,[1] so also, however it may be
weakened by sin, there must be in man a natural love for his
own kind without which the love of the gospel for men of
every race and every condition would be contrary to nature
rather than its exaltation. How should we all be called upon
thus to love one another in God if we were not all equal in
our condition and specific dignity as rational creatures?

Christianity confirms and emphasizes the concrete sense
of equality in nature by affirming its historical and genealogical character, and by teaching that here we are concerned
with a blood relationship, properly so-called, all men being
descended from the same original parents, and being brothers
in Adam before they are brothers in Christ. Heirs of the same
sin and the same weaknesses, but heirs also of the same original greatness, all created in the image of God and all called

to the same supernatural dignity as adopted sons of God, and to coheirship with Christ the Saviour, all redeemed by the same life-giving Blood, and thus destined to become equals of the angels in heaven,[2] what Christian can look upon man with the demented gaze of racist pride? The *unity of mankind* is at the basis of Christianity. Pius XII asserts it from the eminence of the chair of Peter, when he condemns, as the first of the pernicious errors so widespread today, "The forgetting of that law of human solidarity and charity, required and imposed as much *by the community of origin and by the equality of rational nature among all men*, to whatever people they may belong, as by the sacrifice of redemption offered up by Jesus Christ. . . ." After having recalled to mind the insight which St. Paul gives us on this matter, the Pope adds, "Marvellous insight which makes us contemplate the human race in the unity of its origin in God; in the unity of its nature similarly composed in all men of a material body and a spiritual and immortal soul; in the unity of its immediate end and of its mission in the world; in the unity of its dwelling place—the earth, the goods of which all men, by natural right, can utilize to sustain and develop life; in the unity of its supernatural end—God Himself, toward whom all should strive; in the unity of the means to attain this end; . . . in the unity of its relation to the Son of God; . . . in the unity of its redemption worked for all men by Christ."[3]

It is because the Christian conception of life is based upon so concrete, broad, and fruitful a certainty of the equality and community in nature between men that it, at the same time, insists so forcefully on the orderings and hierarchies which spring and should spring from the very heart of this essential community, and on the particular inequalities which they necessarily involve. For in the world of man as in the world of creation, there can be no concourse or communication, no life or movement without differentiation, no differentiation without inequalities.[4]

Christianity fearlessly asserts the necessity of these inequalities; it respects them, furthers them, favours them, for it knows that as long as they remain normal—that is as long as the human will, by a kind of perversion, does not undertake to make them serve as means of exclusion rather than of com-

munication and make them crush the essential equality and
the primordial community which they presuppose—the inequalities, which lend variety to human life and intensify the
richness of life's encounters, in no way injure the dignities
which befit the unity of mankind and the rights which are
grounded on this unity. On the contrary, these inequalities
make such a unity all the more manifest. Every man is a man
in his very essence, but no man is man in essence,[5] that is,
exhausts in himself all the riches of the various perfections of
which human-kind is capable. In this sense all the diversity of
perfections and virtues distributed through the generations
of men in space and time is but a varied participation in the
common and inexhaustible potentialities of man.

The term *unity of mankind* is the Christian name, and the
truest name, of the equality in nature between men. It helps
us to purify the idea of that equality from all erroneous associations and implications, whether they arise from a geo-
metric imagination or from a passion for levelling. An arith-
metic equality between two numbers excludes all inequality
between them, but equality in nature between men, or in the
unity of human nature, for its full flowering demands individual inequalities. To affirm the equality in nature between men is for idealist egalitarianism to wish that all inequality among them should disappear. To affirm the equality
in nature between men, or the unity of human nature, is for
Christian realism to wish that those fruitful inequalities,
whereby the multitude of individuals participates in the common treasury of humanity, should develop themselves. Egalitarian idealism interprets the word equality on a plane surface; realism interprets it with the dimension of depth as
well. Not only should one conceive of equality as something
fundamental from which arises an infinite number of differences, but equality itself is a profound thing—organic, inten-
sive, and qualitative. Let us not say that one man is as good as
another; that is a nihilistic formula which acquires real meaning only from deep religious pessimism (*vanitas vanitatum,
omnis homo mendax*). Let us say that in a man are, *virtuali-
ter*, all men. The Son of Man who "knows what there is within
man" perceives in each man all men.

Thus we must assert both that equality in essence which

unites men in rational nature and those natural individual inequalities which arise from this very unity or equality. But from this very fact we also recognize that it is equality which is primordial, and inequalities which are secondary. Because, speaking absolutely, the community of essence is of greater importance than individual differences; the root is more important than the branches.

The Church gave brilliant testimony to this primacy of equality in nature over derivative inequalities when on October 28, 1939, on the feast of Christ the King and while Europe was going into a period of convulsions which would make us lose hope for her if we had not hope in God, the Pope consecrated over the tomb of St. Peter twelve bishops belonging to the most diverse peoples and groups of peoples, several of whom were men of colour. "Those who enter the Church, whatever may be their origin and their language", said he on this occasion, "must know that they have an equal right as sons in the house of the Lord, wherein reign the law and peace of Christ". But if this equality in the Church is established upon baptism and the grace of divine adoption, who can fail to see that it necessarily presupposes a similar fundamental equality in the order of nature? The exercise of episcopal government brings into play natural gifts and virtues as well as infused gifts. And here we have white men, according to the regions where they happen to live, who can be governed on the road to their eternal destiny by bishops of the yellow or black race, just as yellow or black men can be governed by bishops of the white race.

With regard to social life it is important at the outset to note that there too, and for the same reasons indicated above, there are and must be equality and inequalities; and that inequalities—which are normal, consubstantial with social life, flourishing everywhere—are and must be secondary. Equality is primary, inasmuch as it relates (as equality pure and simple) to the fundamental rights and common dignity of human beings, and (as equality of proportion) to justice.

Indeed, among all peoples that which is thus secondary, the inequalities, most often conceals that which is primary, not only because in general inequalities exist everywhere and are the more apparent, but doubtless also because in the social order men have always made much of inequalities, in themselves fragile and of human origin, by means of marks and insignia, manifestations of power and trappings of fear, thus trying to solidify and stabilize them. It remains true that, whatever may be the forms of a given society and the inequalities they involve, it is not only a denial of the Evangelical virtues, but in the natural order itself a baseness, an offence against creation, to treat as an *inferior man* a man belonging to some inferior part of the social structure, to make him conceive his inferior social condition as an inferiority of essence. To do this is to place in a relationship of effective prevarication both him who scorns and him who is scorned. If a man is of an inferior social condition, he is there not by virtue of one of those pseudo-essential necessities of which we have spoken.* Far from relegating him once and for all to his condition, it is only right to honour in him the powers and potentialities of human nature, thanks to which he might have found himself in a higher position if he had been born in some other cradle, or if the fortunes of life had offered him other opportunities, or if he had taken better advantage of those in fact offered him.

Ever since the New Law brought on earth liberated and energized the natural movement of history—in the very depths of the conflict occasioned by its opposing forces, which themselves became energized—this natural movement has not tended to iron out social inequalities; it has tended rather to bring them back to their proper proportions and to their secondary character with respect to common human dignity. To speak more generally, and concerning the demands of inequality as well as of equality, it can be said that, in the toilsome development of mankind and of reason, in proportion as the normal aspirations of the human personality succeed, under whatever given conditions, in more or less perfectly achieving reality, to the same extent the natural law—taken not as an abstract code but in its historical growth, which is itself natural—tends progressively to make explicit the potential requirements contained within its principles, and the positive

* See *Ransoming the Time*, pp. 7–16.

law tends in its own sphere to open itself more to the influences of nature.

Certain social inequalities result from natural inequalities or are required by them. It is just that that part which by innate or acquired superiority renders more services to the whole should receive more in return. It is also just or equitable that individuals should receive in proportion not to their needs or desires, which tend to become infinite, but to the necessities of their life and development, the means for putting to use their natural gifts. In this sense the more a man has, the more he should receive. The same care that men bestow upon their rare plants or their most beautiful stallions they do not bestow upon the superior persons who are an honour to their own species. This is in itself an offence against nature; even though men's awkwardness is such that it is better for genius not to receive their care.

Other social inequalities, however, are themselves of social origin. It is important to concentrate our attention on these typically social inequalities, of which Pascal liked to point out both the importance and the whimsicality and which egalitarianism least understands. It is from the needs proper to the internal differentiation of the social body, indeed, not from the natural merits of the individuals who happen to be embodied in one or another of its parts, that arise the inequalities in duties and advantages attached to these parts. An imbecile king remains the king. The *orders* of the Old Régime may have given way to the *classes* (in the strict sense of the word)[6] of our present régime, and these in their turn may give way to "bodies" having varied statuses. Always will some inequalities of intrinsically social origin bear witness to the unconquerable originality and vitality which belong to social life as such. It is clear, on the other hand, that such inequalities turn into a perversion of political life and into barbarism if bewildered men wish to erect them into a state of social servitude for the human groups assumed to be inferior.

Social equality itself, in so far as it merits the name, has also a value which is properly and truly social. Although it is based upon unity and equality in nature, it is not to be confused with it; it is rather an expression or development thereof in the social order. This is first of all that equality, recognized and sanctioned by society, in those rights—so hard to specify but none the less real—which we call the fundamental rights of the human person: the right to exist, to keep one's body whole, to found a family (itself assured the enjoyment of its liberties); the right of association, the right to the private ownership of material goods, the right to seek those good things through which a rational creature may perfect himself, the right to travel toward eternal life along the road one's conscience acknowledges as designated by God. It is also that equality in the respect which human dignity requires that social customs show to all men, by treating them all as men, not as things. Then again, it is "political equality, equality of all before the law, whether it represses or protects, the making available to all citizens of public employment".[7] The institution of these last three equalities by the temporal power is derived, as the late Cardinal Verdier wrote, from the "evangelical streams released by Christ throughout the world". It is, finally, that equal conditions as coheirs of the effort of all, in accordance with which all should in so far as possible participate "free of charge" in the elementary goods needed for human life.

This social equality is thus, in its own way and like equality in nature, not a surface thing, but lies deep; and it includes essential differences, not only in degrees and modes, but in its basis in the law. I have said that this equality, with its differing forms and degrees, has, as the term "social equality" sufficiently indicates, a proper and real social value. Let it be added that it possesses this in a different way from the social inequalities, in this sense that, taken all in all, the inequalities proceed from society more than from nature, whereas social equality proceeds from nature more than from society. It is by virtue either of the exigencies or of the wishes of human nature that, taking into account the different degrees I have pointed out in the domain of natural law, common law, or positive law, social equality assumes in society the proper and real social value about which I have spoken. The fundamental rights of the human person are in themselves anterior to civil society, and the equality of these rights has social value only in so far as society recognizes and sanctions them in its own order. The other kinds of equality, although they derive from nature as their principle, as does society itself, rise up progressively in the midst of society, like a social flowering forth or fructifying of the equality of nature. In any case social equality is not a condition of existence set by "nature" for "all men", like their arms and legs or the colour of their eyes, which social life, unexpectedly coming into being, needs thereafter only to protect, as Jean-Jacques Rousseau would have it. Social equality is a condition of existence which, whether in its various degrees it be postulated or desired more or less imperiously by nature, achieves reality in society. "All men" are not born in this effective condition of existence. The members of a sufficiently developed civil community obtain it from the community through natural law or through positive law, either by virtue of being men (if it is a question of the fundamental rights of the person) or, if it is a question of other kinds of equality, by virtue of being citizens.

In itself, and when its nature is not vitiated by absolute egalitarianism, the multiform social equality which we have been discussing favours the development of natural inequalities, because in opening to each a greater number of possibilities, it favours at the same time differences in growth and in development. And on the other hand it requires that these natural inequalities be compensated for by a process of organic redistribution, by virtue of which the weak and the less favoured share in the benefits which the social whole owes to others.

Similarly, in so far as the true character and the true rôle of social equality are effectively recognized, this social equality, serving as a seemingly natural ground for social inequalities of structure and function, gives them more intrinsic stability than the artifices of constraint can give; yet on the other hand it requires that these social inequalities be compensated for in two ways: first, by the fact that the conditions to which they correspond be not closed but open (open for the circulation of elements which come from other levels); and second, by the fact that in each one of these conditions individuals may enjoy a state of life that is truly human and may really be able to strive (I do not say easily, because without obstacles to override there is no progress for us) for the fullness of human development.

If what I have said concerning the indestructible originality of the social life and its proper differentiations is just, it is an illusion to wish that all may have at the start strictly identical opportunities to mount to the highest degrees in social life. (From the fact that everyone is bound up in a different social fabric, the initial opportunities of one differ from those of another; and then again it is naïve indeed to believe that the reward of a good life should consist in a change of social level.) But it is proper that the highest social conditions should not of themselves be closed to any one, and even more important, it is proper that in whatever *social* structure men are involved, they should have the same opportunities to achieve—each one according to his effort and his condition—their *human* fullness, those fruits of wisdom and human virtue whose savour is not identical, but similarly good in each, whether he spends his life in working the earth, in philosophizing or in governing the State. Thus, such notions as equality of opportunity or equality of conditions, which egalitarianism would make chimerical, become true and proper if they are understood in the sense not of an equality pure and simple, but of a *proportional* equality.

This *equality of proportion* plays a capital rôle in the temporal community. What Proudhon and the great egalitarianists did not understand was that in the domain of relations between the social whole and its parts, such a proportional equality is justice itself. Having respect for the differences, and hence the concrete inequalities, associated with the carrying on of personal life in the midst of society— equality, by the very fact that it does not relate to an abstract man-in-himself, but to concrete persons, in a certain fashion seeks to move over into the sphere of these very inequalities. It then becomes the equality of proportion that characterizes distributive justice, which latter deals with each in accordance with his merits. And thus, pervading and reconciling all inequalities, justice to a certain extent restores equality, thereby making civic friendship possible. For, as Thomas Aquinas put it, "friendship is a certain union or society of friends, which cannot exist among persons remote from one another, but has as its prerequisite that they have access to equality. Hence it pertains to friendship equally to use the equality which has been previously established; but it pertains to justice to lead unequals to equality. When this equality has achieved reality, the task of justice is performed. Thus equality is a final end as regards justice, but a principle as regards friendship."[8] Finally, if equality lies at the root and inequality rests in the branches, it is a new kind of equality which, by virtue of justice, friendship, and human compassion and by virtue of the communication they provoke, is realized in the fruit.

It is well to insist upon this last statement, and elaborate its implications. Because social life, while postulated by nature, is the work of reason and virtue and implies, however opposed it may be, a movement of progressive conquest of man over nature and over himself, social equality is not something ready-made; it implies in itself a certain dynamism. Like liberty, it is itself an end to struggle for, and with difficulty, and at the price of a constant tension of the energies of the spirit. If, by postulates of nature, it is, in its most general forms, basic and primary, social equality is yet only a seed which must develop and which works in the direction of fruition. It requires not only the exercise of distributive justice in the temporal community; it requires as wide a measure as possible of free participation by all in the necessary good things, material and spiritual, and that redistribution to persons of the common good of which we spoke above. It requires the progress of social justice; the organic development of institutions of law; the participation, in more and more extensive degrees, of persons as such in political life; the transition to conditions which would really offer to each an equal opportunity (equal in the proportional sense) to bring his gifts to fruit, and which would permit the formation of an aristocracy born of personal work, that pays back the good effects of his labour for common use; the sharing more and more by all in the benefits of culture and the mind, and in that inner liberty which is given by mastery over self and knowledge of the truth.

The civilization which we have before our eyes has sought these things, but because it sought them in the wrong way it has often found their very opposites. Doubtless the illiterate craftsmen of medieval France participated more in the commonwealth of the mind than do the middle classes of today, to whom such rare technical marvels as the movies and the radio, used in disastrous fashion, as far as the masses are concerned, provide the delights of a scattered mind and the uniformity of emptiness. I am well aware of all this. Nor do I think that being illiterate is a good thing in itself. We must then renew ourselves, and we must undertake to seek the good in the good way. Such a leaven of equality as has been disseminated by pseudo-Christian egalitarianism has filled the world with unhealthy fermentations; but there is another leaven of equality[9] which is a leaven of justice and is a proper stimulant of human history, and which tends to raise the human mass toward a way of life more truly human, wherein inequalities are not suppressed, but compensated, and subordinated to that high equality of the common use of the good things which nourish and exalt our rational nature. In sum, the error has been to seek equality in a regression toward the basis set up by "nature", and in a levelling down to this base. It should be sought in a progressive movement toward the end which is composed of the good things of rational life becoming in so far as possible and in various degrees accessible to all, and this, thanks to the very inequalities themselves, by justice and fraternal friendship turned away from seeking domination and toward helpfulness and cooperation.

The equality I have been discussing should be called *Christian equality*, not only because it issues from the Judeo-Christian tradition and conforms with the Christian conception of life, but also because, if it were not for the influence of the Christian leaven injected into secular history, and if it were not for the added stimulus, which in its own sphere temporal civilization receives from Christian energies, this equality could not succeed in coming to pass. As there is a flowering of the natural law which can be attained only with the help of the virtues of the New Law, there is also a human flowering, a real humanism of civil life which can be attained only with the help of these virtues.

The rôle played by the irrational instincts and tendencies

is major in the political life of men. To make possible the existence of a political life in which the dynamism of equality works in the right direction, the habits and customs which spring from the Christian virtues in the human mass must therein tame the irrational with reason and develop right instincts. For the development among men of a real sense of equality without egalitarianism and of that civic love, which is not a gift of nature but an heroic conquest of reason and liberty, in this temporal order which is the very home of conflicts, of weaknesses and of the sins of the world, the sap of the gospel, the sense of supernatural equality of those called to a divine life, the sense of brotherly charity must permeate this temporal order to give it life and lift it up. "Wherever prevails a religion other than ours", wrote Joseph de Maistre, "slavery is the rule, and wherever that religion is weakened, the nation becomes, in exact proportion, less jealous of the general liberty. . . . Government alone cannot govern; it requires either slavery, which diminishes the number of wills operative within the State, or divine energy, which, by a supernatural *grafting* process, destroys the natural violence of those wills and enables them to act together without harming each other."[10]

Finally, to return to the central theme of this study, the realism of our intelligence is so weak, and the natural love of our own kind is so little vigilant, either because of the weakness of our nature or because of the injuries it has suffered, that without the reinforcing comfort of faith and gospel love, it is almost impossible that we should not fall, with regard to the equality and the inequality of men, into one of the two errors—empiricist or idealist—which we have discussed.* Indeed, a realist conception of equality in nature, if it is to be established among men in a sufficiently general way and with enough force to act effectively upon civilization, can be no less than a Christian conception of that equality.

* See *Ransoming the Time*, pp. 7–16.

NOTES

1. Cf. *Summa Theologica* I, 60, 5.
2. *Luke* 20:36.
3. Encyclical *Summi pontificatus*, October 20, 1939. Italics mine.
4. Cf. *Summa Theologica* I, 47, 2.
5. Cajetan, *In Summam Theologicam*, I, 6, 3.
6. Cf. Goetz Briefs, *The Proletariat* (New York: McGraw-Hill, 1937).
7. Cardinal Verdier, *Christian Answers to Social Problems*, p. 62.
8. St. Thomas Aquinas, *In VIII, Ethic*, lect. 7.
9. "That fundamental equality is active and radiant. . . . It creates a kind of egalitarian *dynamism*, a leaven of equality which perpetually raises the human mass to a way of life where the distances that separate ever diminish, where true brotherhood is without end more perfectly realized. . . ." Cardinal Verdier, *op. cit.*, p. 43.
10. Joseph de Maistre, *Le Pape*, t. III, c. 2.

17. WHO IS MY NEIGHBOUR?

The problem I should like to consider in this chapter is a very difficult one, but it is of vital importance. I think that there is a decided advantage for us in courageously facing this problem, and becoming aware of its reality, even if we are unable to do much more. The question is to determine whether the diversity of religious creeds, an evident historical fact, is an insurmountable obstacle to human cooperation.

Surely it is a paradox that despite the state of religious diversion in which mankind lives, good fellowship, brotherly intercourse and a spirit of union can be established between men in the earthly commonwealth, while each of them is bound to his God and is attached with all his heart to his faith in Him and to the form of worship he renders Him. But man himself is a paradox. And more astonishing still appears the "exceeding great love" of Him who loved us first and whose very predilections work for the welfare of all.

Nothing in history, indeed, goes to show that religious feeling or religious ideas have been particularly successful in pacifying men. Religious differences seem rather to have fed and sharpened their conflicts. And yet, if it is true that human society must bring together in the service of the same terrestrial common good men belonging to different spiritual families, how can the peace of that temporal society be lastingly assured if first in the domain that matters most to the human being—in the spiritual and religious domain itself—relationships of mutual respect and mutual understanding cannot be established? I prefer the word fellowship to "tolerance", for it connotes something positive—positive and elementary—in human relationships. It conjures up the image of travelling companions, who meet here below by chance and journey through life—however fundamental their differences may be—good humouredly, in cordial solidarity and human agreement. Well, then, for the reasons I have just mentioned, the problem of good fellowship between the members of the various religious families seems to me to be

a cardinal one for the new age of civilization, the rough outlines of which are beginning to take shape in our present
night. I should like to quote in this connection the words
pronounced by Pope Pius XII at his coronation: "Our
thoughts go out also in this solemn moment to all those who
are outside the Church and who, we should like to think, will
rejoice to learn that the Pope prays to Almighty God for
them also and wishes them every possible good".

A deliberate attempt to bring closer together the believers
of the various religious families is something relatively new.
On a solemn occasion, Pope Pius XI called upon all men of
good will to such an attempt. No doubt this attempt is partly
due to the imminent dangers, to the spiritual evils threatening us: open atheism publicly warring against God, or pseudo-
theism seeking to turn the living God into some protecting
genius for the State or some demon of the race. If that is so,
we must admit that it is a stern lesson for believers. Was it
needful that God permit the frightful degradation of mankind that we are witnessing today, so many persecutions and
so much suffering, to teach those who believe in Him to go
down into the real depth of their own hearts, even into those
mysterious regions where we more or less faintly hear the
hand of the God of love knocking at our bolted doors?

Let me say immediately that this attempt at rapprochement might easily be misunderstood. I shall therefore begin
by clearing the ground of any possible sources of misunderstanding. Such a rapprochement obviously cannot be effectu-
ated at the cost of straining fidelity, or of any yielding in
dogmatic integrity, or of any lessening of what is due to
truth. Nor is there any question whatever either of agreeing
upon I know not what common minimum of truth or of sub-
jecting each one's convictions to a common index of doubt.
On the contrary, such a coming together is only conceivable
if we assume that each gives the maximum of fidelity to the
light that is shown to him. Furthermore, it obviously can
only be pure, and therefore valid and efficacious, if it is free
from any *arrière-pensée* of a temporal nature and from even
the shadow of a tendency to subordinate religion to the defense of any earthly interest or acquired advantage.

I am sure that everyone is agreed on these negative conditions I have just enumerated. But one aspect of the paradox I mentioned at the outset is that, as soon as we pass on to positive considerations, each one sees the very justification and the very reason for being of this good fellowship between believers of different religious families mirrored in his own particular outlook and in his own world of thought. And these outlooks are irreducibly heterogeneous, these worlds of thought never exactly meet. Until the day of eternity comes, their dimensions can have no common measure. There is no use closing one's eyes to this fact, which simply bears witness to the internal coherence of the systems of signs, built up in accordance with different principles, on which human minds depend for their cognitive life. Fundamental notions such as that of an absolute oneness of God have not the same meaning for a Jew as for a Christian; nor has the notion of the divine transcendence and incommunicability the same meaning for a Christian as for a Moslem; nor the notions of person, of freedom, grace, revelation, incarnation, of nature and the supernatural, the same meaning for the Orient as for the Occident. And the "non-violence" of the Indian is not the same as Christian "charity". No doubt it is the privilege of the human intelligence to understand other languages than the one it itself uses. It is none the less true that if, instead of being men, we were patterns of Pure Ideas, our nature would be to devour each other in order to absorb into our own world of thought whatever other such worlds might hold of truth.

But it happens that we are men, each containing within himself the ontological mystery of personality and freedom; in each of us the abyss of holiness of the Supreme Being is present with His universal presence, and He asks to dwell there as in His temple, by manner of a gift of Himself to us. Well, each one must speak in accordance with his outlook. I suppose there are readers of this book who do not share my own creed. I shall try to tell them as briefly, but also as frankly and as precisely as possible—and this frankness is itself one of the characteristics of mutual confidence—how the paradox of fellowship I am at present examining can be solved for me, a Catholic, from the point of view of a philosophy which takes into account the data of Christian theology. I do not apologize for this excursion into the field of theology, it is required by the subject I am discussing.

The Catholic doctrine concerning the status of non-Catholics before God

It is well known that, according to the Catholic Faith, God, after having spoken in various and imperfect ways through the prophets, spoke once and for all, in a perfect and final manner, through His own uncreated Word, who took flesh in the womb of a virgin of Israel in order to die for mankind. And that the deposit of this revelation of the Word of God was confided to a living and visible body, made up both of just men and of sinners, but specially assisted by the Spirit of God in its mission of truth and salvation. Thus authority plays a most important part for Catholics. But apart from dogmas and their connected truths and apart from the discipline of salvation, freedom plays a big part also, and the diversity of opinions in human affairs is far greater in the Catholic Church than is generally realized by those not in it. I know that the teaching of the Church can deal with every matter connected with faith; but in being integrally mindful of this teaching, I can still disagree most sharply with other Catholics about political or social matters: democracy, trade unionism, the late war in Spain or the Second World War, as well as about philosophical or historical questions. This is because it is only to the purity and integrity of the Word of God that the faithful are bound as such; the teaching authority of the Church intends of itself only to safeguard this living deposit of truth, just as the disciplinary authority of the Church has no other object than to enable the faithful to live by that truth. It is to the First Truth in person, speaking to my heart, that I adhere by means of the statements of dogma that bring the revelation to all. As a Catholic and by my Catholic Faith, I am bound in conscience to no human, theological or philosophical opinion, however well founded it may be, and still less to any judgments on contingent or worldly matters, or to any temporal power. Nor am I bound to any particular form of culture or civilization, and still less of race or blood. I am bound uniquely to what is universality itself and superuniversality: to the Divine, to the words and precepts of Him who said, "I am the Truth, I who speak to you".

That in brief is how the Catholic outlook appears to me. Catholic theology teaches that it is upon our love, as Saint John of the Cross says, that we shall be judged; in other words, that salvation and eternal life depend on charity. It teaches that charity presupposes faith and has its roots in faith, in other words, in truth divinely revealed. It teaches that *explicit* faith in Christ, illuminating the human mind regarding the inmost secrets of divine truth and life, is not only the requisite means for souls to attain the highest degree of conformity with God and divine union, and a prerequisite for peoples to achieve a firm position of general morality and perfectly human civilization, but that that faith is also the response of reverence justly due to God's gift, inclining His glory toward us. Explicit faith in revealed truth, therefore, is the first duty of everyone who is not incapable of hearing through his ears and in his heart the word of God. But Catholic theology adds that faith together with grace are offered to all souls, even if they are unable to know the truth explicitly in its integrity. If those souls are in good faith and do not refuse the internal grace offered to them, they have *implicit* faith in Christ and accept implicitly the entire divinely revealed truth, even if they only believe, having no clearer light, that God exists and saves those who seek Him.[1] (And God knows much better than do they themselves whether they believe that.)

If, therefore, Catholics hold that there is no salvation outside the Church, you can see that this maxim can shock only those who understand it wrongly and who are ignorant of what is commonly taught concerning the "soul of the Church". All it means to us is that there is no salvation outside the Truth, which, explicitly or implicitly, is freely offered to all. And does that not seem fully in harmony with the nature of man and his essential dignity? Surely if there were salvation outside the Truth, I should not want such a salvation, for I prefer the Truth to my joy and freedom; or rather I know that only the Truth can give me real joy and set me free.

We believe that there is no salvation outside the Truth, and the fact that all men do not explicitly know the Truth, the fact of religious division, far from being a good in itself, is a mark of the distress of our condition. But we also hold, as I have just explained, that the Truth speaks to every man's heart; and God alone knows who those are, in whatever part of the world they may be born and whether or not they live under the régime of His publicly revealed word, who truly and efficaciously hear His interior and secret word. We believe that there is no salvation outside Christ, but we also believe that Christ died for all men and that the possibility of believing in Him—either explicitly or implicitly—is offered to all. We believe that there is no salvation outside the Mystical Body of Christ, but we also believe that those who visibly belong to that Body by confessing the faith and the sacraments, and are thus designated to continue in time the work of redemption and receive more generous effusions of the vehicles of grace, are not its only members. We hold that every man of good faith and right will, provided he does not sin against the light and does not refuse the grace interiorly offered to him, belongs, as we put it, to the Soul of the Church, or, in other words, is invisibly and by the motion of his heart a member of the visible Church and partakes of her life, which is eternal life. And no man, withal, whether Christian or non-Christian, can know whether he is worthy of love or of hatred.

Catholics are sometimes reproached with speaking to others in a domineering or patronizing manner. Human weakness being what it is, that may well be the case with some. Yet in reality, their position is far from being a comfortable one. They are twice wounded, with the wounds of their faults and with the requirements of their God. Not only does their reason show them that other religions can also transmit to mankind many great truths, although in their eyes incomplete or mixed—and on occasion, if it is a question of certain techniques of natural spirituality or of psycho-physical mastery of self—certain truths which the Gospel did not take pains to teach. But what is more important still, they see that, through the very supernatural truth which they have received—not as a monopoly but as something to give to others—men belonging to other spiritual families, even poor idolaters, can, if they are of good faith and if their hearts are pure, live better than some members of their own religious family. And who would not lose heart, if he were not helped by grace! The tree bends, says Saint Thomas Aquinas, under the fullness of its fruit. The Church rejoices over the testimony she is required to give, and the Christian rejoices in her. She knows that it is a bounden duty to acknowledge the holy reality of privileges received. For the divine freedom gives as it pleases to whomever it pleases. But, as Saint Paul puts it, it is in a fragile vessel that each faithful soul contains grace. That he should have on his pitiable human shoulders some measure of the burden of divine truth in no way justifies the believer in being supercilious or patronizing; rather he feels inclined to excuse himself and to ask forgiveness of every passer-by. *Euntes ibant et flebant*; going, they went and wept. I know well that there are men—and it is perhaps to make up for their little practical faith—who despise others and ceaselessly repeat: we believers, we respectable people, we Christians, we Catholics, at times even we "born" Catholics, as if they were not born sinners like everyone else. They never suspect that, by thus placing their pride in evidence of their religion, they make those who see them want to blaspheme the Almighty.

The basis of good fellowship among men of different creeds, considered on the spiritual level

To return to the question of the fellowship of believers. I think it is clear what the basis of such a fellowship is in the Catholic outlook. This basis is not of the order of the intellect and of ideas, but of the heart and of love. It is friendship, natural friendship, but first and foremost mutual love in God and for God. Love does not go out to essences nor to qualities nor to ideas, but to persons; and it is the mystery of persons and of the divine presence within them which is here in play. This fellowship, then, is not a fellowship of beliefs, but the fellowship of men who believe.

The conviction each of us has, rightly or wrongly, regarding the limitations, deficiencies, errors of others does not prevent friendship between minds. In such a fraternal dialogue, there must be a kind of forgiveness and remission, not with regard to ideas—ideas deserve no forgiveness if they are false—but with regard to the condition of him who travels the road at our side. Every believer knows very well that all men will be judged—both himself and all others. But neither he nor another is God, able to pass judgement. And what each one is before God, neither the one nor the other knows. Here the "Judge not" of the Gospels applies with its full force. We can render judgement concerning ideas, truths or errors; good or bad actions; character, temperament, and what appears to us of a man's interior disposition. But we are utterly forbidden to judge the innermost heart, that inaccessible center where the person day after day weaves his own fate and ties the bonds binding him to God. When it comes to that, there is only one thing to do, and that is to trust in God. And that is precisely what love for our neighbour prompts us to do.

There are some people who do not like that word, "love". It embarrasses them, because it has become hackneyed, and because we hear it as well from lips that have gone to rot, or from hearts that worship themselves. God is not so squeamish. The Apostle John tells us that God is self-subsisting Love.

There is only one proper and fitting way through which peace and union can come to men, and that is through love: first, love springing from nature for beings—for those poor beings who have the same essence as we have ourselves, and the same sufferings, and the same mental dignity. But that love is not enough, for the roots of strife are too strong for it. There must be a love of higher origin, immediately divine, which Christian theology calls supernatural, a love in God and for God, which both strengthens in their proper sphere our various inclinations toward one another in the natural order, and also transcends them to infinity. Charity is very different from that simple human benevolence which philosophers praise, which is noble indeed in itself, yet inefficacious in the end. Charity alone, as Bergson observed in his great book, *The Two Sources of Morality and Religion*, can open the heart to the love of *all* men, because, coming from God who first loves us, charity desires for all men the same divine good, the same eternal life, as it does for ourselves, and it sees in all human beings the summoned of God, streaming, as it were, with the mysteries of His mercy and the prevenient gifts of His goodness.

I should like to dwell a moment on the inner law and the privileges of this friendship of charity, as regards precisely the relations between believers of different religious denominations (as well as between believers and non-believers). I have already made it sufficiently clear that it is wrong to say that such a friendship *transcends dogma* or exists *in spite of* the dogmas of faith. Such a view is inadmissible for all those who believe that the word of God is as absolute as His unity or His transcendence. I know very well that if I lost my faith in the least article of revealed truth, I should lose my soul. A mutual love which would be bought at the price of faith, which would base itself on some form of syncretism or eclecticism, or which, recalling Lessing's parable of the three rings, would say: "I love him who does not have my faith because, after all, I am not sure that my faith is the true faith and that it bears the device of the true ring," in so saying would reduce faith to a mere historic inheritance and seal it with the seal of agnosticism and relativity. Such a love, for anyone who believes he has heard the word of God, would amount to putting man above God.

That love which is charity, on the contrary, goes first to God, and then to all men, because the more men are loved in God and for God, the more they are loved themselves and in themselves. Moreover this love is born in faith and necessarily presupposes faith, at least the implicit faith I mentioned earlier. And it remains within faith, while at the same time reaching out to those who have not the same faith. That is the very characteristic of love; wherever our love goes, it carries with it our faith.

Nor does this friendship of charity merely make us recognize the *existence* of others—although as a matter of fact here is something already difficult enough for men, and something which includes everything essential. Not only does it make us recognize that another exists, and not as an accident of the empirical world, but as a human being who exists before God, and has the right to exist. While remaining within the faith, the friendship of charity helps us to recognize whatever beliefs other than our own include of truth and of dignity, of human and divine values. It makes us respect them, urges us on ever to seek in them everything that is stamped with the mark of man's original greatness and of the prevenient care and generosity of God. It helps us to come to a mutual understanding of one another. It is not supradogmatic; it is suprasubjective. It does not make us go beyond our faith, but beyond ourselves. In other words it helps us to purify our faith of the shell of egotism and subjectivity in which we instinctively tend to enclose it. And it also inevitably carries with it a sort of heart-rending, attached, as is the heart, at once to the truth we love and to the neighbour who is ignorant of that truth. This condition is even associated with what is called the "ecumenical" bringing together of divided Christians; how much more is it associated with the labour of bringing into mutual comprehension believers of every denomination.

I distrust any friendship between believers of all denominations which is not accompanied, as it were, by a kind of compunction or soul's sorrow—which would be easy and comfortable; just as I distrust any universalism which claims to unite in one and the same service of God, and in one and the same transcendental piety—as in some World's Fair Temple— all forms of belief and all forms of worship. The duty of being faithful to the light, and of always following it to the extent that one sees it, is a duty which cannot be evaded. In other words, the problem of conversion, for anyone who feels the spur of God, and to the extent that he is pricked by it, cannot be cast aside, any more than can be cast aside the obligation of the apostolate. And by the same token I also distrust a friendship between believers of the same denomination which is, as it were, easy and comfortable, because in that case charity would be reserved to their fellow-worshippers, there would be a universalism which would limit love to brothers in the same faith, a proselytism which would love another man only in order to convert him and only in so far as he is capable of conversion, a Christianity which would be the Christianity of *good* people as against *bad* people, and which would confuse the order of charity with what a great spiritual writer of the seventeenth century called a police-force order.

The cooperation of men of different creeds, considered at the temporal level

It follows from what I have said that from the Catholic point of view (which is mine) a rapprochement between believers of diverse religious denominations can be accomplished, on the religious and spiritual level itself, only by and in friendship and charity, by and in the pure spirituality and freedom of love. It cannot in any way involve any less intangible, more definite, more visible communion, expressed in the order of the speculative and practical intellect by some community of symbol or of sacred ritual. But on the level of the temporal and profane life (and that is indeed quite another level) it is proper that the effort toward union should express itself in common activities, should be *signed* by a more or less close cooperation for concrete and definite purposes, whether it be a question of the common good of the political community to which we all respectively belong, or of the common good of temporal civilization as a whole.

No doubt in that field it is not as believers but rather as members of a given fatherland, as men bound together by customs, traditions, interests and particular outlooks of a fleshly community, or as men having in common a given concrete historical ideal, that believers belonging to different religions are called upon to do a common work. But even in that common temporal task, ethical and spiritual values are involved, which concern the believer as such. And in that common temporal task itself, the mutual good will and fellowship I have been discussing remain factors of primary importance (I say primary; I do not say sufficient) for the pacification of men. In this sphere of temporal and political life, the most suitable phrase is not the phrase *love of charity*, but rather *civic friendship*, which is a virtue of the natural order, that must, however, be leavened by charity. It is a great pity that in an agonized world, men who believe in the supernatural, enchained as they are by so many sociological prejudices, should be so slow to broaden their hearts and to cooperate boldly in order to save from the inheritance of their fellows the elementary values of threatened humanity. From the English *Blue Book* anyone may learn about the atrocities and abominations committed in Nazi concentration camps, which blaspheme the image of God in the human person. But why were these things, that the British Government had known very well for many years, published only when war had already broken out? Anyone may also discover for himself the similar degradation of the human person practiced in Soviet prisons and concentration camps or during the persecution of the Kulaks. If a true feeling for justice and friendship had, at the appropriate time, brought into play the firm intervention of free peoples against such indignities—not by war, but by normal political or economic pressure and for aims purely and truly disinterested—in place of their seeking business accommodations with butchers, maybe the world could have avoided today's dreadful convulsions.

It is impossible to exaggerate the vital importance, so little understood by the sectarian liberalism of the nineteenth century and by the paganism of the present, of the spirit of friendship in human society. Perhaps by force of contrast the extreme sufferings and the terrible conflicts that men are undergoing today will at least have the effect of awakening in a goodly number of them a feeling for friendship and cooperation.

The cruel anomaly with which we are concerned here lies in the fact that historically, as I have pointed out, religion seems to have done as much to divide men and sharpen their conflicts as it has to pacify them. This anomaly is linked up with what is deepest in man's nature. If man is not drawn above himself toward eternal values, he becomes less than human; and when he makes use of these eternal values for the sake of his own world of weakness and sin, he uses them to feed and strengthen, and to hallow his passions and malice. To this contradictory situation there is only one key; that key is charity. Religion, like everything great and noble and demanding within us, increases the tension in mankind; and together with the tension, suffering; and with the suffering, spiritual effort; and with the spiritual effort, joy. *Tantum religio potuit suadere malorum* (So much evil could religion precipitate), said Lucretius of old in a formula after all am-phibological. He should have added, and how necessary also is it to the very breath of humanity! And what great good it has been able to call forth, what hopes and virtues it has been able to inspire! Nothing that has been done through the substance of the centuries has been lastingly useful to human beings without religion, at least without religion in its purest forms.

It is not religion that helps to divide men and sharpen their conflicts; it is the distress of our human condition and the in-terior strife in our hearts. And without religion we should cer-tainly be far worse than we are. We see today how, when man rejects the sacred tradition of humanity and aspires ei-ther to free himself from religion by atheism, or to pervert religion by deifying his own sinful blood through a kind of racist pseudo-theism or para-theism, the darkest forms of fa-naticism then spread throughout the world. Only by a deeper and purer religious life, only by charity, is it possible to sur-mount the state of conflict and opposition produced by the impact of religion upon human weakness. To bring to an end all fanaticism and all pharisaism will require, I believe, the whole of human history. But it is the task of the religious con-science itself to overcome these evils. It alone is capable of doing so. It is the religious conscience which, by spiritualizing itself in suffering, must gradually rid itself and the world of the leaven of the pharisees and the fanaticism of the sectarians.

I believe that when we think of all these things, we better perceive the dramatic greatness of our time. As has often been pointed out, a certain unification of the world is taking place on the subhuman level of matter and technique, whereas on the human level itself, the most savage conflicts come into being. In an apocalyptic upheaval, which imperils the very foundations of life, the advent of men to a new age of civiliza-tion is thus being prepared, which doubtless will indicate not only an historical transformation of great importance, for good as well as for evil, in the forms of consciousness and culture, but also the coming of a higher state of unity and in-tegration. In the meantime—and it is this which lies at the root of our unhappiness—technical progress has outstripped the mind, matter has gone faster than spirit. And that leaves to those who would hope—I am among them—only one hope: hope in a heroic effort of spiritualization thanks to which all progress in the material and technical order—a progress we must utilize, not condemn—can at least serve to effect a real progress in the emancipation of the human being.

All this is to say that the world itself is serving men an awful summons, and this summons is primarily addressed to those who are believers. The future will be good neither for the world nor for religion unless those who believe understand what is first and foremost required of them. If those very men who wear the insignia of the spirit allow their souls to become subject to those forces of destruction which desperately set evil against evil, and if they enlist religion—even, as some may say, in its own interest—in any undertaking whatever of domination and violence, I think that the disaster for civilization will be irreparable. What is required of believers at the outset and before everything else, even in the struggles of this world, with all the harsh means they imply, is not to dominate but to serve. It is to preserve among men confidence in good will, in the spirit of cooperation, in justice, in goodness, in pity for the weak and the outcast, in human dignity and in the power of truth. These are big words, but it is not enough to let them remain words; they must be made flesh in our lives. If we speak the truth without *doing it*, we run the risk of leading men to regard truth as an imposture. It has been said again and again in recent times, and rightly, that the believer is specially called upon to confess his God in social and temporal life, in the hard work of men. Many things which he accepts today in the earthly state of his fellows and in the conditions of human societies, will appear later to be as little worthy of acceptance as now appears to us the slavery of antiquity. The tragedy of unemployment, the tragedy of the refugee and the émigré, the tragedy of war, are symptoms of a deep disorder which we must work tirelessly to remedy.

Undoubtedly the world needs bread. It is horrible to think that there are so many millions of men on this earth who cannot satisfy their hunger. But what the world needs also and above all are the words that come from the mouth of

God, words of active truth, of effective and fertile truth; it needs—I do not say solely or exclusively, but I do say primarily—the contemplation of the saints, their love and activity. And from us who are not saints it needs that in the patient insignificant acts of our everyday life, and in our social and political activities, each of us should faithfully witness, according as his state of life permits, the love of God for all beings and the respect due to the image of God in each human creature.

The analogical similarities in basic principles and ideas required for the cooperation of men of different creeds in the temporal order

There is still one question about which, in conclusion, I should like to say something. In the first part of this chapter, I emphasized the fact that religious division creates for believers of different denominations a fundamental plurality of points of view, and I drew attention to the illusion of seeking for the basis and purpose of good fellowship in a common minimum of doctrinal identity—a common minimum which would be seen gradually to shrink to nothing while we discussed it, like the wild ass's skin in Balzac's story.

Yet on the other hand I have just said that this fellowship, based on friendship and charity, should extend, on the level of temporal civilization, to common action (doubtless not free from a certain amount of inevitable opposition and conflict); that it should extend real cooperation for the good of temporal society. But how can such common action be possible without common principles, without a certain basic community of doctrine?

Before passing to more concrete considerations, I shall first answer this question in my own philosophical language. We are all bound together by a more primitive and fundamental unity than any unity of thought and doctrine: we all have the same human nature and, considered in their extramental reality, the same primordial tendencies. That sameness of nature is not sufficient to ensure community of action, since we act as thinking beings and not simply by natural instinct. But it subtends the very exercise of our thought. And the nature we hold in common is a rational nature, subject intellectually to the attraction of the same fundamental objects; this unity of nature lies at the deepest foundation of what similarities our principles of action may have, however diverse they may be in other respects. Now, in order to do the same terrestrial work and pursue the same temporal goal, there must be a *certain community* of principles and doctrine. But there need not necessarily be—however desirable and obviously more effective this might be in itself—a strict and pure and simple *identity* of doctrine. It is sufficient that the various principles and doctrines between themselves should have some unity and community of similarity or proportion or, in the technical sense of the word, of *analogy*, with regard to the practical end proposed. Besides, this practical end in itself, although subordinated to a higher end, belongs to the natural order. And no doubt it will be conceived differently according to each one's particular outlook; but in its existential reality it will be placed outside each one's particular conception. Considered thus, in real existence, it will in a measure fall short of, and, at the same time, give actual reality to, each one's particular conceptions.

Therefore, men with different religious convictions will be able not only to collaborate in working out a technique, in putting out a fire, in succouring a man who is starving or sick, in resisting aggression. All that is obvious. But—and this is the problem that concerns us here—if there really is that "analogical" likeness I have just mentioned between their principles, they can also cooperate—at least as regards the primary values of existence in this world—in a constructive action involving the right ordering of the life of temporal society and earthly civilization and the moral values inherent therein. I acknowledge this possibility at the same time— and the two things are not incompatible—as I realize even more keenly my personal conviction that a complete doctrine, based on all principles of Catholic teaching, is alone capable of supplying an entirely true solution for the problems of civilization.

I shall give an example of what I mean from the field I know best, namely Western Christianity, and an example which relates to the religious life itself. The practical problems connected with the relationship between the spiritual and the temporal, and their practical solutions, are so much alike for the Orthodox Church in the Soviet Union, for the Catholic Church and Protestant communities in Germany, that the experience and testimony of believers belonging to these different Christian families are, with their sufferings, a kind of common property. Another example can be drawn from the practical convergence which appears today, in connection with questions of civilization and the defense of the human person, between speculative outlooks as incompatible as Karl Barth's and my own. A Thomist and a Barthian will always clash in theology and philosophy; they can work together within human society.

But we must be even more precise. I have said that the basis of fellowship between believers of different spiritual families is friendship and the love of charity. I now add that it is the implications of love itself that supply us with the guiding idea we need and that make manifest for us the "analogical" likeness of practical thought I referred to earlier.

It is obvious in fact that, if I am right in what I have said, the primary and fundamental likeness between us is the acknowledgement of the fundamental and primordial ethical value of the law of brotherly love, however much this law may have different theological and metaphysical connotations for us, according to the religion or school of thought to which we belong. For the Christian it corresponds to and raises to divine levels a fundamental though terribly thwarted tendency of our nature. It is the second commandment, which forms but one with the first: the commandment to love our neighbour as ourselves. "I feel," wrote Gandhi in a note on the *Satyagraha* in 1920, "that nations cannot be one in reality, nor can their activities be conducive to the common good of the whole humanity, unless there is this definite recognition and acceptance of the law of the family in national and international affairs, in other words, on the political platform. Nations can be called civilized, only to the extent that they obey this law."[2] That, I also believe, is the truth.

Now this very law of brotherly friendship in practice has many implications. The first truth it implies, and which underlies all the rest, is that our existence is directed toward

God and that, in accordance with the first commandment, we must love God above everything. How indeed can the law of love have *absolute* value, transcending all the conflicts and discords which flourish among men, unless all men, whatever their race or colour, their class, their nation, ther social conditions, their natural shortcomings, receive from an Absolute above the world the bond creating between them a more fundamental and far-reaching communion than all their diversities, and unless they are created to love first and foremost this Absolute in which all things live and move and have their being? We see only too readily that, in the great contemporary movements in which God is in practice denied, whether by virtue of an atheism that refuses to admit His existence or by virtue of a pseudo-theism that blasphemes His nature, love and charity are alike rejected as weaknesses and as the worst enemies either of the State or of the Revolution. The theorists of these movements make that abundantly clear in their writings.

The second implication is on the one hand the holiness of truth and on the other hand the eminent value of good will. If man can bend the truth to his own desires, will he not also want to bend other men in like manner? Those who despise charity are also those who think that truth depends, not on *what is*, but on what at each moment serves most effectively their party, their greed, or their hate. And those who despise charity also despise good will. The word to them seems pale and dangerously liberal. They forget—at any rate the Christians among them—that the word has its origin in the Gospels. It is true enough that good will is not sufficient, and that men who mistake that will which is good will for that willingness which is weakness cheat people. But good will is necessary and of primary necessity. It is useful in everything. Real, authentic good will indicates the sacred mystery which spells salvation for men and which makes it possible to say of a man that he is purely and simply good. It enables men to go out of themselves to meet their neighbours halfway. That is why the pharisees and the fanatics, walled up in their whited sepulchres, wherein they would like to enclose the whole world, are not only suspicious of good will; they detest the very idea.

The third implication contained in fraternal amity is the dignity of the human person with the rights it implies and the realities on which it is based. I refer to the spirituality of the human soul and its eternal destiny. In the text from which I have already quoted, Gandhi also pointed out that, "It [Satyagraha] is called also soul-force, because a definite recognition of the soul within is a necessity, if a Satyagrahi is to believe that death does not mean cessation of the struggle, but a culmination." I as a Christian know very well on what my faith in the immortality of the soul and the dignity of the human person is based. I read in the Gospels: "What doth it profit a man if he gain the whole world and lose his own soul?" I read also that the hairs on each of our heads are counted, and that the angels who see the face of the Father watch over each of the children of men, who are equal in that dignity, and that we must love our enemies. And I read the story of the man who went down from Jerusalem to Jericho and whom robbers left half-dead by the roadside. A Samaritan, in other words a foreigner, with whom the Jews did not mix and whose religious beliefs were different from theirs, recognized his neighbour in that man by having pity on him; whereas a doctor of the law and a priest, going on their way with closed hearts, by so doing excluded themselves from neighbourship with men. The mysterious words of Christ on this matter mean that it is up to us really to become the neighbour of any man, by loving him and having pity on him. It is not community of race, of class, or of nation; it is the love of charity that makes us what we ought to be, members of the family of God, of the only community where each person, drawn out from his fundamental loneliness, truly communicates with others and truly makes them his brothers, by giving himself to them and in a certain sense dying for them. Nothing that has ever been said points out more profoundly the mystery and dignity of the human person. Who is my neighbour? The man of my blood? Of my party? The man who does me good? No. It is the man to whom I show mercy, the man to whom is transmitted through me the universal gift and love of God, who makes the rain from Heaven fall upon both the good and the wicked.

The existence of God, the sanctity of truth, the value and

necessity of good will, the dignity of the person, the spirituality and immortality of the soul: these, and all the other implications bound up with them which I shall not mention here, correspond to spontaneous perceptions of our reason and to primary tendencies of our nature; but they are not understood in an identical and univocal way by believers in the various religions of humanity. Thus Christianity and Buddhism have different conceptions of the human person; the survival of the soul has a different meaning for those who believe in personal immortality and in the resurrection of the body and those who believe in transmigration; the sanctity of truth appears in a different light according to the fashion in which both revelation and human reason are conceived; the value of good will has different connotations for the Catholic who believes in sanctifying grace, for the Orthodox who believes in the sanctifying uncreated Spirit but not in created grace, for the Protestant who believes that the merits of Christ are imputed to an essentially corrupt nature, for the Israelite who believes in the Law, for the Moslem who believes in salvation by the mere profession of Islamic faith; and this difference is still greater as between these religious groups and the religious groups who believe in Karma. As regards the existence of God itself, I do not think that Buddhism rejects, as is often stated, the existence of God, nor that it is in reality an atheistic religion. I believe that this apparent atheism comes from the fact that Buddhism has developed historically as a kind of mystical destruction of the Brahmanic affirmation, so that the Buddhist ascesis and Nirvâna are, as it were, like a vast apophatic or negative theology, standing alone in emptiness. But this example does serve to cast light on the extent to which the idea of God may differ among believers of the various religions. It should be added that those who believe that they are non-believers may, in their practical lives, by choosing as the aim of their activity the authentic moral good, choose God, and may do so by virtue of God's grace, without their knowing God in a consciously and conceptually formulated manner.

All this goes to show that there is nothing *univocal* between the various paths travelled by men, and that practical good fellowship is not based on a common minimum of doctrinal identity. In a certain sense, *less* than a common minimum is to be found there, since ultimately no notion appears to be univocally common to all the different religious outlooks. Yet in another sense there is much *more* than a common minimum, since among those who, belonging to different religious families, allow the spirit of love to enter into them, the implications of brotherly love create, for the principles of the practical reason and of action and as regards terrestrial civilization, a community of similitude and *analogy* which corresponds on the one hand to the fundamental unity of our rational nature and is, on the other hand, not merely concerned with a minimum number of points of doctrine, but penetrates the whole gamut of practical notions and of the principles of action of each one. The coming together of such men to cooperate for the good of human society is not based upon an equivocation. It is based upon "analogical" likeness as between the practical principles, motions, and progressions implied in their common acceptance of the law of love, and corresponding to the primary inclinations of human nature.

And why should I, a Christian, according to whose faith a single Name has been given to men through whom they can be saved, even in the temporal order, why should I disguise the fact that this community of analogy itself supposes a *primum analogatum* purely and simply true; and that implicitly and ultimately everything which is authentic love, working in the world for the reconciliation of men and the common good of their life here below, tends, under forms more or less perfect, more or less pure, toward Christ, who is known to some, unknown to others?

In this philosophical attempt to solve a difficult problem, I have spoken in accordance with my faith, and I hope that I have said nothing which might offend the conscience of any of my readers. I shall be glad if I have succeeded in outlining with sufficient clarity what are, from my point of view, the foundations of mutual fellowship and understanding between believers of different religious families and of a constructive cooperation between them for the good of civilization. The good of civilization is also the good of the human person, the recognition of his rights and of his dignity, based ultimately on the fact that he is the image of God. Let no one deceive himself; the cause of religion and the cause of the human person are closely linked. They have the same enemies. The time has passed when a rationalism fatal to reason, which has prepared the way for all our misfortunes, could claim to defend the person and his autonomy *against* religion. Both against atheistic materialism and against an irrationalism drunk with inflicting domination and humiliation, an irrationalism which perverts the genuine instincts of human nature and makes of the political State a supreme idol and a Moloch, religion is the best defender of the person and of his freedom.

And finally if I am asked what I believe to be the reason for God's having permitted the religious divisions in mankind, and those heresies which "must be," according to Saint Paul—I should answer: For the education of mankind, and in order to prepare the way for final religious unity. Because on the one hand it is something above human powers to maintain purity and strength in the collective virtues of any natural community, unless it be within the particular hereditary bias of this earthly, sociologically closed social group. And on the other hand the common life of the Church, the Kingdom of God, is that of a spiritual, supernatural, supra-racial, supra-national, supra-earthly community, open to all humanity as it is open to Deity and divine and deifying blood. Much suffering and many purifications throughout human history are necessary to extricate us from any restriction and adulteration of spiritual unity brought about by fleshly unities.

On the day when all the faithful could live with men of other creeds in perfect justice, love and understanding, and at the same time keep the true faith perfectly whole and pure, on that day men would not need actually to practice these virtues toward people of other creeds, because infidelity and religious division would on such a day have vanished from the face of the earth.

18. THE DISPERSION OF ISRAEL

Let us take up the question of the dispersion of Israel, understood in its ultimate significance. As I wrote in another study[1] from which I am here borrowing several pages, whatever the economic, political or cultural forms which cloak the problem of the dispersion of Israel among the nations, this problem is and remains in truth a mystery, sacred in character, of which St. Paul, in the Epistle to the Romans, gives us the principal elements in his sublime summary.

If there are Jews among the readers of this essay, they will understand, I am sure, that as a Christian I try to understand something of the history of their people from a Christian viewpoint. They know that according to St. Paul, we gentile Christians have been grafted onto the predestined olive tree of Israel in place of the branches which did not recognize the Messiah foretold by the prophets. Thus we are converts to the God of Israel who is the true God, to the Father whom Israel recognized, to the Son whom it rejected. Christianity, then, is the overflowing fulness and the supernatural realization of Judaism.

The vocation of Israel

Referring to the Jews, his brothers in the flesh to whom he expected to be anathema, St. Paul had such a profound and tender love for them "who are Israelites, to whom belongeth the adoption as of children, and the glory, and the testament, and the giving of the law, and the service of God, and the promises: whose are the fathers, and of whom Christ came according to the flesh,"[2] that he wrote that "if the loss of them be the reconciliation of the world, what shall the receiving of them be, but life from the dead?"[3] "For," continues the apostle, "I would not have you ignorant, brethren, of this mystery (lest you should be wise in your own conceits), that a blindness in part has happened in Israel, until the fulness of the Gentiles come in. And so all Israel should be saved . . . As concerning the Gospel, indeed they are enemies for your sake: but as touching the election they are most dear for the sake of the fathers. For the gifts and the calling of God are without repentance. For as you also in times past did not believe God, but now have obtained mercy, through their unbelief; so these also now have not believed, for your mercy, that they also may now obtain mercy. For God hath concluded all in unbelief, that He may have mercy on all."[4]

Thus from the first Israel appears to us a mystery; of the same order as the mystery of the world and the mystery of the Church. Like them it is a mystery lying at the very core of redemption. And we must say that, if St. Paul be right, what is call the *Jewish problem* is an *insoluble* problem, that is, one without *definitive* solution until the great reconciliation foretold by the apostle, which will resemble a resurrection from among the dead.

Between Israel and the world, as between the Church and the world, there is a suprahuman relation. It is only by considering this triad, that one can grasp even an enigmatic idea of the mystery of Israel. It seems to me that we have here as our sole guiding thread a sort of inverted analogy with the Church. We realize that the Church is not a mere administrative organization dispensing religion. According to its own teaching about itself, it is a mysterious body in which living bonds, in order to accomplish a divine task, unite souls with one another, and with God. The Church is the mystical body of Christ. Indeed, Jewish thought is itself aware that in a quite different sense and in its own way, Israel is a *corpus mysticum*, a mystical body. A recent work by Erich Kahler, *Israel unter den Völkern* emphasizes this point particularly. The bond which unifies Israel is not simply the bond of flesh and blood, or that of an ethico-historical community. A sacred and suprahistorical bond, it is one of promise and yearning rather than of possession. In the eyes of a Christian who remembers that the promises of God are irrevocable and without repentance, Israel continues its sacred mission but in the darkness of the world, preferred, on so unforgettable an occasion, to the darkness of God. Israel, like the Church, is in the world and not of the world. But since the day when, because its leaders chose the world, it stumbled, it is bound to the world, prisoner and victim of that world which it loves, but *of which* it is not, shall not be, and never can be. Thus is the mystery of Israel understood from a Christian viewpoint.

The communion of this mystical body is the communion of mundane hope. Israel passionately hopes, waits, yearns for the coming of God on earth, the kingdom of *God here below*. With an eternal will, a supernatural and non-rational will, it desires justice in time, in nature, and in the city of man.

So, like the world and its history, Israel and its action in the world are ambivalent realities; because the longing for the absolute in the world can take all forms, some good, others evil. Hence the fact that, in the astonishing complexity of the forms it assumes, simultaneously pregnant with good and evil, there will always be found something to glorify and something to degrade Israel. "Anti-Semites speak of Jews," said Péguy. "I am aware that I am about to speak paradoxically: the anti-Semites do not know the Jews at all." Again, he said: "I know this people well. It bears on its skin no single spot which is not painful, where there is not some old bruise, some ancient contusion, some secret woe, the memory of a secret woe, a scar, a wound, a laceration of the Orient or of the Occident."

It is not a question of deciding whether you find Jews attractive or repulsive; that is a matter of temperament. But have they a right to common justice and the common brotherhood of man? If men could tolerate each other only on condition of having no complaint against each other, all the provinces of every country would constantly be at war. The most curious fact, moreover, is that many anti-Semites declare that they have only praise for Jews they have known personally, but nevertheless feel hatred for the Jews as a sacred obligation. Which is one way, among others, of paying tribute to the mystery of Israel we are considering.

But what, then, is that vocation of Israel which persists in darkness, and of which we were just speaking? First of all, there is its vocation as a witness to the Scriptures. But more, while the Church is assigned the labor of supernatural and supratemporal redemption of the world, Israel, we believe, is assigned, on the plane and within the limits of secular history, a task of *earthly activization* of the mass of the world. Israel, which is not of the world, is to be found at the very heart of the world's structure, stimulating it, exasperating it, moving it. Like an alien body, like an activating ferment injected into the mass, it gives the world no peace, it bars slumber, it teaches the world to be discontented and restless as long as the world has not God, it stimulates the movement of history.

The spiritual essence of anti-Semitism

It seems to me that these considerations explain something of the spiritual essence of anti-Semitism.

The diverse specific causes which the observer may assign to anti-Semitism, all the way from the feeling of hate for the foreigner natural to any social group, down to religious hatreds—alas! that these two words may be coupled—and to the manifold inconveniences produced by some waves of immigration, mask an underlying spring of hatred deeper down. If the world hates the Jews, it is because the world clearly senses that they will always be outsiders in a supernatural sense, it is because the world detests their passion for the absolute and the unbearable stimulus which it inflicts. It is the vocation of Israel which the world execrates. To be hated by the world is their glory, as it is also the glory of Christians who live by faith. But Christians know that the Messiah has already conquered the world.

Thus hatred of Jews and hatred of Christians spring from a common source, from the same recalcitrance of the world, which desires to be wounded neither with the wounds of Adam nor with the wounds of the Savior, neither by the goad of Israel for its movement in time, nor by the cross of Jesus for eternal life. We are good enough as we are, says the world, we have no need of grace or transfiguration, we ourselves will accomplish our own happiness in our own nature. This is neither Christian hope in a helping God, nor Jewish hope for a God on earth. It is the hope of animal life and its power, deep and, in a sense, sacred, demonic, when it masters the human being who thinks himself deceived by the emissaries of the absolute.

Racial tellurianism is anti-Semitic and anti-Christian. Communist atheism is not anti-Semitic; it is satisfied in being against God universally. In one as in the other, the same absolute naturalism, the same abhorrence for all asceticism and all transcendence, is to be found at work. The mystical life of the world itself aims to blossom heroically, as it were; every mystical body constituted apart from the world must be rejected as such. . . .

Jews and Christians

Have I succeeded in giving some idea of the pathos of the situation of the Jewish people? In explaining how, often despite itself, and while manifesting, sometimes in contrasting forms, a materialistic messianism which is the dark face of its vocation to the absolute, but manifesting also admirable ardor, intelligence and dynamism, the Jewish people bears witness to the divine in human history? Thence come the conflicts and the tension which, under all sorts of masks, necessarily prevail between Israel and the nations.

It is an illusion to believe that such tension can completely vanish. To desire to put an end to the problem by anti-Semitic violence, openly persecutory or politically mitigated, is villainy, one of those villainies natural to the human animal (whether he be an Arab and himself the descendant of Shem, or a Slav, a Latin or a German), and from which only Christianity, to the extent that it is really lived, can deliver the nations. The sole road is to accept the state of tension and to face it in each specific case, not with hatred, but with that concrete intelligence which love demands from each, so that one may come to an early understanding with one's adversary while traveling together, and in the consciousness that "all have sinned and need the glory of God," *omnes quidem peccaverunt, et egent gloria Dei.* "The history of the Jews," said Léon Bloy, "thwarts the history of the human race as a dike thwarts the flood, to raise its level."

On the spiritual plane, the drama of love between Israel and its God, if we are to believe St. Paul, will reach a dénouement only with the reconciliation of the Synagogue and the Church. If there is no earlier truly definitive solution to the problem of Israel, there are nevertheless some partial or provisional solutions, specific responses whose discovery is the task of political wisdom and which each historic age must seek.

The historic age in which we live is a period of accumulated difficulties for the Jewish people. In the economic field the renunciation of free competition, the rise of autarchical and state capitalist régimes, deal a body blow to Jewish economic pursuits. Recently published studies of the economic situation of world Jewry indicate the growing pauperization of the Jewish masses.

In the political and moral fields, the development of various types of totalitarianism, all of which regard the non-conformist as a biological enemy of the secular community, menaces the natural attachment of the Jews to independence and liberty.

In the spiritual field, the upsurge of unprecedentedly ferocious forms of paganism signifies an inevitable conflict, already terribly begun, with that people who, surrounded by the pagans of another age, knew how to pay heroic tribute to the sanctity of the personal and transcendent God.

I have come to believe that if the world should triumph over the errors and evils oppressing it today and should contrive to establish the rule of a civilization, new and more consonant with human dignity, the solutions at once pluralist and personalist which would have to prevail generally in such a régime, will likewise characterize those efforts to regulate the Jewish question which such an historical climate must inspire. As I tried to explain elsewhere,[5] a pluralism founded on the dignity of the human person, and established on the basis of complete equality of civic rights, and effective respect for the liberties of the person in his individual and social life, would then recognize in certain determined matters, an ethico-juridical status proper to various spiritual families, or even, sometimes, to various national communities which enter into the *convivium* of the temporal city. But such solutions, which though far removed from the old Liberalism, are thoroughly opposed to the ignominious medievalist Hitlerian parody, and which tend to strengthen the bonds of justice and brotherly friendship between the various elements of the same civil society, could only be considered in a general new régime of civilization, freed from the ills of capitalistic materialism as well as from the even greater ills of Fascism, Racism and Communism. Those who at present suggest a special status for the Jews are actually thinking of measures of discrimination against them. They are the victims of the absurd illusion, according to which the Jewish question, poisoned as are all questions of today by the general crisis suffered by a civilization which is sick and in a state of transformation, is the only or the principal cause of this crisis; they imagine that the "solution" which consists of sacrificing the Jews would end the evils whose roots plunge, in fact, into the very depths of the economic, moral, spiritual and political structures of our civilization. Infected by the contagion of the errors propagated by the racist mentality, they serve this mentality, whether they wish to or not. Some of them are fierce anti-Semites who pretend to be good apostles. Others protest that they are not anti-Semites, and consider themselves as dispassionate *realists*: they are Mr. Hitler's messengers, who have *not even* the excuse of passion.

Strictly speaking, the only suitable "realism" here would be the one which understands the reality of the horror whereby the cult of hatred and the rejection of all human sentiment threaten the universe; the only realism which a Christian has the right to profess in such a matter is the one that warns us that the least word which might convey the merest shadow of an indulgence or concession toward racism, runs the risk of bearing an ugly complicity, and of dripping with innocent blood.

If we now turn more particularly toward the Christians, it appears, that being themselves grafted onto the olive tree of Israel, they must look on the men involved in the Jewish tragedy with a brotherly eye and, as the apostle Paul teaches them, not without trembling for themselves. It is certainly possible for Christians to be anti-Semites, since one observes the phenomenon frequently enough. But it is possible for them only when they obey the spirit of the world rather than the spirit of Christianity.

Strangely enough certain Christians are heard to remark: "Has the world been moved (they say) by the massacres of so many Christians in Russia, Spain, and Mexico? We will be stirred by the Jewish persecutions when the world will be stirred by the sufferings of our own."

When I hear this manner of reasoning, I wonder how it is that from one day to the next, and without even telling me anything about it my religion has been changed. Does the Gospel teach that if a brother has sinned against me, by omission or otherwise, it is justifiable to sin against him in the same fashion? Jesus said: "These things you ought to have done, and not to leave those undone." Now it is said: "Because these things have been left undone, you ought not to do those." Because certain people have been lacking in justice and in love, others must be similarly deficient . . .

It is not exact to say that the world remained indifferent to the suffering of Christians in Russia, Spain and Mexico. It is, however, exact that many who today are full of indignation because of Racism remained quite cold regarding the discriminatory laws enacted by certain governments against religious Orders, and regarding the anti-Christian persecutions which have raged or are raging in so many countries. I object to such unjust indifference and such one-eyed pity. But I do not want to lay myself open to the same objection.

Among careless or partisan writers many historic confusions arise from the fact of the commingling in mediaeval civilization of the affairs of the Church and the affairs of a secular commonwealth religiously organized, where mundane interests and both the good and evil of human social life were steeped in religion. If one makes proper distinctions, one can see that, in a temporal civilization where the régime of the ghetto—not to speak of the drama of the Marranos and the Spanish Inquisition—lent itself to the worse anti-Semitic passions and excesses, the Church itself and as such, was not responsible for the excesses, even if some of its ministers were. It is well enough known that the Popes repeatedly defended the Jews, notably against the absurd charge of ritual murder, and that all in all the Jews were generally less unhappy and less badly treated in the Papal States than elsewhere.

Western civilization, emerging from the Holy Roman Empire and the mediaeval régime, while in jeopardy of collapsing in other respects, as we know, freed itself from the strong impurities which this régime entailed. And it would be a singular aberration if Christians wished to return to those impurities at the moment when they have lost their historic reason for existing. Today anti-Semitism is no longer one of those accidental blemishes of a secular Christendom in which evil was mixed with the good. It contaminates Christians like an error of the spirit. . . .

It is well known that Pope Pius XI spoke out vigorously against the racist campaign and racist measures inaugurated by the Italian government in imitation of the German government. To the concept and word *race*, figuring in the theories imported from Germany, he opposed magnificently the ancient Latin idea of *gens* and *populus*, the connotation of which belong much more to the moral than to the biological order.

The following passages of a discourse pronounced by Pope Pius XI are also to be noted.[6] Commenting upon the words of the Canon of the Mass, *sacrificium Patriarchae nostri Abrahae*, the sacrifice of our father Abraham, he said, "Notice that Abraham is called our Patriarch, our ancestor. Anti-Semitism is incompatible with the thought and sublime reality expressed in this text. It is a movement in which we Christians can have no part whatsoever . . . Anti-Semitism is unacceptable. Spiritually we are Semites."

Spiritually we are Semites. No stronger word has been spoken by a Christian against anti-Semitism, and this Christian is the successor of the apostle Peter.

As for its moral characterization from the Catholic viewpoint, anti-Semitism, if it spreads among those calling themselves disciples of Jesus Christ, seems to be a pathological phenomenon which indicates a deterioration of Christian conscience when it becomes incapable of accepting its own historic responsibilities and of remaining existentially faithful to the high exigencies of Christian truth. Then, instead of recognizing the trials and shocks of history as the visitations of God, and instead of assuming those burdens of justice and charity demanded by that fact, it turns aside to substitute phantoms relating to an entire race, phantoms which derive a certain consistency from various real or fancied pretexts. And in giving free rein to feelings of hate which it believes justified by religion, it seeks for itself a sort of alibi.

It is no little matter, however, for a Christian to hate or to despise or to wish to treat degradingly the race from which sprung his God and the Immaculate Mother of his God. That is why the bitter zeal of anti-Semitism always turns in the end into a bitter zeal against Christianity itself.

"Imagine," wrote Léon Bloy, "that people about you were to speak continually of your father and your mother with the greatest contempt, and to have for them only insults or outrageous sarcasm. What would be your sentiments? Well, that is exactly what is happening to Our Lord Jesus Christ. We forget, or rather we do not wish to know, that as a man Our Lord was a Jew, the epitome par excellence of the Jewish nature, the Lion of Judah; that His Mother was a Jewess, the flower of the Jewish race; that the apostles were Jews, along with all the prophets; finally, that our whole liturgy is based on Jewish books. How, then, express the enormity of the outrage and the blasphemy involved in vilifying the Jewish race?"

NOTES

1. "L'Impossible Antisémitisme," appeared first in *Les Juifs* (Paris: Plon, 1937), and later in our *Questions de Conscience* (Paris: Desclée de Brouwer, 1938). Editors' Note: For the English version, see "The Mystery of Israel," ch. VI of *Ransoming the Time*. In this study, complementary to *A Christian Looks at the Jewish Question*, Prof. Maritain makes clear that he is writing *as a Christian philosopher*, from a primarily metaphysical and religious standpoint, (pp. 142–43). In a recent work, *Le mystère d'Israël et autres essais*, (Paris: Desclée de Brouwer, 1965), he has gathered together "the scattered pages in a good many books" in which he discussed the destinies of Israel and the persecutions she has suffered; besides a number of revisions, the book contains an important *Post-scriptum* (pp. 241–53).

2. *Rom.* 9:4.

3. *Rom.* 11:15.

4. *Rom.* 11:25, 26, 28–32.

5. "L'Impossible Antisémitisme," in *Questions de Conscience*, pp. 86–89.

6. Discourse pronounced in September 1938 before the directors of the Belgian Catholic Radio Agency.

19. THAT SUFFER PERSECUTION

"Blessed are they that suffer persecution for justice's sake: for theirs is the kingdom of heaven." The eighth beatitude confirms all the others (*est firmitas quaedam omnium beatitudinum*, says Saint Thomas Aquinas) and corresponds to the first; the circle of the Gospel's blessedness, which begins with the poor in spirit, is completed with the persecuted. They are placed under the same banner: theirs is the kingdom of heaven, *ipsorum est*, not precisely a possession to which they have a right, but something much more intimate, inward and personal—for a thing which is *mine* is within me as though belonging to me, more beloved to my heart than is my very self. He, the Poor Man, the persecuted above all who have suffered persecution, is not He, Himself, likewise the Kingdom of heaven? He tells them that He is their treasure.

Those who suffer persecution for justice's sake. We know approximately, or we believe we know, what persecution is. But "for justice's sake"—there we feel the presence of a mystery. What is this justice for the sake of which they are persecuted?

The saints know what is this justice. They are persecuted for the sake of the justice which makes us adopted sons of God and participants in His life through grace; they are persecuted for the sake of the divine truth to which they bear witness and of that Word which was made flesh and came to dwell in the world and "His own received Him not"; they are persecuted for the sake of Jesus Who is our justice. "Blessed are ye when they shall revile you and persecute you and speak all that is evil against you, untruly, for My sake: be glad and rejoice, for your reward is very great in heaven. For so they persecuted the prophets that were before you."

Blessed are the saints. They know wherefor they suffer. Not only do they suffer for justice's "sake" but "for" justice, which they know and which they love and which they will. Throughout their worst sufferings and their darkest nights they are well satisfied to be persecuted, they know that persecution is good for them, they desire it as they might desire an earthly paradise, they are astonished and worried when persecution is lacking to them. But never do they lack it long. Saint Paul reassures them and tells them that all those who seek to live piously in Christ Jesus will suffer persecution. When they are persecuted they have obtained that which they have wanted, they have that blessedness of the Gospel for which they have asked, they are well served.

And when they die abandoned and persecuted, the Holy Ghost Who is called the Consoler reminds them in the depths of their hearts of all the things which their Savior has told to those who are His, and that same Spirit places before the eyes of their souls the image of Him who has opened the way for them and who has loved them first of all, even unto giving His life for them upon that cross of redemption to the partaking of which He has now invited them.

The saints are not the only ones to be persecuted. And the inner justice of the soul is not the only justice for the sake of which men suffer persecution. All those who have sought justice within the earthly community and who have suffered for its sake imprisonment or exile or death, and who, moreover, have been looked upon as fools or bad citizens, have not been offered the promise of the eighth beatitude for such things. The immediate object of their thirst, the immediate cause of their sufferings is not to conform themselves to the Savior who makes man just and holy in the eyes of God; it is rather the imperfect and obstructed labor whereby a little more human justice is introduced into the world. They have battled against the oppression or enslavement in which men have been held by men of another race, another nation, another caste or another class; they have battled with human means and for human ideas; they have very often had to have recourse to force against force, to appeal to the wrath of those who have been humiliated and downtrodden. On occasion their passion for earthly justice has been fevered by hatred and violence, or else led astray by great illusions which made them dream of constructing a Jerusalem of peace without God, or else bemused by a despairing revolt against both Creator and creation. At times they have sought to be titans, at times "grand inquisitors" like the one in

Dostoevski's tale. Unhappy are those who seek for justice in this world and suffer persecution for its sake. To have done so is not sufficient to assure them of the promise of the kingdom of heaven. And the justice they seek and for the sake of which they suffer, they usually see rejected by men throughout the length of their struggle for it, and betrayed by men at the very moment when justice is able to go freely among men.

Nonetheless they also have obtained that which they wanted. For they have labored in time and under the law of time for a thing of the earth and an idea entrusted to history. Time will bring them their reward when they are no longer, their labor and their trouble will bear their own fruits on earth under forms which they themselves had not foreseen, bemused as they were in the eddies of the vast stream of history. I do not mean to say that every effort on behalf of justice automatically succeeds in producing an effect in the history of mankind; I am not so optimistic. To my mind everything depends upon the depth at which the thirst after justice and the suffering on behalf of justice—however mixed these may be—have been brought into life within the secret substance of a heart and of a spirit. If a man's actions, before having been given outward manifestation, have thus been given birth in the very depths of the spirit, they will equally take their place in the depths of history, and there they will go their shadowy way until one day a few of the seeds they contain come to take root and bear fruit among men.

Having granted this, it is clear that if we look upon things in themselves, there is neither separateness nor conflict between thirst after the justice of God's kingdom and thirst after justice in this sad world. The one summons the other. The latter threatens to drive a man out of his mind unless it is accompanied by the former; the former requires and awakens and sanctifies the latter. How could men who daily ask that the will of the Father be done on earth as it is in heaven not thirst after justice on earth and within the human community? How could men who believe in the Gospel as far as eternal life is concerned not believe in it for life here below—how could they resign themselves to men's earthly hope therein being disappointed? So long as abysmal poverty and slavery and injustice exist in the lives of men and in their mortal societies, there will be no rest for the Christian. He knows that his God suffers in the persons of all those who are suffering, all those who are spurned, all those who are persecuted throughout the world.

Hence blessed is he who suffers persecution for the sake of the justice of God's kingdom and for the sake of justice on earth. He suffers abuse for Christ's sake when he is abused for the sake of his brethren. Blessed is he if he is doubly persecuted. The more unhappiness he bears in his temporal existence because of his desire for justice in temporal society and because of his undertaking to "ransom the evil of the days," the more utterly and the more surely is he persecuted; and the more may he consequently hope, if he is faithful, to have in life everlasting, which for the just begins even here below, the blessedness of the persecuted; the more can he hope that his is the kingdom of heaven.

In our own day we have seen monstrous persecutions, persecutions in which hangmen beyond number scientifically organized cruelty and assassination, bending themselves to the task of debasing man in his body and in his soul, not striking down persons condemned by reason of a faith to which at least they gave witness, but masses of men and women guilty only of the fact of their existence and wiped out like rats. And we have been able to verify the truth of the saying that next to the hangmen what men despise most is his victim. Confronted by these great herds of victims left to their fate, the Christian questions his heart and even his faith.

He thinks of his Jewish brethren, of the ancient olive tree with some of its branches broken, among which he has been grafted.[1] Six million Jews have been *liquidated* in Europe. Other masses of human beings have been deliberately exterminated, also in millions, in Poland, in the briefly conquered Russian provinces, in Serbia, and this in the name of "living space" or through political vengeance. These men and women have been put to death because they were hated in their quality as people and because others desired to wipe their race from the face of the earth. This animal hatred possessed supernatural eyes. In truth it was their very election, it was Moses and the prophets who were persecuted in them, it was the Savior sprung from them against whom the grudge was held. It was the dignity of Israel, within which the Catholic Church prays God to have all nations enter, which was buffeted in these despised wretches treated like the vermin of the earth. It was our God who was slapped and scourged in His fleshly lineage, before being persecuted openly in His Church. How strangely knowing a hatred, more aware than the weak love of our own hearts: even before that day foretold by Saint Paul, when church and synagogue would be reconciled, and which would be for the world like life from the dead, they have been reunited in this devilish hatred. Just as Christianity was hated because of its Jewish origins, Israel was hated because of its belief in original sin and in the redemption and because of Christian pity, all of which had their source in Israel. As has been pointed out with deep truth by the Jewish writer, Maurice Samuel, it was not because the Jews killed Christ but rather because they gave Christ to the world that Hitlerian anti-Semitism in its rage dragged the Jews along all the roads of Europe, through filth and blood, tore from their mothers children from thenceforth not even possessed of a name, undertook to dedicate an entire race to despair.

Thus it happened that unwitting Israel has been pursued by the same hatred which also and first of all pursued Jesus Christ. Its Messiah shaped Israel to His own likeness in suffering and humiliation before shaping it, one day, to His likeness in glory. Such are the bloody implications of that fullness of Israel of which Christians, if they think in their hearts, can detect the precursory signs in the sequence of abominable events remembrance of which will ever be burning and yet which are already being pushed into the dungeons of indifference in the hearts of those who survive. Like ill-assorted fellow-travelers, Jews and Christians have together journeyed along the road to Calvary. The great mysterious fact is that the sufferings of Israel have more and more distinctly taken on the shape of the cross.

But could they have any knowledge of this, all these innocent people struck down like pariahs? Blessed are they that suffer persecution . . . these words were not for them, were not yet for them, at least on this earth. They knew not that they suffered persecution for the sake of the Just Man sprung from Jesse's tree and from a daughter of Israel full of grace; they knew not of what "receiving," of what reintegration—wherein the kingdom of heaven would be within reach of their people—the persecution they suffered was the hidden tidings.

At least they did know that they were dying because of their people's vocation and because their people's passion for justice on earth is hated by the world. At least those of them who cherished in their hearts the spirit of prayer and the religion of the Scriptures must have known that they were dying for the hope which is Israel's.

The Christian, however, thinks of other abandoned beings whose lot awakens in the soul an unbearable anguish because of the unrelieved darkness of the night in which death struck them. I do not refer to those who throughout Europe languished in prisons and concentration camps, were shot down as hostages, perished under torture, because they had resolved not to bend their heads to the conqueror; such men and women knew why they were suffering and why they were dying. They chose to fight and to resist, they gave their lives for freedom, for their countries, for human dignity. I am thinking rather of those poorer beings who had done nothing except their humble daily tasks, and upon whom in a flash death pounced like some wild beast. Sacrificed by the whims of war and of savagery, persecuted not for the sake of justice about which they were not even thinking, but for the sake of the innocent fact of their mere existence at an unlucky point in time and space. What are their sufferings and their death except the likeness and brief summary wherein we may see the sufferings of millions of poor wretches throughout the course of the centuries, shattered without defense by that great mechanism of pride and greed which is as old as humanity? The conquered who have been reduced to slavery, the untouchables, the classless, the slaves of all ages, the black men sold at auction by merchants of human flesh, women and children laboring in sweatshops, the workers of the industrial age, all those whom abject misery has stripped of their human condition, all the people damned by the worldly community.

Certain events which took place during the course of the war just ended serve as terrible illustrations of what I am attempting to say. Let us remember the slaughtered people of the village of Lidice, the women and children machine-gunned and burned alive at Oradour on Corpus Christi, those peasants of the Vercors whom the SS, seeking vengeance for the fighting achievements of the underground, suddenly seized in their peaceful homes and hung head downward, encouraging dogs to tear at their faces. Let us remember others who, by every artifice were induced to die in despair, for instance by hanging them just a little above the level of the ground so that they would jump continuously until their strength failed them and the hangman's rope strangled mere shreds and tatters of a human being. Let us remember those Jews overwhelmed with weariness, who after weeks of bloody journeying, would upon arrival at Buchenwald of their own accord lay themselves upon the shelves in the crematorium; let us remember the miserable wretches who were starved to death in sealed railway carriages. Where lay the consolation of these persecuted innocents? And how many others died completely abandoned and alone. They did not give their lives, their lives were taken from them, and under the shadow of horror. They suffered without having wanted to suffer. They did not know why they died. Those who know why they die are greatly privileged.

It all seems to take place as though the passion and death of Jesus were something divinely vast, that it must be shared by men in its various and contrasting aspects in order that some picture of that passion might be available to its members and in order that men might completely participate in this great treasure of love and of blood. The saints of their own wills enter into Christ's passion, by offering themselves along with Him, by knowing the secrets of the divine life, by living in their souls their union with Him, by putting into action, in the depths of their being, the gifts they have received. In any torture of the body or of the spirit, in the abysses of utter abandonment, they are still privileged people. That beatitude addressed to the persecuted illumines their earthly existence. The more they are abandoned, the more can they say with John of the Cross: "Mine are the heavens and mine is the earth, mine are men, the just are mine and mine are the sinners; the angels are mine and the Mother of God and all things are mine; and God Himself is mine and exists for me. What then, O my soul, dost thou ask and dost thou seek? All this is thine and everything exists for thee. . . ."

But those wholly and completely forsaken, the victims of the night, those who die as though they were the outcasts of earthly existence, those who are hurled into Christ's death agony without knowing it and against their wills—all these are making manifest another aspect of that same agony, and surely all aspects must be made manifest. Jesus gave His life because He willed it. But He likewise "hath made sin for us"; He was "made a curse for us, for it is written: cursed is everyone that hangeth on a tree"; He was abandoned by God on His cross of misery, without protection against suffering, without help against those who persecuted Him.[2] As though a legacy left to His saints, He said *into thy hands I commend My spirit.* And as though a legacy left to another flock, He said: *My God, My God, why hast Thou forsaken Me?* The great flock of the truly destitute, of those dead without consolation—would He not take care of those who bear this mark of His agony? How could it happen that their very abandonment itself would not serve as the signature of their belonging to the crucified Savior and having a supreme title to His mercy? In the throes of death, in the moment when they pass to the other side of the veil and the soul is on the point of leaving a flesh for which the world had no use, is there not yet time enough to say to them: Thou shalt be with *Me* in paradise? For them there are no signs, for them hope is stripped as bare as they are themselves; for them, to the bitter end, nothing, even from the direction of God, has shone forth in men's eyes. It is in the invisible world, beyond everything earthly, that the kingdom of God is given to these persecuted ones, and that everything becomes theirs.

NOTES

1. Cf. Chapters IX, X and especially XI of Saint Paul's Epistle to the Romans.
2. *Summa Theologica* III, 47, 3.

PART SIX
THE CREATIVITY OF THE SPIRIT

"As the mystic suffers divine things, the poet is here to suffer the things of this world, and to suffer them so much that he is enabled to speak them and himself out. And when he is most engaged in the act of spiritual communication, it is because then he still suffers attentively an inexorable hand stronger than he, that passes and does not return. The degree of creative strength of poetic intuition is proportional to the degree of depth of such attentive passivity."

Creative Intuition and Poetic Knowledge

20. CREATIVE INTUITION AND POETIC KNOWLEDGE

Because poetry is born in this root life where the powers of the soul are active in common, poetry implies an essential requirement of totality or integrity. Poetry is the fruit neither of the intellect alone, nor of imagination alone. Nay more, it proceeds from the totality of man, sense, imagination, intellect, love, desire, instinct, blood and spirit together. And the first obligation imposed on the poet is to consent to be brought back to the hidden place, near the center of the soul, where this totality exists in the state of a creative source.[1]

Poetic Intuition

Thus, when it comes to poetry, we must admit that in the spiritual unconscious of the intellect, at the single root of the soul's powers, there is, apart from the process which tends to knowledge by means of concepts and abstract ideas, something which preconceptual or non-conceptual and nevertheless in a state of definite intellectual actuation: not, therefore, a mere way to the concept, as was the "impressed pattern" I have spoken of, but another kind of germ, which does not tend toward a concept to be formed, and which is already an intellective form or act fully determined though enveloped in the night of the spiritual unconscious. In other words, such a thing is knowledge in act, but nonconceptual knowledge.

The problem, then, that I should like to discuss now deals with that kind of knowledge which is involved in poetic activity.

Clearly, what we are considering at this point is not the previous (theoretical) knowledge, in any field whatever of human experience and culture, that is *presupposed* by art and poetry, and which provides them with external materials to be integrated in, and transformed by, the fire of creative virtues.

What we are considering is the kind of inherent knowledge that is immanent in and *consubstantial* with poetry, one with its very essence.

Here our first signpost is, I think—the notion of the free creativity of the spirit. In the craftsman the creativity of the spirit is, as it were, bound or tied up to a particular aim, which is the satisfying of a particular need. In the poet it is free creativity, for it only tends to engender in beauty, which is a transcendental, and involves an infinity of possible realizations and possible choices. In this respect the poet is like a god. And in order to discover the first essentials of poetry there is nothing better for us to do than to look to the First Poet.

God's creative Idea, from the very fact that it is creative, does not receive anything from things, since they do not yet exist. It is in no way *formed* by its creatable object, it is only and purely *formative* and *forming*. And that which will be expressed or manifested in the things made is nothing else than their Creator Himself, whose transcendent Essence is enigmatically signified in a diffused, dispersed, or parceled-out manner, by works which are deficient likenesses of and created participations in it. And God's Intellect is determined or specified by nothing else than His own essence. It is by knowing Himself, in an act of intellection which is His very Essence and His very Existence, that He knows His works, which exist in time and have begun in time, but which He eternally is in the free act of creating.

Such is the supreme analogate of poetry. Poetry is engaged in the free creativity of the spirit. And thus it implies an intellective act which is not formed by things but is, by its own essence, formative and forming. Well, it is too clear that the poet is a poor god. He does not know himself. And his creative insight miserably depends on the external world, and on the infinite heap of forms and beauties already made by men, and on the mass of things that generations have learned, and on the code of signs which is used by his fellow men and which he receives from a language he has not made. Yet, for all that he is condemned both to subdue to his own purpose all these extraneous elements and to manifest his own substance in his creation.

At this point we see how essential to poetry is the subjectivity of the poet. I do not mean the inexhaustible flux of superficial feelings in which the sentimental reader recognizes his own cheap longings, and with which the songs to the Darling and Faithless One of generations of poets have desperately fed us. I mean subjectivity in its deepest ontologic sense, that is, the substantial totality of the human person, a universe unto itself, which the spirituality of the soul makes capable of containing itself through its own immanent acts, and which, at the center of all the subjects that it knows as objects, grasps only itself as subject. In a way similar to that in which divine creation presupposes the knowledge God has of His own essence, poetic creation presupposes, as a primary requirement, a grasping, by the poet, of his own subjectivity, in order to create. The poet's aim is not to know himself. He is not a guru. To attain, through the void, an intuitive experience of the existence of the Self, of the Atman, in its pure and full actuality, is the specific aim of natural mysticism. It is not the aim of poetry. The essential need of the poet is to create; but he cannot do so without passing through the door of the knowing, as obscure as it may be, of his own subjectivity. For poetry means first of all an intellective act which by its essence is creative, and forms something into being instead of being formed by things: and what can such an intellective act possibly express and manifest in producing the work if not the very being and substance of the one who creates? Thus it is that works of painting or sculpture or music or poetry the closer they come to the sources of poetry the more they reveal, one way or another, the subjectivity of their author.

But the substance of man is obscure to himself. He knows not his soul, except in the fluid multiplicity of passing phenomena which emerge from it and are more or less clearly attained by reflective consciousness, but only increase the enigma, and leave him more ignorant of the essence of his Self. He knows not his own subjectivity. Or, if he knows it, it is formlessly, by feeling it as a kind of propitious and enveloping night. Melville, I think, was aware of that when he observed that "no man can ever feel his own identity aright except his eyes be closed; as if darkness were indeed the proper element of our essences."[2] Subjectivity *as subjectivity* is unconceptualizable; is an unknowable abyss. How, then, can it be revealed to the poet?

The poet does not know himself in the light of his own essence. Since man perceives himself only through a repercussion of his knowledge of the world of things, and remains empty to himself if he does not fill himself with the universe, the poet knows himself only on the condition that things resound in him, and that in him, at a single wakening, they and he come forth together out of sleep.[3] In other words, the primary requirement of poetry, which is the obscure knowing, by the poet, of his own subjectivity, is inseparable from, is one with another requirement—the grasping, by the poet, of the objective reality of the outer and inner world: not by means of concepts and conceptual knowledge, but by means of an obscure knowledge which I shall describe in a moment as knowledge through affective union.

Hence the perplexities of the poet's condition. If he hears the passwords and the secrets that are stammering in things, if he perceives realities, correspondences, ciphered writings that are at the core of actual existence, if he captures those more things which are in heaven and earth than are dreamt of in our philosophy, he does not do so by knowing all this in the ordinary sense of the word to know, but by receiving all this into the obscure recesses of his passion.[4] All that he discerns and divines in things, he discerns and divines not as something *other* than himself, according to the law of speculative knowledge, but, on the contrary, as inseparable from himself and from his emotion, and in truth as identified with himself.

His intuition, the creative intuition, is an obscure grasping of his own Self and of things in a knowledge through union or through connaturality which is born in the spiritual unconscious, and which fructifies only in the work. So the germ of which I spoke some pages back, and which is contained in the spiritual night of the free life of the intellect, tends from the very start to a kind of revelation—not to the revelation of the *Übermensch* or of the omnipotency of man, as the Surrealists believe, but to the humble revelation, virtually contained in a small lucid cloud of inescapable intuition, both of the Self of the poet and of some particular flash of reality in the God-made universe; a particular flash of reality bursting forth in its unforgettable individuality, but infinite in its meanings and echoing capacity—

> To see a World in a Grain of Sand,
> And a Heaven in a Wild Flower. . . .

Nature of poetic knowledge

I used a moment ago the expression "knowledge through connaturality." It refers to a basic distinction made by Thomas Aquinas,[5] when he explains that there are two different ways to judge of things pertaining to a moral virtue, say fortitude. On the one hand we can possess in our mind moral science, the conceptual and rational knowledge of virtues, which produces in us a merely intellectual conformity with the truths involved. Then, if we are asked a question about fortitude, we will give the right answer by merely looking at and consulting the intelligible objects contained in our concepts. A moral philosopher may possibly not be a virtuous man and know everything about virtues.

On the other hand, we can possess the virtue in question in our own powers of will and desire, have it embodied in ourselves, and thus be in accordance with it or connatured with it in our very being. Then, if we are asked a question about fortitude, we will give the right answer, no longer through science, but through inclination, by looking at and consulting what we are and the inner bents or propensities of our own being. A virtuous man may possibly be utterly ignorant in moral philosophy, and know as well (probably better) everything about virtues—through connaturality.

In this knowledge through union or inclination, connaturality or congeniality, the intellect is at play not alone, but together with affective inclinations and the dispositions of the will, and as guided and shaped by them. It is not rational knowledge, knowledge through the conceptual, logical, and discursive exercise of reason. But it is really and genuinely knowledge, though obscure and perhaps incapable of giving account of itself.

St. Thomas explains in this way the difference between the knowledge of divine reality acquired by theology and the knowledge of divine reality provided by mystical experience. For the spiritual man, he says,[6] knows divine things through inclination or connaturality: not only because he has learned them, but because he suffers them, as the Pseudo-Dionysius put it.

Knowledge through connaturality plays an immense part in human life. Modern philosophers have thrown it into oblivion, but the ancient Doctors paid careful attention to it and established upon it all their theory of God-given contemplation. I think that we have to restore it, and to recognize its basic role and importance in such domains as moral practical knowledge and natural or supernatural mystical experience —and in the domain of art and poetry. Poetic knowledge, as I see it, is a specific kind of knowledge through inclination or connaturality—let us say a knowledge through affective connaturality which essentially relates to the creativity of the spirit and tends to express itself in a work. So that in such a knowledge it is the object created, the poem, the painting, the symphony, in its own existence as a world of its own, which plays the part played in ordinary knowledge by the concepts and judgments produced within the mind.

Hence it follows that poetic knowledge is fully expressed only in the work. In the mind of the poet, poetic knowledge arises in an unconscious or preconscious manner, and emerges into consciousness in a sometimes almost imperceptible though imperative and irrefragable way, through an impact both emotional and intellectual or through an unpredictable experiential insight, which gives notice of its existence, but does not express it.

This particular kind of knowledge through connaturality comes about, I think, by means of emotion. That is why, at first glance, one believes, and often the poet himself believes, that he is like the Ahab of *Moby Dick*: "Here's food for thought, had Ahab time to think; but Ahab never thinks; he only feels, feels, feels; *that's* tingling enough for mortal man! to think's audacity. God only has that right and privilege."[7] Well, in this people are mistaken. The poet also thinks. And poetic knowledge proceeds from the intellect in its most genuine and essential capacity as intellect, though through the indispensable instrumentality of feeling, feeling, feeling. At this point I would wish to insist that it is in no way a merely emotional or a sentimentalist theory of poetry that I am suggesting. First, I am speaking of a certain kind of knowledge, and emotion does not know: the intellect knows, in this kind of knowledge as in any other. Second, the emotion of which I am speaking is in no way that "brute or merely subjective emotion" to which I alluded in another chapter, and which is extraneous to art.[8] It is not an emotion expressed or *depicted* by the poet, an emotion as *thing* which serves as a kind of matter or material in the making of the work, nor is it a thrill in the poet which the poem will "send down the spine" of the reader. It is an emotion as *form*, which, being one with the creative intuition, gives form to the poem, and which is *intentional*, as an idea is, or carries within itself infinitely more than itself. (I use the word "intentional" in the Thomistic sense,[9] reintroduced by Brentano and Husserl into modern philosophy, which refers to the purely tendential existence through which a thing—for instance, the object known—is present, in an immaterial or suprasubjective manner, in an "instrument"—an idea for instance, which, in so far as it determines the act of knowing, is a mere immaterial tendency or *intentio* toward the object.)

How can emotion be thus raised to the level of the intellect and, as it were, take the place of the concept in becoming for the intellect a determining means or instrumental vehicle through which reality is grasped?

That's a difficult question, as are all similar questions dealing with the application of the general concept of knowledge through connaturality to the various particular fields in which this kind of knowledge is at play. I think that in all these cases, where the soul "suffers things more than it learns them," and experiences them through resonance in subjectivity, we have to find out a certain specific way in which the great notion developed by John of St. Thomas apropos of mystical knowledge—*amor transit in conditionem objecti*, love passes on to the sphere of the intentional means of objective grasping—has to be used analogically. Here I would say that in poetic knowledge emotion carries the reality which the soul suffers—a world in a grain of sand—into the depth of subjectivity, and of the spiritual unconscious of the intellect, because in the poet, contrary to other men (especially those involved in the business of civilized life), the soul remains, as it were, more available to itself, and keeps a reserve of spirituality which is not absorbed by its activity toward the outside and by the toil of its powers. And this deep unemployed reserve of the spirit, being unemployed, is like a sleep of the soul; but, being spiritual, is in a state of virtual vigilance and vital tension, owing to the virtual reversion of the spirit on itself and on everything in itself. The soul sleeps, but her heart is awake; allow her to sleep . . .

Well, let us suppose that in the density of such a secretly alert sleep and such a spiritual tension, emotion intervenes (whatever this emotion may be; what matters is where it is received). On the one hand it spreads into the entire soul, it imbues its very being, and thus certain particular aspects in things become connatural to the soul affected in this way. On the other hand, emotion, falling into the living springs, is received in the vitality of intelligence, I mean intelligence permeated by the diffuse light of the Illuminating Intellect and virtually turned toward all the harvests of experience and memory preserved in the soul, all the universe of fluid images, recollections, associations, feelings, and desires latent, under pressure, in the subjectivity, and now stirred. And it suffices for emotion disposing or inclining, as I have said, the entire soul in a certain determinate manner to be thus received in the undetermined vitality and productivity of the spirit, where it is permeated by the light of the Illuminating Intellect: then, while remaining emotion, it is made—with respect to the aspects in things which are connatural to, or *like*, the soul it imbues—into an instrument of intelligence judging through connaturality, and plays, in the process of this knowledge through *likeness* between reality and subjectivity, the part of a nonconceptual intrinsic determination of intelligence in its preconscious activity. By this very fact it is transferred into the state of objective intentionality; it is spiritualized, it becomes intentional, that is to say, conveying, in a state of immateriality, things other than itself.[10] It becomes for the intellect a determining means or instrumental vehicle through which the things which have impressed this emotion on the soul, and the deeper, invisible things that are contained in them or connected with them, and which have ineffable correspondence or coaptation with the soul thus affected, and which resound in it, are grasped and known obscurely.

It is by means of such a spiritualized emotion that poetic intuition, which in itself is an intellective flash, is born in the unconscious of the spirit. In one sense it is, as I said a moment ago, a privilege of those souls in which the margin of dreaming activity and introverted natural spirituality, unemployed for the business of human life, is particularly large. In another sense, because it emanates from a most natural capacity of the human mind, we must say that every human being is potentially capable of it: among those who do not know it, many, in point of fact, have repressed it or murdered it within themselves. Hence their instinctive resentment against the poet.

Of itself poetic intuition proceeds from the natural and supremely spontaneous movement of the soul which seeks itself by communicating with things in its capacity as a spirit endowed with senses and passions. And sometimes it is in mature age, when the spirit has been fed with experience and suffering and turns back toward itself, that it best experiences the sapid sleep in which poetic intuition awakes—and which also exists, in another fashion, and with the acrid taste of greenness, in the child and the primitive. Poetic knowledge is as natural to the spirit of man as the return of the bird to his nest; and it is the universe which, together with the spirit, makes its way back to the mysterious nest of the soul. For the content of poetic intuition is both the reality of the things of the world and the subjectivity of the poet, both obscurely conveyed through an intentional or spiritualized emotion. The soul is known in the experience of the world and the world is known in the experience of the soul, through a knowledge which does not know itself. For such knowledge knows, not in order to know, but in order to produce. It is toward creation that it tends.

"*Je est un autre*," Rimbaud said: "I is another." In poetic intuition objective reality and subjectivity, the world and the whole of the soul, coexist inseparably. At that moment sense and sensation are brought back to the heart, blood to the spirit, passion to intuition. And through the vital though non-conceptual actuation of the intellect all the powers of the soul are also actuated in their roots.[11] . . .

Poetic intuition as cognitive

I should like to add a few remarks in an effort to bring out the main aspects or implications involved in the notion of poetic intuition.

It seems to me that the first distinction to be made in this regard deals with the fact that poetic intuition, which is both creative and cognitive, can be considered especially either as creative, and therefore, with respect to the engendering of the work, or as cognitive, and therefore with respect to *what is grasped* by it.

Let us, then, consider first poetic intuition as cognitive. It is cognitive, as we have seen, both of the reality of things and of the subjectivity of the poet. Now is it possible to try to make more precise that "reality of things" of which I just spoke? In other words, what is the *object* of poetic intuition? But the word "object" is equivocal here, for things are objectivized in a concept, and there is no concept, therefore no objectivization, in poetic intuition. Let us say, then, what is the *thing grasped* by poetic intuition?

Our previous consideration of poetic knowledge already contained the answer: poetic intuition is not directed toward essences, for essences are disengaged from concrete reality in a concept, a universal idea, and scrutinized by means of reasoning; they are an object for speculative knowledge, they are not the thing grasped by poetic intuition. Poetic intuition is directed toward concrete existence as connatural to the soul pierced by a given emotion: that is to say, each time toward some singular existent, toward some complex of concrete and individual reality, seized in the violence of its sudden self-assertion and in the total unicity of its passage in time. This transient motion of a beloved hand—it exists an instant, and will disappear forever, and only in the memory of angels will it be preserved, above time. Poetic intuition catches it in passing, in a faint attempt to immortalize it in time. But poetic intuition does not stop at this given existent; it goes beyond, and infinitely beyond. Precisely because it has no conceptualized object, it tends and extends to the infinite, it tends toward all the reality, the infinite reality which is engaged in any singular existing thing, either the secret properties of being involved in its identity and in its existential relations with other things, or the other realities, all the other aspects or fructifications of being, scattered in the entire world, which have in themselves the wherewithal to found some ideal relation with this singular existing thing, and which it conveys to the mind, by the very fact that it is grasped through its union with, and resonance in, subjectivity spiritually awakened.

Such is, I think, the thing grasped by poetic intuition: the singular existent which resounds in the subjectivity of the poet, together with all the other realities which echo in this existent, and which it conveys in the manner of a sign.

So it is true that poetry, as Aristotle said, is more philosophical than history.[12] Not, surely, with respect to its mode or manner of knowing, for this mode is altogether existential, and the thing grasped is grasped as non-conceptualizable. But with respect to the very thing grasped, which is not a contingent thing in the mere fact of its existence, but in its infinite openness to the riches of being, and as a sign of it. For poetic intuition makes things which it grasps diaphanous and alive, and populated with infinite horizons. As grasped by poetic knowledge, things abound in significance, and swarm with meanings.

Things are not only what they are. They ceaselessly pass beyond themselves, and give more than they have, because from all sides they are permeated by the activating influx of the Prime Cause. They are better and worse than themselves, because being superabounds, and because nothingness attracts what comes from nothingness. Thus it is that they communicate with each other in an infinity of fashions and through an infinity of actions and contacts, sympathies and ruptures. I would think that this mutual communication in existence and in the spiritual flux from which existence proceeds, which is in things, as it were, the secret of creative sources, is perhaps in the last analysis what the poet receives and suffers, and grasps in the night of his own Self, or knows as unknown.[13]

Coming now to the other cognitive function of poetic intuition, I mean poetic intuition as obscurely revealing the subjectivity of the poet, I need not dwell long on this subject. It is clear that poetic intuition is filled with the subjectivity of the poet as well as with the thing grasped, since the thing grasped and the subjectivity are known together in the same obscure experience, and since the thing grasped is grasped only through its affective resonance in and union with the subjectivity. Nay more, as we have seen, it is in order to express the subjectivity of the poet in the work which proceeds from the creativity of the spirit that the grasping of things comes about, together with the awakening of subjectivity to itself. As a result, we may say, it seems to me, that in the attainments of poetic intuition what is *most immediate* is the experience of the things of the world, because it is natural to the human soul to know things before knowing itself; but what is *most principal* is the experience of the Self—because it is in the awakening of subjectivity to itself that emotion received in the translucid night of the free life of the intellect is made intentional and intuitive, or the determining means of a knowledge through congeniality.

As concerns finally the work, it also will be, in indissoluble unity—as the poetic intuition from which it proceeds—both a revelation of the subjectivity of the poet and of the reality that poetic knowledge has caused him to perceive.

Be it a painting or a poem, this work is a made object—in it alone does poetic intuition come to objectivization. And it must always preserve its own consistence and value as an *object*. But at the same time it is a sign—both a *direct sign* of the secrets perceived in things, of some irrecusable truth of nature or adventure caught in the great universe, and a *reversed sign* of the subjective universe of the poet, of his substantial Self obscurely revealed. Just as things grasped by poetic intuition abound in significance, just as being swarms with signs, so the work also will swarm with meanings, and will say more than it is, and will deliver to the mind, at one stroke, the universe in a human countenance.

Il fallait bien qu'un visage
Réponde à tous les noms du monde.[14]

The work will make present to our eyes, together with itself, something else, and still something else, and still something else indefinitely, in the infinite mirrors of analogy. Through a kind of poetic ampliation, Beatrice, while remaining the woman whom Dante loved, is also, through the power of the sign, the light which illuminates him. Sophie von Kühn, while remaining the dead fiancée of Novalis, is also the call of God that seduces him.

Thus it is that poetry captures the secret senses of things, and the all-embracing sense, still more secret, of subjectivity obscurely revealed: in order to throw both into a matter to be formed. And both, the senses perceived in things and the deeper and more vital, unifying sense of the avowal of creative subjectivity, compose together one single complete and complex sense, through which the work *exists*, and which we have called the poetic sense of the work.

Are there some particular observations to be made regarding poetic intuition in the painter, as contradistinguished to poetic intuition in the poet? I would say that in both of them poetic intuition has the same fundamental characteristics, but with further differences which seem to me to have essential significance. The reason for this is the fact that the reality with which the poet is confronted is the very object of intelligence, that is, the ocean of Being, in its absolute universality; whereas the reality with which the painter is confronted is the universe of visible matter, of Corporeal Being, through which alone the ocean of Being in its infinity comes to show through for him. The world of the painter is the world of the eye before being and while being the world of the intellect.

As a result, in order to describe the painter's poetic intuition, we must first remember that he is a captive of Nature, he is bound to her, he cannot escape her—"one cannot go against nature," as Picasso himself put it: and all painters feel the same way. But, as I pointed out in previous remarks[15] (that I should like to resume in giving them now full philosophical bearing), the painter does not look at nature as at a separate thing-in-itself, to be copied or imitated in its external appearances. He looks at nature as at a creative mystery which he tries to imitate in its secret workings and inner ways of operation, and which, by means of poetic intuition, comes through his eyes to the recesses of his own creative subjectivity as a germ or a key[16] of that object which is the work to be produced into existence. What the intellect of the painter grasps in the dark of Things and his own Self together, is an aspect of the infinite depths of Visible Corporeal Being in so far as constructible or feasible in colors and lines, an aspect or element of the mystery of the universe of visible matter or corporeal existence in so far as this aspect or element is meant to fructify into a work—which itself is an object for the eye before being and while being an object for the intellect.[17]

But this very process cannot come about without going at the same time beyond the universe of visible corporeal existence and attaining enigmatically the infinity of the universe of Being and existence. Since in poetic intuition subjectivity is the very vehicle to penetrate into the objective world, what is looked for by the painter in visible things must possess the same kind of inner depth and inexhaustible reserves for possible revelation as his own Self. While grasping some aspect of visible corporeal existence as a reality, he grasps it also as a sign, through which we are brought to him, in a kind of indeterminable fluidity, the same secret meanings, correspondences, echoes, and intercommunications which the poet obscurely catches in the universe of Being and the human universe. Yet the painter catches them still more obscurely, and only in the manner of resonances or overtones. The painter's poetic intuition conveys to him—as a "seminal principle" or key to operation—some of the inexhaustible inside aspects of visible matter, and, by the same stroke, some of the more inexhaustible meanings which make the invisible universe of Being show through—and all this is caught by way of knowledge through connaturality, according to any direction whatever in which an act of spiritual communication with the things of the world can be brought about, and all this can be expressed only by recasting these things into a new visible fabric.

Thus it is that genuine painting, while remaining strictly painting, attains—especially after the "liberation" accomplished in modern times—to a kind of metaphysical vastness and a degree of intellectuality which resemble those peculiar to poetry. It does so through its obscure grasping, by means of creative intuition, both of the workable secrets of the world of visible matter and the implied or suggested inner realities of the world of Being.

Modern painting longs, like modern poetry, for a superior degree of intellectuality, and is intent on the impact of Things on intuitive reason—to the very extent to which it is true to poetic knowledge. But at the same time modern painting (like modern poetry) is tempted to go in the opposite direction, and runs the risk of dispersing in mere sensationalism or in a merely taste-guided and superficial release of imagination, to the very extent to which it mistakes the nonlogical character of poetic knowledge, or the liberation from conceptual reason, for a total break with and liberation from reason itself and the intellect itself, thus losing any spiritual or emotional gravity, and neglecting those "mysterious centers of thought" of which Gauguin spoke. This ambivalence of modern painting seems to me singularly striking, and singularly instructive for the philosopher.

I should like to observe, in addition, that it is not surprising —precisely because of the particular conditions I just tried to point out—that the utterances of painters about the peculiar poetic intuition of their own are poorer than those of the poets. They confess themselves in their canvas, not in their words. And they use as a rule, in point of introspection, a humble vocabulary, in which they choose quite modest (sometimes all the more moving) words that convey in reality a deeper meaning for which they have no expression. They speak in this way of their "little sensation,"[18] as Cézanne put it, of their "Impressions,"[19] their "feelings,"[20] their "interior promptings,"[21] their "vision"[22]—this word "vision" is probably for them a very close equivalent of what in a philosophical perspective we call poetic intuition.

Yet some more significant evidences are not lacking, not to speak of the great testimony of Chinese painters. It is in the full force of the sense with which they are laden that we must understand the words of a painter or a sculptor when he tells us that for him "everything he sees has an inexhaustible fullness and value,"[23] that he has put "as far as possible . . . the logic of the visible at the service of the invisible,"[24] or that "the artist . . . sees; that is to say, his eye, grafted on his heart, reads deeply into the bosom of nature";[25] or that to express the "big forms" in which all the richness of nature is concealed "you have to love these, to be a part of these in sympathy";[26] or the words of van Gogh, when he writes: "Instead of trying to reproduce exactly what I have before my eyes, I use color more arbitrarily so as to express myself forcibly,"[27] "I want to paint men and women with that something of the eternal which the halo used to symbolize, and which we seek to give by the actual radiance and vibration of our colorings";[28] and the words of Poussin when he says that "painting is nothing but an image of incorporeal things despite the fact that it exhibits bodies," and that there are, in the components of the work, "parts" which "are of the painter himself and cannot be learned. That is the golden bough of Vergil, which no one can find nor gather if he is not led by destiny."[29]

On the other hand, if the observations I have submitted are true, we may realize that friendship and community of effort and theories between painters and poets, as developed especially since the time of German Romanticism and of Baudelaire and Delacroix, are of course a blessing, but that they can also be detrimental to both sides. The groups in which they exchange ideas, claims, mutual admiration, and mutual jealousy, serve to stimulate and enlarge the creative instinct in an invaluable manner.[30] But they also may result in having either painters or poets disregard what is most specific in their own particular approach to the work. Poets instructed by painters may see in the poem a mere construction of images. Painters instructed by poets may try to get clear of that concentration on the world of visible corporeal existence which a Cézanne went in for with such heroic tenacity,[31] and thus forget the primary requirement of painting's peculiar poetic intuition. Then, in quest of a direct attainment of the world of Being in its absolute universality, they will endeavor to go out of painting—only to slip into some kind or other of expressionist literature; or else, disappointed and discouraged, they will fall back on any new sort of academicism, covered by a pretense of freedom and a display of ideological tenets.

Poetic intuition as creative

My last remarks will deal with the second of the two aspects that can be distinguished in poetic intuition, namely, poetic intuition as creative.

From the very start poetic intuition is turned toward operation. As soon as it exists, the instant it awakens the substance of the poet to itself and to an echoing secret of the reality, it is, in the depth of the nonconceptual life of the intellect, an incitation to create. This incitation can remain virtual. The poet, because poetic intuition is his ordinary frame of mind, is constantly open to such hidden incitations,

> Tu lis les prospectus, les catalogues, les affiches
>   qui chantent tout haut,
> Voilà la poésie ce matin . . .[32]

and not all of them can pass to the act. Nay more, a poetic intuition can be kept in the soul a long time, latent (though never forgotten), till some day it will come out of sleep, and compel to creation. But at that moment there is no need of any additional element, it is only a question of application to actual exercise. Everything was already there, contained in poetic intuition, everything was given, all the vitality, all the insight, all the strength of creativity which is now in act, like a dart empowered with a power of intellectual direction; and in a certain sense (intensively—whatever part adventitious chance may have in the development) the totality of the work to be engendered was already present in advance, whether this totality is now virtually given in the first line of a poem, as a gift from the preconscious life of the soul, or virtually concentrated in the spiritual germ of a novel or a drama.

With respect to the work made, it might be said, it seems to me, that that element in beauty which is *integrity* has principally to do with poetic intuition as objectivizing itself into the action or the theme, whereas that element which is *radiance* has principally to do with poetic intuition in its native and original state. Hence it is that poetic intuition may happen to appear with striking radiance even in a poem lacking in integrity; and such splintered fragments, transparent to the rays of being, may be enough to reveal the pure essence of poetry. For nothing is more precious than a capture on the high seas of poetry, be it offered in a single line—

L'espoir luit comme un brin de paille dans l'étable . . .[33]

O Thou steeled Cognizance whose leap commits
The agile precincts of the lark's return . . .[34]

Odour of blood when Christ was slain
Made all Platonic tolerance vain.[35]

And I shall always prefer a haikai, if it has this kind of transparency, to a big noisy machine deafening me with ideas. Yet the fact remains that from the very start poetic intuition virtually contains and encompasses the poem as a whole, and demands to pass through it as a whole; when it does not succeed in appearing save in a fragmentary way, it is because it has been betrayed by the art of the poet.

Now a further issue must be examined. If we turn to the useful arts we observe that poetic knowledge or intuitive emotion is not in them the spiritual germ of the work to be made. Poetic intuition can play a part in them—then a concern for beauty will creep into them; but poetic intuition is not the determinative focus of their creativity. This determinative focus is what the Schoolmen called the *idea factiva*, say the "creative idea." They took care, moreover, to warn us that the craftsman's creative *idea* is in no way a *concept*, for it is neither cognitive nor representative, it is only generative; it does not tend to make our mind conformed to things, but to make a thing conformed to our mind. They never even used the word "idea" in the sense of "concept," as we have done since the time of Descartes. And so, if we may continue to speak of the craftsman's creative idea, it is on the condition that we be aware of the fact that this word idea is merely analogous when applied to that creative idea and to what we usually call ideas. The craftsman's creative idea is an intellectual form, or a spiritual matrix, containing implicitly, in its complex unity, the thing which, perhaps for the first time, will be brought into actual existence. And this creative idea pertains to the virtue of art, is involved in the virtue of art, is the initial determinative focus in the exercise of this virtue.

Well, by a most unfortunate occurrence, it happened that this same expression, creative idea, was transferred from the realm of the useful arts to the realm of the fine arts, better to say, of those arts which depend on the Platonic *mousikè*, or on poetry. As a result, the worst confusions came about. Theoreticians of art, mistaking this "idea" for a concept, fancied that the so-called creative idea was an ideal model sitting for the artist in his own brain, the work supposedly being a *copy* or portrait of it. This would make of art a cemetery of imitations. The work is an original, not a copy and never has such a thing as this idea as model existed except in the mind of some aestheticians imbued with spurious Platonism, or some philosophers misreading the theological notion of the divine Ideas.

At the same time the expression "creative idea," which makes sense only as the craftsman's creative idea, was used to designate the poetic intuition itself in its creative aspect, the poetic intuition born in emotion, in the primeval sources of the preconscious life of the intellect. And poor Eckermann was to ask his wonderful Goethe what was the *idea* he had endeavored to embody in Faust. "As if I knew," Goethe answered, "as if I myself could tell! *From Heaven, through Earth, down to Hell*, there's an explanation, if you want one: but that is not the idea, that's the development of the action. . . ."

That was not the idea, for there was no idea, but only poetic intuition, which is in no way an idea. In reality—this is a point I shall emphasize again in the next chapter—poetic intuition transcends the virtue of art. And poetic intuition involves and contains within itself, in a superior state and eminent manner, *formaliter-eminenter*, as a scholastic would say, all that exists—and infinitely more (for it is both cognitive and creative)—in the craftsman's creative idea. It is enough for poetic intuition to pass to actual operative exercise; by the same stroke it will enter the sphere and dynamism of the virtue of art, whose more or less adequate means it will bring into play.[36]

Such is the case, indeed, with every genuine poet. Now not all artists and poets are genuine poets. What I mean is that, at the initial moment of the operative exercise, another process can take place. Then, the poetic intuition becomes a craftsman's creative idea, losing its inherent transcendence and descending, as it were, into the mechanical noise and the merely intellectual concerns for manufacturing with which the craftsman's creative idea is pregnant; and to the extent to which it becomes a craftsman's creative idea, the poetic intuition leaves behind many of its essentials, especially the creative power inherent in the superior unity of the grasping effected by poetic knowledge and intuitive emotion.[37] This phenomenon comes about, it seems to me, when man, in a hurry to display his own energy and to produce something great, or because poetic intuition is weak in him, goes *beyond* poetic intuition, and, instead of listening to it, endeavors to supplement it in his own way—not to speak of those in whom poetic intuition is simply lacking.[38] Thus it is that we meet in bookstores, concerts, and exhibitions so many works which have nothing or little to say; and that in so many dramas there is plot but no action; and that in so many novels the characters are either creatures deprived of freedom which only execute the pre-established plan of a watchmaker god, or creatures wandering on the loose which ceaselessly escape the weak purposes of an impotent god. Only, I think, an exceptionally powerful poetic intuition can cause the relationship between the novelist and his characters to be what it must be—an image, I mean, of the relationship between the transcendent creative eternity of God and the free creatures who are both acting in liberty and firmly embraced by His purpose.

The remarks I just put forward give account, I believe, of a distinction which, like all essential distinctions, can be difficult of application in particular cases, but of which literary and art criticism has always been basically aware: on the one hand, the sons of *Mousikè*, the poets and creators (who can also be perfect craftsmen), and on the other hand the sons of *Technè*, the men of letters, or the professionals (who can also be bad craftsmen).

We may observe, in closing, that the craftsman's creative idea, which is part of the virtue of art, improves from the very fact that this virtue itself improves, both by exercise and by discipline.

On the other hand, poetic intuition can neither be learned nor improved by exercise and discipline, for it depends on a certain natural freedom of the soul and the imaginative faculties and on the natural strength of the intellect. It cannot be improved in itself, it demands only to be listened to. But the poet can make himself better prepared for or available to it by removing obstacles and noise. He can guard and protect it, and thus foster the spontaneous progress of its strength and purity in him. He can educate himself to it, by never betraying it (this is a serious school in discipline) and by making everything second to it (this is a serious school in sacrifice).

As to the operative exercise of poetic intuition, moreover, it can be improved by a certain humility, I don't mean with regard to men, but with regard to this intuition itself—and also by the work of intelligence and of the virtue of art dealing with the ways and means of execution. For poetic intuition, as concerns its operative exercise, perfects itself in the course of the artistic process. I do not mean that at the beginning poetic intuition is something either formless or fragmentary, as Claudel says—too harshly—of the results of inspiration[39] (because he thinks only of what emerges as conceptually seizable into the field of consciousness); I mean that poetic intuition, though full and complete from the very start, involves, at the beginning, a great part of virtuality. It is with the steady labor of intelligence intent on the elaboration of the form that this virtuality contained in poetic intuition actualizes and unfolds itself along the process of production. And then the very exercise of artistic science and intellectual perspicacity, choosing, judging, cutting out all the nonsignificant, the fat, the superfluous, causes—precisely because it is always listening to creative emotion and appealing to it—new partial flashes of poetic intuition to be released at each step of the work. Without this steady labor poetic intuition would not, as a rule, disclose its entire virtue.

But let us return to the intrinsic quality of poetic intuition itself in the poet, and to the question of its higher or lesser degree. What matters most in this connection is inner experience and its deepening into further and further recesses of subjectivity. Since poetic intuition is born in these recesses, where the intellect, the imagination, all the powers of the soul suffer in unity some reality of existence brought to them by intentional emotion, it involves first of all a certain alert receptivity. As the mystic suffers divine things, the poet is here to suffer the things of this world, and to suffer them so much that he is enabled to speak them and himself out. And when he is most engaged in the act of spiritual communication, it is because then he still suffers attentively an inexorable hand stronger than he, that passes and does not return. The degree of creative strength of poetic intuition is proportional to the degree of depth of such attentive passivity. . . .

The creative self and the self-centered ego

All the preceding considerations on poetic knowledge help us to understand the essential disinterestedness of poetic activity. They also oblige us to realize that a crucial distinction must be made between the creative Self and the self-centered ego.

This distinction has something to do with the metaphysical distinction between the human person *as person* and the human person *as individual*. Matter (in the Aristotelian sense of *materia prima*) is the primary root of individuality, and matter both longs for being (as a pure potency which has no determination of itself) and narrows being (which it limits to its own capacity or receptivity under given conditions). In each of us, individuality, being that which excludes from ourselves that which other men are, might be described as the narrowness of the ego, always threatened and always eager to grasp for itself. Personality, on the other hand, is rooted in the spirit inasmuch as the spirit holds itself in existence and superabounds in existence. It is the subsistence of the spiritual soul communicated to the whole fabric of the human being and holding it in unity, and it testifies to the generosity or expansiveness in being which pertains to its spiritual principle. Personality means interiority to oneself and requires at the same time the communications of knowledge and love. By the very fact that each of us is a person and has spiritual inwardness, each of us requires communication with *other* and *the others* in the order of knowledge and love; and the supreme act of the person as such is that giving of oneself which is one with love.[40] The new and eternal name, inscribed on the white stone, which will be given us one day, and "which no one knoweth but he that receiveth it,"[41] reveals our personality. The name by which men know us, and which is inscribed on our passports, is but one of the designations of our individuality. "Thou are thyself though," Juliet said, "not a Montague. . . . Romeo, doff thy name; And for that name, which is no part of thee, Take all myself."[42]

The creative Self of the artist is his person as *person*, in the act of spiritual communication, not his person as material individual or as self-centered ego.

Lionel de Fonseka asserts that "vulgarity always says *I*."[43] Let us add that vulgarity says *one* also, and this is the same thing, for vulgarity's *I* is nothing but the self-centered ego, a neuter subject of predicates and phenomena, a subject as *matter*, marked with the opacity and voracity of matter, like the *I* of the egoist.

But in an entirely different manner poetry likewise always says *I*. "My heart hath uttered a good word," David sang. "Vivify *me* and *I* will keep Thy commandments." Poetry's *I* is the substantial depth of living and loving subjectivity, it is the creative Self, a subject as *act*, marked with the diaphaneity and expansiveness proper to the operations of the spirit. Poetry's *I* resembles in this respect the *I* of the saint, and likewise, although to quite other ends, it is a subject which gives.[44]

Thus, by necessity of nature, poetic activity is, of itself, disinterested. It engages the human Self in its deepest recesses, but in no way for the sake of the ego. The very engagement of the artist's Self in poetic activity, and the very revelation of the artist's Self in his work, together with the revelation of some particular meaning he has obscurely grasped in things, are for the sake of the work. The creative Self is both revealing itself and sacrificing itself, because it is *given*; it is drawn out of itself in that sort of ecstasy which is creation, it dies to itself in order to live in the work (how humbly and defenselessly).

This essential disinterestedness of the poetic act means that egoism is the natural enemy of poetic activity.

The artist as a man can be busy only with his craving for creation. He can say, like Baudelaire: "I don't give a damn for the human race," he can be concerned only with his work, like Proust, he can be an out-and-out egoist, as Goethe was: in his process of creation, inasmuch as he is an artist, he is not an egoist, he is disinterested in his ego.

But the artist as a man can have his craving for creation involved in the movement of expansion and generosity of a soul whose passions and ambitions are not those of an egoist. And such internal abundance and magnanimity is the normal and connatural climate of the virtue of art. Narrowness and avarice in human desires make it live in cold and sleet. After all Shelley was right in writing that the "state of mind" naturally linked with poetic inspiration "is at war with base desire."[45]

It is, I think, an effect of the essential disinterestedness of the poet in the very act of poetry, and an effect of his natural orientation toward creation, that the poets and artists of the past gave us such poor indications of their own inner creative experience. They spoke in the most conventional and shallow rhetoric and the most commonplace stock phrases—*nascuntur poetae*, the Muses, the Caelestial Patroness, the Genius, the Poetic Faculty, the divine spark, later on the goddess Imagination—of this experience, which at least the greatest among them lived in fact, to be sure, but which their conscious intellect did not seek to grasp. They were not interested in reflexive self-awareness. The *reflex age*, the age of *prise de conscience*, which roughly speaking began for mysticism at the time of St. Teresa of Avila and St. John of the Cross, came later for poetry. When it began for it, at the time of Romanticism, it brought to completion the slow process of "revelation of the Self" which had developed in the course of modern centuries.[46]

This revelation of the Self is a blessing inasmuch as it takes place in the genuine line of poetry. It becomes a curse when it shifts from the line of poetry, and of the creative Self in the fire of spiritual communication, to the line of man's material individuality, and of the self-centered ego, busy with self-interest and power. Then the egoism of man enters the sphere of the poetic act, and feeds on this very act. And being there in an unnatural state, it grows boundlessly. The poetic act itself, on the other hand, is insidiously wounded, even in great poets.

The shift in question came about, in fact, simultaneously with the incomparable progress that poetry owes to the definitive revelation of the creative Self. That is one of the usual predicaments of human history. And nevertheless the essential disinterestedness of the poetic act is so ineradicable that the final result of this invasion by the human ego in the universe of art could not possibly be to make the artist into a *creative usurer* (that is a contradiction in terms); it was—I shall return to this point—to make him into a hero, a priest, or a savior, offering himself in sacrifice no longer to his work but both to the world and to his own glory.

NOTES

1. Cf. Raïssa Maritain, "Sense and Non-Sense in Poetry," *The Situation of Poetry* (New York: Philosophical Library, 1955), pp. 1–22.
2. *Moby Dick* (New York: Random House, The Modern Library, 1926), p. 53.
3. Cf. my *Art and Poetry* (New York: Philosophical Library, 1943), p. 89.
4. "This thing which is in me *but* which no efforts of mine can slay!" "Wherefore time and again I stroke my empty bosom in pity for myself: so ignorant am I of what causes the opening and the barring of the door." Lu Chi, Wen Fu, II, (o), 6–7, in *The Art of Letters: Lu Chi's "Wen Fu,"* A.D. 302, trans. and ed. E. R. Hughes (Bollingen Series XXIX; New York: Pantheon Books, 1951), p. 108.

5. *Summa Theol.*, II-II, 45, 2. Cf. my book *The Range of Reason* (New York: Charles Scribner's Sons, 1952), Chap. III.

6. *Summa Theol.*, I, 1, 6, ad 3.

7. *Moby Dick*, p. 554.

8. See *Creative Intuition in Art and Poetry* (New York: Pantheon Books, 1953), pp. 6–8. As I put it in *Art and Scholasticism* (New York: Scribner's, 1930): "I will willingly suffer the domination of the *object* which the artist has conceived and which he puts before my eyes; I will then yield myself unreservedly to the emotion aroused in him and me by one same beauty, one same transcendental in which we communicate. But I refuse to suffer the domination of an art which deliberately contrives means of suggestion to seduce my subconscious. I resist an emotion which the will of a man claims to impose upon me" (p. 66).

See also E. I. Watkin, *A Philosophy of Form* (rev. ed.; London and New York: Sheed & Ward, 1951), Chapter II, Section IV. In his remarkable analysis of aesthetic contemplation, Mr. Watkin rightly points out both the intellectuality and objectivity of artistic intuition, and its essential difference from the emotion or vital pleasure which normally accompanies it. These pages afford us the most correct philosophical approach I have read on the matter—except for the lack of the key notion of intentional emotion, as contradistinguished to ordinary or "vital" emotion.

9. On the notion of intentionality, which is absolutely basic in the theory of knowledge, see my books *Réflexions sur l'intelligence* (Paris: Desclée De Brouwer, 1924), pp. 59–68, and *The Degrees of Knowledge* (New York: Charles Scribner's Sons, 1959, rev. ed.), pp. 114–15.

10. In the case of mystical contemplation, love of charity (which is much more than an emotion) becomes a means of experiential knowledge for the virtue of faith which already tends toward and knows (though not experientally) the reality with which to be united. And a special inspiration of the divine spirit is necessary, because a supernatural object is then to be experienced in a supernatural manner.

In the case of poetic knowledge, on the contrary, no previous virtue of the intellect is already in the act of knowing when emotion brings the enigmatic reality which moves the soul, the world which resounds in it and which it suffers, to the bosom of subjectivity and of the creativity of the spirit. And the entire process needs no inspiration whatever from the outside—no more than the knowledge a mother has of her child through affection or connaturality—because the object as well as the mode of experience are simply natural.

11. Thus it is through the notion and reality of poetic knowledge that the sentence of Novalis quoted in the preceding chapter

(*Creative Intuition in Art and Poetry*, pp. 84–85) takes on philosophical sense, and appears not as a pure élan of lyricism, but as a justifiable statement: "The poet is literally out of his senses—in exchange, all comes about *within him*. He is, to the letter, subject and object at the same time, soul and universe."

Rimbaud's saying "Je est un autre" is found in his letter of May 15, 1871, to Paul Demeny ("Lettre du Voyant"), first published by Paterne Berrichon in *La Nouvelle Revue Française*, October 1912.

12. *Poetics*, Chap. 9, 1451b6.

13. See René Char, *Seuls demeurent* (Paris: Gallimard, 1945), p. 75.

14. Paul Eluard, *L'Amour la Poésie* (Paris: N.R.F., 1929).

15. See *Creative Intuition in Art and Poetry*, pp. 29–30.

16. *Ibid.*, p. 29, note 23.

17. *Ibid.*, p. 49, note 4.

18. Ambroise Vollard, *Paul Cézanne* (Paris: Crès, 1924), p. 102.

19. Edward Hopper; in *Artists on Art* (New York: Pantheon Books, 1945), p. 471.

20. See *Ceative Intuition in Art and Poetry*, p. 119, note 13.

21. Georges Rouault; in *Artists on Art*, p. 415.

22. Albert Pinkham Ryder; *ibid.*, p. 356. Cézanne; *ibid.*, p. 366.

23. Hans von Marées; *ibid.*, p. 388.

24. Odilon Redon; *ibid.*, p. 361.

25. Rodin, *ibid.*, p. 325.

26. John Marin; *ibid.*, p. 468.

27. Van Gogh; *ibid.*, p. 383.

28. *Ibid.*, p. 383.

29. From a letter to M. de Chambray, 1665.

30. See Blaise Cendrars, *Le Lotissement du Ciel* (Paris: Denoël, 1949), p. 226.

31. See *Artists on Art*, p. 363.

32. Apollinaire, "Zone," *Alcools*.

33. Verlaine, in "L'espoir luit," *Sagesse*.

34. Crane, in "Atlantis," *The Bridge*.

35. Yeats, in "Two Songs from a Play," *The Tower*.

36. Let us not be deceived by the language of painters. What they sometimes call the "original idea" is but the sketch itself in which poetic intuition first takes visible form. "The original idea, the sketch, which is so to speak the egg or embryo of the idea, is usually far from being complete. . . ." Delacroix, *Journal*, 1854; in *Artists on Art*, p. 234.

37. *Ibid.*, p. 322.

38. *Ibid.*, p. 230.

39. See *Creative Intuition in Art and Poetry*, pp. 278-79.

40. Cf. my essay, *The Person and the Common Good* (New York: Scribner's, 1947). Chap. III.

41. *Apocalypse* 2:17.

42. *Romeo and Juliet*, II, ii.

43. Lionel de Fonseka, *On the Truth of Decorative Art, a Dialogue between an Oriental and an Occidental.* (French trans., Paris: Chitra, 1930: "La vulgarité dit toujours *je*.")

44. I am afraid that T. S. Eliot, in his essay on "Tradition and the Individual Talent" (*The Sacred Wood*, pp. 47-53), missed the distinction between creative Self and self-centered ego, just as that between creative emotion and brute or merely subjective emotion. (See *Creative Intuition in Art and Poetry*, p. 120, note 16, and p. 143, note 55.

45. *A Defence of Poetry.*

46. See *Creative Intuition in Art and Poetry*, pp. 9-11.

21. ART AND BEAUTY

Saint Thomas, who was as simple as he was wise, defined the beautiful as that which, being seen, pleases: *id quod visum placet*.[1] These four words say all that is necessary: a vision, that is to say, an *intuitive knowledge*, and a *delight*. The beautiful is what gives delight—not just any delight, but delight in knowing; not the delight peculiar to the act of knowing, but a delight which superabounds and overflows from this act because of the object known. If a thing exalts and delights the soul by the very fact that it is given to the soul's intuition, it is good to apprehend, it is beautiful.[2]

Beauty is essentially an object of *intelligence*, for that which *knows* in the full sense of the word is intelligence, which alone is open to the infinity of being. The natural place of beauty is the intelligible world, it is from there that it descends. But it also, in a way, falls under the grasp of the senses, in so far as in man they serve the intellect and can themselves take delight in knowing: "Among all the senses, it is to the sense of sight and the sense of hearing only that the beautiful relates, because these two senses are *maxime cognoscitivi*."[3] The part played by the senses in the perception of beauty is even rendered enormous in us, and well-nigh indispensable, by the very fact that our intelligence is not intuitive, as is the intelligence of the angel; it sees, to be sure, but on condition of abstracting and discoursing; only sense knowledge possesses perfectly in man the intuitiveness required for the perception of the beautiful. Thus man can doubtless enjoy purely intelligible beauty, but the beautiful that is *connatural* to man is the beautiful that delights the intellect through the senses and through their intuitions. Such is also the beautiful that is proper to our art, which shapes a sensible matter in order to delight the spirit. It would thus like to believe that paradise is not lost. It has the savor of the terrestrial paradise, because it restores, for a moment, the peace and the simultaneous delight of the intellect and the senses.

If beauty delights the intellect, it is because it is essentially a certain excellence or perfection in the proportion of things to the intellect. Hence the three conditions Saint Thomas assigned to beauty:[4] *integrity*, because the intellect is pleased in fullness of Being; *proportion*, because the intellect is pleased in order and unity; finally, and above all, *radiance* or *clarity*, because the intellect is pleased in light and intelligibility. A certain splendor is, in fact, according to all the ancients, the essential characteristic of beauty—*claritas est de ratione pulchritudinis*,[5] *lux pulchrificat, quia sine luce omnia sunt turpia*[6]—but it is a splendor of intelligibility: *splendor veri*, said the Platonists; *splendor ordinis*, said Saint Augustine, adding that "unity is the form of all beauty";[7] *splendor formae*, said Saint Thomas in his precise metaphysician's language: for the form, that is to say, the principle which constitutes the proper perfection of all that is, which constitutes and achieves things in their essences and qualities, which is, finally, if one may so put it, the ontological secret that they bear within them, their spiritual being, their operating mystery—the form, indeed, is above all the proper principle of intelligibility, the proper *clarity* of every thing. Besides, every form is a vestige or a ray of the creative Intelligence imprinted at the heart of created being. On the other hand, every order and every proportion is the work of intelligence. And so, to say with the Schoolmen that beauty is *the splendor of the form on the proportioned parts of matter*,[8] is to say that it is a flashing of intelligence on a matter intelligibly arranged. The intelligence delights in the beautiful because in the beautiful it finds itself again and recognizes itself, and makes contact with its own light. This is so true that those—such as Saint Francis of Assisi—perceive and savor more the beauty of things, who know that things come forth from an intelligence, and who relate them to their author.

Every sensible beauty implies, it is true, a certain delight of the eye itself or of the ear or the imagination: but there is beauty only if the intelligence also takes delight in some way. A beautiful color "washes the eye," just as a strong scent dilates the nostril; but of these two "forms" or qualities color only is said to be *beautiful*, because, being received, unlike the perfume, in a sense power capable of disinterested knowledge,[9] it can be, even through its purely sensible brilliance, an object of delight for the intellect. Moreover, the higher the level of man's culture, the more spiritual becomes the brilliance of the form that delights him.

It is important, however, to note that in the beautiful that we have called connatural to man, and which is proper to human art, this brilliance of the form, no matter how purely intelligible it may be in itself, is seized *in the sensible and through the sensible*, and not separately from it. The intuition of artistic beauty thus stands at the opposite extreme from the abstraction of scientific truth. For with the former it is through the very apprehension of the sense that the light of being penetrates the intelligence.

The intelligence in this case, diverted from all effort of abstraction, rejoices without work and without discourse. It is dispensed from its usual labor; it does not have to disengage an intelligible from the matter in which it is buried, in order to go over its different attributes step by step; like a stag at the gushing spring, intelligence has nothing to do but drink; it drinks the clarity of being. Caught up in the intuition of sense, it is irradiated by an intelligible light that is suddenly given to it, in the very sensible in which it glitters, and which it does not seize *sub ratione veri*, but rather *sub ratione delectabilis*, through the happy release procured for the intelligence and through the delight ensuing in the appetite, which leaps at every good of the soul as at its proper object. Only afterwards will it be able to reflect more or less successfully upon the causes of this delight.[10]

Thus, although the beautiful borders on the metaphysical *true*, in the sense that every splendor of intelligibility in things implies some conformity with the Intelligence that is the cause of things, nevertheless the beautiful is not a kind of truth, but a kind of good;[11] the perception of the beautiful relates to knowledge, but by way of addition, *comme à la jeunesse s'ajoute sa fleur*; it is not so much a kind of knowledge as a kind of delight.

The beautiful is essentially delightful. This is why, of its very nature and precisely as beautiful, it stirs desire and produces love, whereas the true as such only illumines. "*Omnibus igitur est pulchrum et bonum desiderabile et amabile et diligibile."*[12] It is for its beauty that Wisdom is loved.[13] And it is for itself that every beauty is first loved, even if afterwards the too weak flesh is caught in the trap. Love in its turn produces ecstasy, that is to say, it puts the lover outside of himself; ec-stasy, of which the soul experiences a diminished form when it is seized by the beauty of the work of art, and the fullness when it is absorbed, like the dew, by the beauty of God.

And of God Himself, according to Denis the Areopagite,[14] we must be so bold as to say that He suffers in some way ecstasy of love, because of the abundance of His goodness which leads Him to diffuse in all things a participation of His splendor. But God's love causes the beauty of what He loves, whereas our love is caused by the beauty of what we love.

The speculations of the ancients concerning the beautiful must be taken in the most formal sense; we must avoid materializing their thought in any too narrow specification. There is not just one way but a thousand or ten thousand ways in which the notion of *integrity* or perfection or completion can be realized. The lack of a head or an arm is quite a considerable lack of integrity in a woman but of very little account in a statue—whatever disappointment M. Ravaisson may have felt at not being able to *complete* the Venus de Milo. The least sketch of da Vinci's or even of Rodin's is more complete than the most perfect Bouguereau. And if it pleases a futurist to give the lady he is painting only one eye, or a quarter of an eye, no one denies him the right to do this: one asks only—here is the whole problem—that this quarter of an eye be precisely all the eye this lady needs *in the given case.*

It is the same with proportion, fitness and harmony. They are diversified according to the objects and according to the ends. The good proportion of a man is not the good proportion of a child. Figures constructed according to the Greek or the Egyptian canons are perfectly proportioned in their genre; but Rouault's clowns are also perfectly proportioned, in their genre. Integrity and proportion have no absolute signification,[15] and must be understood solely *in relation* to the end of the work, which is to make a form shine on matter.

Finally, and above all, this radiance itself of the form, which is the main thing in beauty, has an infinity of diverse ways of shining on matter. There is the sensible radiance of color or tone; there is the intelligible clarity of an arabesque, of a rhythm or an harmonious balance, of an activity or a movement; there is the reflection upon things of a human or divine thought;[16] there is, above all, the deep-seated splendor one glimpses of the soul, of the soul principle of life and animal energy, or principle of spiritual life, of pain and passion. And there is a still more exalted splendor, the splendor of Grace, which the Greeks did not know.

Beauty, therefore, is not conformity to a certain ideal and immutable type, in the sense in which they understand it who, confusing the true and the beautiful, knowledge and delight, would have it that in order to perceive beauty man discover "by the vision of ideas", "through the material envelope", "the invisible essence of things" and their "necessary type."[17] Saint Thomas was as far removed from this pseudo-Platonism as he was from the idealist bazaar of Winckelmann and David. There is beauty for him the moment the shining of any form on a suitably proportioned matter succeeds in pleasing the intellect, and he takes care to warn us that beauty is in some way *relative*—relative not to the dispositions of the subject, in the sense in which the moderns understand the word relative, but to the proper nature and end of the thing, and to the formal conditions under which it is taken. "*Pulchritudo quodammodo dicitur per respectum ad aliquid. . . .*"[18] "*Alia enim est pulchritudo spiritus et alia corporis, atque alia hujus et illius corporis.*"[19] And however beautiful a created thing may be, it can appear beautiful to some and not to others, because it is beautiful only under certain aspects, which some discern and others do not: it is thus "beautiful in one place and not beautiful in another."

If this is so, it is because the beautiful belongs to the order of the *transcendentals*, that is to say, objects of thought which transcend every limit of genus or category, and which do not allow themselves to be enclosed in any class, because they imbue everything and are to be found everywhere.[20] Like the one, the true and the good, the beautiful is *being* itself considered from a certain aspect; it is a property of being. It is not an accident superadded to being, it adds to being only a relation of reason: it is being considered as delighting, by the mere intuition of it, an intellectual nature. Thus everything is beautiful, just as everything is good, at least in a certain relation. And as being is everywhere present and everywhere varied the beautiful likewise is diffused everywhere and is everywhere varied. Like being and the other transcendentals, it is essentially *analogous*, that is to say, it is predicated for diverse reasons, *sub diversa ratione*, of the diverse subjects of which it is predicated: each kind of being *is* in its own way, is *good* in its own way, is *beautiful* in its own way.

Analogous concepts are predicated of God pre-eminently; in Him the perfection they designate exists in a "formal-eminent" manner, in the pure and infinite state. God is their "sovereign analogue,"[21] and they are to be met with again in things only as a dispersed and prismatized reflection of the countenance of God.[22] Thus Beauty is one of the divine names.

God is beautiful. He is the most beautiful of beings, because, as Denis the Areopagite and St. Thomas explain,[23] His beauty is without alteration or vicissitude, without increase or diminution; and because it is not as the beauty of things, all of which have a particularized beauty, *particulatam pulchritudinem, sicut et particulatam naturam*. He is beautiful through Himself and in Himself, beautiful absolutely.

He is beautiful to the extreme (*superpulcher*), because in the perfectly simple unity of His nature there pre-exists in a super-excellent manner the fountain of all beauty.

He is beauty itself, because He gives beauty to all created beings, according to the particular nature of each, and because He is the cause of all consonance and all brightness. Every form indeed, that is to say, every light, is "a certain irradiation proceeding from the first brightness," "a participation in the divine brightness." And every consonance or every harmony, every concord, every friendship and every union whatsoever among beings proceeds from the divine beauty, the primordial and super-eminent type of all consonance, which gathers all things together and which calls them all to itself, meriting well in this "the name χαλός, which derives from 'to call.'" Thus "the beauty of anything created is nothing else than a similitude of divine beauty participated in by things," and, on the other hand, as every form is a principle of being and as every consonance or every harmony is preservative of being, it must be said that divine beauty is the cause of the being of all that is. *Ex divina pulchritudine esse omnium derivatur.*[24]

In the Trinity, Saint Thomas adds,[25] the name Beauty is attributed most fittingly to the Son. As for integrity or perfection, He has truly and perfectly in Himself, without the least diminution, the nature of the Father. As for due proportion or consonance, He is the express and perfect image of the Father: and it is proportion which befits the image as such. "As for radiance, finally, He is the Word, the light and the splendor of the intellect, "perfect Word to Whom nothing is lacking, and, so to speak, art of Almighty God."[26]

Beauty, therefore, belongs to the transcendental and metaphysical order. This is why it tends of itself to draw the soul beyond the created. Speaking of the instinct for beauty, Baudelaire, the *poète maudit* to whom modern art owes its renewed awareness of the theological quality and tyrannical spirituality of beauty, writes: ". . . it is this immortal instinct for the beautiful which makes us consider the earth and its various spectacles as a sketch of, as a *correspondence* with Heaven. . . . It is at once through poetry and *across* poetry, through and *across* music, that the soul glimpses the splendors situated beyond the grave; and when an exquisite poem brings tears to the eyes, these tears are not proof of an excess of joy, they are rather the testimony of an irritated melancholy, a demand of the nerves, of a nature exiled in the imperfect and desiring to take possession immediately, even on this earth, of a revealed paradise."[27]

The moment one touches a transcendental, one touches being itself, a likeness of God, an absolute, that which ennobles and delights our life; one enters into the domain of the spirit. It is remarkable that men really communicate with one another only by passing through being or one of its properties. Only in this way do they escape from the individuality in which matter encloses them. If they remain in the world of their sense needs and of their sentimental egos, in vain do they tell their stories to one another, they do not understand each other. They observe each other without seeing each other, each one of them infinitely alone, even though work or sense pleasures bind them together. But let one touch the good and Love, like the saints, the true, like an Aristotle, the beautiful, like a Dante or a Bach or a Giotto, then contact is made, souls communicate. Men are really united only by the spirit; light alone brings them together, *intellectualia et rationalia omnia congregans, et indestructibilia faciens.*[28]

Art in general tends to make a work. But certain arts tend to make a *beautiful* work, and in this they differ essentially from all the others. The work to which all the other arts tend is itself ordered to the service of man, and is therefore a simple means; and it is entirely enclosed in a determined material genus. The work to which the fine arts tend is ordered to beauty; as beautiful, it is an end, an absolute, it suffices of itself; and if, as work-to-be-made, it is material and enclosed in a genus, as beautiful it belongs to the kingdom of the spirit and plunges deep into the transcendence and the infinity of being.

The fine arts thus stand out in the *genus* art as man stands out in the *genus* animal. And like man himself they are like a horizon where matter and spirit meet. They have a spiritual soul. Hence they possess many distinctive properties. Their contact with the beautiful modifies in them certain characteristics of art in general, notably, as I shall try to show, with respect to the rules of art; on the other hand, this contact discloses and carries to a sort of excess other generic characteristics of the virtue of art, above all its intellectual character and its resemblance to the speculative virtues.

There is a curious analogy between the fine arts and wisdom. Like wisdom, they are ordered to an object which transcends man and which is of value in itself, and whose amplitude is limitless, for beauty, like being, is infinite. They are disinterested, desired for themselves, truly noble because their work taken in itself is not made in order that one may use it as a means, but in order that one may enjoy it as an end, being a true *fruit, aliquid ultimum et delectabile*. Their whole value is spiritual, and their mode of being is contemplative. For if contemplation is not their act, as it is the act of wisdom, nevertheless they aim at producing an intellectual delight, that is to say, a kind of contemplation; and they also presuppose in the artist a kind of contemplation, from which the beauty of the work must overflow. That is why we may apply to them, with due allowance, what Saint Thomas says of wisdom when he compares it to play:[29] "The contemplation of wisdom is rightly compared to play, because of two things that one finds in play. The first is that play is delightful, and the contemplation of wisdom has the greatest delight, according to what Wisdom says of itself in Ecclesiasticus: *my spirit is sweet above honey*. The second is that the movements of play are not ordered to anything else, but are sought for themselves. And it is the same with the delights of wisdom. . . . That is why divine Wisdom compares its delight to play: *I was delighted every day, playing before him in the world*."[30]

But Art remains, nevertheless, in the order of Making, and it is by drudgery upon some matter that it aims at delighting the spirit. Hence for the artist a strange and saddening condition, image itself of man's condition in the world, where he must wear himself out among bodies and live with the spirits. Though reproaching the old poets for holding Divinity to be jealous, Aristotle acknowledges that they were right in saying that the possession of wisdom is in the strict sense reserved to Divinity alone: "It is not a human possession, for human nature is a slave in so many ways."[31] To produce beauty likewise belongs to God alone in the strict sense. And if the condition of the artist is more human and less exalted than that of the wise man, it is also more discordant and more painful, because his activity does not remain wholly within the pure immanence of spiritual operations, and does not in itself consist in contemplating, but in making. Without enjoying the substance and the peace of wisdom, he is caught up in the hard exigencies of the intellect and the speculative life, and he is condemned to all the servile miseries of practice and of temporal production.

"Dear Brother Leo, God's little beast, even if a Friar Minor spoke the language of the angels and raised to life a man dead for four days, note it well that it is not therein that perfect joy is found. . . ."

Even if the artist were to encompass in his work all the light of heaven and all the grace of the first garden, he would not have perfect joy, because he is following wisdom's footsteps and running by the scent of its perfumes, but does not possess it. Even if the philosopher were to know all the intelligible reasons and all the properties of being, he would not have perfect joy, because his wisdom is human. Even if the theologian were to know all the analogies of the divine processions and all the whys and the wherefores of Christ's actions, he would not have perfect joy, because his wisdom has a divine origin but a human mode, and a human voice.

Ah! les voix, mourez donc, mourantes que vous etes!

The Poor and the Peaceful alone have perfect joy because they possess wisdom and contemplation *par excellence*, in the silence of creatures and in the voice of Love; united without intermediary to subsisting Truth, they know "the sweetness that God gives and the delicious taste of the Holy Spirit."[32] This is what prompted Saint Thomas, a short time before his death, to say of his unfinished *Summa:* "It seems to me as so much straw"—*mihi videtur ut palea.* Human straw: the Parthenon and Notre-Dame de Chartres, the Sistine Chapel and the Mass in D—and which will be burned on the last day! "Creatures have no savor."*

The Middle Ages knew this order. The Renaissance shattered it. After three centuries of infidelity, prodigal Art aspired to become the ultimate end of man, his Bread and his Wine, the consubstantial mirror of beatific Beauty. And the poet hungry for beatitude who asked of art the mystical

---

* I feel today that I must apologize for the sort of thoughtlessness with which I adopted this phrase here. One must have little experience of created things, or much experience of divine things, in order to be able to speak in this way. In general, formulas of contempt with regard to created things belong to a conventional literature that is difficult to endure. The creature is deserving of compassion, not contempt; it exists only because it is loved. It is deceptive because it has too much savor, and because this savor is nothing in comparison with the being of God. [1935]

fullness that God alone can give, has been able to open out only onto *Sigê l'abîme*. Rimbaud's silence marks perhaps the end of a secular apostasy. In any case it clearly signifies that it is folly to seek in art the words of eternal life and the repose of the human heart; and that the artist, if he is not to shatter his art or his soul, must simply be, as artist, what art wants him to be—a good workman.

And now the modern world, which had promised the artist everything, soon will scarcely leave him even the bare means of subsistence. Founded on the two *unnatural* principles of the *fecundity of money* and the *finality of the useful*, multiplying needs and servitude without the possibility of there ever being a limit, destroying the leisure of the soul, withdrawing the material *factibile* from the control which proportioned it to the ends of the human being, and imposing on man the panting of the machine and the accelerated movement of matter, the system of *nothing but the earth* is imprinting on human activity a truly inhuman mode and a diabolical direction, for the final end of all this frenzy is to prevent man from resembling God,

> *dum nil perenne cogitat,*
> *sesque culpis illigat.*

Consequently he must, if he is to be logical, treat as useless, and therefore as rejected, all that by any grounds bears the mark of the spirit.

Or it will even be necessary that heroism, truth, virtue, beauty become *useful* values—the best, the most loyal instruments of propaganda and of control of temporal powers.

Persecuted like the wise man and almost like the saint, the artist will perhaps recognize his brothers at last and discover his true vocation again: for in a way he is not of this world, being, from the moment that he works for beauty, on the path which leads upright souls to God and manifests to them the invisible things by the visible. However rare may be at such a time those who will not want to please the Beast and to turn with the wind, it is in them, by the very fact that they will exercise a *disinterested* activity, that the human race will live.

NOTES

1. *Summa Theol.*, I, 5, 4, ad 1. Saint Thomas, it must be added, means to give here only a definition *per effectum*. It is when he assigns the three elements of the beautiful that he gives an *essential* definition of it.

2. "It is of the nature of the beautiful that by the sight or knowledge of it the appetite is allayed." *Summa Theol.*, I-II, 27, 1, ad 3.

3. *Ibid.*

4. *Summa Theol.*, I, 39, 8. "For beauty includes three conditions: *integrity* or *perfection*, since those things which are impaired are by that very fact ugly; due *proportion* or *harmony*; and lastly, *brightness* or *clarity*, whence things are called beautiful which have a bright color." (English translation from *Basic Writings of St. Thomas Aquinas*, edited by Anton C. Pegis, New York: Random House, 1945.)

5. Saint Thomas, *Comment. in lib. de Divin. Nomin.*, lect. 6.

6. Saint Thomas, *Comment. in Psalm.*, Ps. XXV, 5.

7. *De vera Religione*, cap. 41.

8. *Opusc. de Pulchro et Bono*, attributed to Albert the Great and sometimes to Saint Thomas. Plotinus (*Enneads*, I, 6), speaking of beauty in bodies, describes it as "something which affects one sensibly from the first impression, which the soul perceives with agreement, recognizes and welcomes, and to which it in some way accommodates itself."

9. *Sight and hearing* SERVING REASON. (*Summa Theol.*, I-II, 27, 1, ad 3).—Moreover sense itself delights in things suitably proportioned only because it is itself measure and proportion, and so finds in them a likeness of its nature: "Sense delights in things duly proportioned, as in what are like it, for sense too is a kind of reason, as is every cognitive power." *Summa Theol.*, I, 5, 4, ad 1. On the expression "a kind of reason"—*ratio quaedam* (ἡ δ᾽ αἴσθησις ὁ λόγος)—cf. *Comm. in de Anima*, lib. 3, lect. 2.

It is permissible to conjecture that in glorified bodies all the senses, intellectualized, may be of use in the perception of the beautiful. Already poets are teaching us to anticipate in a way this state. Baudelaire has annexed to aesthetics the sense of smell.

10. This question of the perception of the beautiful by the intellect using the senses as instruments would deserve a careful analysis which, in my opinion, has too rarely tempted the subtlety of philosophers. Kant gave it his attention in the *Critique of Judgment*. Unfortunately the direct, interesting, and sometimes pro-

found observations much more frequently met with in this *Critique* than in the other two are vitiated by his mania for system and symmetry, and above all by the fundamental errors and the subjectivism of his theory of knowledge.

11. "Beauty is a certain kind of good." Cajetan, *In* I-II, 27, 1.—So it was that the Greeks used the same word καλοκἀγαθία to express both notions.

12. Denis the Areopagite, *De Div. Nomin.*, cap. 4; Saint Thomas, lect. 9. Let us by virtue of time-honored actual usage, continue to call "the Areopagite" the man whom modern authorities call the *pseudo-Denis.*

13. "Her have I loved, and have sought her out from my youth, and have desired to take her for my spouse, and I became *a lover of her beauty.*" Wisdom, VIII, 2.

14. *De Divin. Nomin.*, cap. 4; Saint Thomas, lect. 10.

15. Let us note that the conditions of the beautiful are much more strictly determined in nature than in art, the end of natural beings and the formal radiance which can shine in them being themselves much more strictly determined than those of works of art. In nature, for instance, there is assuredly a perfect type (whether we recognize it or not) of the proportions of the male or female body, because the natural end of the human organism is something fixed and invariably determined. But the beauty of a work of art *not being the beauty of the object represented,* painting and sculpture are in no way bound to the determined proportions and to the imitation of such a type. The art of pagan antiquity thought itself so bound because of an extrinsic condition, because it represented above all the gods of an anthropomorphic religion.

16. "Τὸν θεοειδῆ νοῦν ἐπιλάμποντα." Plotinus, *Enneads,* I 6.

17. Cf. Lamennais, *De l'Art et du Beau* (Paris: Garnier, 1864), Ch. I.

18. "Beauty, health and the like are in a way said with respect to something else: because a certain mixture of humors produces health in a boy, but not in an old man; and what is health for a lion may mean death for a man. Health, therefore, is a proportion of humors in relation to a particular nature. In like manner beauty [of the body] consists in the proportion of its parts and colors; and so the beauty of one differs from the beauty of another." Saint Thomas, *Comment. in Psalm.*, Ps. XLIV, 2.

19. Saint Thomas, *Comment. in lib. de Divin. Nomin.*, cap. 4, lect. 5.

In an article entitled "Variations du Beau," published in the *Revue des Deux Mondes,* July 15, 1857 (*Oeuvres littéraires,* I, *Études esthétiques,* Paris, Cres, 1923, pp. 37 et seq.) Eugène Delacroix formulated from his painter's point of view some very just observations. Philosophizing on the question with more acumen than many professional philosophers, he had realized that the multiplicity of the forms of the beautiful in no way impairs its objectivity: "I have not said and nobody would dare to say that it can vary in its essence, for then it would no longer be the beautiful but mere caprice or fancy. But its character can change; a countenance of beauty which once charmed a far-off civilization does not astonish or please us as much as one which is more in accord with our feelings or, if you like, our prejudices. *Numquam in eodem statu permanet*, said ancient Job of man." Here we have, in different terms, an affirmation of the fundamentally *analogical* character of the idea of beauty (cf. "Projet d'article sur le beau," *ibid.*, pp. 141 et seq.).

"We must see the beautiful where the artist has chosen to put it," said Delacroix again ("Questions sur le Beau," *Rev. des Deux Mondes*, July 15, 1854; *ibid.*, p. 52); and already in his *Journal* (end of 1823 and beginning of 1824): "A Greek and an Englishman are each beautiful in his own way, which has nothing in common with the other" (*Journal*, Plon, 1893, vol. I, p. 47).

20. In an essay published in 1923 ("L'Esthétique de saint Thomas" in *S. Tommaso d'Aquino*, Publ. della Fac. di Filos. dell'Univ. del Sacro Cuore, Milan, Vita et Pensiero), Father de Munnynck endeavored to cast doubt on this point. To do so is to conceive the *quod visum placet* and the Scholastic teaching on the beautiful in a wholly material manner (cf. Father Wébert's review, *Bulletin thomiste*, II Année, no. 1, Jan. 1925). The classic table of transcendentals (*ens, res, unum, aliquid, verum, bonum*) does not exhaust all the transcendental values, and if the beautiful is not included, it is because it can be reduced to one of them (to the good—for the beautiful is that which in things faces the mind as an object of intuitive delight). Saint Thomas constantly affirms that the beautiful and the (metaphysical) good are the same thing in reality and differ only in notion or idea (*pulchrum et bonum sunt idem subjecto, sola ratione different*, I, 5, 4, ad 1). It is so with all the transcendentals: they are identified in the thing, and they differ in idea. Wherefore, *whoever tends to good, by that very fact tends to the beautiful* (De Ver., 22, 1, ad 12).

21. The analogates (*analoga analogata*) of an analogous concept (*analogum analogans*) are the diverse things in which this concept is realized and which it fits.

22. In God alone are all these perfections identified according to their formal reason: in Him Truth is Beauty, is Goodness, is Unity, and they are He. In the things of this world, on the other hand, truth, beauty, goodness, etc., are aspects of being *distinct according to their formal reason*, and what is *true sim-*

pliciter (absolutely speaking) may be *good* or *beautiful* only *secundum quid* (in a certain relation), what is *beautiful simpliciter* may be *good* or *true* only *secundum quid*. . . . Wherefore beauty, truth, goodness (especially when it is no longer a question of metaphysical or transcendental good itself, but of moral good) command distinct spheres of human activity, of which it would be foolish to deny *a priori* the possible conflicts, on the pretext that the transcendentals are indissolubly bound to one another—a perfectly true metaphysical principle, but one that needs to be correctly understood.

23. *De Divinis Nominibus*, cap. 4; Saint Thomas' *Commentary*, lessons 5 and 6.

24. Saint Thomas, *ibid.*, lect. 5.

25. *Summa Theol.*, I, 39, 8.

26. Saint Augustine, *De Doctr. Christ.*, I, 5.

27. Baudelaire, *L'Art romantique* (Paris: Calmann-Lévy, 1885), p. 167.

28. Denis the Areopagite, *De Divin. Nomin.*, cap. 4 (Saint Thomas, lect. 4).

29. *Opusc.* LXVIII, *in libr. Boetii de Hebdom*, in princ.

30. *Prov.*, VIII, 31.

31. *Metaph.*, I, 2, 982b.

32. Ruysbroeck ("Vie de Rusbrock," in *Rusbrock l'Admirable*, Oeuvres choisies, ed. E. Hello, Paris, Perrin et Cie, 1902, p. lii.).

22. THE FREEDOM OF SONG

Nowhere better than in music does there appear to the philosopher the very mysterious nature of the creative idea, or factive idea, that plays a central role in the theory of art. A pattern, as the scholastics said, *id ad quod respiciens artifex operatur*; that which the creative spirit looks at within itself in order to bring the work into existence. There is nothing truer, but, as with many a scholastic formula, there is nothing easier to kill while believing that one understands it. To academic thought this dictum would mean that the operative idea is a model which the artist carries in his head and sees there ready-made, and of which the work is to be the *copy* or the portrait. This is to make of art a cemetery by definition, a cemetery of imitations. For every copy (I do not say every image) is imitation, without form proper to itself nor formative in itself, of a thing, I say, formed from within, by its form or its soul.

And likewise in the ethical order, the academicism of virtue, which asks of the human being to make himself into the *copy* of an ideal, changes moral life into a cemetery of lies; in the end the ideal will have duped the conscience, and made of every act an hypocrisy: with no other way out than the escape of the unhappy Jean-Jacques into the dream-world of his *inhabitants*. Counter-trace your ideal as much as you wish to, construct, have recourse to compass and to tape-measure, you will be still an imitation; there is no tracing in the world of God. To imitate the Saints is not to copy an *ideal*, and it is not to *copy* the Saints. It is after their example —and by allowing as they did Another to conduct you where you do not wish to go, and love to configure you from within into the Form that transcends all form—to imitate the Saints is to become, precisely, an *original*, not a copy; to imitate the Saints is, like them, to become inimitable. Invent something new? Invent one's self a new face? That's much too little for us, really—and still a lie. I mean for you yourself to become, at the very heart of your being, invention and novelty, the invention of Another and the new earth that He inhabits—for "He has one idea and who can turn Him?"[1] That this idea should be incorporated in you, soul of your soul, should quarter and dissolve you from within in order to remake you without your knowledge, and change you into one dissimilar to others, into a gulf of solitude no longer closed but open and peopled by the gift and thereby the more total—nothing less is necessary for love, and for freedom. *Non est inventus similis illi qui conservaret legem Excelsi.*

Such also is the work of art, in its manner and in the universe of production. It is not the copy nor the duplicate but, rather, the body of the artist's ideas. Astonishing correspondence of divine things! The work lives, outside of the artist, through an idea which is its internal principle of consistency and meaning, and which does not exist as idea except in the mind of the artist and separate from the work. And it is only when the symphony is made and finished that, in the mind of the composer, its creative idea is itself achieved. I mean as to the *expressiblity* of this idea, as to the detail of its determinations and of its contours. A model to copy? The creative idea is an intuitive flash (given at one stroke but unexpressed, and without contours) in which the whole work is potentially contained and which will unfold and explain itself in the work, and which will make of the work itself an original and a model; incomparably more immaterial than is believed by academicism, such an idea is "a moment of intellection altogether spiritual and simple, which in regard to the work is transcendent and unlimited,"[2] and by means of which are formed the representations themselves, the conceptions and images that are, as it were, the raw materials of the work.

The creative idea expresses itself finally in matter, as the speculative intuition of the philosopher does in the concept or mental word. And in truth these are analogous: to perform the inner word in the mind, and the work of art in matter. The majority go and buy this word ready-made in the department stores of language, and that swarm of birds which men exchange among themselves and which you see darkening the sky (this is called the intercourse of ideas) are stuffed words batted back and forth with rackets; lead weights are added by thinkers in the hope of putting out the opponent's eye, or bashing in his head. From time to time a word is really born, emerging from the invisible living waters where the ray of abstractive intuition meets the profound images and sensibility.

As for the creative idea, it appears to consciousness especially, in truth, as a decisive emotion, but an emotion transverberated by intelligence, a little cloud at first, but full of eyes, full of imperious visioning, charged with will, and avid to give existence; and if the affective tone imposes itself before all on our knowledge of ourselves, in reality what is of chief import in this intelligenced emotion is the invisible and intentional dart of intuition. Let us suppose even that it be pure intellectual intuition as in the case of the angel; in any case it has its structure and its contours expressed to the mind, its objectivity fashioned and uttered, only in the work itself that it produces outwardly; subtended by the concepts, born in the midst of them, doubtless even requiring, because of the conditions of mental activity in man, some vague obscure concept in order to come to birth in the mind, in itself the factive or creative idea is not a concept; it is an intellective gaze; it is an intellection having for *concept*, for intelligible fruit engendered—but exterior to the mind and born of matter—the work itself that is made, the object not of knowledge but of creation, or rather, the object of creative knowledge which in its essence is forming and not formed, producing, and not produced.

Where if not in musical creation could be found a better image of the creation of a world? Like the cantata or the symphony, the world was constructed in time (in a time that began with it), and is being preserved all the length of its successive duration by the thought from which it receives existence. There is nothing closer to the abyss of the created than the movement of that which passes, the flux, rhythmed and ordered, of the impermanent blossoming of a sensory joy that yields and fades away. Like the world and like motion, song has its countenance only in a memory; *si non esset anima, non esset tempus*. And no more than the flow of time is music in itself limited and closed. Why should the song stop? Why should a musical work ever finish? "It is not like a painting, there is no reason for it to finish . . . ," was that a paradox? Let us say rather, that as the time of the world shall one day emerge into the instant of eternity, so music should cease only by emerging into a silence *of another order*, filled with a substantial voice, where the soul for a moment tastes that time no longer is.

And how find for uncreated creative knowledge a more instructive image than created creative knowledge? Just as, in His essence eternally seen, God knows all things, so in his factive idea the artist knows his work in a fashion that may be called substantial.

However, have I not said that this existence-giving knowledge is itself not finished, in its representable detail, until the work is finished? Let us venture to say that in one sense the same is true for the divine knowledge. For to give us some intelligence about the properties of the creative knowledge, called *scientia visionis*, it is not only the consideration of what is called God's "antecedent will" (by which He wills that all be good, all be saved), which we must add to the consideration of the divine essence infinitely transparent to the divine intellection, it is also the consideration of the "consequent will" of God, by which He permits the evil of the free creature—and by reason of what circumstances, if not of the refusal brought about by the creature? I mean not only by reason of the general possibility of refusal included in created liberty, I also mean by reason of the initiatives of refusal which in effect emanate from it at a given moment.

If it is true that in the line of evil the creature is the first cause (deficient, not efficient)—first cause of the privation or nothingness that wounds a given moment of his liberty—then it must be said that evil cannot be known save in the same instant when it thus wounds existence, when the creature escapes voluntarily from the influx of being and goodness that descends from creative love:[3] and it is because time is present in its entirety at the immobile and eternal *nunc*, that from all eternity, the free absence, the voluntary non-regulation, the non-being that is the root of the devious act accomplished by me at a given hour of this clock of the universe or the atom, is and was and shall be known of God.

Is this positing a determination of the divine knowledge by the creature, I mean by the irruption of nothingness of which the creature has the first initiative?—But do you then believe that non-being is capable of determining? And furthermore do you believe that created beings are for divine knowledge anything else but a secondary term attained as a mere "material" or factual datum, in no way formative or specifying? Are you forgetting that only the divine essence is for divine knowledge a formal and specifying object, and that neither the things (other than Himself) that God knows, nor the "decrees," nor the "permissions" of His will have the slightest determining role in regard to His act of knowledge? If we do not begin by recognizing the absolute freedom of divine knowledge in regard to its created objects, we had better not discuss these things. Even when it knows that of which it is not the cause—evil as such—it is never formed by what it knows. If its permissions themselves remain formative, it is in this sense that divine knowledge still lays hold of and assumes the initiatives of refusal of the creature in the designs and the forms through which the torrent of being passes.

To say that God knows creatures in His essence, is not to say that God does not know creatures but ideal models of them, idea-pictures, Cartesian ideas, objects known in place of things, of which things are the copy, itself unknown; it is not to make of the divine essence an idol of created things! The divine essence is not the image or the expression of things, it is the things that are themselves and in themselves a similitude and an expression of the divine essence. God does not know them in His essence as if in an image of them, but as in the infinitely transcendent intuition of Him by Him which is also the creative form of things.

In the pure flash of eternal and subsistent intellection which is His being, God knows possible things, He knows them and exhausts them, down to the undersoil of their own essence; and there, in that same flash He knows His "predetermining decrees"; to put it otherwise, He knows, among possible things, certain ones in so far as being freely willed and loved by Him, and thus in so far as existing, loving and acting; and in free creatures thus known exhaustively in their creative idea, and who are before Him like gods of "down below" because He has permitted them to refuse His love if they so wish, He knows the nothingness which they are able to "make" without Him (and only without Him)[4] and which they are making at a given instant on their own initiative, and by which they slip away from Him, fissure their being (and where indeed would He know evil, if not there where, negatively, it takes form—in the good that it wounds?) Thus God knows, by His knowledge of vision, evil—or rather that free non-attention to the rule of action, that pure and very secret "nihilation" which is the metaphysical root of wrong action—God knows evil in the acting creature himself, whom He knows—insofar as existing and freely acting—in the fires of creative love, and—in regard to his nature and to the abyss of his possibilities—in the consubstantial light of the Uncreated essence. Thus, in the light of what God Himself is to Himself, in the very experience of His own beauty and goodness, created things are known by Him and touched by him without touching Him, to the profoundest depth of their being and of their non-being, to the furthest depth of the goodness of their very being (*et erant valde bona*), to the furthest depth of the sweetness of the good, or of the bitterness of the evil of their very doing.

As organic life is a growth of being which is constructed through victories and ruins, as mystical life is a passage constantly accelerated across the squalls of light and of night— so too the life of the creative spirit is a strange experience of growth and deepening—of course I am speaking of something wholly other than the perfecting of technical knowledge and of skill; all is danger in this growth, but the worst danger is that of refusing it.

What is it, definitively, if not a progress in the realization of the metaphysical relationship, pointed out just now, between the creative human idea, in spite of all that it drains from alien servitudes, and the creative idea *par excellence* which is all liberty with regard to the object—formative and not formed? By nature the human creative idea depends in a humiliating manner upon the exterior world and upon all that infinite mass of forms and beauties already made; and furthermore upon all the store of what the generations have learned; and upon the code of signs in use in the tribe; and upon the very rules for the fabrication of the object (insofar as they are yet distinct from the creative idea itself). It has need of all these and all these are alien to it. While purifying itself it must subject all these to itself: subject them, therefore separate itself from them; *segregatus ut imperet*.

The movement of operative spirituality which is the essential of the creative idea, *as such* is free of all, and receives nothing from anything nor from anyone (save from the first poet), in order to form the object uniquely to its own resemblance. This movement must constantly increase; likewise will the night increase, sometimes transluminous and sometimes shadowy; likewise will solitude be brought about; likewise—uprootings, ruptures, a destruction that would be universal.

It is understandable that there are grounds for hesitation. When the heart is not rich in powerful constellations, when it is not a universe in itself capable of holding its own before the universe, then the ravages of the spirit will be merely destructive and devouring, there will be nothing other than destruction.

But am I God, then, to make a divine work and to form without being formed? Am I asked to create out of nothing? If my work is a kind of concept or word that my creative intuition fashions for itself outside of me out of the dust, what then will it express?

In proportion as the artist approaches his pure type and realizes his most fundamental law, it is indeed himself and his own essence and his own intelligence of himself that he expresses in his work; here is the hidden substance of his creative intuition.

Is it himself, that is to say his states or his phenomena, his emotion as *material* to enclose in a work? This is the case for the commercial or idealistic corruption of art. I have just said that the creative emotion is not the matter but the *form* of the work, it is not a thing-emotion, it is an intuitive and *intentional* emotion, which bears within it much more than itself.

It is the self of the artist insofar as it is a secret substance and person in the act of spiritual communication, that is the content of this formative emotion. It has been written[5] that vulgarity always says I: it says *one* also, and this is the same thing, for vulgarity's I is nothing but a neuter subject of phenomena or of predicates, a subject-matter like that of the egoist. But in an entirely different manner poetry likewise always says I: "*my* heart hath uttered a good word," "vivify me and *I* will keep Thy commandments . . . ," poetry's *I* is the substantial depth of the living and loving subjectivity, it is a subject-act, like that of the saint, and likewise, although in another fashion, it is a subject which gives. The art of China and of India, like that of the Middle Ages, shelters itself in vain behind the rite or the simple duty of ornamenting life, it is as personal as, and more personal at times than that of the individualistic Occident. The more or less rigorous canonicity of art is here a secondary condition; in the days of old it was a condition favorable for hiding art from itself. But the consciousness of itself and at the same time the freedom which art acquired a taste for, are fine dangers which mobilized poetry.

But man does not know himself through his own essence. His substance is hidden from him, he perceives himself only as refracted by the world of his acts which itself refracts the world of things: if he does not fill himself with the universe he remains empty to himself; thus it is not in the light antecedently possessed of an intuition of the self by the self that he has his creative intuitions, as have the pure spirits, he cannot express himself in a work except on condition that things resound in him, and that in him, at the mutual wakening, they and he come forth together out of sleep. Hence the perplexities of the poet's condition. If he hears the passwords and the secrets that are stammering in things, if he perceives realities, correspondences, figures of horror or of beauty of a very certain objectivity, if he captures like a spring-finder, the springs of the transcendentals, it is not by disengaging this objectivity for itself, but by receiving all this into the recesses of his sentiment and of his passion—not as something other than he, according to the law of speculative knowledge, but on the contrary as inseparable from himself, and in truth as part of himself; and it is thus to seize obscurely his own being with a knowledge which will not come to anything save in being creative, and which will not be conceptualized save in a work made by his hands. His knowledge nourishes itself "on a captive intelligibility"[6]: thus knowledge by affective connaturality, knowledge by resonance in subjectivity, is by nature a poetic knowledge, tending of itself to a work of sounds or colors, of forms or words. It is not without reason that the mystical experience, while incommunicable by its very nature (insofar as it is mystical) superabounds so frequently (insofar as it is knowledge by connaturality) in poetic expression. And as for the poet himself, it is not without reason either that he believes himself chosen to suffer more than other men;

> J'ai l'extase et j'ai la terreur d'être choisi.[7]

As the mystic endures divine things, the poet is here to suffer the things of the temporal world, and to suffer them so much that he is enabled in expressing them to express himself. And when he is the most engaged in the act of spiritual communication, it is because he suffers still attentively an inexorable hand stronger than he, that passes and does not return.

In order that the life of the creative spirit should grow unceasingly, conforming to its law, it is necessary that the center of subjectivity should continuously be deepened to a point where, in suffering the things of the world and those of the soul, it awakens to itself. In following this line of reflections one would doubtless be led to ask whether, beyond a certain level, this progress in spirituality can continue without, under one form or another, a religious experience properly so-called that would aid the soul of the poet to quit the surface-levels. Continuing at any price, refusing heroically to renounce the growth of the creative spirit, when such an experience postulated by the whole being had nevertheless been rendered impossible, wasn't this perhaps the secret of Nietzsche's disaster? In any case, what I want to keep in mind here, is that creation forms at different levels in the spiritual substance of the soul, everyone by this very fact confesses what he is; the more the poet grows, the deeper the level of creative intuition descends into the density of his soul. Where formerly he could be moved to song, he can do nothing now, he is obliged to dig down deeper. One would say that the shock of suffering and vision break down, one after another, the living sensitive partitions behind which his identity is hiding. He is harassed, he is tracked down, he is destroyed pitilessly. Woe to him if in retiring into himself he finds a heaven devastated, inaccessible; he can do nothing then but sink into his hell. But if at the end of ends the poet turns silent, it is not that there is ever achieved the growth of which we speak, it is not that of itself the song does not still ask to be more deeply born in him, less distant from the creative uncreated spirituality, archetype of all creative life, it is that the last partition of the heart has been attained, and the human substance consumed.

I have spoken of the poet, but of the one that every artist should be, and not only of the one who versifies. And here, again, it is the composer who in truth offers to the speculations of the philosopher a privileged experience. Less bound to the universe of human ideas and human values than he who creates with the vocables of the language of men, less bound than the painter and the sculptor to the forms and images of things, less bound than the architect to the conditions for the use of the thing to be created, it is in the composer that are verified in the clearest fashion the metaphysical exigencies of poetry. So that when *he* falls short of them, the gap is most apparent. None other than a maker of operas could instruct a Nietzsche by so perfectly decisive a disappointment.

This question concerning the depth of the formation point of the creative impulse is of greater moment than all the others. A thousand other conditions are of import to the work of art, this matters above all. If the musical work of Arthur Lourié appears to me so rich in sense, this is because it seems to me that in no other artist today is the creative intuition born at a deeper level.

This is pure music, in truth, and this the purest music is at the same time the fullest. The philosopher finds in it an admirable illustration of the law that on condition of being born deep enough in the soul, and of being strong enough also to survive great perils, music or poetry is the most truly pure music or poetry (because the deepest level where it generates is a level of factive spirituality, of the spirit of music or poetry), precisely when it abounds with human and divine sap (because to be hollowed out to that point, the soul must have suffered much from itself and from without).

Because art is, also, spirit in the flesh, from the time it becomes conscious of itself it begins to suffer from the torment of freedom. Is it too not called to a certain deliverance? Being the quintessence of the energies of the created, is not art engaged in the travail of parturition like all creatures? The unhappy epoch which is passing to its end under our eyes was conscious of this vocation, and on that account it moved us. But how badly it set about its work! A great poet of whom "stupidity is not the strong point"[8]—was to place a feeble and dejected hope in that sovereign art of dodging all that is most dear which has always been the refuge of the classical French spirit. Both the fear of the soul and the search for a compensating victory, of an illusory eternity in the reign of surfaces unfailingly arranged, and the irremediable humanistic and Jansenistic dualism in the classical spirit, rightly indicated by Charles Du Bos[9]—a spirit which is altogether secularized nowadays and emptied of substance—at last could not but reduce poetry to the impeccable and delectable form of an absence. It is also, despite appearances, in the region of words and mechanisms of expression (in seeking this time to lay bare their subconscious origins—but to destroy a machine is still to mechanize) that the surrealists have searched for freedom. Dissimulated by a somewhat suspicious fervor for mystery, it is still a taste for Cartesian experimentation that was at work. They failed to produce a composer.

It is in music that poetry had its best chance. It sought with more sensitive antennae; it touched several times what can hardly be seized.

Debussy or music rediscovered,[10] yes, that was a first deliverance; what a marvel! Wrung were the necks of eloquence, of mystagogy and magical pretensions; creative force and humility found once more the genuine conditions of art, opened the fountainheads of the working intelligence, broke the rules of the schools, restored to the work its truth as a fruit spiritually ripened for delectation. It was a deliverance however of art still more than of poetry, which remained too closely linked to psychology, to affective appearances, diluted now and then in the too fleeting flow of an emotion that did not reach the soul. With the exception of some penetrating artists, learned and sensitive like you, my dear Roland-Manuel, the experience of Debussy did not deliver up its secret; and a work of genius the particular tendency of which was directed toward factive objectivity, was, however, to deceive, and to appear to surrender to the influence of sentiment.

The work of Satie seemed less great, his lesson went further; it was the lesson of a Socrates cunningly awakening virtue, troubling bad consciences and pricking good ones, he cleansed music of all pretension and all pedantry, he profoundly purified it, I think that in this order of the purification of means he descended much deeper than Debussy; but it was still above all a purification of the virtue of art, the modesty and the dissimulations of his irony are from this point of view significant indeed; poetry, and of what freshness, slipped slim and disguised, through the half-open doors; she was there, admirably living and vivacious, along with tenderness; constrained however, shy as a beggar-woman, she waited her turn. It is not to calumniate Satie's successors to avow that in what concerns them, that turn has rarely come about. After brilliant promises, and a little more than promises, the mechanics of address, of intelligence and taste began again to deal out surprises; the monotony of this exercise was to take on quickly a fatal aspect. The most certain talents, and God knows if they are numerous in our time, do not succeed in breaking the charm. Fallen into the inertia of a new formalism—stopped short on another route by the great experience of Stravinsky, which leaves nothing to be done where it has passed—or shaken by tentatives, sometimes astonishing, of galvanization—modern music finds itself once more in a critical phase, which might seem without issue.

From his uneasy retreat in the Alhambra of Granada, a recluse burning with ardor and faith has however shown the way. Harsh and knowing as is passion, discreet, secret, precise, and little by little transfigured within the deserts of prayer, the song of Manuel de Falla makes an eternal spring gush from the rock. At first attuned to the violence, after all a little thin, and close to the picturesque, of popular melody, the De Falla of *Master Peter's Puppet-show* is now taming, like an ascetic speaking to the birds, the universe of poetry. Is he too exceptional a composer to be made much of as an example by the philosopher seeking to note the wind-shifts of the contemporary spirit? Another solitary answers him, whose example is also significant.

I do not know whether our time is disposed to receive what Lourié brings to it. I know well that he brings it a delivered music.

Others[11] have retraced the singularly instructive curve of his experiments and researches since the time of the refined Futurism of the circles of Petersburg and of the manifesto of the *Spontaneous Spectre*.[12] What I wish to stress here is the force of *traction*, if I may so call it, and of enfranchisement, of such a work. It draws to itself and reassembles nearly all of what the music of our time has sought, and not only music, but poetry too, revolution, all that belabors our culture in the nervous centers of its pain. And now we see all this assembled booty (with all the armaments soon mastered of the technique and sensibility of our time) on which falls an unknown fire, beginning to throw up its highest flame.

Nothing makes more manifest the laws of growth which we have been discussing. Please don't take what I am saying as a sign of a one-track mind, I am rather embarrassed, so precise is the confirmation, to have to state that the great influx of the soul and inspiration which is renewing music today through the invasion of a murmur coming from the depths of substance, through a small cloud on the horizon which is to drench with a rain as fresh as fire the energies of the creative intellect, was produced in Lourié at the time that another breath, this one contemplative, came to intensify the vital unity in the depths of a spirit long since religious.

It has been said of the music of Lourié that it is an ontological music; in the Kierkegaardian style, one would say also "existential." It is born in the singular roots of being, the nearest possible to that juncture of the soul and the spirit, spoken of by Saint Paul. Ontology as metaphysical knowledge is at the highest degree abstractive intuition; but as for poetry, on the contrary, the more ontological poetry is, the more nearly does it gush from the impenetrable recesses of individuality, I mean the individuality of that spiritual soul one in substance with the flesh. And it is thus that it gives to the work produced the most powerful though still concrete charge of universality. If it is true, as I remarked before, that a resonance of the universe in the creative *self* is required by the operative idea, this contrast is easily understood. By the same token we can explain certain errors of philosophers who demand for their philosophy the privileges of a knowledge reserved to the composer, the painter, the poet.

"Ontological" music is "erotic" music—here again I am speaking Danish—I mean that it owes its substance to the Eros immanent in being, to that internal weight of desire and regret which all created things bemoan, and that is why such music is naturally religious, and does not entirely waken save under a touch of the love of God. Finally, it does not advance in the fashion of a horse or an ox, a snake, a bird or a projectile, it advances—for being is of itself transcendentally true, and reflected or reflectible in intelligence—by a movement of organically related words and responses and, as it were, of intelligible echoes; to put it another way, in the fashion of a dialogue, in the fashion of that inner dialogue by which we converse continually with ourselves or with God. It is in this sense (and without the least reference to any logical play at all of thesis and antithesis) that one of Lourié's works is entitled *Dialectical Symphony*. There is indeed found in him, though he is of the spirit rather than of the word, that characteristic of substantial conversation which is carried to the highest degree in Mozart, angel of the word.

It is, as I see it, with the *Liturgical Sonata* that the period opens in which Lourié's art attains its plenitude and verifies in an unimpeachable way the Pauline axiom—where the spirit is, there is liberty. In the *Spiritual Concerto* the specifically religious music, free of all traditional form, rediscovers, together with its essential inspiration, an astonishing spontaneity. The Dialectical Symphony is also religious but in an entirely different manner, and in the absence even of any

Christian theme: by the lineage of the work alone. Thus it answers to what one could call a religious sense of profane existence. The rhythm beats like the heart of the great night, with a vital inexorable necessity; the song traverses, envelops this night like a gaze that is contained by nothing, like a love that makes the law, that *is* the law. Along with the *Festival During the Plague* the same spiritual sense penetrates to the heart of the perversity of the creature, of the too much cherished delicacy of his delectations and his nostalgia before they see rising over them the tranquil wings of death; the profound Baudelairian affinities of Lourié, what there is in him of dandyism and cruelty, but broken by what sweetness, appear with a singular intensity in this admirable festival of agonies of our world. Now what strikes me here is the progressive stripping and sharpening of intuition in the course of these three great works, which had logically to be born in this order, and in which the creative gaze becomes more acute as the object itself is more somber. But then it happens that the most recent work, at the date of writing, a song for two voices, a setting for a religious poem, *Procession*, is nothing but pure humility and fidelity, a perfect freeing in the movement of the soul, advancing to give itself.

Is it another effect of that analogy in spiritual position with Baudelaire of which I have just spoken? I find in Lourié's work an aspect that I can only characterize by taking the risk of saying, for want of better words, that there is in this music "magic"—this being a dangerous word, a dangerous and desirable thing, it is proper to make some reflections on it.

All works of art are made of body, soul and spirit. I call *body*, the language of the work, its discourse, the whole of its technical means; *soul*, the operative idea, the "verbum cordis" of the artist—it is indeed born of the abundance of the heart; and *spirit*, the poetry.

It goes without saying that the body is the instrument of the soul. But I think—after all, the definitions of words are free—that there is "magic" in a work when the spirit transcends the soul, is in a way separate from it—like the *Nous* of Aristotle that entered by the door—and when the soul and the body find themselves in regard to the spirit as it were annihilated, I mean to say they become together, the soul like the body of the work, the pure *instrument* of an alien spirit, a sign through which passes a superior causality, the sacrament of a separate poetry that makes a game of art.

And what is there to say, now that we are furnished with these notions? We will first remark that there are (because beauty is a transcendental and analogical thing) three almost independent lines, if I may so put it, along which aesthetic emotion and admiration can rise; for a work can be beautiful through the body or through the soul, or through the spirit (which is to say, poetry). And there is a fourth line which is no longer precisely beauty, but grace, in the sense in which Plotinus said that grace is superior to beauty; and in this line it is the magic of the work that is important. It is good to find here again the old master of magic of the *Enneads*. His teaching is uncertain when he proposes to conduct us to mystical contemplation and to introduce us to divine things; but if it is removed to the region of things of poetry and beauty, its true force is then assumed. It is there Plotinus must be listened to.

After this I have no intention of proposing classifications or of undertaking a distribution of palms; moreover, certain work without magic can be more beautiful, greater and more accomplished, and richer in poetry than other work that is endowed with magic; it does not seem to me without interest, however, to test in the contact with experience the value of our instruments of prospection.

Fearing to lay a parricidal hand on the greatest of musicians, dare I say that there is little of magic in Johann Sebastian Bach? Yes, I shall say that this most sublime of music, this mother-music, is a music without magic: in Bach (and this is perhaps the secret of his power and of his fecundity), the spirit and soul are but one—the poetry of the work is consubstantial to its creative idea, which is not instrument but queen and goddess always. That is why the music of Bach prays with a great vocal prayer that is elevated to the contemplation which mystic theology calls "acquired contemplation"; it does not pass the threshold of mystical or infused orison.

The danger of magic arises from the fact that it is the gift of an order exterior or superior to art. He who has it without having sought it receives something from heaven or from hell—something difficult to bear, and which extracts an art strong enough to obey. He who seeks it inevitably alters his art, fabricates counterfeit money. Wagner lived only for magic; if we except *Tristan*, there is no magic in his music, not even the shadow of black magic—only the frauds and the drugs of a head drunk with science and genius.

The case of Satie is the reverse. Through the passion for probity, he detests, he excommunicates in himself all possible magic, he ferociously cleanses his work of it. Repressed, magic then disguises itself in the queer taste for mystification that disarms the enterprise of mystery, and that protects the ironic snows of a virgin music.

With Stravinsky the spirit or poetry of the work is not consubstantial to its soul, but transcends it. But it is the spirit proper to the composer, his dominating intellect, his own will. Thereby it is understood how, the more he becomes himself, the further he removes himself from magic. Compare the *Rites* and the *Wedding*, where so many spirits of earth and of the waters still haunt him, to other masterpieces like *Apollo* or that *Capriccio* of which the brilliant poetry depends in its entirety on the made object.

There is no magic in Beethoven; and yet who makes himself loved better than he? Different indeed from Wagner, he does not seek for magic; how resist this great heart that gives itself, spirit and soul confounded, and which supplements a certain want of the workman's invention by the generosity of his personal substance dispensed without measure?

There is magic in Schubert, in Chopin, in Moussorgsky. Magic is not always white. The magic of Lourié rises from the shadows of the human depths traversed by the pitiableness which assumes everything from a sort of catastrophe of being which has all the weight of tragedy but whose character, properly tragic, that is to say hopeless, remains problematic and so to say in suspense, because of the face of God who passes through the doors. His music, when it prays, crosses the threshold of supernatural orison. The marvel, with him as with the other princes of magic is that magic makes stronger and more dense the art through which it passes, which obeys without ever bending. The magic of the chief of princes is an angelic magic—I do not say that with

Mozart an innocent angel is alone at work; in this miracle of heroic childhood the cruelty of the child and the angel, a murderous grace, traverses at times the transparency and lucidity of infused knowledge, of the infallible play.

There is finally a sacred magic, the altogether white one, which has its source in the unutterable desires of the Holy Spirit, it is the magic of Gregorian melody. But it belongs to another universe.

To recognize certain families of spirits, other principles of differentiation could be sought, drawn chiefly from the analogy of the world of art with the world of moral life. In certain of these spirits, the virtue of art appears to be more akin to prudence, in others to contemplation. Here are two families which hardly understand each other, here as elsewhere the prudent one dreads the contemplative and distrusts him, sometimes feels resentment against him. Like the old Descartes, Péguy, Rouault, Satie are prudent; whence circumspections, susceptibilities, fears, and the passion for admirable invention for the good turn of genius brooded on in solitude. Bergson or Léon Bloy, Lourié, Jean Hugo are contemplative, they have an unconstrained manner, exigencies and detachment, the luck or the mischance of the privileged; their fortune or misfortune depends upon a transcendental, on which they have gambled.

Don't you think, dear Lourié, that there are strange correspondences between Music and Philosophy? Both, when their center is in themselves, are capable of speaking out and of going whither they will, they attain their goal, they believe in themselves, they spread out their tails, like the peacock, with the apparatus of their fine techniques; they install themselves, they are installed.

We prefer that they have outside of themselves and higher than themselves (to speak truth, infinitely higher than themselves) the point of fixity to which they hold, the center of their vitality. This is less convenient for them, they can no longer believe in themselves, they are condemned to move constantly, to detach themselves, to deracinate themselves, they never finish starting, they have palpitations of the heart, they are properly speaking *eccentric* virtues. Well, they have a chance to see the country, and to live a little, and perhaps thus they will approach that "Love that we will recognize by wounds that we have given it".

Their goal flees continually before them. The more they advance, the more they see it retreat, it is behind them that they would perceive their nearness to it, but they cannot turn their heads. With no shade of esotericism in them, they are nonetheless masked. What does this mean? They must follow an evangelic way, mask themselves with light and with simplicity, that is what obfuscates most surely the eyes of men. They must cross dangerous zones where the spirit of vertigo can seize them, before arriving there where there is no more path, but the great firmament—the freedom of the peaceful.

NOTES

1. *Job* 23:13.

2. See *The Degrees of Knowledge*, p. 398 (1959 Edition).

3. The good also of the free creature cannot be known save in the same instant when it is willed, but for another reason, because in a general way the constellation of all the created causes is incapable of giving foreknowledge with certitude of the act of free will, which as such depends only on the will itself and on the first cause.

4. "Sine me *nihil* potestis facere." *John* 15:5. (Note: See *Saint Thomas and the Problem of Evil* Milwaukee: Marquette University Press, 1942 and MR 7 above).

5. Cf. Lionel de Fonseca, *De la vérité dans l'Art, dialogue entre un Oriental et un Occidental* (Paris: Chitra, 1930).

6. *Les Degrés du Savoir*, p. 5 (*The Degrees of Knowledge*, p. 2).

7. Paul Verlaine.

8. Paul Valéry.

9. Cf. Charles Du Bos, *Approximations*, VIe serie.

10. Cf. Louis Laloy, *La Musique retrouvée* (le Roseau d'or), Paris, 1928.

11. Cf. Boris de Schloezer, *Courrier des îles*, no. 4, July 1934; Henri Davenson, *Esprit*, February 1935.

12. (1914). Lourié there recognized as principles special to music: "(1) The elimination of linearity (of the architectonic) by means of internal perspective (the primitive synthesis), (2) The substantiality of the elements." Since then he has taken more cognizance of the importance of construction.

PART SEVEN

FAITH, CONTEMPLATION, AND LOVE

"To wish paradise on earth is stark naïvete. But it is surely better than not to wish any paradise at all. To aspire to paradise is man's grandeur; and how should I aspire to paradise except by beginning to realize paradise here below? The question is to know what paradise is. Paradise consists, as St. Augustine says, in the joy of the Truth. Contemplation is paradise on earth, a crucified paradise."

Action and Contemplation

23. THE WAYS OF FAITH

The wonders of faith

I am only a philosopher—not even one of those theologians whom the Cartesian Minerva ironically described as supermen. In order to tell you something of the virtues of faith, I shall let someone speak for me who stands above philosophers and theologians—the Apostle Paul himself.

In the Epistle to the Hebrews, which, if it was not drafted word for word by him, nevertheless conveys to us faithfully his doctrine and his thought, Saint Paul, speaking of Faith (*Hebrews* 11: 1–39), says: "Faith is the substance of things to be hoped for. . . . By faith Abraham, when he was tried, offered Isaac. . . . By faith also of things to come, Isaac blessed Jacob and Esau. . . . By faith Moses, when he was born, was hid three months by his parents. . . . By faith he left Egypt, not fearing the fierceness of the king. . . . By faith they [the Israelites] passed through the Red Sea, as by dry land. . . . By faith the walls of Jericho fell down. . . . By faith [the heroes of God and the prophets] conquered kingdoms, wrought justice, obtained promises, stopped the mouths of lions, quenched the violence of fire, escaped the edge of the sword . . . put to flight the armies of foreigners. Women received their dead raised to life again. . . ."

One would like to be able to draw a picture in our times of comparable wonders. This we cannot do. Is it because we are men of little faith? Is it because the present day is for faith itself a time of anguish and of purifying night? It is as though, while awaiting a new Enoch, a new Elijah, the signs and wonders are become so rare among us that the Queen of Heaven herself feels compelled to bear witness from time to time, intervene herself, and write upon the ground of this planet letters of fire proffered to the inattention of human beings.

The average functioning of intelligence in our time: the crystallization in the sign

Faith is itself a mystery. It is a gift from heaven, but a gift received within ourselves. One may observe first of all, it seems to me, that the very way of functioning which characterizes as a rule the state of the intellect in a period such as ours tends of itself, if we are not careful to react unconsciously upon the manner in which faith is received within us, upon the paths faith follows within us. Preceding the formulation of any atheistic philosophy, sometimes even in philosophies which pride themselves on making room for religion, even indeed on protecting it, there is a *way of functioning* of the intellect which in itself is atheistic, because instead of aspiring to being, it eliminates being and voids it. Perhaps this is why Kierkegaard, faced with an intelligence functioning in such manner, and, moreover, fully aware of the rights of reason, thought that faith exacted an anguished division of the soul and must always propose a perpetual challenge to reason.

But the remarks I would like to make are of a less general nature; they concern two typical aspects of the average functioning of intelligence in our times. I am not speaking of philosophical theories of knowledge, for in that case I would call the two aspects in question idealism and empiricism. I am speaking of the practical way in which a large number of thinking human beings are led by the tendency of the day to make use of their intellect—a way which perhaps the philosophical theories of knowledge do no more than reflect. This practical way of putting intelligence to use seems to me revealed in two symptomatic tendencies, one of which I shall call *mental productivism* and the other the *primacy of verification over truth.*

The productivism in question deals with concepts and conceptual statements, signs and symbols. Judging by the intellectual behavior of many of our contemporaries, one can say that they neglect and disregard as much as possible the moment of passive receptivity in which we *listen* before we *speak*, in which reality, grasped by sense and experience, engraves itself upon the intelligence before being brought in a concept or an idea to the level of intelligibility in act. We concern ourselves only with the productive aspect of the activity of intelligence, with the manufacture of concepts and ideas. The result is that what interests us above all are the signs thus manufactured, and not the being of which they are the expression. We go to meet reality with a gush of formulas. Ceaselessly, we launch prefabricated concepts. At the slightest provocation a new concept is formed of which we make use in order to take advantage of being, while protecting ourselves from it and avoiding having to submit to it. We do not try to see, our intelligence does not *see*. We content ourselves with signs, formulas, expression of conclusions. We seize upon some information about reality which can be of use to us, and that is all we want. But there is no question of using the information as a means of obtaining a view of reality itself. I read today's temperature on the thermometer: I shall, or shall not wear my overcoat; to try from there to learn what is heat itself is all the more out of the question because the quality of heat is such that we can get no intelligible grasp of it. In the same sense, I learn that one of my friends has lost his father; I shall write him a few words of sympathy; there will be no question of my seeing *into* his grief.

This way of functioning of the intellect—let us call it "crystallization in the sign"—is all very well for the physico-mathematical sciences, for these ask nothing of reality except that it furnish a base for the *entia rationis* on which they are working. But it does not suffice philosophy. It does not suffice faith. In both, the way the intelligence works is not through "crystallization *in the sign*" but through a "transition to the reality signified," as when knowing that my friend has lost his father I truly see into his grief, I understand that my friend is in sorrow. "Faith," says Saint Thomas (*Summa Theol.*, II-II, 1, 2, *ad* 2), "does not stop at words, at conceptual signs; its object is nothing less than reality itself attained by means of these signs"—in other words, the actual mystery of the Godhead communicating Himself to us.

Well, it is this very thing that we are actually disregarding when we allow our faith to become contaminated by the

mental productivism of which I have just spoken and follow
the road taken by the modern intellect. For when we do this
our faith crystallizes in the sign, it does not progress beyond,
or as little beyond as possible, into the reality signified. And
thus it trespasses against the formulae of dogma, those infinitely precious conceptual signs whereby the living God
tells of Himself in our language, and whose sacred virtue and
dignity lie precisely in the fact that they are the vehicles of
divine reality. There have always been Christians for whom
to know that Christ redeemed the sins of the world is a piece
of purely intellectual information of the same caliber as the
information that the temperature this morning was 54 degrees Fahrenheit. For them, stating the fact is enough, just
as the reading of the thermometer is enough. They have
every intention of using the information to get to heaven; but
they have never been face to face with the reality of the mystery of the Redemption, with the reality of the sufferings of
the Savior. They have never experienced the shock of recognition of faith, the scales have not fallen from their eyes.
What I mean is that the way the modern intelligence functions risks making this manner of living our faith appear
normal whereas it tends to empty faith of all content.

The primacy of verification over truth

The second typical aspect of the way of functioning of the
contemporary intellect arises naturally from the first; I called
it the primacy of verification over truth. We take more interest in verifying the validity of the signs and symbols we
have manufactured than in nourishing ourselves with the
truth they reveal. Has not the word truth itself become suspect to many contemporary philosophers? In fact our intelligence cares very little for the delights and enchantments of
the truth, any more than for those of being; rather, our intelligence fears both; it stops at the level of verification, just
as it stops at the symbol.

What are the consequences entailed by this attitude of
mind with regard to belief? Belief is based on testimony.
Well, for us, belief will not be that we are sure of a thing
as though we had seen it, on the oath of a trustworthy wit-

ness. Belief, for us, will be only that we have verified something that a trustworthy witness tells us, *leaving entire responsibility to him*, and that we accept it, of course, but without vouching personally for its truth. That is all very well for history. But it will not do for faith. For when it comes to faith I myself vouch for the veracity of what has been told me. I am more certain of it than of my own existence, since Primordial Truth itself has told me through the intermediary of the Church, which here is merely an instrumental cause, an instrument for the transmission of the revealed and is itself an object of faith: *id quod et quo creditur.* "There are three things," writes Saint Thomas, "which lead us to the faith of Christ: natural reason, the testimony of the Law and the Prophets, the preaching of the Apostles and their successors. But when a man has thus been led as it were by the hand to the Faith, then he can say that he believes for none of the preceding motives; not because of natural reason, nor the witness of the Law, nor because of the preaching of men, but only because of the First Truth itself. . . . It is from the light which God infuses that faith derives its certitude." (*In Joann.* IV, lect. 5, a. 2)

Thus it is that he who receives the grace of faith hears in his heart the voice of the Father, and is supernaturally enlightened by the *lumen fidei.* In one single impulse he adheres to the objective truths presented by the Church, entrusts himself wholly to God, Primordial Truth, in an ineffable relation of person to person, and clings to Christ the Savior.

There are believers, however, whose faith consists merely in accepting what the Church teaches them, while leaving the responsibility to the Church, and without risking themselves in this adventure. If they inquire as to what the Church holds to be the truth, it is in order to be advised as to the properly authenticated formulas which they are asked to accept, not in order to learn the realities which are given them to know. God said certain things to His Church; in turn the Church said them to me; it is the priests' business, not mine; I subscribe to what I am told, and the less I think about it, the happier I am. I have a deaf and merely mechanical faith, the faith of a "charcoal burner" and I am proud of it. A faith of this kind if it was put to the extreme would be no longer a matter of knowledge at all, but merely one of obedience, as Spinoza saw it. And in that conception of faith I do not believe because of the testimony of Primordial Truth teaching me from within, by means of the truths universally presented by the Church. I believe because of the testimony of the Church *as a separate agent*, because of the testimony of the apostles taken apart from the testimony of Primordial Truth which they heard, but which means nothing to me; I believe because of the testimony of men. But then where is the theological virtue of faith? Here again the way in which intelligence functions within faith leads, practically speaking, to emptying faith of its content. Here again we have to do with an intelligence which in its general way of functioning has given up *seeing* and thus betrays the conditions necessary for the exercise of faith. For faith, which believes and does not see, dwells—dependent on the will moved by grace—in the intelligence, the law of which is to see. From this it follows that it is essential for faith not to be quiet, to suffer a tension, an anxiety, a movement which beatific vision alone shall end. *Credo ut intelligam.* Essentially, faith strains toward seeing; that is why it needs to flower here below in contemplation, to come to be through love and gifts, *fides oculata*, to enter into the experience of that which it knows through riddles and "in a glass darkly." Actually, faith's eyes are never closed. It opens its eyes in the sacred night and if it does not see, it is because the light which fills this night is too pure for sight which is not yet one with God.

Precisely because faith is a supernatural virtue infused in the intelligence, it is not surprising that the fortuitous ways in which the intelligence functions at this or that moment in the evolution of humanity should tend to affect faith itself in the conditions in which it is exercised. It is for evil rather than for good, as I have just pointed out, that faith is affected by the manner of functioning of our contemporary intelligence. A priest, a friend of mine, told me that he had learned in the confessional that many of the cases of doubt and vacillations in faith, having nothing to do with the authentic trials of faith, reveal the mental habits of modern intelligence which I tried to describe a moment ago. He often asked himself whether the souls of whom he was speaking had ever truly had faith. In any case, it is clear that today the spirit of faith must climb back up the slopes of an intelligence no longer accustomed to the knowledge of being. And it is doubtless possible that a heroic faith is all the more pure and sublime, the more it dwells in an intelligence the general tenor of which is alien to it. Nevertheless the fact is that faith itself, in order to find normal conditions for its exercise, needs to dwell in an intelligence which has itself regained its normal climate. An intelligence patterned exclusively on the mental habits of technology and the natural sciences is not a normal climate for faith. Natural intelligence, the kind which is to be found in common sense, is spontaneously focused on being, as philosophy is in a systematic and premeditated way. Never have men had a greater need for the intellectual climate of philosophy, for metaphysics and for speculative theology; without doubt this is why they appear so fearful of them, and why such great care is taken not to frighten men with them. Yet they are the one and only way of restoring the intelligence to its most natural and deep-rooted functioning, and thus to bring back the paths of intelligence into the main highway of faith itself.

Faith and unity of inspiration

Faith is an obscure communion with the infinitely luminous knowledge which the divine Abyss has of itself. Faith instructs us in the depths of God. Faith stands above any human system, no matter how valid; it is concerned with revelation, with that which cannot be named by man, yet has desired to make itself known to us in terms which all may understand. The transcendence of faith leads to a strange paradox: faith in its own domain—in the things which are *of faith*—unites minds absolutely and upon certainties absolutely essential to human life; it alone can create such a unity of minds. But faith only creates unity of minds from above; it does not create unity of doctrine or of behavior in any of the categories of our activities which touch only human affairs, affairs which are not *of faith*.

All Catholic intellectuals are united in the Faith and in

the discipline of the Church; for all other things, whether it be philosophy, theology, esthetics, art, literature, or politics (although there are certain positions which none of them would hold since they are incompatible with Faith), they can and doubtless do hold the most various opinions. The unity of faith is too lofty to impose itself upon human affairs, unless they have an immediate connection with faith. Faith itself insists that reason should be free in human affairs and it guarantees this freedom. And intelligence is willing to be held captive but by God alone, the Subsistent Truth.

Faith creates unity among men but this unity is in itself a divine, not a human unity, a unity as transcendental as faith.

And yet is it not in the very nature of good that it should diffuse itself? Could it possibly be that from the peak of the eternal mountains divine unity does not come down into our plains, carrying with it continually its unifying virtue? Indeed, it does diffuse itself among us, it does communicate itself. Indeed, had we the spirit of faith; were our faith not anemic and ailing; were it to find in us those full conditions of exercise which it naturally demands; were that faith informed by charity and thus become perfect virtue, it would inform also in its turn all our intellectual and moral life. The transcendent unity of living faith would then provide us with a unity at every level of our human activities, yet still in the mysterious and secret way, free and internal, and after the transcendent fashion inherent in faith itself, not by any external conformity or regimentation; not in a visible, formulated or tangible manner, but by the wholly spiritual springs, the invisible breath of the working of grace. This would be a unity brought about by faith in the things which are not of faith, in other words a unity of inspiration rather than of objective doctrine or guidance. There exists no code or system capable of expressing such a unity; it arises at the wellsprings of the soul like that peace which Jesus gives and which the world cannot give.

Can we attempt to describe it still further? I would say that it requires a certain attitude in regard to truth, to wisdom, to freedom, that faith alone can produce; I would also say that it depends on the degree of depth to which the Gospels penetrate us.

A certain attitude in regard to truth

The unity of which I speak requires a certain attitude toward truth, a very simple attitude, evangelically simple, the attitude of the simple in spirit. To have the candid integrity to prefer truth to all intellectual opportunism and to all trickery, whether in philosophy, theology, art, or politics, to have such integrity demands a purification more radical than one might think. Every philosopher loves truth, but with what admixtures? The super-ego of the philosopher is there to intrude into that love all sorts of monsters in disguise. If you analyze the philosophical systems from that point-of-view, you will find that a number of them embrace not only a sincere search for the truth but at the same time a shrewd desire to discover the most advantageous intellectual standpoints or to connive with the times, or the passion to rule tyrannically over a fictitious universe in order to compensate for various secret frustrations. If our love of the truth were purified by the flame of faith, even though we would not all adhere to the same doctrine, we would be set free from an appreciable number of parasitical motives that can cause division among us.

I should like to point out, with regard to theology, another way in which intellectual opportunism can commingle with the pursuit of the truth. We know that theology, rooted in supernatural faith, makes use of purely rational discipline and of philosophy as an instrument in order to acquire some understanding of the revealed mysteries. For theology, philosophy is a *means*; therefore, theology chooses to put to its service the philosophy most *useful* for its own purposes. What philosophy, then, will be the most useful? Shall theology choose the philosophy, more or less true, more or less false, which has, the strongest hold on our times, and is, therefore, most easily able to reach men's souls and turn them to God? If theology makes that choice, then in the very sphere of the highest knowledge you have opportunism taking the place of truth. For the philosophy *the most useful* to theology can only be the philosophy which is *the most true*, regardless of whether or not it pleases our contemporaries. The instrument of knowing placed in the service of theological truth cannot be other than philosophic truth, such as we attain it first of all in its proper order, entirely natural and rational. As disproportionate as it is before the divine mystery, philosophy is raised up in its regard by the very use which theology makes of it, as the instrumental cause is raised above itself through being moved by the principal agent. But it is philosophic truth, not philosophic error, which can be thus elevated. In order to be a useful instrument, philosophy needs only to be true; all that is asked of it is that it be true.

At this point I ask permission to say something parenthetical, because I seem to hear some voices which are somewhat shocked. "Ah, we see what you have been leading up to! You want us all to be Thomists." Would to God that, philosophers and theologians, we were all Thomists; assuredly that is (as French pulpit orators used to say) the grace that I wish for us. But I do not seek to compel everyone to be a Thomist in the name of Faith. I do not reproach theologians who are distrustful of Saint Thomas with a lack of faith at all; only with a lack of intelligence. They may be much more intelligent than I, that I do not doubt. They are still not intelligent *enough*. Their faith is not in question. My remarks on the subject of theology go no further than those I proposed a while ago on the subject of philosophy. In both cases I do not claim that the unity which comes down from faith will produce a unity of system or of doctrine. But there is another sort of unity, one that cannot be seen nor formulated, that in the human domain itself of theology and philosophy would be a unity of spirit, a similar basic attitude of spirit. There is no doubt that it would diminish, but it would not suppress the diversity and opposition of systems. We would not all be Thomists, but in the love of truth which is in all of us there would be less mixed elements. . . .

I have reached the end of my parenthesis. I would add that this attitude toward truth which I have attempted to describe, and which is induced in us by living faith, would be brought, were the spirit of faith more widespread, not only into the domains of philosophy and theology, but also into the domain of art—a domain in which truth is no longer the universal truth, but the truth of the creative intuition of the artist, of his own individual treasure to which he must be faithful at the cost of sacrificing all else. The spirit of faith would also bring this attitude toward truth into the domain of politics, a domain in which the name of the truth in question is justice.

A certain attitude in regard to wisdom

I have spoken of the first attribute—the attitude toward the truth—of the unity brought down in our midst by transcendent faith. The second attribute of this unity is, it seems to me, a certain attitude toward wisdom. Wisdom is a savory science, *sapida scientia*; it is fruition; and of the three wisdoms discussed by Saint Thomas, metaphysical wisdom, theological wisdom and the wisdom of contemplation, this last, which functions in the superhuman way of the Gift of Wisdom and is rooted in the living faith, preeminently deserves the name of wisdom. Well then, does not faith itself, as I described it a while ago, tend inevitably toward contemplation, toward the contemplative experience which faith alone however does not suffice to procure, since this experience depends also upon love and the gifts of the Holy Ghost? Had we more faith, we would all reach out, each according to his own fashion, toward that experience of union with God which is the highest Wisdom; we would understand that this alone makes action truly seminal. Moreover, infused contemplation, since it is achieved by and in charity, tends to superabound in action; but contemplation alone, with the trials it imposes, truly dispossesses man of himself, truly makes a man an instrument, a fellow-laborer with God. Even the most generous activity, if it is not mystically dispossessed, if it does not somehow spring from the experience of contemplation—no matter how hidden, how disguised—run the unavoidable risk of ending up in disillusion or in bitterness.

I firmly believe that the spirit of contemplation is called upon to assume new forms, to make itself more pliable and bolder, to clothe itself in the love of one's neighbor in proportion as it spreads out into ordinary life. This means that action can be a disguise for mysticism, but it does not mean there can be a mysticism of action. There is no more a mysticism of action than there is one of inertia. Stop now, says the Lord, wait a minute, keep quiet a little; be still and learn that I am God.

Those of us who believe only in activity will doubtless have some surprises. We have all read Bergson's book on *The Two Sources of Morality and Religion*. We know the lesson taught by Aldous Huxley, who understands nothing of our dogma, but has grasped the supreme importance of spiritual experience for humanity. We know, in the activity of a Gandhi, how much was due to a certain mystical meditation, even though perhaps it could belong only to the natural order. Allow me to draw your attention to the fact that a book on the subject of contemplation written by a poet who became a Trappist is now selling tens of thousands of copies in the United States, as is also the book by the same author in which he tells of his conversion.[1] This is only the most trifling indication, but it interests me particularly because I have the highest regard for Thomas Merton, and because for many years I have thought that the most active land in the world is obsessed with a latent desire for contemplation. Where will that desire lead? One thing is certain, and that is that all over the world, no matter where, wisdom and contemplation are daughters of God whom the human race cannot do without.

A certain attitude in regard to freedom

The third attribute of the unity brought us by faith is, it seems to me, a certain attitude toward freedom. If it is true that grace makes us the adopted children of God, then the more profoundly faith works in us the more intensely it leads us to seek the liberty of those children, that autonomous liberty which means independence with regard to creatures and dependence with regard to God. Thus the theologian is free with respect to theology, the philosopher with respect to philosophy, the artist with respect to art, the politician with respect to politics. And this kind of freedom through which we transcend whatever makes each one of us most inflexibly committed is also a mysterious way, ironic and winged, of transcending our differences.

Then, too, we are free so far as the world is concerned. We place the invisible above the visible. We put social and legal consideration in their true place which is doubtless important, but still secondary. It is to the forces at work in human souls that we give primary importance. We respect in them the liberty which we have become aware of in ourselves. We do not desire the conversion of heretics to ashes, but rather to the living God. We grasp the meaning of Saint Augustine when he said: "You think you hate your enemy, when it is your brother whom you hate." In the most arduous conflicts our awareness of the rights and dignity of our adversary is never obliterated. That internal liberty, when it is mutually recognized and respected, is the sign of a unity of the mind which touches the very heart of human relations and which in a certain way reflects in us the transcendent unity of supernatural faith.

The descent of the Gospel within us

Thus it is by relationship to the truth, to wisdom, to liberty that the unity we seek to define is characterized; it goes down to the heart of human things; it is only concerned with an attitude of mind and is too subtle and tenuous to have an expression which can be formulated. Nevertheless, it is also of central importance and of overpowering significance: all this because it stems from a supernatural virtue which itself unites men through their adherence to divine truth, but through that adherence alone—in other words because it is that transcendent unity as radiating beyond itself, and being poured into the fragile vessels that we are.

It is clear that this additional unity produced by faith, this spread-out unity, depends on how deeply the Gospel has penetrated us. Each time one rereads the Gospel, one sees a new reflection of its demands and its freedom, as terrible and sweet as God Himself. Happy is he who loses himself forever in that forest of light, who is ensnared by the Absolute whose rays penetrate everything human. The greater our experience, the more inadequate we feel in the practice of the evangelical teachings, yet at the same time the more we are impressed with their mysterious truth, the more deeply we desire it. That is what may be called the descent of the Gospel within us. When we meditate upon theological truths, it is we who do the meditating upon theological truths, but when we meditate upon the Gospels, it is the Gospels which are speaking to us; we need only give heed. And no doubt, when we are thus walking with Matthew, Mark, Luke and John, the One whom the Gospel tells of draws near us, to awaken us a little. *Mane nobiscum, Domine, quoniam advesperascit.* "Abide with us, Oh, Lord, for the evening comes."

It seems to me that if a new Christendom is to come into being, it will be a time when men will read and meditate upon the Gospel more than ever before.

About a new Christendom

I have just alluded to the idea of a new Christendom. Actually, I have been alluding to it throughout this chapter: for what else are those roads that faith travels through the depths of human activities; what else is that unity brought down among us by faith which I referred to, if not one of the preliminary conditions for the coming of a new Christendom?

The dearer our hope, the more we must beware of illusions about it. The hope of the coming of a new Christian era in our civilization is in my opinion a hope for a distant future, a very distant future. My opinion about this was already intimated in a book written many years ago.[2] The events which have occurred since that time have only served to confirm these surmises—which are pessimistic as to the present, optimistic as to the future. After the war it would have been impossible for the spirit to assume control over the forces unleashed in the sick world save by a kind of heroism which could not be demanded of the nations. Since human intelligence has thus inevitably failed in its task, one can only hope that for the immediate future things will somehow settle themselves, thanks to the unconscious and passive resources of human mediocrity, in other words thanks to a kind of animal shrewdness adjusting itself to the natural pressures of history. But taking as a whole the phase of the world's history which we have reached, it has become a mere platitude to say that we have crossed the threshold of the Apocalypse. The atomic bomb is a brilliant advertisement for Léon Bloy.

But does that imply that the end of the world is due tomorrow, and that after the great crises no new phase of world history is to begin? As for me, I believe that a new phase will begin, and it is to that phase that I delegate my hopes for the coming of a new age of Christian civilization, more successful than the Middle Ages. But it will come *after* the general liquidation of which we have seen the beginnings, and especially *after* the major event prophesied by Saint Paul, the reintegration of Israel which, according to the Apostle, will be for the world like a resurrection from the dead. Let us admit that from now till then there are still too many poisons to eliminate. Let us also admit that things have come to such a pass that for Christianity again to take the lead in history the Gentiles could well afford to receive help from the ancient spirit of the prophets.

NOTES

1. Thomas Merton, *Seeds of Contemplation* (Norfolk, Connecticut: New Directions Books, 1949), and *The Seven Storey Mountain* (New York: Harcourt, Brace and Company, 1948).
2. *True Humanism* (New York: Charles Scribner's Sons, 1938).

24. ACTION AND CONTEMPLATION

Greek Philosophy

The debate between action and contemplation not only concerns each of us personally, but is also of vital importance to human culture and to the destiny of civilization. I hold it to be of special moment to this continent, as I shall try to suggest at the end of this chapter.

We know well enough how emphatic the East is about its calling to the contemplative life and how proud of it; while the West with no less pride—a pride which is beginning to suffer much—boasts that it has chosen action. Could this lead us to affirm without more ado that the East is contemplation and the West action? Such an affirmation would be all too simple. Things do not tell their secrets so easily. Occidental activism might be, in its misery and agony, a degenerated and pathetic form of what was once an incomparable sentiment of life and human values. The West, I believe, had once a habit of contemplation in harmony with the deepest postulations of spiritual reality.

In philosophical language the problem of action and contemplation is that of *transitive* (or *productive*) and *immanent* activity (immanent activity in its most typical and purest function).

Transitive activity is that which one being exercises upon another, the so-called patient, in order to act upon it, imparting to it movement or energy. This activity, which is quite visible, is characteristic of the world of bodies; through it all elements of material nature intercommunicate, and through it we act on matter, transforming it. It passes away in Time, and with Time. Not only is it transitory, it is transition. The Greeks were right in saying that in this activity, the action in which the agent and the patient intercommunicate is accomplished in the patient, *actio in passo*, and being common to both, makes the agent (notwithstanding its being as such the nobler of the two) dependent on the patient, in which alone it obtains perfection. The Agent is itself *in actu* and attains its perfection only by acting on another than itself, and in the instant of this action. Transitive action is a mendicant action, which achieves itself in another being, and is essentially in need of another being. On the other hand, while the agent's perfection is also, in fact, that of the patient, the agent as such does not seek the patient's good, but its own (this is a typical characteristic of purely transitive action). Hence its 'egotism'. People who exercise philanthropy as a transitive activity need the poor to help if they want to be helpful, sinners to preach to if they want to be preachers, victims whose wrongs they can redress. They need *patients*.

Immanent activity is of quite a different order. It is the characteristic activity of life and spirit. Here the agent has its own perfection in itself; it elevates itself in being. Immanent action is a self-perfecting quality. The acts of knowing and of loving are not only within the soul, they are for the soul an active superexistence, as it were, superior to the merely physical act of existence. Thus the soul, when it knows, becomes thereby something that it is not, and when it loves, aspires toward what it is not, as to another self. This action, as such, is above time.

It speaks for Aristotle's greatness to have known and taught that immanent (or vital or interiorizing) action is nobler and more elevated than transitive (or non-vital or exteriorizing) action.

In their doctrine of immanent action, the Greeks held that the immanence of the intellectual act is, as such, more perfect than that of the act of will; that is why, according to a thesis which St. Thomas made classical, intelligence is nobler than will, from the sole point of view of the degrees of immanence and immateriality of the powers of the soul.

All this led the Greeks to a twofold conclusion, which, in its first part, formulated a most valuable truth; and, in its second part, transformed that truth into a great error.

The great truth which the Greeks discovered (and which their philosophers conceptualized in very divers spiritual ways) is the superiority of contemplation, as such, to action. As Aristotle puts it, life according to the intellect is better than a merely human life.

But the error, follows. What did that assertion mean to them practically? It meant that mankind lives for the sake of a few intellectuals. There is a category of specialists—the philosophers, who lead a superhuman life; then in a lower category, destined to serve them, come those who lead the ordinary human life, the civil or political one; they in turn are served by those who lead a sub-human life, the life of work —that is, the slaves. The high truth of the superiority of contemplative life was bound up with the contempt of work and the plague of slavery. Even the work of freemen, of the artist or the artisan, was scorned. Plutarch wrote: 'Who, having the choice, would not prefer enjoying the contemplation of Phidias' works, to being Phidias himself?' 'All artisans have a despicable occupation, because there can be nothing noble in a workshop', said 'the good Cicero'. And farther to the East, the Brahmin's contemplation reposes socially on the untouchables' misery; wisdom, on offence and humiliation.

Christianity

Christianity has transfigured everything.

What innovations did Christianity introduce on the subject with which we are dealing? I should say they are fourfold.

First, it teaches us that love is better than intelligence. St. Thomas admits, like Aristotle, that considering the degrees of immanence and immateriality of the powers of the soul in themselves, intelligence is nobler than will, but he adds that considering the *things* we know and love, these things exist in us by knowledge according to the mode of existence and their own dignity, and therefore it must be said that to love things that are superior to man is better than to know them. It is better to love God than to know him; it is also better to love our brethren, in whom the mystery of God's likeness is concealed, than to know them. And the love which is *Caritas* is, not in the moral order only, but in the ontological as well, that which is most excellent and most perfect in the human soul and in the Angel.

Second, Christianity has transfigured the notion of contemplation, and endowed it with a new meaning. Albert the Great sums it up in his admirable treatise *De Adhaerendo*

Deo: 'The contemplation of the philosophers', he writes, 'is concerned with the perfection of the contemplator, and hence does not go farther than the intellect, so that their end is intellectual knowledge. But the contemplation of the saints is concerned with the love of the one who is contemplated—of God. And this is why, not content with the intellect, with knowledge as its ultimate end, it attains the heart through love, *transit ad affectum per amorem.'* And love indeed is its own instrument, love's dark fire is its light. *Quia ubi amor, ibi oculus.* This leads to consequences, which we shall presently see, and which make the word 'contemplation' rather unsatisfactory.

Third, Christianity has also transfigured the notion of action and has given it a new meaning. Christian wisdom has seen, better than the wisdom of philosophers, that the action which man exercises on matter or other men, though it is transitive, cannot be reduced to transitive action such as is found in the world of bodies. It is essentially human activity. It has not only been thought and willed before being exercised—being born in the heart before being made manifest in the external world; it not only necessarily proceeds from an immanent act, but, moreover, it goes beyond the work it serves, and by an instinct of communication which demands to be perfected in goodness, proceeds to the service of other men. You can give high wages to a workman for work manifestly useless—for instance, the task, which used to be imposed on convicts, of digging holes and then filling them up—and this workman will be driven to despair. It is essential to human work that it be useful to men.

As has often been remarked, Christ in assuming for Himself the work and condition of an artisan in a small village, rehabilitated labour, and manifested its natural dignity, a dignity which Antiquity had denied. The *hardship* of work is a consequence of the Fall and of the loss of privileges proper to the state of innocence, but not *work* in *itself.* Adam in the state of innocence, worked—without any pain—and had the mission of cultivation and keeping the Garden.

Man's labour in its first and humblest stage is a co-operation with God the Creator, and Christianity's rehabilitation of labour in the moral order is bound up with revelation, in the dogmatic order, of creation *ex nihilo*. *Pater meus usque modo operatur, et ego operor.* My Father worketh hitherto and I work too. Here is the foundation of labour ethics, which the modern world is seeking and has not yet found. The work which Antiquity most despised, manual work, imposes the forms of reason on matter, and delivers man from the fatalities of material nature (provided however he does not turn his industry into an idol which enslaves him even more); thus, work has a value of natural redemption; it is like a remote prefiguration of the communications of love. Man is both *homo faber* and *homo sapiens*, and he is *homo faber* before being in truth and actually *homo sapiens* and in order to become the latter.

Fourth, and this is a consequence of the preceding considerations, another innovation which Christianity has introduced, relevant to our subject, is that contemplation (supernatural contemplation, which would be better called *entrance into the very states of God, of God Incarnate*) is not only the business of specialists or of the chosen few. This was an astounding revolution in the spiritual order. Greeks and Jews, masters and slaves, men and women, poor and rich (but the poor, first), souls who have known evil and souls (if there be such) who have not, whatever their condition, race and wounds—all are called to the feast of divine Love and divine wisdom. That wisdom calls them all, it clamours in the public places and in the roadways. All, without exception, are called to perfection, which is the same as that of the Father who is in heaven; in a manner either close or distant, all are called to the contemplation of the saints, not the contemplation of the philosophers, but to loving and crucified contemplation. All without exception. The universality of such an appeal is one of the essential features of Christianity's *catholicity*.

At the same time and symmetrically, all are bound by the law of work. There are no more privileged by pain and labour. Work is for everyone, as well as the sin of which everyone must be cured. If any will not work, neither shall he eat. It is St. Paul who said this, and the evolution of modern societies shows more clearly every day how universal that assertion is. I know well that some people who have adopted it as a motto, not knowing its author, perhaps, give it a wrong interpretation, believing that there is but one kind of work—that which creates economic values. They fail to see the admirable analogical variety of the notion of work. According to the social conscience which the Christian leaven has awakened, no one can be dispensed from activities directed to the good of men, be it to clothe or feed their bodies, to teach them or guide them, to bring them to truth and beauty or delights of the spirit, to feed them with the words of God, or, like those dedicated to contemplative life, to wear oneself out in praying for them. All those varied activities are fraternal, and communicate analogically in that notion of work which the Christian spirit has renewed.[1]

I have just said that the notion of work is verified in a most refined way, even in those dedicated to the contemplative life. It is true that contemplation itself is in fact not work, not a thing of utility. It is a fruit. It is not ordinary leisure; it is a leisure coinciding with the very highest activity of the human substance. According to the profound views of St. Thomas Aquinas, following Aristotle, those who go beyond the socio temporal life achieve in themselves the supra-social good to which the social tends as to a transcendent term, and by that very act are free from the law of labour. There remains no more for them but Thee and I, Him whom they love, and themselves.

But in virtue of that generosity which is inherent in immanent activity at its highest degrees, loving contemplation overflows as a protection and a benediction to society. And though not itself a useful service or a work, even in the widest meaning of the word, that which is beyond usefulness superabounds thus in a usefulness, in which the notion of work is still realized at the extreme limit of refinement.

Thus, it will be understood why I have said above that all activities, from manual labour to the gratuitously added utility of contemplative leisure, are fraternal activities, in which the notion of work can be found at very different degrees of analogy.

Christianity has not condemned slavery as a social and juridical form, save in its most extreme modes, which are absolutely incompatible with human dignity. It has done bet ter by annihilating, from within, its functional necessity in human conscience. It has evacuated that necessity from conscience, and is evacuating it progressively from existence (for ancient slavery is not the only form of servitude), and it will require the entire history of mankind to have completely finished with it. For Christian conscience, as I have just pointed out, there do not exist two categories in humanity, *homo faber* whose task is to work, and *homo sapiens* whose task is the contemplation of truth. The same man is both *faber* and *sapiens*, and wisdom calls us all to the freedom of the children of God.

Superabounding contemplation

The contemplation of which I have been speaking is Christian contemplation—what Albert the Great, in the text quoted above, called *contemplatio sanctorum*. The Christian doctors tell us that it is supernatural, that is to say, it is achieved by the gifts which Sanctifying Grace—formal participation in us of divine nature—brings to the soul; and not only by its object, but in its mode as well, it goes beyond anything that the energies of human nature, left to themselves, can achieve.

It can be called Christian in a historical sense, since for nearly two thousand years Christian contemplators have made it manifest to us. It can be called Christian in a different sense, ontological or metaphysical, since it lives by the grace of Christ. In that sense it can even be found—substantially the same, whatever the difference of mode, degree, purity, or human setting—in eras or lands where Christianity is not professed. It is the supernatural contemplation of the Old Testament and the New, of Moses and St. Paul, such as is exercised by the living faith and supernatural gifts. The existence of these divine gifts is taught us by Christian revelation, but they are alive in all who have the grace of Christ, even when not belonging visibly to His Church (for instance, some of the Jewish Hassidim whose story was told by Martin Buber, or that great Mohammedan mystic Al Hallaj, whom Louis Massignon has studied).

At the same time, supernatural contemplation achieves and fulfills a natural aspiration to contemplation which is consubstantial to man, and to which the Sages of India and Greece bear witness. According to Albert the Great, this natural contemplation, as such, has its term in intellect and knowledge. No doubt, love can crown *gnosis*, but here it remains an effect; it does not constitute the proper end of the contemplative act itself, nor the proper mean of it.[2]

It must be remarked that there are in the spirit many activities, discursive activity and activity of desire, which are neither repose nor contemplation.

But while being a labour, this labour of the intelligence and of the heart tends toward contemplation and prepares for it, and in this measure participates in the end to which it is directed. It follows that there is a vast region of the life of the spirit, where contemplation is prepared, even outlined, not being, for all that, disengaged from active life and laborious activity. In this wider sense, the philosopher and the poet can be said to be already contemplative on the plane of natural activities.

This should help us to resolve a rather difficult problem. In the order of the Kingdom of God and eternal life, many are surprised by the theological teaching that action is directed to contemplation. In the order of temporal life and terrestrial civilization, the philosopher has to acknowledge that same law of work being directed in the end to contemplation and to the activities of repose. But what activity of repose and what contemplation? The contemplation of the saints is not a proper and direct end of the political life. It would be more than a paradox to give as a direct end to the life of men, as members of a terrestrial community and as part of the temporal universe of civilization, the transcendent and superterrestrial end which is their absolutely ultimate end as consorts with the saints, and souls redeemed at a great price; in other words, to solve the question of the workman's leisure by saying that work has for its end, on the ethico-social plane, mystical union, preluding the ultimate end. And yet, even in the ethico-social order, work is not its own end; its end is rest. Is it then directed to leisure and holidays, understood as a mere cessation of work, a pleasure, or honest pastime, a family party, winter sports, or the movies? If so, it would then be directed to something less noble and less generous than itself. We are far from looking with scorn on rest and relaxation which recreates the worn-out human substance. But that rest is but a preparation to a renewed labour, just as sleep prepares for the toils of the day.

In reality, human work, even on the plane of social terrestrial life, must be accomplished with a view to an active and self-sufficient rest, to a terminal activity of an immanent and spiritual order, already participating in some measure in contemplation's supertemporality and generosity. For all that, such active rest is not yet the rest of contemplation properly speaking; it has not yet attained to contemplation. Let us say it is the active rest of the culture of the mind and the heart, the joy of knowing, the spiritual delectations which art and beauty offer us, the generous enthusiasm supplied by disinterested love, compassion and communion, zeal for justice, devotion to the commonwealth and to mankind. The very law of work to which every member of the commonwealth has to submit, demands that all should have access to that leisure. There is nothing here that is contemplation, properly speaking. But if in this kind of leisure, instead of shutting up human concerns in themselves, man remains open to what is higher than himself, and is borne by the natural movement which draws the human soul to the infinite, all this will be contemplation in an inchoate state or in preparation.

But enough of this. Let us ask St. Thomas and the theologians what they think of supernatural contemplation.[3] In a famous passage, St. Thomas says first that, absolutely speaking and in itself, contemplative life is better than active life. This is a thesis characteristic of any conception of life worthy of the human person's dignity—the fundamental thesis of the intrinsic superiority of contemplation. St. Thomas proves it by eight reasons drawn from Aristotle and illuminated by eight texts from Scripture. And there is, he says, a ninth reason, added by the Lord when He says: 'Mary has chosen the better part.'

After this, there is a second point of doctrine to be considered: contemplation, being the highest degree of the life of the soul, cannot be an instrument of the moral virtues and the operations of active life, but the end to which those things have to be directed as means and dispositions.

A third point, made manifest by the example of Christian contemplatives and by the teaching of theologians, is that the contemplation of the saints does not merely attain to the heart through love. Not being confined to the intellect, being the fruit of love in act through which faith becomes as it were a thing of experience, thus contemplation also enters the sphere of action, in virtue of the generosity and abundance of love, which consists in giving oneself. Action then springs from the superabundance of contemplation, *ex superabundantia contemplationis,* be it by the very reason of the *nature* of the work it produces, (thus preaching things divine must overflow from a heart united to God or be vain), or by reason of the *mode* of the production, which makes a work, whatever it is, an instrument employed by sovereign Love to touch and vivify the heart.

It is by virtue of such a superabundance, which comes from the supernatural ordination of human life to the fruition of God, that Christian wisdom, unlike that of the philosophers, is not merely speculative, but practical as well, and directive of human life, for this life is not regulated by human measures only, but by divine as well, and thus becomes the object of that very knowlege which contemplates God. More excellent than any purely intellectual wisdom, because it attains closer to God, being a wisdom of love and union, the act of the gift of wisdom is not a self-sufficing contemplation, but one which, as St. Paul puts it, walks toward them that are without, redeeming time.

When explaining the words of Jesus: 'Know ye not that I must be about my Father's business?' St. John of the Cross, the great doctor of contemplation, liked to recall Dionysius's sentence: the divinest of all things divine, is to co-operate with God in the salvation of souls; which means, St. John of the Cross tells us, 'that the supreme perfection of every creature, in its own hierarchy and degree, is to ascend and grow according to its talent and resources in the imitation of God; and it is most admirable and most divine to co-operate with Him in the conversion and salvation of souls. God's own works are resplendent in that.'

We have arrived here at a fundamental truth: Christian philosophy is a philosophy of being; more than that, a philosophy of the superabundance of being; and in this it stands incomparably higher than other great philosophies of being, such as Hindu metaphysics, where being does not give being and can but absorb in itself—*maya* and soul itself. Christian philosophy, better than the Greek, has seen that it is natural that immanent activity should superabound, since it is super-existing. Purely transitive activity is egoistic, as I have said at the beginning of this chapter. Immanent activity is 'generous', because, striving to be achieved in love, it strives to achieve the good of other men, disinterestedly, gratuitously, as a gift. Christian theology is a theology of divine generosity, of that superabundance of divine being which is manifested in God Himself, as only revelation can tell us, in the plurality of Persons, and which is also manifested, as we could have discovered by reason alone, by the fact that God is Love, and that He is the Creator. And God, whose essence is His own beatitude and His own eternal contemplation, God who creates, gives, has never ceased to give, He gives Himself through Incarnation, He gives Himself through the Holy Ghost's mission. It is not for Himself, St. Thomas says, it is for us that God has made everything to His glory. When contemplation superabounds in efficacious love and in action, it corresponds within us to that divine superabundance communicative of its own good.

The call to contemplation

That is what philosophers can be taught about supernatural contemplation both by theology and by the experience of the saints. Properly speaking, such a contemplation is a participation in the divine life and perfection itself—an entrance, as I said above, into the very states of the Word Incarnate. It is the purely and simply terminal freedom of exaltation and of autonomy.

But have I not said that Christianity's great novelty is its universalism, which calls all men to what is most difficult, to perfect life, a life of union and contemplation? Let us consider this more closely. It was much discussed, some years ago, whether contemplative graces are exceptional not only *de facto* but also *de jure*, whether it is temerarious to desire or hope for them, or whether they are the normal flower within us of the living grace of virtues and gifts. This discussion, momentous to all who are anxious to know man, has been complicated by many extraneous considerations springing either from inadequate vocabulary, or practical preoccupations. I shall say a word about it before finishing.

The anti-mystical tendencies, which have developed since the sixteenth and seventeenth centuries, were generated by an all too legitimate fear, that of shame and quietism; the wine of the Holy Ghost is apt to go to one's head when mingled with the alcohols of imagination. Books of spirituality, not those only which make commonplace literature out of the saints' experiences, but even those of authentic spirituality, are apt, when falling into impatient and weak hands, to cause many a victim which psychiatry claims as its own. It is terrible to throw anything divine to men, who make use of everything to feed their chimeras.

And yet God, who is wise, has dared to do that terrible thing; and at what risk, when giving us His Truth. If books were judged by the bad uses man can put them to, what book has been more misused than the Bible? Let us live dangerously, says Nietzsche; that is a pleonasm. One is out of danger only when dead. To turn souls away from aspiring to the graces of contemplative union, to deprive them of the teaching and advices of a St. Therese or a St. John of the Cross, is to deprive them of the channels of life, to condemn them to a parching thirst. If anti-mystical tendencies were completely systematized, they would turn Christianity into a mere moral system, while it is, first of all, a theological communion.

And this is why in the discussion to which I referred, theologians are coming to an agreement (though with many differences of nuance) on the point that all souls are called, if not in a proximate manner, at least in a remote one, to mystical contemplation as being the normal blossoming of grace's virtues and gifts.

For if we define mystical life (or life according to the spirit) as a coming of the soul under the regimen in which the gifts of Grace, called in sacred terminology gifts of the Holy Ghost, predominate (so that henceforth the soul is docile to the spirit of God, who disappropriating it of itself, takes it into His own charge), then it is clear that every soul is called—at least in a remote manner—to mystical life *thus defined*. Why is that so? Because all are called to the perfection of love. And that perfection cannot be attained without the radical purification and substantial remouldings which are the mystical life's sacrificial privilege. St. Thomas teaches us that the gifts of the Holy Ghost are necessary to *salvation*, because we are so foolish that we could not, on certain difficult occasions to which we are all exposed, make by ourselves the proper use of theological and moral virtues to avoid *mortal sins*; then it must be said with still more reason that we are too foolish and too miserable to make by ourselves the proper use of those virtues to *attain perfection*, and hence it is necessary for this aim that the gifts of the Holy Ghost should govern our life as directive habits.

We must now observe that among the inspiring gifts which Catholic theology has learned to enumerate from Isaiah, some, like those of Counsel, Fortitude, Fear, mainly concern action, while others, like those of Understanding and Wisdom, are mainly related to contemplation.

It follows that souls which have entered upon the ways of spiritual life will behave in very different manners, each according to its calling. Some will be favoured in a pre-eminent manner with the highest gifts, those of Wisdom and Intelligence; these souls will represent mystical life in its normal plenitude, and will have the grace of contemplation in its typical forms, be they arid or comforting. In the case of other souls it will be primarily the other gifts of inspired freedom; their life will be indeed a mystical and disappropriated life; but it will be such pre-eminently in relation to their activities and works, and they will not have the typical and normal forms of contemplation.

They will not be, for all that, deprived of contemplation, of participating and experiencing lovingly the divine states. For St. Thomas teaches us that all the gifts of the Holy Ghost are connected and therefore cannot be present in the soul without the gift of Wisdom; though in the case we are dealing with, it will be exercised in a less apparent way, and in an atypical, attenuated, or discontinuous mode. The contemplation of the 'active' souls will be *masked* and inapparent, but they will have contemplative graces; perhaps they will be capable only of saying rosaries, and mental prayer will bring them only headache or sleep. Mysterious contemplation will not be in their way of praying but in the grace of their behaviour, the gentleness of their hands, perhaps, or in their way of walking or of looking at a poor man or at suffering.

It should perhaps be added that contemplative life is superhuman, whereas the active life is connatural to man and better adapted to the equilibrium of his natural energies. It appears that the forms of contemplation to which souls faithful to grace will actually attain most often, will not be the typical one, where the supernatural sweeps away everything, at the risk of breaking everything, but rather the atypical and masked forms which I have just mentioned, where the superhuman condescends in some measure to the human and consorts with it.

We see now with what nuances and distinctions we should understand the theological doctrine, which we have been reviewing, of every single soul being called to contemplative graces. Each is called, if only in a remote manner, to contemplation, *typical or atypical*, apparent or masked, which is the multiform exercise of the gift of Wisdom, free and unseizable, and transcending all our categories, and capable of all disguises, all surprises.

In this sense, if all this is borne in mind, the Thomist theses about contemplation—its necessity for the perfection of Christian life and its intrinsic superiority over action—appear in their manifest truth.

The doctrine I have stated summarily means that Christian contemplation springs forth from the Spirit which bloweth where it listeth, and one hears His voice and no one knows whence He comes or whither He goes. It means that Christian contemplation is not the affair of *specialists* or *technicians*. The active ways through which the soul disposes itself to it are not techniques, but only fallible preparations to receive a free gift, fallible preparation which this gift always transcends.

Natural spirituality has techniques which are well determined and are, moreover, good and useful. This apparatus of techniques strikes everybody who begins to study comparative Mysticism. Now, the most obvious difference between the Christian and the other mystics is the freedom of the former from any techniques, recipes or formulas. It is, essentially, not esoteric or *reserved to specialists*.

We meet here with two difficulties which I should like to mention, and which are due, the one to vocabulary, the other to the masters.

There is a difficulty which comes from vocabulary. It is that *words* are specialists. They cannot have the amplitude of transcendentals. They particularize what they denote, in virtue of their past, and of the associations, sometimes extremely heavy, which they drag along with them. That word 'mystic' for instance, which I have used all through this essay because I had to, is not satisfactory. It evokes a procession of phenomena, ecstasies, and extraordinary gifts belonging, when they are genuine, to what theologians call *charisms* or gratuitous graces—which has nothing to do with the essence of the mystical or disappropriated life, as we understand that word: since we have (following the theologians) defined mystical life by the dominating regimen of the Holy Ghost's gifts —the *habitus* of inspired freedom—which are quite different from charisms. The word 'contemplation' is hardly better. I have already said it is quite unsatisfactory. It leads a good many people into error, making them believe that it pertains to some spectacular curiosity. It carries with it a Greek past, the Greek notion of theoretical life. We have seen, at the beginning of this essay, with what care we ought to strip the great truths of Antiquity of the errors which grow parasitically on them. Shall we then try to find other words? That would be vain. The new words would soon become clichés as misleading as the old ones. We must accept the fact, and particularly in this matter, that words cannot relieve us of the effort of thinking.

Nor can the masters! This is the second difficulty I wish to note. The masters, too, are inevitably specialists, specialists of what they teach. St. John of the Cross is a specialist of contemplation and heroism. He teaches a common way, a way

open to all (to 'all those who have heard' in a proximate
manner the call of God); but he teaches this common way
according to the purest and *most typical* paradigm of the
states through which it leads. In brief, he speaks to all, to all
those who have entered on the road, by addressing himself to
a few Carmelite nuns of the noblest trend. Through them, he
speaks to all. This means that we who read him are expected
to hear him according to a whole key-board of analogical values, to hear with *universal resonances*, and in a non-special-
ized sense, what he says as a specialist of genius. To understand him differently would be to betray him. Thus, for
instance, concerning the nights and the passive purifications
which he describes, one must grasp the fact that in other circumstances and in other states of life, these typical forms can
be supplemented by other ordeals originating in events or in
men, and which play an analogous purifying role. By pursuing
this line of reflections one would see many things become
more plain. One would also begin to see what is the role of a
St. Therese of Lisieux, teaching in truth the *same doctrine* as
St. John of the Cross, and the same heroism, but in the simplicity, entirely denuded and *common*, of the 'little way.'

Orient and Occident

To come back to where we started, to the debate of East and
West, we see, if what we have said be true, that activism and
pragmatism, the rejection of contemplative values, the de-
thronement of Wisdom, are the West's greatest woe. It seems
as if today the West seeks a remedy in the frantic exaggeration of this evil. The attempts to create new civilizations
which are taking form before our eyes—where the civil community becomes the soul of a dynamism which is purely ac-
tivistic, industrial and warlike, and mobilizes for that active
end both science and thought—do not make our prognostica-
tions optimistic. The West has here much to learn from the
East and from its fidelity to the primacy of contemplative
values.

But, at the same time, what I want to point out is that,
while denouncing the errors and shortcomings of our unhappy West, the Christian feels for it a piety that is filial,

and can plead its cause in the face of the East. For this activism and pragmatism are the catastrophe of a truly great thing which the spirit of separation from God has led astray. I mean the generosity, the propensity to give and communicate, the sense of ontological superabundance springing from Evangelical Love, and of holy contemplation superabounding in activity.

Let us remember the great words which St. Thomas wrote about the Incarnation, and which to my mind throw the deepest light upon those problems: 'In the Mystery of the Incarnation,' he says, 'the movement of *descent* of divine plenitude into the depths of human nature is more important than the movement of ascent of human nature toward God.' This is a truth that holds good, not only for the Head but for the whole of the Body. It explains to us how supernatural contemplation, proceeding thus from the descent within us of divine plenitude, superabounds within us in love and activity.

We hold that the West will not surmount the crises in which it is engaged, unless it reconquers that vital truth, and understands that external activity must overflow from a superabundance of internal activity, by which man is united to truth and to the source of being. If the East, perhaps because its efforts toward contemplation aspired above all toward philosophical forms of contemplation, has given great importance to natural contemplation and spirituality, even in things that belonged to the secular and temporal order; one might ask if in the West, by a sort of division of labour, spirituality and contemplation—not philosophical but supernatural contemplation—have not been too much the exclusive preoccupation of souls consecrated to God and to the things of His Kingdom; while the rest of mankind was abandoned to the law of immediate, practical success and the will to power. If a new age of Christian civilization should dawn, it is probable that the law of contemplation superabounding in action would overflow in some way into the secular and temporal order. It will thus be an age of the sanctification of the profane.

As I have said at the beginning of this chapter, the debate between action and contemplation is particularly important to this continent. Is it not a universally repeated commonplace that America is the land par excellence of pragmatism and of the great undertakings of human activity? There is truth in this, as in most commonplaces. Whitman celebrates the pioneers in a manner which is certainly characteristic of the American soul. But, in my opinion, there are in America great reserves and possibilities for contemplation. The activism which is manifested here assumes in many cases the aspect of a remedy against despair. I think that this activism itself masks a certain hidden aspiration to contemplation. To my mind, if in American civilization certain elements are causing complaints or criticisms, those elements proceed definitely from a repression of the desire, natural in mankind, for the active repose of the soul breathing what is eternal. In many unhappy creatures, good but wrongly directed, nervous breakdown is the price of such repression. On the other hand, the tendency, natural in this country, to undertake great things, to have confidence, to be moved by large idealistic feelings, may be considered, without great risk of error, as disguising that desire and aspiration of which I spoke.

To wish paradise on earth is stark naïveté. But it is surely better than not to wish any paradise at all. To aspire to paradise is man's grandeur; and how should I aspire to paradise except by beginning to realize paradise here below? The question is to know what paradise is. Paradise consists, as St. Augustine says, in the joy of Truth. Contemplation is paradise on earth, a crucified paradise.

NOTES

1. I do not think that the word "work" and the concept of work must be reserved only to manual work and to intellectual activities preparing for or regulating the latter. I consider the fact of a thing being *per se*, or in itself, related to the utility of the human community, as the true criterion of work in the ethico-social sense. And lawyers, statesmen, teachers have an activity no less related to the usefulness of the community than the activity of farmers or miners.

2. For a more detailed analysis of these questions see my essay "The Natural Mystical Experience and the Void," in *Ransoming the Time* (New York: Charles Scribner's Sons, 1941), pp. 255–89.

3. Cf. Jacques and Raïssa Maritain, *Prayer and Intelligence* (New York: Sheed & Ward, 1928).

25. LOVE AND FRIENDSHIP*

A *necessary distinction within disinterested love*

At the very heart of disinterested love, or love-for-the-good-of-the-beloved (which St. Thomas calls *amor amicitiae*[1] in contrast to *amor concupiscentiae*, i.e., love-for-the-good-of-the-subject, or love of desire), Raïssa distinguishes two kinds of love which she calls, simply following the common and accepted everyday usage, *love* and *friendship*. But she uses these ordinary words with a rigor and depth that goes beyond everyday usage. "The essence of love lies in the communication of the self with a fullness of joy and delight in the possession of the good loved. The essence of friendship lies in benevolence extending even to the sacrifice of oneself for the beloved. God gives us His friendship in coming to our aid in all our necessities and in dying for us on the cross.[2] God gives us His love in making us partakers of His nature through grace—in making the sanctified soul to be His dwelling place. . . ."

It is difficult to restrict the words rich in meaning for human life. Such words tend either to contract or enlarge the thought behind them. Keeping this in mind, let us try to make some precise distinctions, even at the price of some clumsiness. Every disinterested love is a gift of self. But even this is ordinarily understood in two different ways: there is, on the one hand, the love of benevolence or of self-surrender in which the lover gives himself to the beloved by giving to the loved one his goods or what he has—in various degrees extending to that perfect love of self-surrender in which one gives all that he has, all his goods, and even his very life. This is *friendship*; and in this friendship the lover in giving what he has unquestionably gives, but *in a certain way*, his very subjectivity inasmuch as what he is has need of what he has, possibly so far as to give his very life. That he gives himself there is no doubt; and he gives himself really, but he does so *in a veiled and indirect manner*, through something other than himself. In other words, he gives himself by means of and through the intermediary of goods that hide his gift of self and more or less break up that gift into small pieces. For the goods allow him to hold back to some degree his own self so that he has not given absolutely all that he has.

In *love*, on the contrary, love that reaches the full human dimensions, the love in which the spirit is pledged—I am speaking of love in its most far-reaching and absolute form (for in its ordinary form the giving of self of which I speak is always headed in this direction)—the person or subjectivity is given directly, openly, without a mask, not hidden under the appearances of any other less total good. From the very outset, the person gives himself totally by giving or communicating to the beloved, pouring forth to him, all that he *is*. It is the very person of the lover that is the Gift made to the beloved, simple, unique and without any reserve. This is why love, especially in the extreme sense in which we here understand it, is the giving of self *absolutely and par excellence*.

The difference between love and friendship is not necessarily a difference in the *intensity* or depth of disinterested love. Any one friendship can be just as intense or more intense than any one love. The difference between love and friendship is a difference in the *intrinsic quality* of disinterested love or in the ontological level on which it is constituted in the soul. In other words, the difference lies in the capacity for giving one's very soul to another.

In God *friendship* and *love* are but two aspects of one and the same infinitely perfect disinterested love—which is the transcendent God himself—two aspects which we distinguish and understand by analogy with what manifests itself in human disinterested love, all of whose qualities and perfections are supereminently contained in their uncreated Exemplar.

In the creature (when we consider things in the natural order), *friendship* and *love* between two human beings are two different kinds of disinterested love. And what is more, in *love*—since on this strictly human level the difference in sexes comes into play and the flesh is concerned—love of desire is joined to disinterested love.

The different kinds of human love

I have already made it quite clear that in speaking of love I was speaking of that love in which the spirit is pledged, that love on a par with man and his dignity—and that I was speaking of it in its extreme and quite absolute form.

We should note that if we take the word in its everyday meaning where love and friendship are distinguished, there is in man a kind of love of the purely animal order and not properly human—the love around which many masculine conversations revolve, the love that is exclusively carnal, the love that refers exclusively to the pleasure of the senses. This kind of love falls *solely* under the love of desire, and has nothing to do with disinterested love. We will not consider it here.

Love of the properly human order begins at the point where, at least incipiently, there is joined to the attraction of the senses that direct and open giving of the person himself of which we spoke above and which proceeds from disinterested love. It is true to say that at the moment this threshold is crossed and just because of the gift by which the lover gives himself to the beloved, the meaning of the word "to exist" becomes twofold: the beloved alone exists fully and absolutely for the lover and the existence of all else is stamped with a kind of invalidity.

This love in the properly human order manifests itself in quite varying forms which, for lack of space, we cannot analyze here. We will confine ourselves to three typical cases. First of all there is the love called sensual passion (*amour-passion*); the love that in its higher form can also be called romantic love. This love plays a central role in human life; it is a mirage which brings out a nostalgia that lies in every human being; its entwined initials are carved on all the trees of the world. It lives the life of a lie, of an illusion; it is a mirage, a semblance, of the love *that is truly love* ("mad-boundless love" [*amour fou*]). It believes itself to be eternal, but it is ephemeral. Here, it is true, the lover gives himself to his beloved (herself to her beloved), but in imagination or dream rather than in reality; here the love of carnal desire holds (often without its being known) the essential and predominant place; the total gift of self which one quite sincerely imagines himself to have made is not real but dreamt. In all truth it is nothing but a disguise whereby our minds cover the desire of the senses with royal finery in which the species serves its own ends while deceiving the individual. It is good for a human being to pass through this exultation which reminds one of the courting songs and dances of birds—but on condition that he does not seek to remain there, for a man is not a bird.

Secondly there is authentic love which one rarely attains immediately (though this is not impossible). Man ordinarily does not arrive at this love except after a certain maturing in life and suffering. This is the love in which one really gives to another not only what he has, but what he is (his very person). In the ordinary form of this authentic love (let us say quite simply, in *happy love*), such a gift is without doubt made, but only initially and like a sketchy blueprint.

Lastly, when such a gift is made in its fullness, we find authentic love in its full and absolute form. This love in which the very person of each is given to the other in all truth and reality is the pinnacle of love between man and woman in the order of natural and ontological perfection. Here the lover truly gives himself or herself to the beloved *as to his Whole*; in other words, he pours himself out to her and she to him, he makes himself—while remaining ontologically a person—a part that does not exist except through and in this Whole that is his Whole. This extreme love is mad-boundless love; and such a name properly belongs to it, for it attains precisely (in this special order or, if you will, in the magic and spiritual "superexistence" of love) what is of itself impossible and mad in the order of simple existence or of mere being where each person remains a whole and cannot become a simple part of another whole. Here is the paradox proper to love: on the one hand it demands the ontologically indestructible duality of persons; on the other it demands, and *in its own way* achieves an unbroken unity, an effectively consummated unity, of these very same persons ("in but one spirit and love," says St. John of the Cross of the supernatural mystical union; but this is already true, on a quite other level and in an analogical sense, of the natural union between man and woman[3] in mad-boundless love). On this terrestrial level (human) mad-boundless love, differently from mad-boundless love for God, belongs to the merely natural order; it is, as I noted above, a natural ontological perfection—it can be used for better or for worse from the moral point of view. This is its splendor and its ambiguity. Its object is a created object. He who loves with mad-boundless love gives himself totally; the *object* of his love is a limited creature, fragile and mortal. We would fail to recognize the grandeur of our nature if we believed that the creature who is loved with mad-boundless love *necessarily* becomes an idol for the lover and is *necessarily* loved more than God. But we would fail to recognize the wretchedness of our nature if we believed it *impossible* that a creature be loved more than God by one who loves with mad-boundless love and become an idol for him. Human mad-boundless love can be found at the heart of a morally right life, or a life subject to the order of charity. It can also be found (and not only outside marriage, but also in marriage), at the heart of a life of sin.

Let us make three remarks here: 1) Mad-boundless love always implies and presupposes (not as necessarily prior in time but as necessarily prior in being) love of self-surrender or of friendship even in going quite beyond it. 2) Mad-boundless love goes beyond friendship for it is on a deeper level—in its very roots—in the soul by the very fact that it is a direct, open, unmasked giving of the very person in his entirety, making himself *one in spirit* with the other. But by reason of the very nature of the human being who is flesh and spirit, of itself[4] it also admits at least the desire of union *in the flesh* and carnal joy, the pleasure of the senses *par excellence* that accompanies that union. A human person cannot give himself to another, or pour out himself to another to the point of making that other his Whole unless he gives or is ready to give to that other his body when he gives his soul. 3) Nevertheless, mad-boundless love is infinitely more than sensible desire. Essentially, primordially and principally, it is disinterested love; love of desire (love for the advantage or joy of the subject that loves rather than for the thing loved) is in this case secondary, completely subordinated to disinterested love. Principally and before all, the person is spirit, and hence before all and principally as spirit gives himself in giving himself totally. As spirit transcends the flesh, so mad-boundless love, authentic love in its extreme form, transcends sensual passion.

Love of charity and uncreated Love

When Raïssa distinguished between *love* and *friendship* she was thinking of mad-boundless love, of love in its extreme form. Moreover, she understood the word in an analogical and transcendent sense, for she was thinking not of the human mad-boundless love which I have been treating, but above all, of the love of God for man (uncreated Love) and the love of man for God (the love of charity).

The object of the love of charity is Spirit subsisting of itself in its transcendent unity, the inscrutable deity itself, the three uncreated Persons—a gift of grace and so belonging to the supernatural order. Here friendship and love (mad-boundless love) evidently are not two distinct species but two differing capacities for giving one's soul to another, rooted in the same disinterested love. Does mad-boundless love still involve, at least in an analogical sense, a certain love of desire of the wholly spiritual order, the desire to possess the Be-loved and to be intoxicated with him and to feel loved by him? No doubt it does: this love claims for itself a fullness of joy and delight in the possession of the "well-beloved." But in this case the desire, having God as its object, is not only absolutely pure of any carnal element; it is not only entirely subordinated to disinterested love; but beyond this it has ceased and must cease from having the good of the subject himself as its *raison d'être* (as in love of desire properly so called); it is not for itself that the soul wishes to bring God *to* itself or desires to possess him, it is *for* God, who is loved first of all. And the more this is so, the more desperate is this desire. Here below this desire cannot be completely fulfilled. This desire will have to pass through nights that can be terrifying. Because disinterested love demands total and absolute sovereignty and one after another relentlessly destroys every root that the desire to possess the well-beloved has in the lover, to the extent he instinctively loves himself,

agony and death rather than joys and delight, will sometimes
be the answer to this desire.

In reference to the love of God for man, I have already
noted that in God friendship and love are but two aspects,
distinguished according to our human manner of knowing,
of one love, a love that is perfectly one, a love that is God
himself. The characteristics of this love in us, this love which
I call mad-boundless love, are found in God in a supereminent manner, infinitely purified and analogically transferred
to the degree compatible with the divine transcendence.

In God there is no love of desire whatsoever, for God has
no need for anything. He has only disinterested love, friendship certainly, and an infinitely generous friendship, but also
mad-boundless love in which he gives himself to a whole (the
created person) who is other than he, a whole he has made
capable by his grace of receiving him and of loving him in
return. Thus the created person in this boundless giving by
which he gives himself entirely in return, can become one
spirit and love with the Love by which God loves himself
eternally and reflect back to God, so to say, the Joy by which
he eternally rejoices in himself.

And if God asks our love in return for his love, it is solely
in the name of disinterested love: not because he has need
of being loved by us but because he loves us. God seeks his
glory, says St. Thomas Aquinas, not for himself, but for us.
It is for us, not for himself, that he asks us to give him our
hearts. *Praebe mihi cor tuum.*[5] "I think with wonder upon the
value the Savior attaches to our poor love. It would be true
to say that the end that he has set for himself is to take
possession of our hearts: 'It is not for nothing that I have
loved you.' Is this not like a metaphysical necessity? Uncreated love, in pouring itself out upon creatures, remains love
and consequently is not satisfied unless to its expansiveness
there be an answering expansiveness that makes union
possible."[6]

Human mad-boundless love and mad-boundless love for God

Let us return now to human love. We have said that mad-boundless love is present in us, emerges like Venus being born from the sea, when the person gives himself wholly, openly and without a mask to another person as to his Whole, in which giving he pours himself out and becomes a part of that Whole. In this context Raïssa's *Journal* puts in relief a central truth upon which I must dwell in the language I am using here. But first of all, a preliminary observation that I will state once and for all: in the following remarks one condition is presupposed—what is spoken of in the human being is not what momentarily springs up from time to time, or if lasting is at the mercy of obstacles and contrariety, but is an habitual state, a way of life in which he can make constant progress.

Keeping this in mind we must say that a man or woman who has for his or her beloved a perfect and full *friendship* (love or self-surrender), and an authentic *love* in its ordinary form, can have at the same time *mad-boundless love* for God; but a human being cannot at one and the same time give himself fully, absolutely, to two objects in such a way that each constitutes his Whole. In other words, if a soul has arrived at mad-boundless love of God, then it must renounce any human mad-boundless love—whether as in the religious state it renounces the flesh completely—or whether living in the bonds of marriage it renounces, not that unique and sacred love by which man and woman are two in one flesh, but that love which is the pinnacle and perfection of conjugal love in the order of natural ontological perfections, mad-boundless love. The reason for this is that a disinterested love of that kind in which the Beloved really and truly becomes the Whole for the Lover must dwell alone in the soul and if such a love (mad-boundless love) is given to God, it cannot be given to anyone but him.

The human soul can have but one Spouse if we understand this word to refer to the ultimate espousals in which mad-boundless love reigns as master. That is why the soul's love i a jealous love if God is this Spouse for God must be, Jesus must be the *Only Well-Beloved*, the *Only One* loved with mad-boundless love.

"How will I prove my love for him?—By giving myself to him from the depths of my heart, in such a way that no other love will ever dwell there. . . . God is jealous of that particular gift of the heart that is love, that gift which of its nature is total and exclusive. . . ."[7]

Model saints and hidden saints

In heaven there are, without doubt, many more, very many more saints than we can imagine.

This is true, in the first place, of Saints in the ordinary sense of this word, that is to say of *model* Saints, heroes of the moral and spiritual life whose lives and example (even though it be only during the last days of their existence here on earth, as in the case of certain martyrs who may have been given to grave faults before becoming witnesses in their blood, or in the case of the Good Thief, who spoke his great act of love only a moment before his last breath) have surpassed the ordinary mode of human living and can exercise upon humanity that sovereign *attraction* of which Bergson spoke. These model saints do not live as the rest of men in the sense that, sometimes even in their external behavior, the measure of their acting, being that of the gifts of the Holy Spirit, surpasses that of the acquired or infused moral virtues; they astonish us, they always baffle us in one way or another; their heroism, no matter how secret its sources, cannot but show in some way. These are the saints who can be canonized. A certain number of them have been canonized. Others, an incomparably greater number, will never be canonized. All of them passed under the sign of mad-boundless love at a certain moment of their lives, and from that point advanced toward the perfection of charity, taken absolutely or under all aspects. At the same time, perhaps only in the last hours of their lives they crossed the threshold of the mystical state and received the manna of unfused contemplation (open or veiled). All were co-redeemers with Christ for they were united to him here below, not only by their membership in the mystical Body, but also in an immediate relation or immediate mutual giving of person to person—as to the Spouse of their souls.

And when I say that in heaven there are very many more saints than we can imagine, I am thinking also of saints who can be called *hidden* because, except in their secret hearts, they lived among us a life like that of any other man. If there was heroism in their lives, and without doubt there was, it was a heroism that was completely hidden. And yet the name "saint" is properly theirs, in this sense that, having walked with perseverance on the path of friendship with God to the point of attaining here below the perfection of charity (under the aspect of intensity), they passed from this earthly life straight into heaven. Thus as I have already observed, their last moment was a moment of triumph of mad-boundless love, and this will continue throughout eternity. I have no doubt that such saints (who cannot be canonized) are much more numerous even than the saints who can be canonized but never will be. It is for these saints, and for them especially, that the Church each year celebrates the feast of All Saints. Here we must think of the great mass of the poor and of the little people of God; I am speaking of all those among them who, to the very end, have practiced self-abnegation, dedication to others and firmness in virtue. Throughout the ages (this is but one example among others) there have been peasant families where work was sanctified by the sacraments, common prayer and the daily reading of the lives of the saints, and where the fear of God, the virtue of religion and a certain rigor of morals served as a sanctuary or tabernacle for the theological virtues. Such families must have given a quite large percentage of the saints who, after "living like any other man," passed straight into heaven. Father Lamy, "the saintly curé," always insisted upon this. Without doubt most of the saints of whom I am now speaking neither crossed the threshold of the mystical state nor experienced even diffused or veiled contemplation (except in the passing *experiences*, more or less rare and usually unnoticed by them, of which I have spoken). Nevertheless they also fulfilled in their own way the vocation to be co-redeemers that was imprinted on their souls by baptism as every Christian who has charity fulfills this vocation. There can be no doubt they did this, not with the full freedom and supreme sacrifices of mad-boundless love that are the privilege of the saints who can be canonized, but by carrying with Jesus, as do the canonizable saints, their own crosses, as members and parts of that unimaginably grand human-divine Whole that is the mystical Body of Christ.

Is it true to say that, to the extent that evening is descending and the old Christianities are crumbling, it is becoming more difficult for the majority of men to preserve charity and to remain faithful to the end under the simple sign of friendship with the Savior, and to people heaven with saints who "lived like any other men?" At the same time, to compensate and more than compensate for these losses, there is a growth, whether in quality or in quantity, on the part of souls who live under the sign of mad-boundless love; and their role in the economy of salvation goes on increasing in importance because (and this is especially true, no matter how small the number may be of those in whom infused contemplation freely develops) their lived intimacy with Jesus, their renunciation and their self-abasements are more and more necessary to purchase the salvation of the many, and to make present and accessible to their sight the depths of the goodness, of the innocence and of the love of God.

I would like to believe it. It was a long time ago that I wrote that a day would come when the world would no longer be habitable except for inhuman brutes and for saints —for great saints.

NOTES

This study was written to replace a footnote to the private edition of Raïssa's *Journal* which Jacques Maritain edited and issued in 1962. Close friends suggested that a longer note be written as an appendix to the trade edition. After complying with the suggestion, Maritain decided instead to publish the "footnote" as a chapter in his "Notebook." It appeared originally in the Swiss periodical *Nova et Vetera* and subsequently as chapter VII of his *Carnet de Notes*.

1. *Amor amicitiae* is *amor benevolentiae* or disinterested love (love for the good of the beloved) that is mutual (S. T., II-II, q. 23,

a. 1). In the perspective in which we find ourselves, it is this *mutua benevolentia* that we have to consider in our discussion; the expression *love of friendship* is thus the one that is proper here.

2. Cf. John 15:13. "Greater love than this no one has, that one lay down his life for his friends."

3. "In but one spirit,"—I say *spirit*, I do not say temperament, character, tastes, etc.

4. But I do not wish to say that a man cannot, by an act of his free will—just as he can, if he wishes, mutilate his body—do violence to nature and separate carnal desire from his mad-boundless love, either for a spiritual motive and by renouncing the flesh if she whom he loves, and indeed always will love with mad-boundless love, asks it of him, or if both of them feel themselves called to it by God (we see fiancés so separating themselves to enter religion, or spouses so making the vow of continence), or for some other motive (if, for example, the woman he loves with mad-boundless love is married to another; to tell the truth, in this case he will more probably bring about the separation in a quite opposite sense—by freeing himself from dissolute living).

5. Prov. 23:26.

6. Raïssa's *Journal*, p. 69.

7. *Journal*, p. 150 (April 20, 1924). The renunciation (in mad-boundless love) that is here involved is that renunciation which Raïssa, in another context, admirably called "to abolish or exceed the limits of the heart." (p. 221).

SUGGESTIONS FOR FURTHER READING

The following list of books is meant to furnish a guide for those who may wish to pursue further the study of Jacques Maritain's philosophy. It includes his most important works on a variety of philosophical subjects plus the more significant books that have been written about his life and thought.

I. CHRISTIAN WISDOM AND METAPHYSICS
(Readings for Parts I, II, VII)

The Degrees of Knowledge Tr. under the supervision of G. B. Phelan (New York: Charles Scribner's Sons, 1959). Maritain's greatest work on metaphysics and theory of knowledge in which he relates the various zones of knowledge through which the mind passes in its quest of being.

A Preface to Metaphysics: Seven Lectures on Being (New York: Sheed & Ward, 1939; paperback, Mentor-Omega, 1962).

Existence and the Existent Tr. by Lewis Galantière and G. B. Phelan (New York: Pantheon Books, 1948; Image Books, 1957).

Approaches to God Tr. by Peter O'Reilly (New York: Harper and Brothers, 1954; Collier Books, 1962).

Saint Thomas and the Problem of Evil (Milwaukee: Marquette University Press, 1942).

God and the Permission of Evil Tr. by Joseph W. Evans (Milwaukee: The Bruce Publishing Company, 1966).

The Sin of the Angel Tr. by William Rossner, S.J. (Westminster, Maryland: The Newman Press, 1959).

An Essay on Christian Philosophy Tr. by Edward H. Flannery (New York: Philosophical Library, 1955).

St. Thomas Aquinas Newly translated and revised by Peter O'Reilly and Joseph Evans (New York: Meridian Books, 1958).

Science and Wisdom Tr. by Bernard Wall (New York: Charles Scribner's Sons, 1940).

The Philosophy of Nature Tr. by Imelda C. Byrne (New York: Philosophical Library, 1951).

II. MORAL, POLITICAL AND SOCIAL PHILOSOPHY
(Readings for Parts III, IV, V)

Moral Philosophy (New York: Charles Scribner's Sons, 1964). Maritain's *magnum opus* on moral philosophy. Complementary to it is *Neuf Leçons sur les Notions Premières de la Philosophie Morale* (Paris: Pierre Téqui, 1951) which has not been translated into English.

True Humanism Tr. by Margot Adamson (New York: Charles Scribner's Sons, 1938). Maritain's most important work on social philosophy in which he envisages a new civilization exemplifying the ideal of brotherhood.

Man and the State (Chicago: University of Chicago Press, 1951; Phoenix Books, 1956). Maritain's most complete work on political philosophy in which he redefines the basic political concepts of body politic, state, the people, sovereignty, human rights, the democratic charter, relationship between church and state, and world government.

Freedom in the Modern World Tr. by Richard O'Sullivan (New York: Sheed & Ward, 1936).

The Twilight of Civilization Tr. by Lionel Landry (New York: Sheed & Ward, 1943).

Religion and Culture Tr. by J. F. Scanlan (London: Sheed & Ward, 1931).

Christianity and Democracy Tr. by Doris C. Anson (New York: Charles Scribner's Sons, 1944).

The Rights of Man and Natural Law Tr. by Doris C. Anson (New York: Charles Scribner's Sons, 1943).

The Person and the Common Good Tr. by John J. Fitzgerald (New York: Charles Scribner's Sons, 1947; Notre Dame, 1966).

On the Philosophy of History Ed. by Joseph W. Evans (New York: Charles Scribner's Sons, 1957).

The Social and Political Philosophy of Jacques Maritain Selected readings edited by Joseph W. Evans and Leo R. Ward (New York: Charles Scribner's Sons, 1955; Image Books, 1965).

III. THE PHILOSOPHY OF ART
(Readings for Part VI)

Creative Intuition in Art and Poetry (New York: Pantheon Books, 1953; Meridian Books, 1955). Maritain's masterwork on the philosophy of art. Text of the Mellon Lectures in the Fine Arts delivered at the National Gallery in Washington.

Art and Scholasticism and the Frontiers of Poetry A new trans. by Joseph W. Evans (New York: Charles Scribner's Sons, 1962; Scribner Library Books, 1962).

Art and Poetry Tr. by Elva de Pue Matthews (New York: Philosophical Library, 1943).

Art and Faith: Letters Between Jacques Maritain and Jean Cocteau Tr. by John Coleman (New York: Philosophical Library, 1948).

The Situation of Poetry Tr. by Marshall Suther (New York: Philosophical Library, 1955).

The Responsibility of the Artist (New York: Charles Scribner's Sons, 1960).

IV. OTHER WORKS

On Education

Education at the Crossroads (New Haven: Yale University Press, 1943; paperbound edition, 1960).

The Education of Man: The Educational Philosophy of Jacques Maritain Edited with an introduction by Donald and Idella Gallagher (Garden City, New York: Doubleday & Company, 1962).

On Philosophers

Bergsonian Philosophy and Thomism Tr. by Mabelle L. Andison and J. Gordon Andison (New York: Philosophical Library, 1955).

Three Reformers: Luther, Descartes, Rousseau (New York: Charles Scribner's Sons, 1929).

The Dream of Descartes Tr. by Mabelle L. Andison (New York: Philosophical Library, 1944).

Important Collections of Essays

Scholasticism and Politics Tr. edited by Mortimer J. Adler (New York: The Macmillan Company, 1940; Image Books, 1960).

Ransoming the Time (New York: Charles Scribner's Sons, 1941).

The Range of Reason (New York: Charles Scribner's Sons, 1952; Scribner Library Books, 1963).

On the use of Philosophy (Princeton: Princeton University Press, 1961; New York: Atheneum, 1965).

V. BOOKS ABOUT JACQUES MARITAIN

Bars, Henry. *Maritain en notre temps.* (Paris: Bernard Grasset, 1959).

Fecher, Charles A. *The Philosophy of Jacques Maritain.* (Westminster, Maryland: Newman Press, 1953).

Maritain, Raïssa. *We Have Been Friends Together and Adventures in Grace. The Memoirs of Raïssa Maritain.* Tr. by Julie Kernan (Garden City, New York: Image Books, Doubleday & Company, 1961).

Michener, Norah Willis. *Maritain on the Nature of Man in a Christian Democracy.* (Hull, Canada: Editions "L'Eclair," 1955).

Phelan, Gerald B. *Jacques Maritain.* (New York: Sheed & Ward, 1937).

Tamosaitis, Anicetus, S.J. *Church and State in Maritain's Thought.* (Chicago: 2345 W. 56th St., 1959).

Jacques Maritain: The Man and His Achievement Edited by Joseph W. Evans (New York: Sheed & Ward, 1963). A collection of essays concerning various aspects of Maritain's philosophy.

The Maritain Volume of the Thomist (New York: Sheed & Ward, 1943). Contains four essays on the life and thought of Jacques Maritain.

The Achievement of Jacques and Raïssa Maritain: A Bibliography 1906–1961 Compiled by Donald and Idella Gallagher (Garden City, New York: Doubleday & Company, 1962). An extensive bibliography of the works by and about Jacques and Raïssa Maritain. Contains over 1500 items.